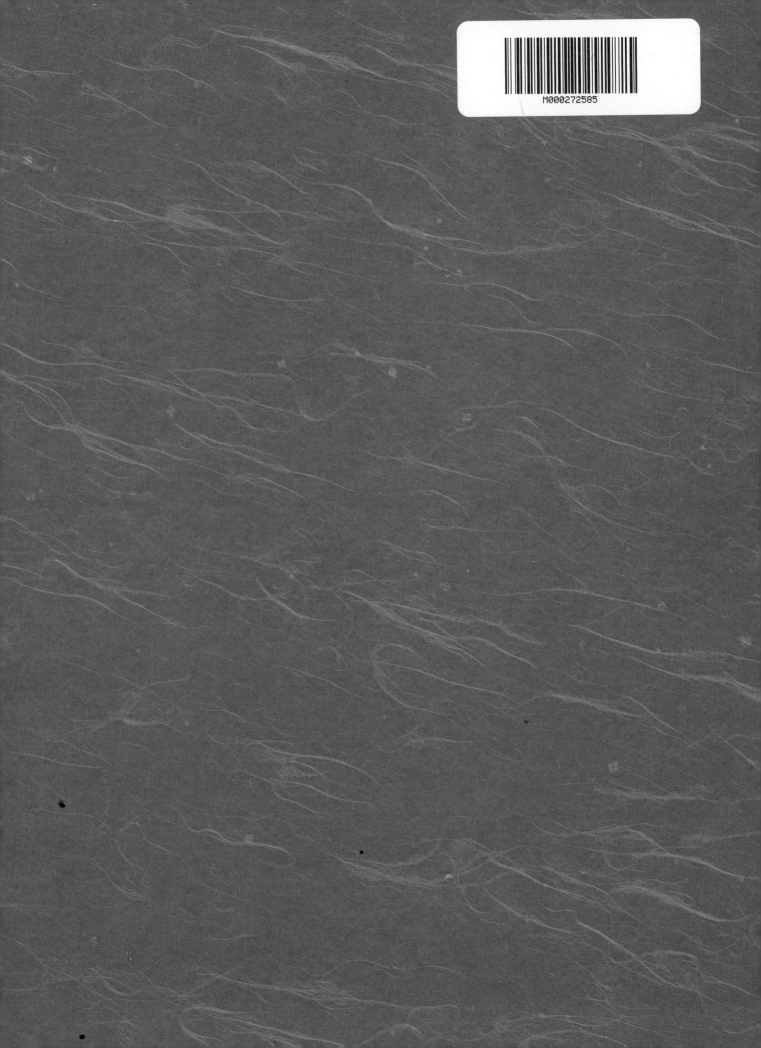

Down to Earth

Down to Earth

The 507th Parachute Infantry Regiment in Normandy

17 Dec. 2004

Descende ad Terram!

Martin K.A. Morgan

Schiffer Military History
Atglen, PA

Dedication

This book is dedicated to the memory of two men: Robert Dempsey Rae and John Carson Smith. They served when called, and were among those chosen by fate to parachute into Normandy on June 6, 1944.

Robert Dempsey Rae
(1913 - 2003)

John Carson Smith
(1923 - 2003)

Book Design by Ian Robertson.

We are interested in hearing from authors with book ideas on related topics.

Published by Schiffer Publishing Ltd.
4880 Lower Valley Road
Atglen, PA 19310
Phone: (610) 593-1777
FAX: (610) 593-2002
E-mail: Info@schifferbooks.com.
Visit our web site at: www.schifferbooks.com
Please write for a free catalog.
This book may be purchased from the publisher.
Please include $3.95 postage.
Try your bookstore first.

In Europe, Schiffer books are distributed by:
Bushwood Books
6 Marksbury Avenue
Kew Gardens
Surrey TW9 4JF
England
Phone: 44 (0) 20 8392-8585
FAX: 44 (0) 20 8392-9876
E-mail: info@bushwoodbooks.co.uk.
Free postage in the UK. Europe: air mail at cost.
Try your bookstore first.

Contents

Acknowledgments

The author is deeply indebted to a number of individuals who provided great assistance in the completion of this project. Bill Rentz, Robert Segel and Bruce Canfield were very generous in making photographs of their personal collections available for use in this book. Several good friends demonstrated a great deal of trust and made artifacts available to the author, namely Jewitt Short, Robert J. Carr, Tom Czekanski and Seth Paridon. Scott Smith Photography of Shreveport, LA, Moorman Photographics of St. Petersburg, FL, Jackson Hill Photography of New Orleans, and Jeff Petry Photography of Vancouver, BC, made many of the modern photographs that appear in the following pages possible.

Several other photographs appear courtesy of Heidi Stansbury-Paridon. Phil Nordyke was also very helpful in providing photographs from the 82nd Airborne Division Museum. Dennis and Barbara Maloney were very helpful and cooperative in providing information about their father, Lt. Col. Arthur A. Maloney. The following 507th veterans were exceptionally generous with their time and always provided greater willing cooperation than any historian/author could ever have hoped for: Paul F. Smith, Frank Naughton, Roy Creek, Robert S. Davis, Gordon K. Smith, John Marr, Paul Mank, William D. Bowell, John Hinchliff, Edward J. Jerziorski, and George Leidenheimer. This book would not have been possible had it not been for their assistance. John Carson Smith, Lou Horn and Robert Dempsey Rae also demonstrated a great deal of willing cooperation and it will always be a source of deep sorrow to me that they passed away shortly before this project came to its inevitable conclusion. They were each great men and it was one of the deepest privileges of my life to have gotten to know them in the last years of their lives.

Great assistance also came from France throughout this project. Paul Le Goupil, Fernand François, Gerard Guegan, Marthe His and Odette Lelavechef each made a great contribution to this project. The original 507th historian, Dominique François, assisted by providing a number of the photographs that appear on the pages that follow. Scott Carroll not only made all of the maps that appear here-after, but also converted frames of film footage into a number of the still images reproduced in the Normandy chapters. His technical knowledge and skill were a great asset. Much of the material that contributed to the chapters dealing with Alliance, Nebraska was made available thanks to Gloria Clark, author of *World War II Prairie Invasion*, and Becci Thomas of the Knight Museum in Alliance. Airborne authors Patrick O'Donnell and Mark Bando contributed their vast personal expertise in a way that was most helpful. Phil Walker and David Druckenmiller of Jump/Cut Productions in Atlanta were very helpful in sharing information and the two of them have made an outstanding film about the 507th. In addition to writing the forward to this book, Lt. Col. Aidis Zunde provided his special expertise in addition to great motivating encouragement. Special thanks also go to the officers and NCOs of the 1st/507th Parachute Infantry at Fort Benning, GA – their professionalism and dedication should make us all sleep better at night.

Moral support for this project came from a number of very important people. Piper Lanier, Nathan McArthur, Tracy Bruno, Elizabeth Bugbee, Jeremy Collins, Betsy L. Plumb, and Colleen O'Donnell were all kind enough to listen to and show great interest in endless stories about the 507th. Dr. Gordon "Nick" Mueller and Sam Wegner made it possible for me to pursue this project. Special thanks also goes to Hugh Ambrose, who provided irreplaceable guidance and encouragement. Mr. Albert "Bud" Parker of Atlanta brought me into the 507th family in late 2001. Had it not been for him, I would never have known the remarkable men whose experiences are described in the pages that follow. Thank you very much Mr. Parker. My brother, Joe W. Morgan, III, and my mother, Mildred "Pete" Morgan, were equally instrumental in keeping me motivated about this project. Special thanks also go to Joe W. Morgan, Jr. In addition to being a soldier, a scholar and the best father ever, he is the person that sparked my interest in history many, many years ago. Finally, this book could never have been completed without the assistance of Deborah L. Stoddard. As cheerleader, copy-editor, translator, research assistant and companion, she is unsurpassed.

Foreword

In the hot August days of 1940, the United States paratrooper tradition was born with the first jumps of the Parachute Test Platoon. The troopers of that unit, under the leadership of Lieutenant Ryder, lit the torch of U.S. airborne forcible entry capability on the fields of Fort Benning.

Soon after, the U.S. Army quickly built up its airborne force, forming a series of parachute and glider regiments. The 507th Parachute Infantry Regiment (PIR) was one of those initial formations, activated in Ft. Benning, Georgia on 20 July 1942.

U.S. paratroopers distinguished themselves during World War II with a series of awe-inspiring airborne operations, the most legendary of which was the jump onto the fields of Normandy in the early morning hours of 6 June 1944 as the prelude to the D-Day landings. The 507th PIR, part of the 82nd Airborne Division, played a pivotal, though sometimes forgotten, role in this operation, as is so dramatically chronicled here by Martin Morgan. In these pages, he tells the story of the first combat experience of this heroic unit – during thirty-five days of combat, this regiment accomplished all assigned missions, though it suffered 938 casualties in so doing. For its accomplishments in Normandy alone, the 507th PIR earned the Presidential Unit Citation (streamer embroidered Cotentin), the French Croix de Guerre with Palm (streamer embroidered Ste.-Mère-Église), the French Croix de Guerre with Palm (streamer embroidered Cotentin), and the fourragere to the French Croix de Guerre, as well as the Normandy campaign streamer with arrowhead device.

The Normandy campaign, however, was only the beginning for this regiment. Reassigned to the 17th Airborne Division, the 507th PIR went on to fight in the Allied counterattack during the Battle of the Bulge. Later, on 24 March 1945, the regiment was the first unit to parachute into Germany as two airborne divisions (the 17th U.S. Airborne Division and the 6th British Airborne Division) were dropped across the Rhine River near Wesel in Operation Varsity.

Not long after the end of the war, the 507th PIR, along with many other distinguished units, was inactivated, but other remaining formations continued the great airborne tradition – a tradition that leads up to today, with airborne assaults in Grenada, Panama, and, most recently, Afghanistan and Iraq.

In 1985, the U.S. Army reactivated the 1st Battalion (Airborne), 507th Infantry. Today, the 1-507th PIR has the mission to train and qualify paratroopers, jumpmasters, and pathfinders in order to provide the Department of Defense with qualified personnel to conduct airborne operations. Unusual in having its own parachute riggers organic to the unit, the battalion also provides rigger support

Millett Hall, the Headquarters of the 1st-507th Infantry (Abn) at Fort Benning. It is named for Colonel George V. Millett, Jr., the officer who commanded the 507th Parachute Infantry Regiment from its formation in 1942 until his capture in Normandy in June 1944. (*Photo by the author*)

The 1st-507th Infantry (Abn) uses Fort Benning's 34-foot towers (*foreground*) during the three-week Basic Airborne Course (BAC) to train parachutists for their first jump. One of Fort Benning's World War II vintage 250-foot towers is visible in the background. (*Photo by the author*)

Trainees attached to the 1st-507th Infantry (Abn) receive instruction on the 34-foot tower at Fort Benning, Georgia in March 2003. (*Photo by the author*)

to itself, the Ranger Training Brigade, the 75th Ranger Regiment, and numerous smaller units.

In carrying on the tradition and the standards set by our predecessors, we strive to produce paratroopers who are physically fit, mentally tough, competent, and courageous – ready to contribute to their units immediately upon arrival. Every year, we train 18,000-20,000 soldiers, sailors, airmen, and marines and send them out to units throughout the U.S. Armed Forces.

To accomplish this mission, the 1-507th PIR has over three hundred cadre members, organized into six companies – HHC, Alpha, Bravo, Charlie, Delta, and Echo.

Four of these companies – Alpha, Bravo, Charlie, and Delta – are responsible for the three-week Basic Airborne Course (BAC) which trains and qualifies approximately 18,000 soldiers, sailors, airmen, and marines for static line parachute operations each year. This course teaches the basics necessary to safely exit a USAF high-

A "Black Hat" airborne instructor of the 1st-507th Infantry (Abn) offers a young Marine trainee some suggestions on how to be a more effective parachutist: Fort Benning, March 2003. (*Photo by the author*)

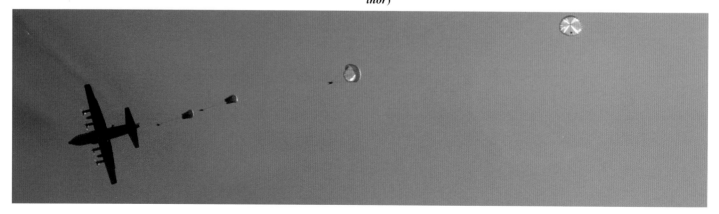

A Pennsylvania Air National Guard C-130 *Hercules* dropping parachutists attached to the 1st-507th Infantry (Abn) for the Basic Airborne Course (BAC): Fort Benning, March 2003. (*Photo by the author*)

Right: Pennsylvania Air National Guard C-130 *Hercules* dropping parachutists attached to the 1st-507th Infantry (Abn) for the Basic Airborne Course (BAC). Fort Benning, March 2003. (*Photo by the author*)

performance aircraft at low altitudes (1000'-1250') with a static line parachute (hooked to a cable in the aircraft by a 'static line' so that when the trooper jumps out of the aircraft, this line automatically deploys the parachute). These troopers graduate after conducting five qualifying jumps, the last one usually at night. To conduct this training, each company has approximately 25-30 cadre. The instructors wear either a maroon beret or the coveted "blackhat." To earn the latter, an instructor must be thoroughly proficient in all aspects of the course, as well as being able to give a formal block of instruction. He is awarded his blackhat after a successful test before the command sergeant major.

Headquarters and Headquarters Company (HHC) is responsible for the Master Trainers, the Jumpmaster Course, the Pathfinder Course, the battalion staff, the maintenance section, and the "holdover" detachment. The Master Trainers – the "eyes and ears" of the battalion commander and command sergeant major – are expert instructors who maintain the consistency of standards across the battalion as each of the BAC companies rotates through airborne training.

Jumpmaster Branch conducts the two-week long Jumpmaster Course, which teaches experienced paratroopers advanced airborne skills. Students learn how to prepare jumpers for an airborne operation, how to inspect a jumper's equipment, and how to safely exit jumpers from an aircraft. These are very demanding tasks – a mistake could easily mean death for a jumper – and we train jumpmaster students to very rigorous standards. This is a "zero-defects" envi-

Students attached to the 1st-507th Infantry (Abn) for the Basic Airborne Course (BAC) descending on Fryer Field in the Alabama training area of Fort Benning, March 2003. (*Photo by the author*)

ronment and the graduation rate, consequently, is quite low – approximately 55%, producing just over 400 jumpmasters each year.

Pathfinder Branch conducts the three-week long Pathfinder Course, which trains personnel how to prepare and inspect equipment to be lifted by helicopters, how to prepare drop zones and landing zones, and how to conduct air traffic control around these zones. Each class culminates with a field problem that puts the student's new skills to the test. This branch produces approximately 500 new pathfinders each year.

Echo Company is the rigger company, with over 120 soldiers. It is composed of a pack platoon (which packs up to 600-800 parachutes daily), a control and issue platoon (which stores and issues parachutes), a maintenance platoon (which repairs parachutes and other equipment), and a ranger support platoon (which is deployable and directly supports the 75th Ranger Regiment). As mentioned, Echo Company supports not only the rest of the battalion, but several other units, to include the 75th Ranger Regiment, packing over 80,000 parachutes a year. The riggers wear the distinctive red "baseball" caps.

In addition to this, the 1-507th PIR is the Department of Defense proponent for military static-line parachuting and pathfinder operations. As such, we are responsible for how these operations are conducted throughout the U.S. military.

The brave men of the Parachute Test Platoon (of which only four survive today) lit the torch of U.S. airborne forcible entry capability more than sixty years ago. That torch was carried forward

Open canopy over the drop zone at Fryer Field in the Alabama training area of Fort Benning, March 2003. (*Photo by the author*)

Open canopies over the drop zone at Fryer Field: Fort Benning, March 2003. (*Photo by the author*)

A Basic Airborne Course (BAC) student about to execute a Parachute Landing Fall (PLF) on Fryer Field in the Alabama training area: Fort Benning, March 2003. (*Photo by the author*)

Student attached to the 1st-507th Infantry (Abn) for the Basic Airborne Course (BAC) leaving the drop zone after completing his first jump. (*Photo by the author*)

and made to burn ever brighter by the paratroopers that followed and "put their knees in the breeze" over such faraway places as North Africa, Sicily, Italy, France, Holland, Germany, New Guinea, the Philippines, Corregidor, Korea, Vietnam, Grenada, Panama, Afghanistan, and Iraq, among others. The men of the 507th PIR did their share in contributing to this glorious history and passing the torch to succeeding generations.

Today, we – the troopers of the 507th – are privileged to carry on this airborne tradition. As we forge men and women into paratroopers, we hold them to exacting and uncompromising standards, knowing that they join a tradition of honor and glory that shines bright in the pages of U.S. military history. We work hard to make our veterans – who were prepared to make the ultimate sacrifice for their country and comrades – proud of these new generations of paratroopers, many of whom will most likely be called upon to again 'chute-up' and jump out into the darkness above some distant land in the service of our great country.

Hunters from the Sky!

Lt. Col. Aidis L. Zunde
Commanding Officer
1-507th Parachute Infantry

Student attached to the 1st-507th Infantry (Abn) for the Basic Airborne Course (BAC) leaving the drop zone after completing his first jump. (*Photo by the author*)

1st-507th Infantry (Abn) Commander's Coin for excellence. (*Author's Collection***)**

Lt. Col. Aidis L. K. Zunde Commanding Officer 1st-507th Infantry (Abn) (*Courtesy of Lt. Col. Ides L. Zunde***)**

Introduction

The American Cemetery in Colleville-Sur-Mer, France is the final resting place for 9,386 of the Americans who lost their lives in the campaign that began in Normandy on June 6, 1944. The rows of graves are not arranged according to unit within the cemetery's 172 acres because here there is no segregation. Here you will find Californian buried next to Pennsylvanian, General buried next to Private, Jew buried next to Gentile, and combat engineer buried next to paratrooper. Among the headstones of the paratroopers at Colleville-Sur-Mer, 129 bear the unit designation 507th Parachute Infantry Regiment, 82nd Airborne Division. Their dates of death begin on June 6th and continue on an almost daily basis until July 22nd, mute testimony to the fact that the men of this particular regiment were engaged in almost constant heavy combat in Normandy for over a month.

Although nearby interpretive text panels tell the big picture story of the overall Normandy campaign, there is nothing to explain the individual circumstances of those 129 507th deaths. In other words, there is no text explaining that when 1st Sgt. George P. Pettus and 2nd Lt. Donald E. Paterson were killed on June 9, 1944, they were fighting for control of a causeway at a place called La Fière. There is no text connecting the death of Cpl. Russell Blair Dillard to fighting around the village of Vindefontaine on D+17 (June 23rd). The headstones of Pvt. Walter L. Choquette and Pvt. Jesus Casas say nothing about how they were first captured, then

The Normandy American Cemetery in Colleville-Sur-Mer, France. (*Photo by Jeff Petry*)

forced by their murderers to dig their own common grave, and then shot in the back of the head and dumped into that hole along with several of their comrades. These details remain untold at the cemetery. However, each one of the 129 507th headstones is a story of a life cut violently short by the Second World War. When the European component of that war began with the German invasion of Poland on September 1, 1939, none of those 129 men could have possibly known that their mortal existence would end the way it did. Yet, the invasion of Poland triggered a sequence of events that ultimately delivered those 129 young American men to an early grave in France overlooking a beach named Omaha.

But the German invasion of Poland decided the fate of more than just the 129 507th paratroopers buried in the Normandy American Cemetery, for it affected the lives of millions of people. Fourteen-year-old Odette Rigault and her 7-year-old little sister Marthe were living a simple rural life near a village called Graignes on September 1, 1939. They had no way of knowing that, four years

Pvt. Walter L. Choquette is among the 129 paratroopers of the 507th Parachute Infantry Regiment buried in the Normandy American Cemetery. (*Photo by Heidi Stansbury-Paridon*)

and nine months later, the war that was just starting in Poland would ultimately come to their family's farm and turn them into refugees. On September 1, 1939, seventeen-year-old Paul le Goupil was living in the city of Rouen. He had no way of knowing that he would be betrayed by one of his own countrymen and that, five years later, he would end up in a concentration camp in Germany near a place called Buchenwald. On September 1, 1939, ten-year-old Anne Frank was living with her family in Amsterdam. She had no way of knowing that, three years later, she would be forced into hiding. She had no way of knowing that after twenty-five months in hiding, an informant would betray her family, leading first to arrest, then deportation and finally, imprisonment. On September 1, 1939, Anne had no way of knowing that her life would end all too early, five years and six months later during a typhus outbreak in the concentration camp at Bergen-Belsen. But it did.

On September 1, 1939, fifty-nine-year-old Jeanette Rankin was known as one of the leading feminist activists in the United States. She first made a name for herself before World War I as an outspoken proponent of women's suffrage and a host of other social welfare issues. In 1916, she scored a major victory for feminism when she became the first woman to serve in the United States Congress. But her election to the House of Representatives was cheapened by the great hypocrisy that women still did not have the right to vote in America. At a time when war was raging across Europe, Rankin established herself as a self-declared pacifist and cast her lot with the anti-war isolationists. When President Wilson asked for a declaration of war against Germany in 1917 following the re-introduction of unrestricted U-Boat warfare, Rankin and forty-nine other isolationist members of Congress voted against it. Because of her opposition to entry in World War I as well as some of her other controversial views, Rankin's popularity rapidly declined to the point that she lost a Republican Senate nomination in 1918. On September 1, 1939, Rankin had no way of knowing that her breed of pacifism was about to undergo a brief renaissance. She had no way of knowing that the isolationism that was so popular in 1916 was about to become popular all over again as Americans sought to keep their country out of the European war that had just begun.

But the war in Europe did breathe new life into the American pacifist movement, and it was enough to carry Jeanette Rankin back into the U.S. House of Representatives in 1940. Thirteen months later, the Japanese Imperial Navy conducted a sneak attack against the U.S. Pacific fleet anchorage at Pearl Harbor in the Territory of Hawaii, killing 2,403 Americans. The emotional fury aroused by the attack on Pearl Harbor was such that the fledgling anti-war movement disappeared literally overnight. When President Franklin Roosevelt asked a joint session of Congress for a declaration of war against Japan the day after the attack, only one member of

Congress voted against it: Jeanette Rankin. Her pacifist convictions were such that, even after the most infamous belligerent act of the 20th century, she would not support the idea of war. Despite the fact that the Japanese attacked the United States while the two nations were at peace, Rankin would not approve military response. On the day she cast the only vote against war with Japan (Monday, December 8, 1941), hundreds of thousands of American men choked recruiting stations across the country, desperate to join the U.S. military. Thousands among them lied about their age just to get a chance to fight. Of the thousands of men who were not accepted into military service because they failed the entrance physical, a large number were so disconsolate to be turned away that they committed suicide. Clearly, Jeanette Rankin did not represent them.

Four days after Pearl Harbor, Adolf Hitler unilaterally declared war on the United States, citing the mutual defense treaty that Germany had signed with Japan and Italy. Thus as of the second week of December 1941, America was at war with the most powerful militarized societies in the world at the time. As 1941 turned to 1942, Jeanette Rankin watched the war that she thought the United States should have nothing to do with as it intensified. As 1941 turned to 1942, she watched the incredible mobilization of the American industrial economy as it occurred simultaneously with the incredible expansion of the American military. Under these circumstances, Rankin astutely realized that her pacifist message would probably not meet with popularity. For that reason, she chose not to seek reelection in 1942.

At about the same time that Rankin chose not to run again, a regiment of paratroopers designated the 507th was born at Fort Benning, Georgia. At about the same time that she was re-adjusting to the private life of a *former* Congressional Representative in early 1943, the 507th moved from Georgia to Nebraska to continue its preparations for war. Late that year, the 507th went to Europe to join the fight against totalitarianism while Jeanette Rankin enjoyed the kind of peaceful, secure lifestyle that was available in only a few places in the world at that time. Then, thirty months after Pearl Harbor, 2,004 men of the 507th jumped into combat for the first time in the early morning hours of D-Day. When the 507th was pulled out of Normandy after thirty-five days in combat, it had suffered approximately 400 killed in action, 129 of which lie buried today at Colleville-Sur-Mer.

Each and every one of the 129 men buried there had chosen their fate, for the parachute infantry was composed exclusively of volunteers. They made the choice to become paratroopers knowing full well that it could lead to death. Those 129 dead men stand in stark contrast to Jeanette Rankin. She believed that nothing was worth fighting for. They obviously believed otherwise. She lived on into old age. They enjoyed no such luxury. She naively moralized that it was wrong to use force even to resist the aggression of nations being driven by men with destructive ideologies. They accepted the unpleasant responsibility of defeating the destructive ideology that had delivered blood and suffering to Europe. They voluntarily accepted the risks of taking up that crusade. They accepted the notion that oppression was worth fighting against and that the peace and dignity of the world was worth fighting for. The pacifism of Jeanette Rankin in the face of Axis aggression was as foolishly optimistic and counterproductive as Neville Chamberlain's attempts at appeasement had been before the war. Her philosophy was toxic because it was blindly tolerant of tyranny. Pacifism must be at all times prepared to accept that which inevitably feeds off of it: the opportunism of criminals. Utopianists like Jeanette Rankin must be prepared to face the reality of Ann Frank.

The Normandy American Cemetery is the final resting place for 9,386 of the Americans who lost their lives in the campaign that began on June 6, 1944. (*Photo by Jeff Petry*)

The great invasion of Normandy is now sixty years behind us and the American history memory of that event is strong. Through the work of people like Steven Spielberg and the late Dr. Stephen E. Ambrose, the public seems to be more interested in the subject now than it ever has. But the present level of interest is no guarantee for the future. The importance of certain other American conflicts has faded into remote memory. Despite their significance, most people do not know much about the wars with Mexico or Spain. Despite its significance and importance in the history of the 20th century, the war that was fought in Korea between 1950 and 1953 is all but forgotten as well. Filmmakers and historians have the power to keep the level of human understanding of these and other historical moments high. Within them, there are more amazing stories to be told than can be comprehended.

The Normandy invasion has been the subject of countless films and books, and yet the subject remains rich and unexhausted. Its stories of teamwork, courage and sacrifice are so multitudinous that all of them have still not been told to the fullest extent possible. The stewardship of those memories must be active. It must be handed from generation to generation so that a century from now, our progeny will still be talking about D-Day. The role of the 507th Parachute Infantry Regiment in that invasion is just one story among many. It is the story of just 2,004 men out of the 150,000 that assaulted northern France on June 6, 1944. Although only one story among many, in it are all of the quintessential elements of remarkable human drama: daring, camaraderie, suffering, triumph over adversity and tragic dénouement. This book was written in an effort to tell that story. It is hoped that after reading this book you will develop an admiration for those 2,004 men and that, each year on June 6th, you will pause to remember what they did for you in Normandy. It is also hoped that after reading this book you will be inspired to visit the American Cemetery at Colleville-Sur-Mer and that during your moments of reflection among the crosses and stars of David, you will remember the regiment's 129 honored dead that lay buried there.

Martin K.A. Morgan
New Orleans, Louisiana
September 2003

1

The Beginning

The 507th PIR was activated on July 20, 1942 at Fort Benning, Georgia, Colonel George V. Millett, Jr., commanding. The new regiment's distinctive insignia was created soon thereafter by Sgt. Kenneth Jenkins of the regimental intelligence section. The insignia was in the form of a shield bearing a white parachute on a blue background and a blue streak of lightning on a white background denoting the infantry. Below the shield was a scroll bearing the regimental motto, which was conceived by Chaplain John J. Verret. The motto appeared as the Latin phrase *Descende Ad Terram*, which translated into English means *Down to Earth*.

Lt. Frank Naughton before a jump at Fort Benning in 1942. He is wearing the early Riddell football helmet. (*Courtesy of Dominique François*)

Distinguished unit insignia of the 507th Parachute Infantry. (*Author's Collection, photo by Scott Carroll*)

Frank Naughton
Headquarters Company, 3rd Battalion
(*Photo by Jeff Petry*)

Paul Smith
F Company
(*Photo by Jeff Petry*)

The first step in the regiment's formation was building a cadré of jump qualified NCOs and officers. Twenty-four-year-old Lieutenant Frank Naughton was among the first officers to become a part of the 507th. He entered U.S. Army service voluntarily in August of 1941 because he did not want to be drafted. "I thought I'd better get in this year and get it over with," Naughton recalled.[1] Upon completing basic training at Camp Wheeler, Georgia, he volunteered for the U.S. Parachute Troops and was then sent to Fort Benning to Jump School. Monday, December 8th was to be his class's first jump, but because of the events of December 7th, that was delayed thirty days. As a result of Pearl Harbor, Naughton's Jump School class did not make their first qualifying jumps until the latter part of January 1942. After Jump School, Naughton se-

Early World War II postcard celebrating the Army's new airborne forces. (*Collection of The National D-Day Museum*)

cured a slot for himself in Officer Candidate School. He graduated from OCS on July 28th and then joined the 507th a few days later when it was just forming. At that time, the regiment was "just a few officers and three or four hundred enlisted men." As a newly commissioned 1st Lieutenant, Naughton was assigned to Headquarters Company, 3rd Battalion.

Paul Smith joined the regiment at about that same time. Born in Taunton, Massachusetts in 1915, Smith enrolled in the Citizens Military Training Corps program in the mid-1930s and, by virtue of that program, was commissioned as a U.S. Army officer in March 1942. His first assignment was to the Armored School at Fort Knox, Kentucky. After finishing, Smith was assigned to a unit there at Fort Knox. Like many men, he was anxious to get into the war. "All my buddies were going to the 1st Armored Division, which was scheduled to go overseas, and I volunteered for that," Smith remembered.[2] When nothing happened, he volunteered for the airborne and went to Fort Benning.

The first weeks of the regiment's life were spent in the 'Frying Pan' area at Fort Benning as the ranks of each company filled-out with new paratroopers. Paul Smith was put in charge of F Company and was able to develop a strong familiarity with his men as the strength of the company grew. It was a position that he found particularly satisfying:

I liked my job, I was a Company Commander and that's the last job you can have in the Army where you know the men intimately, and I just loved it. I knew the first name of every man in my Company and I knew most of their serial numbers and I knew their wive's names, I knew where they were from...I thought it was great.[3]

"When the 507th was born, we had probably five or six officers that were regular Army officers – the rest of our people were citizen soldiers," Smith remembered.[4] In the summer of 1942 the U.S. Army's parachute force was still quite new, having been established at Benning just two years prior. It was an all-volunteer force that grew in size with each passing month as the United States geared up for war. The airborne vertical envelopment concept itself represented a revolutionary military doctrine at the very cutting edge of technology. Vertical envelopment made it possible to drop a large autonomous combat team behind enemy lines that could disrupt enemy operations and seize otherwise inaccessible objectives deep in enemy territory. With a reputation for being composed of the best of the best, America's airborne began attracting attention as it grew. Even before Pearl Harbor, the American public and the American media sat up and took notice of what was being developed at

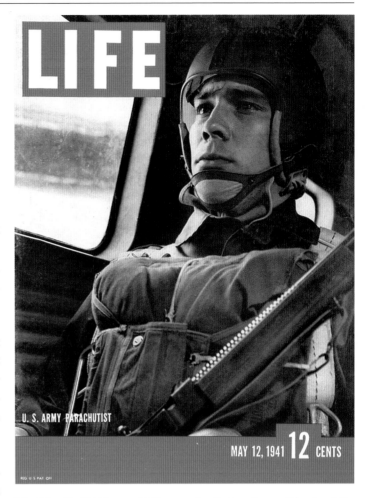

The May 12, 1941 issue of *Life* magazine featured an article about the Army's parachute troops. To many U.S. Army soldiers, this article constituted their introduction to the growing strength of the nation's airborne forces. *(Courtesy of Jewitt Short)*

Johnny Marr
G Company
(Photo by Jeff Petry)

This photograph of Edward R. Barnes was taken shortly before he volunteered for the airborne. Before jump school he served in the 4th Infantry Division; after jump school, he was attached to the 507th Parachute Infantry Regiment. *(Courtesy of Edward R. Barnes)*

Robert S. "Bob" Davis left college immediately after Pearl Harbor and joined the U.S. Army. He was one of the regiment's original members. *(Courtesy of Bob Davis)*

Lou Horn
C Company
(Photo by Jeff Petry)

Roy Creek
E Company
(Photo by Jeff Petry)

Fort Benning. The May 12, 1941 issue of *Life* magazine featured an article about the burgeoning strength of the American Airborne:

> Last summer, in the dusty Georgia air above Camp Benning, there were 48 U.S. parachutists, who day after day, at peril of their lives, jumped from Army transport planes 750 ft. in the air. Last week there were 521 such parachutists, jumping, going to ground school, learning a dangerous new job. By fall there will be 4,084 of them, divided into eight battalions, as well as about 400 in the Marine Corps. In another year there may be several thousand more. In an amazingly short time, the U.S. will have organized and trained an effective parachute force, ready for action.[5]

The article went on to outline the required qualifications a soldier would have to meet to be eligible for the Airborne.

> A parachutist must be tough. Because the job is dangerous. All must volunteer, and entrance requirements are strict. A man must be between 21 and 32, unmarried, athletic, have a high I.Q. He must realize that he is likely to get hurt.[6]

Despite the intimidating tone of the requirements, there was no lack of volunteers. This was largely due to the fact that the Army advertised. Men read about the parachute troops in Army newspapers and on flyers posted on bulletin boards and in clubs. In addition to that, jump-qualified officers circulated among regular Army units throughout the country, calling for soldiers to sign up for the new branch of the Army. Johnny Marr had been drafted into the Army on June 19, 1941 and was in basic training at Camp Roberts, California when he first heard about the paratroopers. A Major by the name of Robert F. Sink spoke to Marr's Infantry Replacement Training class during the early Fall of 1941 and appealed to the men to volunteer. Sink, who would go on to command the 506th Parachute Infantry Regiment, convinced Johnny Marr and two hundred other men in his training class to sign up for the Airborne.[7]

Such efforts met with great success, with the result that thousands of soon-to-be paratroopers were recruited out of the ranks of those already in uniform. This made the job much easier because these men had already received at least their basic training and consequently already had a familiarity with Army life. John J. Hinchliff was one of those men. He was born and raised in Park Rapids, Minnesota. When he was just seventeen years old, he lied about his age to join the Minnesota National Guard. In the guard, Hinchliff was assigned to a Coast Artillery Anti-Aircraft unit, which he found it to be somewhat lacking in excitement:

> Duty was very boring, you were on duty twenty-four hours, off duty twenty-four hours, and that went on for some time, and then one day they came around asking for volunteers for the Airborne. Hell, we didn't even know what the Airborne was at that time but just to get out of that environment about nine of us volunteered.[8]

Edward R. Barnes was also already in the U.S. Army before the war. Like John Hinchliff, he was not entirely happy with the

John Carson Smith joined the Army as a Private in 1940, and by the time he was assigned to the 507th two years later, he had been promoted to the rank of Sergeant. *(Courtesy of Dominique François)*

path upon which his military career was leading him prior to volunteering for Jump School. He was serving in the 4th Infantry Division when a call went out for a soldier that could play the bugle. Barnes stepped forward because he had learned the bugle when he was in the Boy Scouts. He was then ordered to report to the division's bandleader, at which time he began to feel reservations. "I thought, I don't want to be a soldier in a band," he recalled.[9] Not long thereafter, he volunteered for the airborne.

The pay was another issue that motivated men to volunteer for the parachute infantry. Paratroopers received an additional stipend that was referred to as "jump pay" – for enlisted men it was $50 per month and for officers, $100.[10] In 1941, a Private in the U.S. Army earned a mere $21 per month. "Jump Pay" would more than double his income. While it was not the sole motivating factor, the extra $50 per month certainly did not hurt. John Hinchliff remembered that, "The fact that they were going to pay us $50 a month "jump pay" – which was a lot of money at that time – sounded pretty

interesting to me."[11] Robert S. "Bob" Davis was also drawn to the parachute troops partly because of that extra $50. Davis was a six-foot tall, 160-pounder that was born and raised in Vermont. Immediately after Pearl Harbor he chose to depart the sophomoric diversions of his college fraternity and attempted to join the U.S. Army Air Corps, but flunked the physical due to colorblindness. He then went to the U.S. Marine Corps, and flunked that entrance physical for the same reason. Next he went to the U.S. Navy and flunked their physical as well. At that point he was growing desperate for a branch of U.S. military service to accept him, so he traveled into Boston and went to see a U.S. Coast Guard recruiter. Davis described what happened next:

> The Coast Guard said, "Well, yeah, OK. We'll give you a job, we'll accept you, but you'll be in there for inshore patrol for the duration of the war." In other words you can't go out to sea, you'll just be checking boats as they come into the harbor. So I said, "Well, that's not for me."[12]

At that point, Davis turned to his last choice, the regular ground army. While he was waiting in line at the Army induction center in Worcester, Massachusetts, he spotted a sign that called for volunteers for the parachute infantry. He got in that line and was accepted into the U.S. Army on February 2, 1942: colorblindness and all. He went to Camp Cross, South Carolina for basic training, then to Jump School at Fort Benning, after which he was assigned to Regimental Headquarters Company/507th as a radio operator.

Lou Horn started his Army career as a Teletype operator in the Signal Corps. Just like so many other men, he was dissatisfied with what he was doing too. Then one day, one of the other men in his unit showed him an advertisement for the Airborne. The ad read, "join the paratroops, transfer in grade, best paid, best fed men in the Army."[13] Without hesitating, Horn applied. Two weeks later he was directed to take a physical, which he did and passed. Soon thereafter, he was on his way to Fort Benning for parachute training.

For many men, membership in the airborne promised an elite status that had a strong appeal. Roy Creek was one of those men. He was born in New Mexico in 1918. He grew up there and ultimately took an ROTC commission in the U.S. Army in 1940 after graduating from New Mexico State University with a degree in agriculture. As his assigned unit began to take on more and more draftees during the expansion of the American military that occurred in anticipation of the coming war, Creek noticed that the quality of the troops he was dealing with had "deteriorated considerably."[14] He was not alone in that assessment. John Carson Smith was born in Winston-Salem, North Carolina in 1923. Like Roy Creek, he joined the Army in 1940, before the U.S. entered the fighting war. Smith quickly rose to the rank of Sergeant and before long he had a similar experience as his unit began receiving an influx of recent draftees. When Smith realized that he would be responsible for training these raw recruits, disillusionment set in and he decided that he could not stand any more. Then he read in an Army newspaper about the formation of the parachute troops down at Fort Benning:

> I had two real good buddies there and we talked and I went down to see the Company Commander and he said that, well I told him that I wanted to transfer into the Paratroops, and he said, "Man, that's a suicidal outfit! You don't want to go that course! I need you to help me train these guys, I want to send you to OCS and come back and help me train these guys." I said, "That's exactly what I want to get away from! I don't want to train these guys." I was really afraid I'd get stuck there and everybody would be going overseas and all with me stuck there training GIs.[15]

Many men felt a strong desire to get into the war as soon as possible. This was especially true in the months immediately after Pearl Harbor when patriotic sentiment was at an all-time high. Unlike Carson Smith and Roy Creek, Lou Horn was not yet in the Army in December 1941. The Long Island, New York native was a 17-year-old high school student when the Japanese attacked the U.S. Pacific Fleet anchorage in the Territory of Hawaii. Like so many thousands of other young Americans, he wanted to join the military as soon as possible after Pearl Harbor. Within weeks of the United States entering the war, Horn went to an induction station, but he could not get in:

> I was 17 and went to enlist and they wouldn't take me, so I had to wait until my 18th birthday which is May the first, and when I became 18 I enlisted in the Army, I did not wait to be drafted, I enlisted.[16]

On a level that seems universal, Americans wanted to go overseas to right the wrongs that Japanese and German aggression had wrought on the world. These were men driven by a deep sense of duty and responsibility to defend their country. These were men anxious to be personally involved in the destruction of totalitarianism. Jack Summer was one of those men. Born in 1921 in South Carolina, he was just twenty years old in December 1941. Soon after Pearl Harbor, he joined the Army. "I guess I was angry like everybody else – I was twenty-one and patriotic," he recalled.[17] Like Summer, Roy Creek was also motivated to action by the Japanese attack and was consequently determined not to be a spectator:

Jack Summer
Regimental Headquarters Company
(*Photo by Jeff Petry*)

Pvt. Jack Summer as a young 507th paratrooper in 1942. (*Courtesy of Dominique François*)

The *Wincharger* allowed airborne trainees to practice collapsing an open parachute canopy in simulated high wind conditions. (*National Archives and Records Administration 111-SC-188260*)

I wanted to get into the war. I was looking for the most sure route to becoming a combat infantry officer. I really wanted to get with troops that I thought would result in my playing a very active role in the war. I volunteered for the parachute troops.[18]

The first step of life in the Airborne was jump qualification. The volunteers all reported to a training battalion at Fort Benning where they began going through the concentrated instruction that would ultimately earn each man a pair of sterling silver jump wings. As soon as Johnny Marr completed basic training in California in September 1941, he was packed aboard a troop train with hundreds of other men – destination Fort Benning. Upon arrival in October,

he became a student in the eighth class to cycle through Group Parachute School (or GPS) – which was in charge of training all parachute troops in the Army. Thus, he received his training through GPS-8. During the next three weeks the soldiers assigned to GPS-8 learned to be parachutists. The first week was spent in ground training. The men practiced and perfected their "parachute landing fall" – a body position that would tend to distribute the shock of hitting the ground evenly over the entire body as opposed to focusing it only on the legs. It was also during week one that the men trained with the *Wincharger*, a large wind-producing fan that made it possible to practice collapsing an open parachute canopy in high wind conditions. Week two emphasized training and instruction on Fort Benning's 34-foot and 250-foot jump towers. The third week

Using one of Fort Benning's 250-foot towers, parachute trainees were able to practice the proper technique for descending under an open canopy. (*National Archives and Records Administration 111-SC-188263*)

Packing shed at Lawson Field, Fort Benning, in 1942. *(Courtesy of Gordon K. Smith)*

of GPS was jump week, when each man was required to jump out of a perfectly good airplane five times.

After completing the required five jumps, the men earned a pair of the coveted jump wings, and the privilege of being called "paratrooper." *Life* magazine described some of the details associated with these training jumps:

> Most practice jumps today are made from an altitude of 750 ft. A human body, falling from that height, will take about 8 1/2 seconds to hit the ground. As a parachutist jumps, his static line, attached to the plane, opens his parachute before he has fallen 100 ft. As he jumps, however, he starts to count-one … two … three … four. If by the time he reaches "four," his

regular parachute has not opened, he pulls the ripcord on the emergency chute strapped to his chest. This should open in two seconds – giving him 2 1/2 seconds of leeway before death.[19]

Naturally, Jump School emphasized an advanced level of physical conditioning mainly because of the rigorous demands associated with parachute operations. Intense physical training was obviously designed to toughen each volunteer's strength, but it also tested mental toughness. Paratroopers had to be capable of coping with and overcoming the harshest adversities that a combat environment could offer. They had to be able to respond effectively at all times, under extreme circumstances. The result was that their specific spe-

Partial View of Lawson Field, the Infantry School, Ft. Benning

Left: Pre-war postcard showing Lawson Field's hangar number 7. The 1st-507th Infantry (Abn) continues to use this hangar today. *(Collection of The National D-Day Museum)*

Opposite: Paratroopers about to make a training jump at Fort Benning. *(Collection of The National D-Day Museum)*

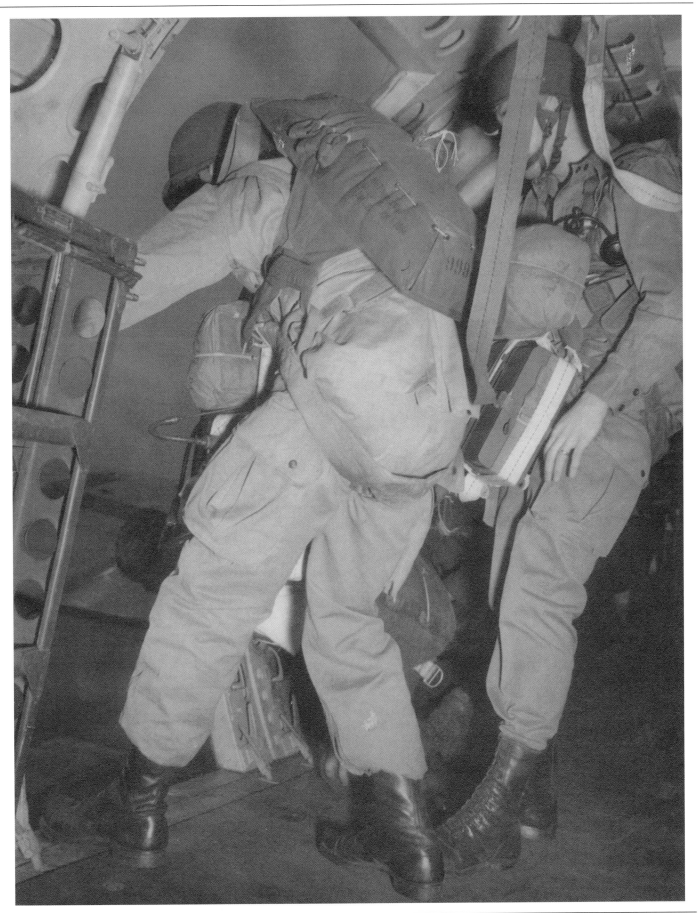

Three Douglas C-47s dropping parachutists during a training jump at Fort Benning in 1942. *(Courtesy of Gordon K. Smith)*

cialized training was more challenging and demanding than any other training in the Army. Carson Smith remembered just how challenging it really was to become a paratrooper:

> It was rough getting your wings back in those days, I mean pushups, twenty-five or fifty pushups wasn't anything for punishment. They'd try you every way in the world to see if you were going to give up or you were going to be a good Paratrooper.[20]

In addition to lots of physical training (referred to as "PT"), airborne volunteers had to do some cross-training as well. The *Life* magazine article went on to describe some of the other aspects of Airborne training.

> Before he is allowed to jump, a parachutist must go to ground school. He must run, tumble and do calisthenics until he is in better shape than a football player. Then he must learn how to jump off a 12-ft. platform without getting hurt, how to guide his falling parachute right or left, how to squirm quickly out of his chute if he finds himself landing in the water. Long after he makes his first jump, his studying goes on, for a parachutist landing in strange country must be ready to read maps, operate a radio, seize an airfield, blow up a bridge.[21]

• • •

507th jumpers just after exiting the aircraft over the drop zone. *(Courtesy of Dominique François)*

A large training jump at Fort Benning. *(Courtesy of Dominique François)*

Three jumpers descending toward the drop zone at Fort Benning. *(Collection of The National D-Day Museum)*

A large training jump at Fort Benning. *(Courtesy of Dominique François)*

Detail shot of a paratrooper in mid-oscillation. *(Collection of The National D-Day Museum)*

The moment of truth: a parachutist about to touch down on the drop zone. (*Collection of The National D-Day Museum*)

"Making a body turn" (*Collection of The National D-Day Museum*)

A trooper collapses his T-5 parachute after landing on the drop zone. *(Collection of The National D-Day Museum)*

One of the many hazards associated with parachute operations was the very serious hazard of landing among trees. In the forests of central Georgia, that could mean being suspended as much as fifty feet above the ground. *(Collection of The National D-Day Museum)*

A pair of sterling silver jump wings on the black and orange oval distinctive to the 507th Parachute Infantry Regiment. Five jumps from a C-47 would earn a young soldier his wings and the privilege of being called "paratrooper." (*Author's Collection, photo by Scott Carroll*)

George H. Leidenheimer, Jr. was born and raised in New Orleans, Louisiana. He volunteered for the U.S. Army immediately after Pearl Harbor and was soon thereafter assigned to the 507th Parachute Infantry Regiment. (*Courtesy of George H. Leidenheimer*)

Sgt. Leidenheimer poses with his mother during a visit home to New Orleans in 1943. Before the year was out, he would be sent overseas with the regiment. (*Courtesy of George H. Leidenheimer*)

George Henry Leidenheimer, Jr. went through Jump School just a few weeks before the 507th was formed. Born on October 23, 1922, Leidenheimer grew up and received a traditional Catholic school education in New Orleans, Louisiana. Ironically, it was during his Catholic school days that he learned all of the four-letter words that he was not supposed to use in a church environment. In 1936, Leidenheimer had finished elementary school and started at S. J. Peters High School on South Broad Street in New Orleans. "It was there that I started playing football," he remembered.[22] This athleticism was something that he would continue later in life when assigned to the 507th Parachute Infantry. Although very busy with school and athletics, Leidenheimer nevertheless worked at a local variety store on Saturdays, holidays and during summer vacation. His home life also placed demands on his time because his mother

Sgt. Leidenheimer poses on the front sidewalk of his family's home on Frenchman Street in New Orleans in 1943. *(Courtesy of George H. Leidenheimer)*

The 507th yearbook was published in 1943 by The Bradford-Robinson Printing Co. of Denver, Colorado. *(Collection of The National D-Day Museum)*

was quite ill throughout his high school years. As the oldest of four children, he had to go home early each day to take care of her and his three siblings. "I cooked, washed clothes, and cleaned the house until Dad arrived home," he recalled.[23] His aspiration was to one day play football for Louisiana State University, but only Southwestern Louisiana Institute in Lafayette showed any interest in his gridiron skills. For that reason, he chose not to go to college, but to work instead. He took a job as a salesman for the Hormel Meat Packing Company. To supplement his income from Hormel, Leidenheimer also started playing football for an independent team in New Orleans at $10.00 per game.[24]

He continued living this way until, in December 1941, his life underwent a dramatic change. "When Pearl Harbor was hit, I immediately went to the U.S. Army's recruitment center to volunteer

for parachute duty," Leidenheimer remembered.[25] Four months later, he was sent to Camp Livingston, Louisiana for basic training which was followed by temporary assignment to Camp Wolters near Mineral Wells, Texas where he went to Morse code school. Then in June 1942, he was transferred to Fort Benning for Group Parachute School. After the five hundred men of his GPS class qualified, half of them were assigned to the ranks of the 505th Parachute Infantry Regiment and the other half were assigned to the 507th.[26] Leidenheimer was assigned to B Company/507th as one of the regiment's original members.

The 507th continued with routine training exercises throughout the rest of July and August 1942. Then in September, the regiment moved across the Chattahoochee River into the Alabama Training Area near Uchee Creek to begin a rigorous 22-week training cycle. The training in Alabama naturally consisted of such obligatory basics as calisthenics, obstacle courses and forced marches. There were also more specialized training missions. For example, on October 30, 1942, nine officers of the 507th Parachute Infantry made a "premeditated" water landing at Lower King's Pond, Georgia. This exercise was described in the 507th yearbook:

> The jump was under the direction of Lt. Colonel Maloney and its object was to dispel any fears of water landings that men or officers of the regiment might have. The men who made the jump were: Lt. Colonel Maloney, Major Smith, Major Pearson, Captain Keller, Captain Brakonecke, Captain Fagan, Lt. Farnham, Lt. Higgins, and Lt. Hathaway. The jump was made with clothing, steel helmet, and jump boots fully laced. Of the nine men that jumped seven managed to land in the water, while the other two were carried off into the trees by the wind. The men were supposed to slip from their harness when they were 10 feet from the water and inflate their life preservers. Some managed to slip from their 'chutes, and others didn't. However, the important thing is nobody got hurt.[27]

Although they did not know it at the time, many of the men of the 507th would ultimately have experience with such water landings in combat.

During this "Alabama Renaissance" the regiment's official newspaper was born. The paper was called *Boots and Wings* and it

Sgt. George Leidenheimer and other soldiers gather around a boxing ring to participate in one of the many sporting activities that 507th men enjoyed. *(Courtesy of George H. Leidenheimer)*

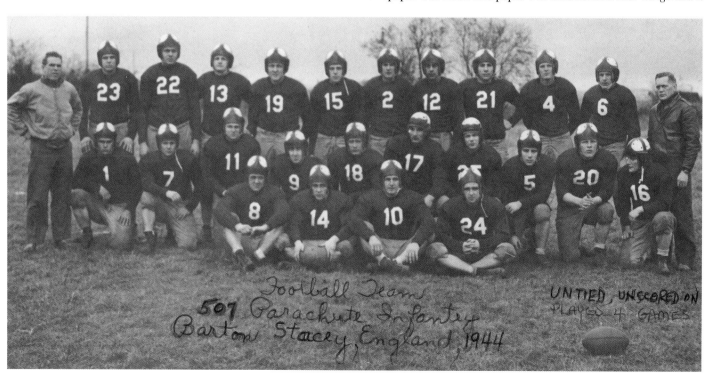

The 507th football team was coached by G Company commander, Captain Floyd Burdette "Ben" Schwartzwalder (far right). Schwartzwalder would later go on to coach Syracuse University to a National Collegiate Championship in 1959. *(Courtesy of George H. Leidenheimer)*

The 507th basketball team in 1943. *(Courtesy of Gordon K. Smith)*

The 507th *Spiders* in action during their one and only winning season. *(Courtesy of Gordon K. Smith)*

was run off on a hand operated mimeograph machine. 1,500 copies of the first issue appeared on November 1, 1942. *Boots and Wings*, which was published regularly until the regiment was deployed overseas, represented just one of the many peaceful fixtures in the life of the regiment before it went to war.

The 507th was still in the Alabama Training area as 1942 turned into 1943. For nearly six months, the daily routine of the men of the regiment had been some of the most vigorous and demanding training seen in the U.S. Army. As the New Year rolled around, the 507th was beginning to take shape as a well-honed combat force and it was ready to be inspected. On January 20, 1943, the commander of the 2nd Airborne Infantry Brigade, General George P. Howell, reviewed the regiment. Following a regimental parade, General Howell awarded prizes to those troopers who had demonstrated superior ability with the mortar, machine gun and rifle. Pvt. William E. Stoler of H Company, Second Battalion was recognized as being the regiment's finest marksman with the standard issue service rifle – the M1 Garand. Pvt. Stoler shot 293 out of a possible three hundred, the highest score of anyone in the 507th. Prior to the parade, the men who were to receive marksmanship awards made a parachute jump under the direction of Lt. Lilborn B. Jackson of E Company. After the conclusion of ceremonies, the men of the regiment enjoyed a southern barbecue.[28]

In addition to its rigorous schedule of combat training, some of the regiment's members also participated in certain extracurricular activities. With so many young men at the peak of their physical condition, athletics were especially popular in the ranks of the 507th.

Pvt. William D. Bowell poses in his class A uniform shortly before volunteering for the airborne. After he completed jump school at Fort Benning, he was assigned to Headquarters and Headquarters Company/507th. *(Courtesy of William D. Bowell)*

Members of the regiment participated in organized boxing, swimming and wrestling on a competitive basis. The 507th football team was coached by G Company Commander, Captain Floyd Burdette "Ben" Schwartzwalder. A former high school coach, Schwartzwalder had personally played three seasons for Muhlenberg College in Allentown, Pennsylvania. His coaching experience gave the 507th football team an edge that made them particularly successful. Of all of the different 507th sports teams though, the basketball team was the most accomplished. Nicknamed the 507th *Spiders*, the team played against several of the leading universities in the Southeast including the University of Georgia, Auburn University, the University of Florida and Georgia Tech. On January 23, 1943, the Spiders even played the New York Celtics, defeating them 42 to 39.

When the season ended on Saturday, February 27, 1943, the 507th Spiders had won 24 out of 26 matches, scoring a grand total of 1,160 points against the 540 points scored by the team's various opponents.[29]

For the men of the regiment who did not participate in sports, there were apparently other extracurricular activities that allowed them to blow off a little steam and sometimes get into a little bit of trouble. A weekend pass off post was evidently where such trouble frequently began. While stationed at Fort Benning, the men would descend on the peace loving populations of the cities of Columbus, Georgia and/or Phenix City, Alabama on weekend pass. These trips inevitably lead to much drinking and carousing. Lieutenant Frank Naughton of Headquarters Company, 3rd Battalion recalled what it was like:

Pvt. Bill Bowell poses in front of the Jefferson County Courthouse in Birmingham, Alabama. This photograph was taken in October 1942, shortly after he became a paratrooper. *(Courtesy of William D. Bowell)*

Pvt. Bill Bowell wears the boots and wings that distinguish him as a U.S. Army paratrooper. *(Courtesy of William D. Bowell)*

Oh gosh, you used to have a lot of people that went to town, got drunk, got in a fight, got brought back by the MPs.[30]

Naughton also recalled an especially amusing incident that occurred while the 507th was still at Fort Benning. One afternoon in January 1943, he was in his quarters when a call came in relating to some 507th men who had gotten into trouble in Columbus. He was instructed to go into town to "try to get everybody out."[31] Having been given his mission, Naughton proceeded to the Police Chief's office to negotiate the release of the 507th men being held in city lock-up. Much to his surprise, Naughton found that 98 men from the 507th were in that jail. Following tense deliberations with the Columbus Chief of Police, Naughton was allowed to call a local judge at home in the middle of the night to secure authorization to release the men. The men were thereafter turned over to the custody of Lt. Naughton, loaded onto a pair of buses, and then driven back onto post – all except for one man, that is. As the paperwork was being completed to process the 98 men out of the Columbus City Jail and into Naughton's custody, one man attempted to escape. The paratrooper turned escapee did not get very far though. After being recaptured the chief of police reneged on that man's release agreement. Naughton recalled the circumstances:

Well, then I had all of them sprung, they were getting the names and all when this one guy broke out of the jail. He was a little bit meaner than the rest. I remember the police chief saying, "Well, he was your prisoner, but he's mine now."[32]

Clearly, some of the men of the regiment burned-off their excess energy through leisure activities other than basketball.

Soon after the basketball season ended, the 507th left Alabama to participate in the Louisiana Maneuvers. On March 7, 1943, the regiment was flown from Fort Benning to Barksdale Field near Shreveport where, after arriving, it began to prepare for deploy-

Pvt. Bowell frequently drove up to Birmingham from Fort Benning to visit the young lady pictured at left – Dorothy Logan of Russelville, Alabama. *(Courtesy of William D. Bowell)*

Pvt. Edward R. Barnes *(left)* **poses for a portrait with two of his 507th comrades.** *(Courtesy of Edward R. Barnes)*

This photograph of Sgt. George H. Leidenheimer, Jr. was taken in the 507th bivouac area at Barksdale Field near Shreveport, Louisiana. The 507th was there to participate in the 1943 Louisiana Maneuvers. (*Courtesy of George H. Leidenheimer*)

Cpl. Ratliff, Pvt. Durnion, and Sgt. Leidenheimer in their encampment at Barksdale Field near Shreveport during the 1943 Louisiana Maneuvers. (*Courtesy of George H. Leidenheimer*)

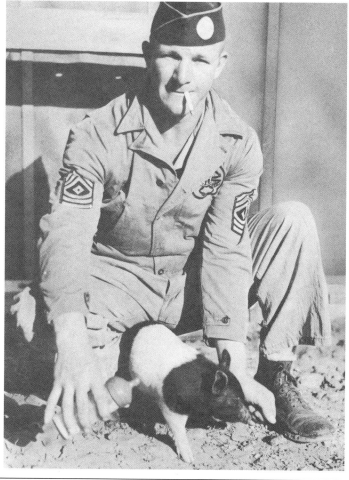

ment. On March 11th, Col. Millett was ordered by the Red Task Force commander to commit the 507th to the maneuver and was given a series of outlined objectives. The regiment was ordered to destroy an enemy held bridge over the Sabine River, to destroy enemy emplacements northeast of that bridge and finally to destroy all enemy forces in the immediate vicinity. Ahead of the full regimental deployment, Millett sent in an intelligence team on the evening of Sunday, March 13th. Consisting of one officer, six intelligence and two communications men, this team observed the opposing force's disposition of men and weapons in the deployment area and then radioed that information back to Col. Millett's headquarters. Armed with that vital information, Millett prepared to deploy the entire regiment.[33]

Right: 1st Sgt. Harrel E. Thompson and "Jumpin' Jimmy" – C Company's mascot. (*from the 507th yearbook, collection of The National D-Day Museum*)

Geronimo on the drop zone following one of his many successful parachute jumps. The reserve parachute canopy that he used is collapsed on the ground behind him. *(Courtesy of William D. Bowell)*

Cpl. Joseph J. Kopacz and Herman the goat, the S-2 mascot. *(Courtesy of William D. Bowell)*

Late the next day, the regiment's 1st and 3rd Battalions flew from Barksdale Army Air Field and air assaulted into a pair of drop zones located approximately fifteen miles northeast of the objective area. The heavily wooded terrain proved to be a significant problem though as hundreds of jumpers ended up coming down in the trees. Although this happened to a large number of the regiment's troopers, only a few injuries resulted. Despite this complication though, the 1st and 3rd Battalion paratroopers did manage to assemble into a single organized force that then proceeded to march ten miles, and successfully attack the objective. Having captured the bridge over the Sabine River, the 1st and 3rd Battalions were soon reinforced by further air assault. The following morning, 2nd Battalion/507th and Regimental Headquarters Company/507th

The regiment's jumping mascot Geronimo and his handler, Pvt. Ken Williams, on the drop zone just after a successful parachute jump. Note Geronimo's specially modified harness and reserve chute. *(Courtesy of William D. Bowell)*

Geronimo and Pvt. Ken Williams. *(Courtesy of William D. Bowell)*

jumped, assembled and then made their way to the bridge to help their comrades hold the position against a possible counterattack. When it was all over, the Red Task Force Army had been judged the winner of the Louisiana Maneuvers and the 507th PIR had received some absolutely practical experience.

During the maneuvers a 507th mortar section, bivouacked in the forests of north Louisiana, crossed paths with a baby pig. The little animal was quickly "adopted" by the mortar men and given the sobriquet "Jumpin' Jimmy." Their affections for Jimmy evidently did not run terribly deep though, because they soon thereafter lost him in a card game to a machine gun squad in B Company/507th. The B Company boys did not keep Jimmy long either though and traded him to C Company for a case of beer. Jumpin' Jimmy finally ended up being taken care of by 1st Sgt. Harold Thompson of C Co. Jimmy was not alone among the many mascots that 507th men adopted before being sent overseas though. As an example, B Company/507th briefly kept a baby coyote named Jackie and Lt. Maitland Higgins of Service Company owned a German shepherd named Buck that ultimately went on to serve in the canine corps.

Other regimental mascots included a pair of dogs named Boots and Wings as well as the 3rd Battalion's canine mascots Penny and Myrtle. But the most celebrated 507th war dog was Geronimo.

In addition to its pig, its coyote and its dogs, the 507th had still another mascot: fourteen-year-old Fred Toohey, Jr. of North Troy, New York. Fred wrote to the regiment during the latter half of 1943 requesting that he be appointed the regiment's mascot. In support of his request, Fred mentioned that a boy in his homeroom had been made the mascot of a Military Police Battalion and he even related a verbal altercation he had gotten into while defending the honor of the airborne infantry. The 507th yearbook described Fred's unique status:

Fred Toohey, Jr. is the only civilian member of a parachute infantry regiment. Freddie has been an ardent follower of the 507th since its activation. His youthful admiration, and spirituous ambition to become a member of the paratroopers, prompted his appointment by our Commanding Officer, Colonel George V. Millett, Jr. He received the coveted wings and

Geronimo descends under an open reserve parachute canopy in early 1943. *(Courtesy of William D. Bowell)*

Geronimo and Pvt. Williams, who was badly injured during the demonstration jump in Denver on the 4th of July 1943 and consequently was not able to go overseas. *(Courtesy of William D. Bowell)*

Geronimo and Sgt. John Carson Smith of Headquarters and Head-quarters Company/507th suited up for a training jump in 1943. *(Courtesy of Albert "Bud" Parker)*

Lt. Col. Roy Lindquist, Lt. Col. James Gavin and Mrs. Gavin at the 507th going away party in late 1942 at Fort Benning. In Normandy, Lindquist would command the 508th Parachute Infantry Regiment and Gavin, after being promoted to Brigadier General, would serve as the Assistant Division Commander for the 82nd Airborne Division. *(Courtesy of Gordon K. Smith)*

boots and his official papers properly signed and bearing the official stamp of the regiment, designating him as its choice for ideal mascot, on October 27, 1943.[34]

Sports and mascots represented merely distractions that helped keep the morale of the men of the 507th high throughout the different phases of their rigorous training. Although these pursuits certainly showed the human side of the young American boys of the strengthening regiment, they were nevertheless young American boys preparing to go to war.

James Gavin (left) and George Millett (right) when they were Majors early in 1942. *(Collection of The National D-Day Museum)*

2

After the Night of Darkness

The next phase of the regiment's training period began immediately after the conclusion of the Louisiana Maneuvers. On March 20, 1943 the 507th arrived in its new home: Alliance, Nebraska – population 6,669. On April 15, 1942, the U.S. Secretary of War authorized the establishment of an air base in Alliance to serve as a training center for Troop Carrier units, Glider Infantry troops and Parachute Infantry and work on the new base began almost immediately. That summer over 5,000 construction workers descended on the city to begin building what would ultimately become a large military facility. Interestingly, the ranks of the workforce were mostly composed of Lakota and Sioux tribesman from the nearby Rosebud Indian Reservation and the Pine Ridge Reservation in South Dakota. A large number of Mexican and African American laborers were also employed in the construction of the base.[1] Because of the sudden, large influx of construction personnel, Alliance experienced a serious housing problem. Before air base construction began, the population of the city had been shrinking for close to ten years, the result of acute drought conditions in the area.

Above: Construction at Alliance Army Air Field. By the time it was finished, the base consisted of 645 buildings and four 9,000-foot runways occupying 5,001 acres of a dried-up lakebed. (*Courtesy of the Knight Museum, Alliance, NE*)

Left: The control tower at Alliance Army Air Field. (*Courtesy of the Knight Museum, Alliance, NE*)

Waco CG-4A gliders parked on the apron at Alliance Army Air Field. Construction of the base was authorized in April 1942 to provide a place for Troop Carrier units, Glider Infantry troops and Parachute Infantry to train. *(Courtesy of the Knight Museum, Alliance, NE)*

Then when construction workers began migrating to Alliance by the busload during the latter half of 1942, they quickly filled all of the local hotels and boarding houses. Some citizens began renting empty rooms to the workers and there were even cases where bidding wars erupted between workers as they bartered over the limited accommodations available in town. To relieve the housing crisis, a sprawling tent city was established at the south end of town.[2]

The military reservation at Alliance, which was 25,000 acres in overall size, was leased to the government at $1 per year. The functioning base facility area itself consisted of 645 buildings occupying 5,001 acres of a dried-up lakebed called Boyer's Meadow.

Included among the base's structures were a sewerage plant, a power plant, a laundry facility and a hospital. Two access roads led to the base and a railroad spur connected the base to the Burlington & Missouri Railroad main line in Alliance. The heart of the base though was its airfield facilities. With an elevation of 3,926 feet, the field consisted of a control tower and eight hangars flanked by four runways, which were the longest in all of Nebraska. All four were fifty feet wide and 9,000 feet long. By the time it was finished, Alliance Army Air Field had cost the U.S. government a total of $15,392,533.[3]

In late 1942 the soldiers and airmen began arriving. The first unit to take up residence was the 403rd Troop Carrier Group. Then

A group of 507th enlisted men pose in the barracks area at Alliance Army Air Field in 1943. *(Courtesy of the Knight Museum, Alliance, NE)*

Paratroopers of the 507th Headquarters Company Demolition platoon in front of their barracks at the airfield in Alliance. *(Courtesy of the Knight Museum, Alliance, NE)*

Paratroopers of the 507th Headquarters Company Communications platoon in front of their barracks at the airfield in Alliance. *(Courtesy of the Knight Museum, Alliance, NE)*

came the 326th Glider Infantry Regiment and the 434th Carrier Group. The 507th Parachute Infantry Regiment followed. Bob Davis, then serving as a radioman with Regimental Headquarters Company, remembered that, "All of the parachute regiments that had received their full complement of men had to go somewhere to train as a unit." In Alliance, the 507th would be able to do just that. There the regiment was teamed up with the 403rd and the 434th Troop Carrier Groups. The Douglas C-47 Skytrains operated by these units made it possible to conduct joint training operations.

The intense physical training that began when each man joined the airborne continued as a daily reality in Alliance. The officers and men of the regiment maintained their peak conditioning just as they had back at Benning – with a regimen of PT (physical training): calisthenics, obstacle courses and forced marches. Their continued training in the sand hills of Nebraska also included repetition of the oh-so important folding and packing of the T-5 parachute. As the standard parachute of U.S. airborne forces in World War II, the T-5 was a 28-foot canopy made of 28 silk panels. The

Right: 1st Sgt. Sandy E. Pipolo poses in front of the NCOs' barracks for regimental Headquarters Company/507th at Alliance. *(Courtesy of the Knight Museum, Alliance, NE)*

3rd Battalion/507th staff officers in Alliance, Nebraska, in 1943: (*left to right*) Lieutenant E.F. Hoffman, Lieutenant G.M. Dillon, Major J.T. Davis, Lieutenant Colonel W.A. Kuhn, Lieutenant H.E. Wagner and Lieutenant W.E. Chambers. (*Courtesy of the Knight Museum, Alliance, NE*)

Capt. Robert D. Rae of Service Company/507th prepares for a training jump in Alliance during 1943. Note the M3 trench knife he is wearing on his right hip. (*Courtesy of Albert "Bud" Parker*)

507th regiment commanding officer, Col. George V. Millett, Jr. (*right*) and 507th regimental adjutant Capt . William J. Miller, Jr. (*left*) suit up for a practice jump in Alliance in 1943. (*Courtesy of the Knight Museum, Alliance, NE*)

Capt. Robert D. Rae (pointing) and five other 507th paratroopers prepare for a training jump in Alliance during 1943. *(Courtesy of Albert "Bud" Parker)*

Sgt. William L. Tippett of Regimental Headquarters Company/507th ready for a training jump. He is armed with the M1A1 Thompson sub-machine gun. *(Courtesy of William D. Bowell)*

Three C-47s dropping 507th paratroopers over the drop zone in Alliance. *(Courtesy of the Knight Museum, Alliance, NE)*

panels were conjoined in such a way as to form an 18-inch hole at the canopy's apex, which was supposed to reduce the oscillation or swinging effect during descent. The canopy was designed to open in the prop blast of the troop carrier aircraft, creating an opening shock of approximately five Gs. Twenty-eight suspension lines extended twenty-two feet from the canopy, connecting it to four cotton web risers, which in turn attached to the harness worn by the parachutist. The harness was designed to have a tightening effect around the body during deployment. Like Chinese finger cuffs, the harness would absorb the sudden shock of the opening parachute canopy.[4]

Seven Douglas C-47s in flight over western Nebraska. *(Courtesy of the Knight Museum, Alliance, NE)*

Paratroopers and equipment bundles falling away from a Douglas C-47 during a training jump in Alliance. *(Courtesy of the Knight Museum, Alliance, NE)*

One of the countless 507th training jumps that were conducted while the regiment was stationed in western Nebraska. *(Courtesy of William D. Bowell)*

"A day without a malfunction" – another successful training jump in Alliance. *(Courtesy of William D. Bowell)*

507th troopers PLF on the drop zone at Alliance. *(Courtesy of William D. Bowell)*

In addition to the daily PT, the T-5 familiarization and all the various other important areas of conditioning and training, the regiment also made numerous training and demonstration jumps in the immediate region. On Sunday, April 4th, the 507th executed a mass jump before 20,000 spectators at Alliance, officially marking the unit's arrival in the town. The jump demonstration was followed by a parade and review down Box Butte Avenue in downtown Alliance with the Alliance High School band. This demonstration and parade was the first of several stateside public demonstration jumps that the regiment would conduct throughout 1943.

Above: Box Butte Avenue in downtown Alliance, Nebraska as it looked before the war. *(Collection of The National D-Day Museum)*

Left: Training with an open T-5 canopy in Alliance in 1943. *(Courtesy of the Knight Museum, Alliance, NE)*

A paratrooper about to collapse his T-5 parachute. *(Collection of The National D-Day Museum)*

The 507th parades down Box Butte Avenue in March 1943. *(Courtesy of the Knight Museum, Alliance, NE)*

Lt. Horace J. Cofer, one of the staff officers of 1st Battalion/507th, poses in the door of a C-47 at Alliance. For public demonstrations, Lt. Cofer would jump with the American flag he is seen holding here. *(Courtesy of the Knight Museum, Alliance, NE)*

Lt. Cofer and flag on the drop zone after a successful jump. *(Courtesy of the Knight Museum, Alliance, NE)*

Lt. Cofer and flag as seen from inside the fuselage of a C-47. Note his T-5 parachute and AN 6513-1 reserve chute. *(Courtesy of the Knight Museum, Alliance, NE)*

On May 23, 1943, Geronimo and sixteen 507th paratroopers thrilled 25,000 spectators when they jumped in a 23-mph wind at Omaha, Nebraska in connection with the annual Field Club Dog Show. To honor Geronimo, the American Women's Volunteer Services gave him a blanket in regimental colors and the Nebraska Kennel Club gave him a collar with jump wings. Geronimo was also presented with a certificate promoting him to the rank of Sergeant in the K-9 Corps. His handler in the 507th was Pvt. Ken Williams of Chester, Pennsylvania. In July, the regiment participated in two demonstrations: one in South Dakota and one in Colorado.

The South Dakota demonstration was done before 18,000 assembled public spectators at the July Bond and Stamp Sale celebration at Gregory. For this mission, three C-47s flew from the Army Airfield at Alliance to drop approximately sixty paratroopers before a "highly enthusiastic" crowd. However, the event was somewhat marred by the fact that two of the men were injured on landing and were rushed to nearby Mother of Grace Hospital for treatment. Although tainted by the injuries, the Gregory, South Dakota demonstration generated "great patriotic sentiment." Soon thereafter an article ran in *The Gregory Times-Advocate* describing the event:

The celebration gave the public an opportunity to witness a military demonstration of the more hazardous type and brought home to every person who witnessed the jump the seriousness of the war and great amount of courage and fortitude one must have to train for this division of the armed forces.[5]

The largest public demonstration jump that involved the 507th was the Denver, Colorado jump on Saturday, July 3, 1943. The event was sponsored by the Kiwanis Club of Denver and was staged with the hopes that it would result in the donation of increased amounts of blood to Denver's two blood banks. The Denver Municipal Airport was selected as the site of the mock attack and the price of public admission was one pint of blood per person. More than 100,000 Denverites crowded the grounds of the municipal airport to watch the show, which began when twelve C-47s of the 73rd and 74th Troop Carrier Squadrons of the 434th Troop Carrier Group appeared over the field at 3:00 pm. These C-47s had flown a distance of over two hundred miles from the airfield at Alliance to deliver their payload of approximately 250 paratroopers of the 507th to the drop zone in Denver.

As the paratroopers descended down to earth, Colonel Millett was on the ground serving as the announcer for the demonstration and his comments were broadcast live on KLZ radio. In addition to the action at the airport, there was also a public display of "everything from carbines to parachutes" at Denver's Courthouse Square.[6] This display featured not only the weapons, but also the equipment of the Airborne. The Denver Red Cross contributed to the public

507th color guard during the July 1943 demonstration jump at Denver, Colorado. *(Courtesy of William D. Bowell)*

507th color guard leads the parade on the regiment's first birthday. *(Courtesy of William D. Bowell)*

display too with a "living tableau" that detailed the battle uses of blood plasma.

With the regimental CO serving as the master of ceremonies on the ground, Maj. Charles D. Johnson of 3rd Battalion was in charge of the jump and the mock assault on the airfield. The first man to step out the door that afternoon was Lt. Horace Cofer, who jumped carrying an American flag on an 8-foot pole. The rest of the 250 paratroopers descended to the drop zone after him. As they reached the ground, the troopers quickly assembled, and then launched their attack.

The plan of action called for one group of men to move against the north gate while a second group moved to the center of the field, covering the advance of the first. The third group deployed on the south gate, thereby enveloping the airport in a viselike pincer movement.[7]

The overall realism of the event was enhanced by the fact that the paratroopers fired blank ammunition to simulate the sounds of the battlefield. The 507th men then assaulted toward their imaginary objectives firing blanks from their rifles and machine guns. Taking the realism of the demonstration a step further, a group of

Commander of the 2nd Airborne Infantry Brigade, General George P. Howell (*left*) and 507th Regimental Supply Officer Captain Gordon K. Smith (*right*) at the 507th birthday Bar-B-Que in Alliance on July 20, 1943. (*Courtesy of Gordon K. Smith*)

Lt. A.L. Stephens leads Headquarters Company, 3rd Battalion/507th on Sunday, August 23, 1943, during grand opening festivities for the Alliance Army Airfield. (*Courtesy of the Knight Museum, Alliance, NE*)

B-24 Liberators from nearby Lowry Field circled the airport at an altitude of 3,000 feet as the troop carriers performed the drop. The B-24s were there to simulate an aerial bombardment of the objective area.

The demonstration apparently had a very strong inspirational impact on the 100,000 public spectators. Immediately after the successful jump, over 2,500 blood donation pledges were received at the city's two blood banks. Donations were collected at the airport by a Red Cross Mobile Unit and were then flown to the Fitzsimons General Hospital by the Colorado Civil Air Patrol for preparation into plasma. Following the demonstration, the Kiwanis Club of Denver entertained the men of the 507th "in royal fashion" in a demonstration of their patriotic spirit. While it was a great success in the eyes of the public, the demonstration was also a success in the eyes of the military observers present:

Two hundred military observers from Lowry Field witnessed the jump and were favorably impressed by the manner in which the men handled themselves after they had hit the ground.[8]

Though the Denver jump may have looked good, it turned out to be a bit of a foul-up for the 507th because it produced a number of injuries. Bob Davis of Regimental Headquarters Company described the nature of the problem:

The battalion went down there and used the same chutes they used in Alliance, where I think the terrain is about 1,100 feet above sea level. The airport in Denver, Colorado is a mile above sea level. The canopy we were using was a twenty-eight foot canopy. Very quickly, we learned henceforth to use a larger parachute canopy for, at five thousand feet above sea level, the air is considerably thinner than it is at 1,100 – you descend a lot faster.[9]

A Jeep and trailer passing the reviewing stand during t he grand opening of the Alliance Army Airfield. Note the single M2 .50-cal. machine gun mounted in the Jeep's trailer. *(Courtesy of the Knight Museum, Alliance, NE)*

When the paratroopers descended through the thin air over the field at Denver, they descended much faster than they would have closer to sea level. Since they were falling at a faster rate of speed than normal, the men hit the ground much harder than was reasonably safe. Even with a perfectly executed parachute landing fall (PLF), the impact energy that resulted from the increased descent speed caused serious problems for each parachutist. Luckily, the 507th suffered no fatalities. However, there were numerous broken legs and broken arms among the jumpers. Bob Davis recalled what he observed in the weeks immediately after the demonstration:

I remember taking the overnight train trip to Denver, Colorado for a weekend pass, maybe two or three weeks after that. And we'd meet our fellow paratroopers on the street in wheelchairs; many others were trying to get around in casts, not necessarily in wheelchairs. It was just a categorical foul-up and another learning experience.[10]

Soon after the Denver event, the 507th observed its first birthday and on July 20, 1943, a special event was held in Alliance to celebrate the occasion. Festivities began when the regiment passed in review before Brigadier General Leo Donovan, commanding general of the 1st Airborne Brigade, which had been activated on Wednesday, April 14, 1943 with the 507th as its nucleus. The General flew down from brigade headquarters at Fort Meade, South Dakota just to be a part of the activities. Following the martial phase of the event, "wives, sweethearts and friends of 507th men were guests of the regiment" for a barbecue cookout. According to the 507th 1943 yearbook, it was "a 4-B classification" event: beef, beer, blondes and brunettes.[11]

The following month, the 507th participated in a very special public ceremony. After over one year of construction, the air base at Alliance was finally complete. Accordingly, an official dedication ceremony was planned for Sunday, August 23, 1943. Since the Allied invasion of Sicily had occurred only the month prior, it was decided that the base dedication ceremony would feature a re-enactment of the airborne element of that invasion. On August 10th, the *Alliance Times and Herald* described what the public would see during the dedication re-enactment:

The Parachute Infantry will fill the sky over the Base as the blossoming chutes descend and make the first spearhead of an invasion. Then the Glider Infantry will be landed from gliders when turned loose by troop carrier tow planes in great numbers to consolidate and hold the airfield. Presently the Field Artillery will move in to enlarge the holdings while the Airborne Engineers will rehabilitate the captured field. The Signal Company will set up inter-outfit communications; so es-

Douglas C-47s approaching the flight line at Alliance Army Airfield on Sunday, August 23, 1943 during the installation's grand opening festivities. *(Courtesy of the Knight Museum, Alliance, NE)*

C-47s making a low pass at Alliance Army Airfield on Sunday, August 23, 1943 during the installation's grand opening. *(Courtesy of the Knight Museum, Alliance, NE)*

sential to a successful mission. In the short space of four hours from one in the afternoon to five o'clock, the period during which the public will be admitted to the field, the complete tactical mission, used in Sicily and inevitably to be used in any landing on the continent, will be demonstrated.[12]

When August 23rd arrived, thousands of people from all over the Panhandle of Western Nebraska flocked to the Army Air Field at Alliance. 12,602 cars filled the designated parking areas at the base as 66,080 people streamed in to watch the show.[13] In front of

the field's four runways, a reviewing stand and press box area was set up and decorated with the flags of all the Allied nations. In addition to that, an area was set aside for static displays of the weapons and equipment of the Airborne. Because much of what was on display that day was material of a "restricted" nature, cameras were not allowed on base. At 1:00 pm, the official ceremony began. Lt. Col. R.T. Jenkins served as master of ceremonies and presented the distinguished guests, which included Col. Reed Landis, commanding officer of the 1st Troop Carrier Command and Dwight Griswold, Governor of the State of Nebraska. After some speeching by the

A flight of five Boeing B-17 Flying Fortresses, two North American P-51 Mustangs and one Lockheed P-38 Lightning passing over Alliance Army Airfield during the installation's grand opening. *(Courtesy of the Knight Museum, Alliance, NE)*

Major Gordon K. Smith and his wife Marty on the front step of the ranch house that they rented while the 507th was training in Alliance. *(Courtesy of Gordon K. Smith)*

Capt. Robert D. Rae of Service Company/507th and his wife Mrs. Dorothy (Dot) Gammell Rae in 1943 in Alliance. *(Courtesy of Albert "Bud" Parker)*

Major Gordon K. Smith seen next to his car in Alliance. Note the gas rationing stickers displayed in the windshield. *(Courtesy of Gordon K. Smith)*

A large number of 507th men established relationships with local girls in Alliance, as in the case of the two troopers pictured here. *(Courtesy of William D. Bowell, Sr.)*

Pvt. William D. Bowell and two Alliance girls pose in front of the recently completed sculpture on Mount Rushmore in South Dakota. *(Courtesy of William D. Bowell, Sr.)*

T-4 James B. Roudebush and Cpl. Edward R. Barnes, both of Headquarters Company, 3rd Battalion/507th, in their Class A uniforms in downtown Alliance in mid-1943. *(Courtesy of Edward R. Barnes)*

Even Geronimo was popular among the ladies of Alliance. Here he is seen with Ms. Gladys Nielsen. *(Courtesy of William D. Bowell, Sr.)*

distinguished guests, the demonstration commenced. The *Alliance Times and Herald* described it:

> The entire program was carefully arranged and just as carefully executed. The schedule of events was maintained with army-like precision and there were no dull delays or tedious waits for something to happen. It was as fast and thrilling as a three-ringed circus and while the largest crowd ever assembled in western Nebraska had to stand in the hot sun during the entire afternoon, they did it willingly and were loathe to leave the grounds.[14]

When the 507th paratroopers assembled on the ground after the jump, they formed up by companies and conducted a pass in review before the reviewing stand at which time they received the accolades of the admiring crowd. The demonstration was a big hit

B Company Sgt. George H. Leidenheimer, Jr. poses at parade rest with an M1 Garand rifle in the company area at Alliance Army Airfield. *(Courtesy of George H. Leidenheimer)*

Sgt. Leidenheimer strikes a dramatic pose with an M1A Thompson sub-machine gun at Alliance Army Airfield in 1943. *(Courtesy of George H. Leidenheimer)*

and a great inspiration for the people there to witness it. A few days after the event, the *Alliance Times and Herald* summed it up:

> Had it been possible for the nation to have witnessed what the people of the Panhandle of Nebraska saw Sunday afternoon, the morale-building bureaus at Washington could have closed shop for the duration of the war. And it is safe to predict that western Nebraska will willingly accept its next War Bond quota as a privilege rather than a chore.[15]

• • •

Throughout the intensity of the regiment's training and the various public demonstrations, the men of the 507th were nevertheless typical young men with strong interests in the opposite sex. Some of the men had wives and girlfriends back home, while some of the men had their wives with them in Nebraska. Captain Robert D. Rae of Service Company was one of the lucky ones who had his

Right: Cpl. George Gillen, Cpl. Ed Atkinson (*with cigarette*), **Sgt. Bill Moricz, Cpl. Carl Cherry and Sgt. Leidenheimer. Cpl. Atkinson was the clown of B Company/507th.** *(Courtesy of George H. Leidenheimer)*

Sgt. Leidenheimer (*center*) carrying an M1919A4 .30-cal. machine gun during a field training exercise near Alliance. (*Courtesy of George H. Leidenheimer*)

new bride, the former Ms. Dorothy "Dot" Gammell, in Alliance with him. When the 507th left Fort Benning earlier in 1943, the wives were discouraged from following their husbands to Nebraska. "They told the women it wasn't going to be any place for them because it was going to be a little town and they better stay where their families were," Dot Rae remembered.[16] Undeterred by those discouraging words, none of the wives followed that advice and soon they had all shown up in the thriving metropolis of Alliance. Dot Rae and four other 507th wives drove across country from Georgia just to be there. They even drove through a snowstorm to reach their destination; such was their determination to be with their husbands.[17]

John Hinchliff was also a married man when the regiment moved to Alliance. He met his wife-to-be, Muriel, while passing through his hometown of Park Rapids, Minnesota on his way to Camp Hulon, Texas. At that point, Hinchliff had already volunteered for the Airborne but was still in the Coast Artillery because he had not yet been notified of his acceptance. John and Muriel went on a couple of dates before his leave ended and he had to report to his next duty station. His developing relationship with Muriel seemed promising, but there was a complicating situation; she was engaged to another man. Even after he left Park Rapids,

This photograph of Sgt. Leidenheimer (*left*) and another trooper was taken while they were both patients at the base hospital at Alliance. Leidenheimer broke his left forearm during a 507th football game and was forced to convalesce for two months in the post infirmary. (*Courtesy of George H. Leidenheimer*)

This is how Sgt. Leidenheimer passed his days in the base hospital while recovering from his broken arm. *(Courtesy of George H. Leidenheimer)*

1st Battalion/507th Pvt. Robert L. Vannatter poses with an example of the wildlife indigenous to the Alliance area. *(Courtesy of William D. Bowell, Sr.)*

Hinchliff "kept the wires hot" with Muriel because, despite her involvement with another man, he had fallen in love with her. Hinchliff then went off to Fort Benning for GPS and, three weeks later he was a paratrooper.[18]

After Jump School he was assigned to the 507th Parachute Infantry Regiment and not long after that, he returned to Park Rapids to see Muriel. During that stay, he met her parents, she met his and the relationship grew stronger. Hinchliff thereafter returned to Fort Benning and as December 1942 approached, he invited Muriel down to Georgia to spend Christmas with him. When her bus arrived at the station in Columbus, Hinchliff was there to meet her with a wedding license in hand. They were married on New Years Day 1943 in Phenix City, Alabama by the Justice of the Peace. All was not perfect though because Hinchliff's staunchly Catholic family

Hunting was a favorite pastime for men of the 507th while they were stationed in Alliance. This group of troopers, equipped with non-military weapons, was about to leave on one of many hunting expeditions. *(Courtesy of Gordon K. Smith)*

Above: Troopers of the regimental Headquarters Company communications platoon posed this photograph with the help of some of the platoon's lineman equipment. *(Courtesy of William D. Bowell, Sr.)*

wanted something more religiously substantial than what the Alabama Justice of the Peace had provided. "When we got to Alliance, I had to go see Father Manning at the Catholic Church and get married all over again," Hinchliff remembered.[19] During those months in Alliance, Muriel stayed in an apartment in town and John stayed with her whenever he could get away from the airfield.

For the unmarried men of the regiment though, Alliance offered very little in the way of female companionship. The single men were largely forced to rely on the occasional weekend pass to Denver to mix and mingle with single women. George Leidenheimer was able to spend a little time with some ladies in that city after sustaining a broken arm during one of the regiment's football games. He first spent two months in the base hospital at Alliance, then the 507th regimental surgeon, Maj. George K. Vollmar, gave him a three-day pass to Denver to improve his morale after his prolonged convalescence. He arrived there on Armistice Day (November 11th) 1943 with $1,000 in his pocket – the winnings from a craps game. That is when the fun really began:

> I went into a bar loaded with about thirty WACs and bought them all a drink. We went bar hopping where I matched up all the WACs with soldiers. Finally only one beauty was left and she was a real pin-up. She posed for war posters. I'd saved her for myself, when she informed me there was only one hour left in her pass. I hailed a cab and rode back to the base with her. We kissed goodbye, the cab was about to pull away, when a cute little blond came running to the cab. After discovering that she wanted to go into town, I invited her to hop in. She had a three-day pass and we had a good time![20]

Right: Troopers of regimental headquarters company pose outside their barracks at Alliance: T-5 Robert G. Smith, T-5 Kenneth F. Robinson, Pfc. William A. Ormsby, Plummer, T-5 Robert S. Davis, Pfc. Thomas J. Arkinson and T-4 Robert L. Byrnes. *(Courtesy of William D. Bowell, Sr.)*

Nine C-47s from Alliance Army Airfield overfly the recently completed sculpture at Mount Rushmore in the Black Hills National Forest near Rapid City, South Dakota. *(Courtesy of the Knight Museum, Alliance, NE)*

507th Regimental Headquarters Company troopers during the regiment's bivouac in the Black Hills of South Dakota in September 1943. *(Courtesy of William D. Bowell, Sr.)*

507th Regimental Headquarters Company troopers Pvt. Stanley Drapala (*wearing helmet*), T-5 Earle R. Kirker (*with pipe*) and Cpl. John H. Summer (*far right*) during the Black Hills bivouac in September 1943. (*Courtesy of William D. Bowell, Sr.*)

Back in Alliance an event was organized to offer a wholesome opportunity for the men of the regiment to socialize with the young ladies of the town: the 507th Sweetheart Contest. Dozens of young ladies from Alliance entered the contest to compete for the title of regimental sweetheart. With music provided by the 507th orchestra, the competition provided the men with an evening's worth of distraction from the daily grind of training. In the final round, the total number of contestants was reduced to five finalists. When the final decision was handed down, Miss Kay Watson of Alliance was named the first and only Sweetheart of the 507th.[21]

In addition to women, there were other distractions that broke the monotony of training and offered the men some degree of social relaxation and morale development. Obviously the regiment's various competitive sporting teams did this as well as the regimental newspaper *Boots and Wings*. The "Prop Blast" organization was another distraction that gave the officers of the regiment a chance to unwind. The 1943 yearbook described it:

> The Prop Blast is an organization for officers which meets whenever there is a sufficient number of new candidates to warrant a mass initiation. The men are prop blasted before they are accepted into the club and the party usually is run off as a satire with the luckless novices being cast in the role of embryo paratroopers at jump school. They are constantly browbeaten by their fellow officers who are dressed as jump school instructors…padded accordingly. The evening is climaxed with a dance and entertainment, and is always a memorable evening especially for those who were inducted.[22]

Despite the serious work that had become their daily routine, even the officers of the 507th took the opportunity to relax occasionally.

In September, the regiment moved into bivouac along the banks of Stockdale Lake, Custer State Park in the Black Hills of South Dakota. This was done to offer the men some rest and recreation before overseas deployment. While in the Black Hills, men of the 507th traveled in all directions to visit places like Wind Cave, Twin

507th Regimental Headquarters Company troopers returning to Alliance from the Black Hills bivouac in September 1943. (*Courtesy of William D. Bowell, Sr.*)

Tunnels, Balanced Rock and Mount Rushmore. Then, on September 24th, two composite groups from A Company, 326th Glider Infantry Regiment and the 3rd Battalion/507th participated in a mock tactical assault on Sedalia Army Air Field in central Missouri. The composite force was designated the Black Task Force for the exercise and the 507th detachment was lead by Maj. William A. Kuhn, commanding officer of 3rd Battalion. The troop carrier C-47s carrying the 507th took off at 4:00 am in the pre-dawn hours to make it possible for the assault force to arrive over the drop zone in Missouri by 6:30 am. One squadron from the 437th Troop Carrier Group arrived over the drop zone at 6:20 am, ten minutes ahead of the main element of the Black Task Force. The purpose of this vanguard element was to create a diversion by dumping dummy parachutists to the west of the airfield in an effort to lure the defenders into committing a counterattack and thus reveal their positions. In the execution, the decoy ruse succeeded in drawing the defenders out of their positions and, when the real Black Task Force jumped at 6:30 am, "the enemy was temporarily caught off balance." In the resulting confusion, the Black Task Force captured the airfield at 10:00 am. Frank Naughton of Headquarters Company, 3rd Battalion described the Sedalia operation:

> That jump went off pretty well. We landed where we were supposed to and assembled properly. I remember the critique afterwards. The critiques we had following several of our maneuvers were anything but good, but I remember this one being particularly good.[23]

But the success of the jump was marred by a tragic accident. During its training phase, the 507th suffered numerous casualties. Dozens of troopers were injured in training accidents as well as in the demonstration jumps at Denver and Gregory, South Dakota. Sadly, the regiment suffered fatalities as well. One of those fatalities occurred during the tactical exercise at Sedalia. After the assault force assembled on the ground, the 3rd Battalion S-3 officer, Captain Dave Brummitt, decided that it was necessary to get the intelligence section up to the airfield's operations tower. Brummitt directed Staff Sgt. August W. Viehl to follow him, and the two men raced off for the tower. As they began to climb, the barrel of Staff Sgt. Viehl's rifle hit a live power line and the voltage was transmitted directly into his body, electrocuting him. Staff Sgt. Viehl had formerly served in Naughton's platoon where he had proven himself to be an exceptionally motivated NCO. His accidental death was sorely felt within the battalion, as Naughton recalled:

That was a sad episode. He was a heck of a good soldier, a wonderful soldier. As a matter of fact, he probably would have been one of those who would get a battlefield commission. Very intelligent. Really a great young man.[24]

On October 23, 1943, the 507th was reviewed for the last time before being sent overseas. The reviewing officers were Brigadier General Donovan and Major General Eldridge G. Chapman, Commanding General, Airborne Command. Following the obligatory parade, General Chapman decorated Pfc. Clifford Worme of Headquarters Company with the Soldiers Medal for heroism. Pfc. Worme was awarded this medal for his extraordinary efforts to save the life of a fellow paratrooper at Fort Benning. Ten months earlier, while the men of the demolitions platoon were on a hike on December 30, 1942, they were given the order to cross the swollen and turbulent water of Uchee Creek. The crossing was not bad at first, but then the swirling water proved to be too forceful. Corporal Stanley S. Fordyce of A Company/507th was one of the men there to witness what happened next. Most of the men wisely turned back, but Fordyce and four others continued on across the creek. "We literally had to swim for our lives," he recalled.[25] When Pvt. Richard Lake was sucked under by the strong current, Pfc. Worme unhesitatingly dove into the water after him and attempted rescue despite the fact that Pvt. Lake was not visible. After struggling for

507th Regimental Headquarters Company troopers returning to Alliance from the Black Hills bivouac in September 1943. Note musette bags and carbine scabbards hanging off of the truck's tailgate. *(Courtesy of William D. Bowell, Sr.)*

H Company/507th passes in review before Brigadier General Leo Donovan, Commanding General of the 1st Airborne Brigade, and Major General Eldridge G. Chapman, Commanding General of Airborne Command at Alliance on October 23, 1943. This was the regiment's last inspection before its overseas deployment. *(Courtesy of the Knight Museum, Alliance, NE)*

several minutes in the water, Pfc. Worme barely managed to reach land himself. The incident proved yet again that even training for the military was very hazardous business.

• • •

The hazards of training though were nothing to compare with the deadly hazards of the overseas war against Germany, Japan and Italy. That war had raged on throughout 1943 while the 507th trained in Nebraska and the year had proven to be a pivotal moment in the struggle against totalitarianism. In January, the Japanese finally gave up the fight for the island of Guadalcanal in the Solomons. In February, 107,000 soldiers of the German XI Corps were surrendered at Stalingrad. In May, 250,000 German and Italian soldiers surrendered to Allied forces in Tunisia. Following the defeat of Axis forces in North Africa, the Allies had conducted amphibious landings at Sicily in July and Salerno in September. At about the same time that the 507th yearbook was being completed, the 2nd Marine Di-

vision was half a world away paying a heavy price for winning the first battle of the Central Pacific Campaign at a place called Tarawa. Up to that point, the 507th had known only the demands of training. As they prepared to join the battle that had been raging around the world for nearly two years without them, the men of the regiment paused to remember those who lost their lives even before that battle was joined. When it was completed, the 1943 yearbook began with these words:

• This book is dedicated to those men who lost their lives while in training with the 507th Parachute Infantry. The sacrifice that they made was not in vain, but shall serve the purpose of en abling the rest of us to grasp the issues at stake more readily … establishing and fixing in our minds the principles for which we are fighting. Because of this clarification, for which they are responsible, we must and shall, be determined to carry out and fulfill whatever tasks may be required of us with the greatest possible zeal and dispatch.

- Their memories shall be with us wherever we go, constant reminders of our duties and obligations. Unaware though we may be of their presence, their vigil shall be constant. From the Valhalla of brave men they shall urge us on when we falter, give us strength when we tire, and lift us when we fall. Our victories shall be their victories – our defeats their defeats. These brave men shall never die so long as comrades live to keep their memories bright and the things they fought for intact.

- To the families of the deceased we offer a word of comfort, a promise of victory. It must be a consolation to know that because of your sons, the tomorrow shall give rise to a better world, after the night of darkness.[26]

Major General Eldridge G. Chapman awards Pfc. Clifford Worme of Headquarters Company/507th with the Soldiers Medal for his extraordinary efforts to save the life of Pvt. Richard Lake at Fort Benning the year before. (*from the 507th yearbook, collection of The National D-Day Museum*)

3

An Honorary Catholic

In November 1943, the 507th finally received orders transferring it overseas. After almost a year and a half of nothing but the most intense training, the regiment was on its way to the war. That year and half had produced a team of highly skilled and motivated officers and men. Through endless repetition, the men had mastered each of their individual occupational specialties. As an example, Staff Sergeant Carson Smith of Regimental Headquarters Company/507th was like many of the men in the regiment and was qualified in the care, maintenance and operation of every firearm in the regiment's armory. Many of the men had developed that same impressive level of expertise. Finally, all of the men had at least five jumps. The incredible amount of demanding training that they had undergone had developed a high level of self-confidence and esprit de corps. "We'd gone through all this difficult training for about a year and half and we thought we were hotshots," remembered Bob Davis.[1] According to Frank Naughton, the men were "cocky."[2] Considering the harsh year and a half of conditioning they had completed, they had certainly earned that. "The armored people, they thought they were the best, but the Airborne *knew* they were the best," Naughton rembered.[3] Lt. Johnny Marr also described general feeling among the men of the 507th:

Jump boots were perhaps the greatest distinctive status symbol of the parachute infantry. After earning his jump wings, a paratrooper was allowed the privilege of blousing his trousers inside his jump boots, something that represented his successful completion of the rigors of airborne training. When the 507th transitioned through Camp Shanks, New York, the troopers were ordered not to blouse their trousers into their boots. (*Courtesy of Tom Czekanski*)

A pre-war post card picturing the passenger liner RMS. *Strathnaver* **– the ship that took the 507th to Europe in December 1943.** (*Author's Collection*)

P. & O. Electric Ship STRATHNAVER, 22,500 TONS.
Carrying First-class and Tourist-class Passengers.
India and Australia Mail Service.

There was a level of confidence amongst all of our soldiers and officers that we were going to do well whatever it was. I think that level of confidence permeated the entire regiment.[4]

Though cocky and self-assured, the men of the 507th were indeed a band of elite, professional soldiers that were among the best in the world. Frank Naughton assessed them by saying, "Talking about the quality of our troops, they were outstanding."[5]

In late November, the 507th left the sand hills of western Nebraska and traveled by rail to Camp Shanks near Orangeburg in Rockland County, New York, arriving there on the 23rd. Built between September 1942 and May 1943, Camp Shanks served as the

Above: Another distinctive uniform item worn by the men of the airborne was the garrison cap with the blue and white sewn-on parachute infantry patch. As a precaution against intelligence leaks, the men of the 507th were made to remove the parachute infantry patches from their garrison caps when the regiment was at Camp Shanks. (*Courtesy of Bill Rentz*)

Right: Cpl. Edward R. Barnes (*left*), **T/5 George B. Rodney** (*center*) **and T/4 Joseph M. Schieble** (*right*) **of Headquarters Company, 3d Battalion/507th at a nightclub in New York City in November 1943. While the regiment was at Camp Shanks preparing to go overseas, many of the men took the opportunity to visit the city.** (*Courtesy of Edward R. Barnes*)

Another pre-war view of the *Strathnaver*. She was 683 feet long with an 80-foot beam and she was equipped to accommodate 500 first class and 670 tourist class passengers. (*Author's Collection*)

final stateside stop for more than a million U.S. Army personnel bound for the European Theater of Operations. The only other staging areas on the eastern seaboard of the United States were Fort Hamilton in Brooklyn, New York and Camp Kilmer in New Brunswick, New Jersey. When combined with Camp Shanks, the three facilities represented the largest military staging area in the world. The purpose of a staging area encampment was to ensure that outbound personnel received all of the proper equipment they would need on the other side of the Atlantic. Transient personnel were housed at Camp Shanks in a series of 20' x 100' barracks, each one of which was equipped with two rows of bunks and three pot-belly stoves for heat.

The Camp Shanks staging area was subject to tight security. Because of the enormous volume of troops being funneled through the facility, it was feared that details would leak pertaining to the names and types of units being prepared to go overseas there. To minimize the risk, every effort was made at the camp to conceal what units were there and where they were going. In the case of the 507th, the Army did not want to give the impression that an airborne parachute element was going overseas.[6] The men of the regiment were therefore required to remove their jump wings and the cap insignia that identified them as paratroopers. They were also prohibited from blousing their trousers into their jump boots – something else that could identify them as airborne men at a glance. Such precautions temporarily stripped the men of the pride and *esprit de corps* they felt as paratroopers with a resulting negative impact on morale. Though well intentioned, the ruse was nevertheless seriously flawed. "I don't think we fooled anybody," recalled

A pre-war picture postcard of the port side of the *Strathnaver*. She was built by Vickers-Armstrong in Barrow-in-Furness, England, and was launched on February 5, 1931. (*Author's Collection*)

A post-war view of the starboard side of RMS *Strathnaver*. This photograph was taken after her two dummy funnels were removed in a reconditioning in Belfast, Northern Ireland, in 1948-1949. (*Author's Collection*)

Frank Naughton.[7] Early each morning, each 507th company went through its daily routine of rigorous pre-dawn PT: something that certainly advertised the fact that this was no ordinary infantry unit.

Before departing a staging camp like Camp Shanks, each unit underwent a final inspection that was designed to identify any problems with its uniforms, weapons or equipment. If a particular piece of equipment needed repairs, the work was done there on post. If a particular piece of equipment was unserviceable and/or beyond repair, the camp quartermaster department replaced it. It was necessary for such facilities to be developed in the U.S. because, at the time, there were no such depot facilities in England that could meet the needs of the growing American Army there. Thus, personnel being deployed to the European Theater of Operations had to carry everything they would need in their backpacks and duffel bags.[8]

After remaining at Camp Shanks for only two weeks, the men of the 507th were marched approximately four miles to Piermont Pier on the west bank of the Hudson River. There, they boarded a ferry that carried them south toward the Verrazano Narrows. Proceeding down the Hudson, they passed Yonkers, then Fort Lee, then Harlem and Hoboken. As the ferry came alongside the upper west side of Manhattan, many of the men of the 507th saw the skyline of New York City for the very first time. For many, it would also be the last time. The ferry continued on past the mouth of the East River, Ellis Island and Governors Island. Then off the starboard

A pre-war picture postcard of *Strathnaver*. By the time that the 507th boarded her in December 1943, she was already a veteran of four years of military service. She was requisitioned as a troopship in 1939 and she later participated in the Operation Torch landings in North Africa in November 1942. (*Author's Collection*)

side, the Statue of Liberty came into view. Dedicated in October 1886, the statue had been given to the United States by the government of France as a symbol of the two country's mutual devotion to the philosophies of freedom and liberty. Now, the men of the 507th were about to begin a journey that would ultimately take them to the soil of France as a part of the crusade to defend those philosophical principles. Many of the men of the regiment would never see the United States again, soon sacrificing their lives in defense of the very principles symbolically represented by that statue.

The ferry offloaded the regiment at Fort Hamilton on the Brooklyn side of the Verrazano Narrows. On December 5, 1943, it outprocessed through the New York Port of Embarkation and boarded the 22,270-ton passenger liner *Strathnaver*. Built by Vickers-Armstrong in Barrow-in-Furness, England on the Irish Sea north of Liverpool, the *Strathnaver* was 683 feet long with an 80-foot beam and she was equipped to accommodate five hundred first class and 670 tourist class passengers. Twin screws powered the ship to a maximum speed of 21 knots and she had three funnels and twin masts. *Strathnaver* was launched on February 5, 1931 and departed on her maiden voyage eight months later on October 2nd of that year. She had been built for the Peninsular & Oriental Steam Navigation Company, a shipping firm with roots dating back to the early 19th Century.

P&O began its life in 1836 by offering regular service to and from London, Spain, Portugal and the Mediterranean. In 1840, P&O opened service to Alexandria, Egypt that offered a connection to an overland route to Port Suez on the Gulf of Suez. This route made possible a connection from the Gulf of Suez, to the Red Sea, the Gulf of Aden and finally the Indian Ocean. At the time, P&O's Alexandria/Port Suez route was the quickest way to get to such places as Bombay, Colombo, Melbourne and Sydney. When the Suez Canal opened in 1869, travel time got even faster. From these humble beginnings, P&O grew to become one of the leading passenger lines providing service to India and Australia. By breaking into the Indian market at a time when the British colonial presence there was growing with each passing year, P&O had established a profitable commercial venture that the company would stay with right up to World War II. When *Strathnaver* joined the P&O fleet, she began operating on the London – India – Australia route until 1939. After England declared war on Germany following the invasion of Poland in September of that year, the Royal Navy requisitioned *Strathnaver* to serve as a troopship. She carried troops to Oran and Algiers in North Africa in 1942 and Anzio on the west coast of Italy in late 1944.

As the men of the 507th boarded the *Strathnaver* at Fort Hamilton they found that the ship's crew consisted of British officers and Indian deck hands and laborers. The Indian crewmembers were mostly from Sri Lanka, and were well organized along the lines of the various castes of Indian society. Aboard *Strathnaver*, the higher castes worked as stewards or attendants in the officers' mess, and the lower castes did all the "dirty work."[9] John Hinchliff recalled that, "everybody knew what caste they belonged to and what his job was."[10] As more and more GIs boarded, the ship became more and more overcrowded. The sheer number of soldiers aboard quickly exceeded *Strathnaver*'s comfortable passenger carrying capacity and accommodations rapidly became somewhat cramped. *Strathnaver* had six decks labeled A through F. For the officers, the experience of crossing the Atlantic would not be altogether unpleasant because they were at least able to enjoy the luxury of cabins on A deck and B deck. Because he was an officer, Frank Naughton enjoyed the relative luxury of a stateroom that he shared with only one other Lieutenant. But conditions for the enlisted men were far less luxurious down in steerage. They were quartered on the lower three decks of the ship in communal bunk areas for large numbers of men. They were packed in "like sardines," according to Bob Davis. The uncomfortably close quarters were so bad that the men began to refer to *Strathnaver* as a "slave ship."[11] Of the six decks aboard ship, F deck was the worst. It was the lowest – just above the ship's keel and propeller shaft. That far below decks, there were scarce few portholes, and many of those had been painted over to prevent light from escaping. Ventilating airflow for the lower decks was produced by large scoop ventilators all the way up on A deck. But the volume of that airflow was significantly weakened for the bottommost decks because of the distance the air had to travel through ventilation ducts to reach the bowels of the ship. Thus, there was little or no ventilation on F deck, a situation that produced a sweltering and stifling environment. The discomfort of this situation was most acutely felt by the unfortunate souls who suffered from seasickness. For most of the 507th paratroopers, this was their first voyage on the high seas. Consequently, these first-timers had to deal with the ugly reality of unrelenting motion sickness.

Making conditions even more unpleasant, the food aboard *Strathnaver* was unspeakably bad. According to Bob Davis "It was slop, worse than anything that we had encountered up to that point." B Company's Sgt. George Leidenheimer remembered that, "Every evening we endured a miserable meal of stinking, greasy mutton."[12] The unfortunate design of the ship was such that a rather unsanitary bathroom – or "head" – was located immediately adjacent to the galley. This proximity meant that a familiar stench was ever present as the men moved through the chow line. Practically everyone was both sick and hungry at the same time. Because of the poor quality of the food and the unsanitary situation with the toilets, many 507th men chose the alternative of living off of the cookies, crackers and candy on sale in the ship's store. Reduced to desperation by the food aboard ship, Sgt. Leidenheimer came up with a plan. One day during the voyage, he borrowed a fatigue jacket without the stripes that would identify him as an NCO. Then he went to the galley where he reported to a mess Sergeant that did not know him with the cover story that he had been assigned to peeling potatoes. As soon as the mess Sergeant walked to the other end of the galley, Leidenheimer grabbed a cardboard box, hefted it onto his shoulder and headed for the door. He had only gone a couple of steps when the mess Sergeant yelled for him to stop and then took off after him in hot pursuit. But Leidenheimer had planned for just such a development and had positioned two men from his squad at the doorway leading into the galley. On cue, the two men began a fake shoving match right at the exact moment that the mess Sergeant reached the door. Their choreography was perfectly timed, perfectly executed and according to the plan they "accidentally" pushed him hard

The regiment's Catholic Chaplain, Captain John J. Verret. He was the man who made Bob Davis an "honorary Catholic" to help cure his chronic seasickness during the difficult voyage on board *Strathnaver*. During the days immediately preceding the invasion, Verret provided great spiritual leadership and comfort to the men of regiment. He was later killed in action by German artillery fire on January 8, 1945 during the Battle of the Bulge. (*Courtesy of Gordon K. Smith*)

enough to knock him against a bulkhead. The diversion slowed the mess Sergeant down long enough for Leidenheimer to disappear among the thousands of other GIs on board ship. When he reached his cabin, he received a pleasant surprise. "The box contained 4-gallon cans of pork and beans," he recalled.[13] Leidenheimer and his partners in crime then proceeded to devour two of the cans immediately. Compared to what they had been eating to that point on board the *Strathnaver*, the pork and beans were delicious.[14]

The daily cycle of serving and preparing meals in the galley was an around the clock function. So many men were crammed aboard ship that they had to be fed in shifts. The men in the hold would eat first, followed by the men on the deck above. The schedule of feeding would, thereby, work its way up from the lower decks to A deck, and then back down to the hold again. The men would first draw their dry rations and then on the next dining cycle, they would draw wet rations. They were constantly feeding.[15]

As a result of the effects of seasickness combined with the awful food, Bob Davis was beginning to question whether or not he was going to be able to complete the trip across to England.[16] Three days after departing from Fort Hamilton, *Strathnaver* joined a protected convoy for the North Atlantic crossing. As the convoy proceeded at the snail's pace speed of seven knots, it moved into increasingly rougher and rougher seas. Davis consequently grew sicker and sicker as the seas got worse and worse. On the fourth day out, he reached a breaking point. He decided to leave F deck in the bowels of the ship and climb to A Deck to get some fresh air. "I don't remember anyone ordering us to stay down there on F deck, although I think it was more or less understood," he recalled.[17] He grabbed a couple of loaves of bread – for him, the only edible food aboard – and stumbled up the spiral staircase: destination A deck. While climbing from C deck to B deck, Davis encountered Captain John J. Verret who, like him, was a native of Vermont. Together, Captain Verret and Davis constituted the only Vermonters in the entire regiment. It also just so happened that the Captain was a priest and was serving as the regiment's Catholic Chaplain. As Davis was ascending the stairs to get to the higher deck, Captain Verret was descending to a lower deck, and the two men met in the middle. Verret stopped, took one look at Davis and asked, "Where are you going?" Cleverly, Davis responded with, "hopefully to heaven, sir." Sensing that Davis was suffering miserably from seasickness, the Captain showed compassion and said, "Well, perhaps I have certain qualifications to be of some assistance to you in that endeavor." With that, Verret motioned for Davis to follow, and he started back up the stairs. Davis followed him all the way up to A deck and then down a long corridor on the starboard side of the ship to a door. Capt. Verret opened the door, and inside was a pair of portholes and a big white bathtub. He told Davis he would find him some cushions to sleep in the bathtub. Meanwhile Davis was not to appear in public except in the event of a boat drill. If anyone asked who he was and what he was doing there, Verret told Davis to, "just tell them that you're my altar boy."[18] As a Protestant, Davis felt that he could not conscientiously do so and he expressed that sentiment to the Chaplain. Verret responded by saying "Oh, that's alright Bob, for the duration of this voyage you're an honorary Catholic."[19]

While Davis was lucky enough to have the circumstances of his situation improved by the compassion of another person, not everyone was able to benefit from such good fortune and they languished down in steerage. As if the cramped quarters, poor ventilation, seasickness and bad food were not enough to make the conditions of the voyage utterly intolerable, the men also had to deal with sheer boredom. "There wasn't much to do on the ship," Frank Naughton remembered, "There was no room for the men to move around."[20] For the most part, the men could only pass the time by reading, playing cards or talking. There were however occasions when that monotony was broken. From time to time, all of the passengers and crew on the ship would have to participate in an emer-

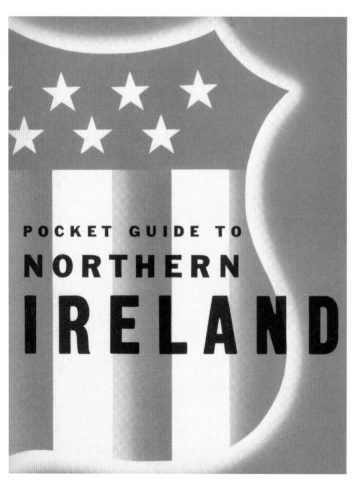

The *Pocket Guide to Northern Ireland* was distributed to American military personnel who were stationed there. *(Collection of The National D-Day Museum)*

gency lifeboat drill. For the 507th this involved each man putting on a life vest and mustering on deck. Then, with everyone assembled on the ship's main deck, officers came around and checked every life vest to insure that they were being worn correctly. Because of the cold, cutting wind of the North Atlantic in December, this was the greatest irritant of all. Although it offered a break to the monotony of life aboard ship, lifeboat drill brought so much discomfort that it offered no relief.

• • •

The regiment's maritime ordeal continued for almost two weeks. After ten miserable, seasick days at sea, *Strathnaver* arrived in Liverpool on December 16th. The men were then taken north by train to Greenock, Scotland on the Clyde River just northwest of Glasgow.[21] There the 507th immediately boarded the liberty ship SS *Susan B. Anthony*, which transported it on to Belfast, Northern Ireland. From Belfast, the regiment was taken by train to the summer resort town of Portrush, arriving there shortly before Christmas 1943. There the regiment occupied some of the resort's buildings that were vacant for the winter. It was so cold living in those rustic accommodations that each room occupied by the regiment's troopers was allotted a ration of coal for heating purposes.[22]

The first activity in which the 507th participated after its arrival was a three-day field training exercise. The real challenge of this particular exercise was that the regiment was only given one day's rations to complete it. "We were to get anything else we needed through our own devices," recalled Sgt. Leidenheimer. Some of the men met this challenge by pilfering eggs, chickens and ducks from local farmers. "At first we felt badly about stealing," Leidenheimer recalled, "but that guilt was alleviated when we learned they were being reimbursed for their losses – quite generously it seemed."[23] The paratroopers soon learned that if they had stolen one dozen eggs, the Irish farmers reported that three-dozen were missing.[24] In the end the accounting worked to the farmers' favor and neither hostility nor animosity developed in relation to the Americans that were suddenly thrust in their midst.

There was little for the men of the 507th to do in Northern Ireland. Without C-47s, it was not possible for the regiment to make practice jumps. For that reason, all training exercises took place on the ground. The regiment participated in one live ammunition field problem and even conducted maneuvers on a golf course at one point. Because sunrise was at 9:00 am and sunset was at 3:00 pm each day, most of the regiment's training in Portrush was conducted at night. With such limited options, the focus was necessarily on weapons familiarization (American *and* German), infantry tactics and PT. When asked what the regiment did while there in Ireland,

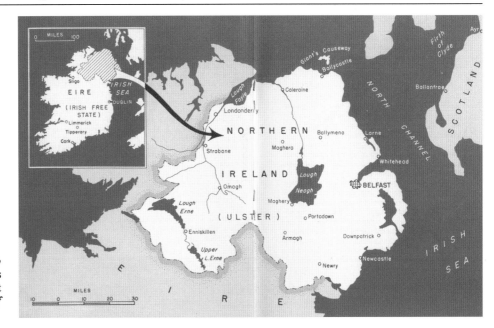

Map in the center of the *Pocket Guide to Northern Ireland*. Although Portrush does not appear on the map, it is on the coast just north of the city of Coleraine. (*Collection of The National D-Day Museum*)

Bob Davis answered, "not much except calisthenics."[25] Every morning the companies fell out early, did calisthenics and ran. They ran in the wind and the rain; they ran when it was cold and when it was colder. In fact, they ran so often and so far that it seemed like all they did was run. "I'm sure if we hadn't beaten the Germans, we could have out-run them," Leidenheimer remembered.[26]

Since Ireland was obviously not the regiment's final destination, the men knew that Portrush was little more than a holding station. The regiment had been diverted there because its base in England was not ready. Three months would pass before the trip back over to England. During that time, the men of the regiment got to know the country and its people. Corporal Stanley Fordyce, an A Company trooper, described what it was like there:

> The weather was cold, damp and cloudy. The country was fascinating. The people were friendly and seemed contented with their simple way of life. Many of their homes were adobe style with thatched roofs and heated with peat. That ever pungent smell. On occasions the families would invite us into their homes for tea and crumpets, then to stay for a little card game.[27]

The 507th even interacted with Irish children during the Christmas season while they were based in Portrush. From the time they arrived, the men saved their candy, apples and oranges and then presented them to the local youth during a Christmas party hosted by the regiment. Among the town's children, there were several, some as old as six years, that had never eaten an orange in their lives – such were the privations of life in wartime Ireland. Those privations only made the children all the more appreciative of the gifts the American paratroopers gave them.[28]

Some 507th men had a different kind of interaction with the natives while in Ireland. For entertainment, they enjoyed visiting the local pubs and sometimes they would share a pint of ale with some of the local girls. But at night, one major factor interfered with the process of selecting attractive young ladies to invite to the pub. As a wartime precaution against German U-Boats and bombers, Portrush was blacked-out at night, so the men were not always able to tell what the ladies looked like when they stopped to talk to them in the street. But Sgt. Leidenheimer came up with a clever scheme to overcome that challenge. Whenever he went into town, he always carried a pack of Lucky Strike cigarettes, even though he did not smoke. "Upon seeing girls on the street, we'd offer them a cigarette, then light it to see whether we'd invite them to join us for a pint of ale," he remembered.[29] It was through this method that Leidenheimer met and dated a British sailor. "There were nine WRENS (British female sailors) who took care of the lighthouse and I was lucky enough to get a date with the cutest of the group, a little blonde," he remembered.[30] One night he took her to a movie and, afterward walked her back home to the lighthouse where she and the other eight girls lived. "I was kissing her in the foyer and she fainted," he remembered.[31] Then he picked her up and rang the doorbell with his elbow. The highest ranking of the ladies – an "old" chief that looked like a bulldog – answered the door and, seeing the unconscious girl in Leidenheimer's arms, asked what happened. "I was telling her goodnight and she passed out," was his answer. With that, the old chief said, "She's done it again! Lay her here on the sofa."[32] Evidently, Leidenheimer was not the young lady's first.

During its stay in Northern Ireland, the ranks of the 507th were bolstered by a large number of additional personnel. Chris Courneotes Kanaras joined the regiment at that time. Kanaras was born in 1922 to a Greek family in Baltimore, Maryland. His father had served with the 1st Infantry Division in France during World War I and – like his father – he entered the service of the U.S. Army. After joining up in 1943, he went to Camp Sibert, Alabama for basic training, after which he was assigned to the 122nd Chemical Impregnating Company. His unit's job was to impregnate uniforms with an anti-chemical agent to lessen the potential affects of exposure to poison gases. In May 1943, flat-top rail cars delivered the unit's heavy equipment, which was marked with the words "American Laundry." Kanaras knew right then and there that he needed to get out of that outfit. There were two options available to him: Army Air Corps gunnery school or the Airborne. He chose the Airborne. Thereafter, Kanaras was sent to Group Parachute School at Fort Benning and then assigned to the 541st Parachute Infantry Regiment at Camp MacKall, North Carolina. In December 1943, the 541st was deactivated and Kanaras was then transferred to Fort Meade, Maryland and then on to Camp Shanks, New York where he boarded the ship *Santa Rosa* for Europe. Upon arriving in Belfast, Kanaras and several hundred other men were taken by truck up to Portrush. Together with Ezro Fontanella and Marty Freedman – men he had served with back in the states – Kanaras was assigned to 3rd Platoon, B Company/507th.

Edward J. Jeziorski also joined the regiment while it was stationed in Ireland. Born in Little Neck, Long Island, New York in November 1920 and raised in Freehold, New Jersey, Jeziorski enlisted in the National Guard in April 1940. Five months later he was a Sergeant and the New Jersey National Guard had been federalized into U.S. government service. Jeziorski's unit was on its way back from the Carolina maneuvers in 1941 when, on the evening of December 7th, it arrived in Culpeper, Virginia and began setting up camp. At that point, some civilians told the men about Pearl Harbor. "We were thunderstruck," Jeziorski remembered, "We couldn't figure out where in the world Pearl Harbor was located."[33] After hearing the news, Sgt. Jeziorski and the men in his unit knew that they were going to be in federal service for an extended period of time.[34]

Over the course of the next fifteen months, Sgt. Jeziorski's unit shuttled up and down the East Coast from Montauk Point, Long Island to Brunswick, Georgia while attached to the Eastern Coastal Defense Command. Then in April 1943, he volunteered for the Airborne. In July, Sgt. Jeziorski was assigned to the 541st Parachute Infantry Regiment at Camp McCall, North Carolina. But toward the end of the year, the 541st was broken up to provide replacements for all of the Airborne units currently deployed in the ETO and the PTO.[35] Consequently, Sgt. Jeziorski was sent overseas. At about the same time that the men of the 507th were arriving in Great Britain aboard the SS *Strathnaver*, he was leaving the U.S.

on board the liner SS *Mariposa*. Upon arriving in Belfast just after Christmas, Sgt. Jeziorski was sent to Portrush where he was made a machine gunner in 2nd Squad, 2nd Platoon, C Company, 1st Battalion/507th. Unfortunately, C Company's Table of Organization for non-commissioned officers was, at that time, full and Sgt. Jeziorski was necessarily reduced in rank to buck Private. "After three years as a non-comm, it was back to step one," he remembered.[36] Despite losing his stripes though, morale was not a problem for Jeziorski because he really liked the outfit and he knew that sooner or later he would get his rank back.[37]

While there in Portrush, Pvt. Jeziorski and a couple of other 507th men discovered a nearby treasure. Bushmill's Distillery was located in Coleraine, only 14 miles inland from Portrush. On several occasions, Pvt. Jeziorski and a few other C Company men traveled down to the distillery where the guards on duty there would give each man a bottle. At that time of the year, the climate in Northern Ireland was far from ideal. The temperature was naturally very low to begin with, but then strong winds blew in off the North Sea

On January 14, 1944, the 507th Parachute Infantry Regiment was attached to the 82nd Airborne Division for the upcoming invasion of Europe. (*Author's Collection*)

to make conditions all the more unpleasant. Finally, the high moisture associated with frequent snowfall made the relentless, inescapable cold the source of great misery for the men. Under such conditions, where a bottle of distilled spirits could add at least a little warmth on a hopelessly cold night, the men were glad to have the good will of the distillers on their side.[38] "They made things just a little more endurable," Jeziorski remembered.[39]

• • •

On January 14, 1944, the 507th Parachute Infantry Regiment was attached to the 82nd Airborne Division. The 82nd Division was born in August 1917 at Camp Gordon near Augusta, Georgia and was given the nickname "All American" because it consisted of men from all forty-eight states. In late April 1918, the first elements of the division departed the U.S. for Europe to fight in the trenches of World War I. During the war, the 82nd spent 105 days on the front line (more than any other U.S. division) and suffered 1,035 killed in action. It was inactivated in 1919 following the conclusion of the war. As a part of the U.S. Army's World War II mobilization in early 1942, the 82nd Division was reactivated at Camp Claiborne, Louisiana on March 25, 1942. It was then re-designated in May as the 82nd Infantry Division and then re-designated again on August 15, 1942 as the 82nd Airborne Division under the temporary command of Major General Omar N. Bradley. The division moved from Camp Claiborne to Fort Bragg, North Carolina in October, where it began preparing to go to war under the leadership of Major General Matthew B. Ridgway. It pre-staged for overseas deployment at Camp Edwards, Massachusetts on April 18, 1943 and then left the United States via the New York Port of Embarkation ten days later. After the division departed New York on April

Sgt. George H. Leidenheimer, Jr. with three other B Company/507th troopers in Portrush in early 1944. *(Courtesy of George H. Leidenheimer)*

28th, it was taken directly to North Africa where it landed at Casablanca, French Morocco on May 10th. While in North Africa, the 82nd began training for what was about to be its first combat mission, Operation Husky – the invasion of Sicily. The 82nd Airborne's operational plan for Husky called for the division to make two separate combat parachute jumps: the first would be on D-Day (July 9, 1943) and the other would be on D+2 (July 11, 1943). For the July 9th combat jump, elements of the division air-assaulted to take the high ground above the Ponte Olivo airfield

A group of 507th officers and men in Northern Ireland during the winter of 1944. *(Courtesy of George H. Leidenheimer)*

B Company/507th Sgt. George H. Leidenheimer, Jr. poses in his wool overcoat with an M1 Garand rifle in Northern Ireland during the winter of 1944. *(Courtesy of George H. Leidenheimer)*

northeast of Gela. Despite the wide scattering of that parachute drop, designated objectives were taken and elements of the division linked up with the 1st Infantry Division the following day. On July 11th the division's 504th Parachute Infantry Regiment (together with attached support units) parachuted into the Gela area, but suffered heavy losses from anti-aircraft fire. These losses were only partly produced by German air defenses; the balance of the regiment's

casualties resulted from numerous incidents of friendly anti-aircraft fire being directed at the incoming troop carrier aircraft. The 82nd thereafter remained in combat in Sicily until the conclusion of that campaign. After securing the crossings of the Fiume delle Canno on July 18th, the division then pushed along the coastal highway and seized the Marsala-Trapani area on the west coast on July 23rd.[40]

In September 1943, the 82nd Airborne supported the Operation Avalanche landings at Salerno on the west coast of Italy. For this operation, the 504th Parachute Infantry Regiment parachuted south of the Sele River on September 13th, the division's 325th Glider Infantry Regiment made an amphibious landing over the Salerno beachhead on July 15th and the 505th Parachute Infantry Regiment dropped in the same area as the 504th the following night. The 504th began an attack on Altavilla on September 16th, it reached Naples on October 1st and then captured Gallo on October 29th. Although the rest of the division returned to England in December 1943, the 504th remained in Italy and made the amphibious landing at Anzio on January 22, 1944. From there, the regiment was engaged in heavy combat along the Mussolini Canal until late March when it returned to England and joined the rest of the division.[41]

By the time the 504th returned from Italy, the 507th had taken its place as a part of the division and was preparing for the upcoming operation. In the end, a large number of 504th men were attached to the 507th for the upcoming invasion, especially in the regiment's three Pathfinder teams. In March 1944, the 507th traveled from Portrush to Glasgow, Scotland where the men boarded trains that moved them to a training and bivouac area near Nottingham, England.[42] There in the iridescently verdant Nottingham countryside, the men lived out of six-man pyramidal tents and the

The 507th Parachute Infantry Regiment encampment at Tollerton Hall near Nottingham. This was the regiment's last home before moving to the airfields for the Normandy invasion. *(Courtesy of George H. Leidenheimer)*

officers slept inside the castle at Tollerton Hall.[43] It was there that preparations began in earnest for D-Day. "We conducted field exercises practically every day," remembered Bob Davis.[44] According to Chris Kanaras, the afternoons were used for map reading, French and German lessons and first aid instruction.[45] While based near Nottingham, the men of the 507th made one day jump and, on May 12th, one night jump. As Frank Naughton remembered, the regiment "had a very intense training period from March to early June."[46]

But it was not all work during the regiment's stay in the area. While there, the men interacted with a local population that showed them great hospitality. "The Brits were always so nice to us, always making us feel welcome," remembered B Company's Sgt. George Leidenheimer.[47] Nottingham was a city about the same size as New Orleans and it was noted for its beautiful women. In addition to preparing to go to war, Leidenheimer continued his world tour of women while in Nottingham. "I dated the prettiest gal in town, Sheila Purdue," he remembered.[48] Sheila's father was a local medical doctor and she worked as his secretary. George and Sheila made a good pair because they both loved to dance. On one particular outing, they entered and won a jitterbug contest and received a bottle of champagne as their prize.[49] Although he was having a good time with Sheila, each night Leidenheimer had to return to a tent at Tollerton Hall that he shared with five other 507th paratroopers.

The closest civilization to the 507th encampment at Tollerton Hall was the nearby village of Plumtree. Like every other township in England, Plumtree had a neighborhood pub: Griffin's Inn. For some of the men of the 507th, the gravity of that pub was too much to resist during their brief stay in the area. Immediately after the regiment's arrival, Col. Millett designated Plumtree off-limits, but a small group of the regiment's enlisted men ignored that ban and made Griffin's Inn their nightly destination. Early each evening, eight bold troopers would slip away from their company area and proceed directly to the pub for a communal pint or two. The locals, aware of Col. Millett's quarantine of the township, became willing co-conspirators and began to harbor the so-called "Plumtree Eight" actively. They did this by standing sentry whenever the 507th men were in the pub. If an MP Jeep was spotted approaching the estab-lishment, the appointed sentinel would sound the alarm, whereupon the "Plumtree Eight" would scramble out the back door to hide behind the men's backyard lavatory. When the MP threat was gone, the "all clear" would be sounded and the paratroopers would return to their place at the bar. "Night after night, this highly complex and profoundly ingenious tactical maneuver was executed with impunity," recalled T/5 Bob Davis, one of the "Plumtree Eight."[50]

Over the course of just a few weeks, the relationship between the "Plumtree Eight" and Griffin's Inn's patrons became a great bond of Anglo-American wartime friendship. The driving force in forging that friendship was the pub's barkeep, Florence. She made sure that everyone in the establishment knew one another and uniformly showed everyone warmth and kindness. She even encouraged the young Americans to write home often. Bob Davis remembered that, "Florence became our mother *in loco parentis* and we began addressing her accordingly; she loved it."[51] Throughout March, April and into the month of May, the "Plumtree Eight" interacted with Florence and the pub's patrons on such an amicable level that an exceptional, strong relationship was born. During this brief period, Griffin's Inn was an oasis of dark, bitter ale and a temporary home away from home.[52] But the date of the invasion was fast approaching and that relationship was about to come to an abrupt end.

By late May 1944, just over 2,000 young Americans from the 507th Parachute Infantry Regiment were training at their base near Nottingham, England. Though none of them had seen combat, they were waiting for the order that would finally send them into it. The accelerated training regimen that began for them in March was the last phase of their pre-combat history. By then, all that could be done in the way of preparation had been done. All that was yet to be done was to perform. Although France had been under enemy occupation for four long years by the summer of 1944, the hour of deliverance was closing in. Soon, the 507th would drift down out of the sky and into the valley of the shadow of death in Normandy and the people of France were about to see the tide turn. For the men of the 507th, their appointment with fate was at hand. Soon, they would be delivered to the hedgerows and marshes of the Cotentin peninsula where lives would be lost and legends would be born.

4

Death by Labor

The 507th was training for the invasion that would ultimately liberate northwest Europe from the tyranny of German occupation. By 1944, World War II had been raging in Europe for several years. It had all started in September 1939 when Germany began its war of expansion by invading Poland. When Hitler's forces thereafter invaded Norway, Denmark, France and finally the Soviet Union, it appeared that the political future of Europe would be dominated by National Socialist Germany. At first, the weapons, equipment and tactics of the Wehrmacht seemed unbeatable as the mighty German military accomplished its strategic goals quickly and efficiently. As of the summer of 1942, most of the European continent was under Hitler's control and Germany was poised threateningly within striking distance of the oil-rich Middle East and the Caucasus. In those dark days before Stalingrad and El Alamein, the world had every reason to suspect that Hitler's legions would continue to march. But the progress of German expansion stalled in late 1942 and then turned into retreat on all fronts. By mid-1943, the Germans had been defeated and driven out of North Africa and the invasion of Soviet Russia had likewise fallen to pieces. By July the Allies had invaded Sicily and in September, Italy itself. Thus, as of early 1944 the Germans were being attacked on their eastern front in Soviet Russia and on their southern front through Italy. Under those circumstances, Allied leaders decided that the time was right to open yet another front to accelerate the collapse of Nazi Germany. This was the genesis of Operation Overlord – the Normandy Invasion. It was to participate in this operation that the 507th had been sent to Europe.

The Europe that the 507th would have to help liberate had been suffering under the tyranny of German domination for close to five years by mid-1944. In countries like Poland and France, German occupation was marked by several basic injustices that stood as the direct result of the exportation of Nazism. The Nazi philosophy was fueled by a belief in self-supremacy that manifested itself in an intense hatred of certain political doctrines, ethnic groups and religions. The movement itself had been born in the beer halls of post World War I Germany and ultimately became Adolf Hitler's National Socialist German Worker's Party. When Hitler was elected Chancellor by plurality in 1933, the Nazi Party became the licit controlling political authority of Germany. Before 1933, the Nazi Party had a reputation for bigotry, intolerance and racism that, after 1933, was realized to the fullest extent possible. In the early years, any person not in conformity with the Nazi ideal was an outcast and subject to exclusion from mainstream society. In the later years, the price for not being a Nazi was much worse. While this certainly applied to foreign nationals in the countries that Germany would ultimately occupy, it also applied to certain Germans as well.

Harry Openheimer was born in Alzey south of Mainz in 1921, and was a teenager when the Nazis took control of his country. He was a butcher's apprentice and a German Jew. Because of his age and religion, he was in a position to be an eyewitness to what was becoming the grim reality of life under Adolf Hitler. Before Hitler came to power, many of Openheimer's closest friends were Gentiles. After Hitler came to power, his gentile friends would no longer associate with him. Also, there were certain things that Jews were not permitted to do after the National Socialists came to power. Openheimer remembered that, "You couldn't go to swimming pools, and there were signs all over Germany saying *Jews Unwanted*."[1]

He observed the re-armament over which Hitler presided and noticed the extent to which German society was becoming heavily militarized. He recalled that, as a result of the Nazi influence, "everything was military oriented in Germany at that time." In spite of the fact that they were Germans, Openheimer and the members of

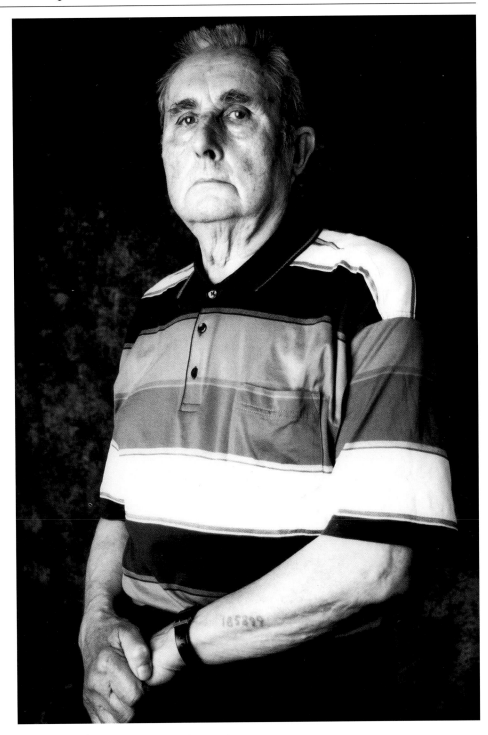

Paul Le Goupil was a schoolteacher in Rouen when World War II began. He joined the Resistance after the Germans executed 48 French hostages at Chateaubriant and Nantes in October 1941. Two years later, Le Goupil was turned in by an informant and was deported to become a slave laborer in Poland and Germany. He was interned first at Auschwitz-Birkenau, then at Buchenwald and, when the war ended, he was an inmate in the concentration camp at Coswig on the Elbe River north of Dresden. (*Photo by Jeff Petry*)

his family suffered the full wrath of Nazi bigotry because of their religious beliefs. Openheimer's father had served in the German military during the First World War. Although German veterans of World War I were normally exalted in Nazi culture, Jewish veterans received little or no appreciation. One day in 1937, Nazi bigotry and intimidation reached a disgusting climax when some SS men publicly humiliated Openheimer's father.

The SS storm troopers made him clean the sidewalk where the Communists wrote things against the Nazis and then the young guys urinated on him. It was quite bad.[2]

The incident was enough to convince his father that the time had come to get his family out of Germany. They fled to the United States where a family in New York City took them in. Oppenheimer and his father, mother and brother made it out just in time and the entire family had to make a fresh start from nothing. In the beginning, each member of the family had it tough, but ultimately things worked out for them.[3] In 1943, Openheimer was drafted into the U.S. Army. He received his basic training at Camp Livingston, Louisiana and ended up back in Europe in the 343rd Infantry Regiment of the 86th Infantry Division. His unit was ultimately deployed in combat against the very same people that had driven his family away from their home country:

> For me I loved to go into the Army, I loved to go into the war, because of what I went through in Germany. They were my enemy, right from the beginning.[4]

The 507th had a member who, like Harry Openheimer, was born in Germany and then left the country after Hitler came to power. Like Openheimer, Cpl. Wolfgang George Sklarz of the regimental intelligence section left his homeland in late 1933 after having "had a taste of Nazi rule."[5] Sklarz first toured the world as a concert pianist and then settled in New York City before ultimately joining the U.S. Army in 1942. With an ability to speak German, Italian, French and English fluently, Sklarz was obviously a great asset to regimental intelligence. To Cpl. Sklarz, Harry Openheimer and a minority of other native-born Germans that had the good sense to recognize it from the start, Hitler was a bitter enemy.

• • •

To most of the people in the various countries occupied after 1939, the Germans were similarly viewed as the bitter enemy. Some people responded to occupation by collaborating with the Nazis and others tolerated their occupiers grudgingly with minimal cooperation. Then there was the resistance. Members of the resistance movements in countries occupied by the Germans were both active and passive. People who participated in active resistance efforts were often armed, frequently engaged in acts of sabotage and employed guerilla warfare tactics. People who participated in passive resistance efforts made a contribution that was every bit as important. Paul Le Goupil was born in Rouen in 1922. He grew up there and ultimately became a schoolteacher. In 1940 he was an eyewitness to the German invasion and occupation:

> When the Germans invaded France, my parents and I evacuated to the region of Cherbourg, to Saint Floxel, which is

near Montebourg. After a time we went back, but my feeling at first was that the Germans didn't appear to be as mean as the propaganda led you to believe. I met them for the first time at my aunt's farm in Saint Floxel where I was staying. They were nice. They were just young guys like me who joked around. There was never any problem in the beginning.[6]

At first, Le Goupil harbored no great animosity toward the Germans individually. As a twenty-year-old, he was more concerned with organizing "clandestine" dances, since such things were prohibited under the occupation. He was "just a kid having fun."[7]

But that situation changed dramatically in late 1941 when the Resistance assassinated two German officers: one in Nantes on October 2nd and then another in Bordeaux a few days later. In the days immediately after the assassinations, German occupation forces took 48 hostages in reprisal. These hostages were held briefly without benefit of trial or representation, and then on October 22nd, the Germans shot them all. Twenty-on hostages were summarily executed in Nantes and twenty-seven were summarily executed at Chateaubriant. "At that moment I decided I had to do something to free my country," Le Goupil remembered.[8] Soon thereafter, he joined the French Resistance:

> I became a Section Chief and then I became head of the department for all of the Lower Seine: Rouen, Le Havre, Dieppe, etc. I became Department Head of the Front Patriotique de la Jeunesse.[9]

The Front Patriotique de la Jeunesse, or Patriotic Front of the Youth, was not a paramilitary organization but a civil organization that recruited young people and workers who "had decided to do something against the German occupation."[10] The front organized young French citizens in order to prepare them for action at the moment of anticipated Allied beach landings. Because the Allied invasion had not yet taken place, the Front Patriotique de la Jeunesse was mostly dedicated to generating anti-German propaganda.

> The main objective of our organization was to prevent the youth from going to Germany. Because for all the young people who went to Germany, there were that many more German soldiers at the front, since young people who worked in Germany replaced the Germans who otherwise would have worked in the factories. So in preventing the French youth from going to work in Germany, we hurt the German military potential. It meant a few soldiers less for Germany.[11]

As a propagandist, Le Goupil was involved in printing, editing and distributing a newspaper called *L'Espoir du Jeune Patriote Normand* (*The Hope of the Young Norman Patriot*). When such propaganda efforts convinced someone to join the resistance, the organization could then offer different types of assistance:

> We hid people, we gave them false papers, we gave them supplies. Those who wanted to do more, who wanted to work with the sabotage teams, well I could help them join these teams because I was in liaison with the principal military chiefs in the region.[12]

Le Goupil was in contact with several military organizations within the Resistance. These organizations were known by several different titles and actually engaged in making war against German occupation forces:

> These organizations were the ones who blew up the railroad tracks and the warehouses, etc. And if people in my organization preferred to do something like that, I steered them toward the responsible party of the military organization. But I was the chief of the organization. I guided people from one place to another according to where they wanted to participate.[13]

With over four hundred people in his department, Le Goupil directed a large group of underground operatives capable of creating significant amounts of trouble for the German occupation:

> The Germans knew very well that the young people in our organizations were the same young people who would shoot them in the back when the Allied invasion took place. So they [the Germans] fought against it with all their might. And they also knew that we were preventing the French youth from going to Germany. For example, hundreds of young people that I successfully prevented from going to Germany, these young people, at the moment of the Allied invasion, were found in organizations of the Resistance.[14]

The Germans actively sought to crush the Resistance, and often did so by infiltrating the movement's various organizations with spies. These spies were French citizens who were paid by the Gestapo to get inside suspected resistance networks. In October 1943, a French Gestapo agent managed to work his way into the inner circle of the Front Patriotique de la Jeunesse. At that time, Le Goupil was staying at his parish priest's home because the priest was helping him to print *L'Espoir du Jeune Patriote Normand*:

> So this young French man introduced himself to the priest saying that he had an American parachutist to hide (because we also took care of getting the parachutists to organizations who would care for them). So the parish priest said, "Oh, well I know someone. I have a chief of the Resistance staying at my place." Two days later, the Gestapo surrounded the parsonage and we were captured. It was a Frenchman who got us arrested![15]

Thanks to the information provided by this one collaborator, the Gestapo rounded up a total of twelve members of the Resistance. In addition to Le Goupil, his Section Head in Rouen, three of his associates and seven others were taken away for interrogation. Despite this setback though, the Resistance survived:

> For me, it was over, but others took our places. The movement went on after us. It didn't stop because some of the bosses were arrested. The Section Head of Dieppe and of Le Havre were not arrested.[16]

Before France was finally liberated in 1944, this one Frenchman had turned in over two hundred members of the underground. He used the same story every time: he told each of his victims that he had a parachutist at his house that needed to be hidden. The worst part of it all was that he only did it for the money.

Le Goupil was in prison in Rouen for the first six months after his arrest. For three of those six months a "well-mannered" Gestapo agent, who had previously taught French, interrogated him. Le Goupil recalled:

> I didn't think I would come out of it alive – I believed they would kill me. But I never gave in. I never gave them a name or anything.[17]

In the end, neither Le Goupil nor the other eleven members of the underground arrested with him were executed. Instead, they were all deported to Germany without the benefit of representation or a fair trial.

> There were no trials at that time. The Gestapo didn't have trials. Whatever the infraction, they sent everyone to Germany. They needed people to dig ditches for the foundations of the factories that made the V1s and V2s.[18]

Soon thereafter, Le Goupil and hundreds of others like him were loaded onto a train for the trip to Germany. He spent the next four days and three nights packed in a freight car with approximately one hundred other miserable people. On April 27, 1944 the train arrived at its destination: Auschwitz in occupied Poland.

There, he became a slave laborer: "The Germans had decided to kill us, to exterminate us, by working us to death. It was death by labor." Le Goupil remained in the camp at Auschwitz-Birkenau for only a brief interval though. Two weeks later, he was moved back across the border into Germany to the concentration camp at Buchenwald in Thuringia. When the European war ended in May, he was liberated at Coswig on the Elbe River north of Dresden:

> We were between the American Army and the Russian Army. And the first soldier I saw was an American in a Jeep and he asked me if I was Russian because my clothes didn't match very well. I said, "No, I'm French."[19]

Paul Le Goupil returned to France on June 1, 1945. More than one full year of his life had been spent in German concentration camps. He had been deported from his home country as punishment for resisting the tyranny of the people who had conquered it. Although one year of his life was gone forever, he was nevertheless one of the lucky ones. Of the eleven people that had been arrested with him, only five returned to France in 1945 – the others had died in the camps.

• • •

While some French men and women resisted the Germans through either active or passive means, for others it was not possible to be involved in the Resistance. For example, parents with small children were in no position to do anything against the occupation because such activity could endanger their lives and perhaps even the safety and security of families. For such people, all they could hope for was that the war Germany had started would not affect them. However the unfortunate reality of the circumstances was that it often did and husbands lost wives, wives lost husbands and children were orphaned as a result of what German aggression had brought to French soil.

Fernand François was born on a small farm just outside the village of St. Marcouf in 1934. St. Marcouf sits approximately four kilometers from the eastern coast of the Cotentin peninsula on a gentle roll of topography that rises above the surrounding countryside. Soon after the invasion in 1940, the Germans began building defensive artillery positions near strategically important coastal areas that could potentially support amphibious landing operations. The eastern shore of the Cotentin peninsula between St. Vaast-La-Hougue in the north and La Madeleine in the south was one of the important areas that the Germans would ultimately fortify as a part of the so-called Atlantic Wall. The Germans therefore planned to build a number of long-range coast artillery batteries in the area that would be capable of showering accurate artillery fire on any ships attempting landings along that stretch of coast. Accordingly, German labor troops arrived in 1941 to begin construction of a permanent battery on a site near St. Marcouf. That site just so hap-

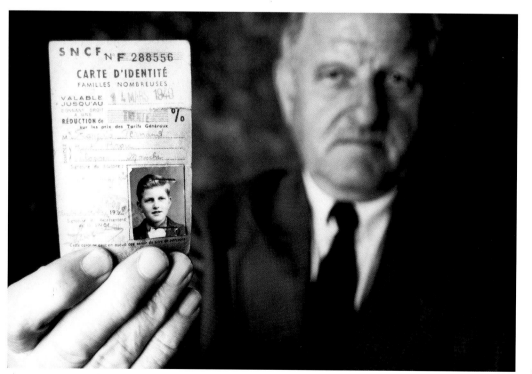

Fernand François was born in the village of St. Marcouf in 1934. He was only ten years old when Allied bombers attacked the nearby battery at Crisbecq late on the night of June 5, 1944. Bombs intended to knock out the battery's three 210mm guns destroyed his home instead, killing his father and his eighteen-year-old cousin. (*Photo by Jeff Petry*)

One of the three reinforced concrete casemates of the battery at
Crisbecq near St. Marcouf. Each
casemate protected one 210mm
(8.27 inch) Czechoslovakian *Skoda*
gun capable of directing accurate
artillery fire along practically the
entire length of the east coast of the
Cotentin peninsula. Although the
battery was heavily bombed before
June 6th, its guns were protected
by their concrete casemates and
were therefore capable of firing on
the invasion fleet off of Utah Beach
on D-Day. (*USCG photo by Albert
Thompson, National Archives and
Records Administration, War and
Conflict #1046*)

pened to be a few hundred yards away from the farm where Fernand
François and his family lived:

> I remember the first Germans that arrived very well. They
> came over the high point that overlooked our farm. They were
> marching, I remember this very well. I was young. I was less
> than ten years old.[20]

What the Germans built there was not just a battery, but a military complex of great size. It was called Batterie Crisbecq and it
was centered around three separate reinforced-concrete casemates
inside of which were mounted three long-range Czechoslovakian
210mm guns made by Skoda. In addition to the 210mm Skodas,
the Crisbecq battery would ultimately include additional armament:
a pair of 155mm guns, six 75mm and three 20mm anti-aircraft guns.
An all around defensive perimeter was also built up to protect the
battery from infantry attack and/or sabotage. This included
minefields, barbed wire and seventeen machine gun nests. The care,
maintenance and operation of the variety of weapons at Crisbecq
required a force of some four hundred men. Although on land, the
force that garrisoned the Crisbecq battery was a detachment of naval infantry of the *Kriegsmarine* – the German Navy. These three
hundred men were under the command of 1st Class Ensign Walter
Ohmsen.[21] With so many men assigned to the post, the Crisbecq
battery lacked adequate facilities to house them all. For that reason,
some of the naval infantrymen at Crisbecq were quartered in private homes, including the nearby farm where Fernand François lived.

> I remember it like it was yesterday...I remember that the
> farm was occupied by the Germans. There was a room in our
> house reserved for them. My parents had to give them a room.[22]

With naval infantrymen living in his house, it was inevitable
that François would end up interacting with the Germans. He had a
great deal of contact with them and that contact was actually not
altogether unpleasant: "They were like family these Germans; they
didn't want the war."[23] Although Fernand François experienced
somewhat positive contact with the people who had conquered his
country, the circumstances of occupation created negative and dangerous situations. When Fernand's mother developed a life threatening illness, the family was not able to get her proper medical
attention:

> During the German occupation there were no more doc-
> tors. The hospitals were mobilized by the Germans. That is to
> say, people could no longer get operations, or be treated like
> they could during peacetime.[24]

With all the local doctors away at the war, the only alternative
was to transport her to a larger city like Cherbourg or Caen. However, that too was not possible as a result of the German occupation. There were no vehicles to take her to a hospital and even if a
car had been available, there was no gasoline. Sadly, Fernand's
mother died for lack of proper medical treatment.

An American soldier is dwarfed by one of the three casemates of the battery at Crisbecq near St. Marcouf. Despite the fact that Allied bombers dropped over 800 bombs on the battery between April 19 and June 6, 1944, the guns were so well protected by reinforced concrete that they were still capable of firing. The German garrison at Crisbecq abandoned the battery on June 12th after which American forces occupied the position, which is when this photograph was taken. (*National Archives and Records Administration*)

After the death of his mother, an 18-year-old niece moved in to the house to help Fernand's father take care of him and his two brothers. Time went by and the motherless family settled into a new routine. As the date of the Normandy invasion approached, things began to change at Fernand's family farm. Shortly before D-Day, more infantry arrived at St. Marcouf and the Crisbecq battery itself began to draw progressively more and more attention from Allied combat aircraft:

> We had some bombings eventually and planes that dove out of the sky, spraying machine gun fire. It happened frequently because planes flew out of the sky to do reconnaissance.[25]

Allied intelligence had astutely recognized that the powerful 210mm Skodas at Crisbecq could potentially wreak havoc among the ships of an invasion armada off the coast in the immediate proximity of the battery. In connection with the plans for Operation Overlord, a nearby stretch of beach north of La Madeleine, just to the east of Ste.-Marie-du-Mont, had been selected to be one of the invasion beaches – a beach codenamed Utah. Unfortunately, the Utah Beach landing area was barely ten kilometers south of St. Marcouf – well within the umbrella of artillery fire of the Skodas at the Crisbecq battery. It was therefore realized that, for an amphibious landing to occur at Utah Beach, the Crisbecq battery would have to be neutralized. Allied planners also recognized that the heavily defended battery would be almost impossible to take using

the vertical envelopment tactics of parachute or glider forces, so they settled instead on an unsophisticated plan: the battery would be the target of a heavy bombing mission the night before the landings. Although they did not know it, the war was about to come to Fernand François and his motherless family:

> It was about ten o'clock at night on the night between June 5th and 6th. We were in bed, and had been for about fifteen or twenty minutes – my father, my two brothers, as well as my cousin. All at once, we heard airplane motors above our house and my father said to the kids, to us, he said to put our clothes on quickly. And my cousin, who was 18 at the time, was faster than we were. She went down to the first floor. The whole house fell upon her.[26]

U.S. Army bombers proceeded to drop six hundred tons of bombs in the area immediately around the Crisbecq battery. Although their target was the battery's casemates, many of the bombs fell off course. Some fell on Fernand's home, destroying it:

> I found myself blasted onto a pile of stones without even a scratch, nothing. My brother, Joseph, found himself under a marble table and my father was lying unconscious under the same table, as if he had been struck in the back of the head by it. Joseph told me, "Papa is dead." I guessed that he was because he had been losing so much blood.[27]

That bombing mission inflicted a terrible amount of destruction on innocent civilians near Crisbecq. In addition to claiming the lives of Fernand's father and 18-year-old cousin, two entire families living in houses near the battery were killed.[28] The battery, though, was not even touched. In fact, Crisbecq's guns located fired on the invasion armada the next morning, sinking the destroyer USS *Corry* (DD-463).

• • •

When the Germans invaded in 1940, Odette and Marthe Rigault were living on their family's dairy farm in Le Port St. Pierre just north of the village of Graignes (ten kilometers south of Carentan) in Normandy. At the time, Odette was fifteen years old and Marthe was just eight. Although young, the two girls were in a perfect position to observe the impact of life under Nazi occupation. One significant change that took effect soon after the German invasion related to the availability of food. After the Germans came, certain food items became very hard to come by, which resulted in the implementation of a food-rationing program. Odette described the details:

> We had ration cards at the time. We could get one hundred grams of butter, one hundred grams of meat; everything was rationed like that because they (the Germans) took everything from us when they came. We had nothing left. The shops were all emptied.[29]

In 1944, Marthe and Odette Rigault were living on their parents' farm near the village of Graignes, ten kilometers south of Carentan. They had been living under German occupation for four long years when eleven planeloads of paratroopers from the 3rd Battalion/507th Parachute Infantry landed all around them at 2:20 am on D-Day. For them, the drama was about to begin. (*Photo by Jeff Petry*)

Not having a ration card meant that you could not purchase food. To obtain a ration card, you had to be registered. This was the Germans way of insuring that everyone was accounted for. During this time, Odette's future husband was a fugitive from the Germans and had to hide from them for four years without a ration card.[30] But rationing was apparently not enough, because the Germans also confiscated food items directly from farmers. Marthe remembered

Four U.S. Army soldiers pose with one of the three 210mm (8.27 inch) Czechoslovakian *Skoda* guns of the battery at Crisbecq near St. Marcouf. Shells from these guns contributed to the sinking of the destroyer USS *Corry* (DD-463) off of Utah Beach on D-Day. (*National Archives and Records Administration 111-SC-190388*)

that, "If you had ten chickens, you had to give them some of the eggs; if you had milk, you had to give it to them."[31] In fact, a German soldier on a bicycle came to the Rigault farm on a regular basis just to pick up eggs from their chicken coop. If you had something they wanted, you had no choice but to give it to them.[32]

Although they could not stand the thought of the occupation, neither could they rally too overtly against it.[33] If a person refused to cooperate, that person was usually deported to Germany where they would become a forced laborer in a concentration camp.[34] At the time, Germany was desperate for laborers to work in the factories producing the materiel supplying its war machine. Faced with such a need, the automatic sentence for practically any offense in the occupied countries was deportation. If you were singled out for this, you had no recourse. Odette recalled what it was like:

> When they wanted to send our French people to Germany to work in the factories, you didn't ask any questions. They took you and they sent you – no one could say anything.[35]

Under these circumstances, simple rural farm families like the Rigaults had absolutely no choice but to cooperate with their occupiers. Otherwise, they would face being sent away from their homes and their loved ones with no promise of being returned. Through this oppressive practice, the German forces occupying France (and their Vichy collaborators) stifled the people's freedom of speech and their freedom of expression. Seeking to protect their citizens and parishioners, many town mayors and parish priests even encouraged cooperation. In helpless frustration, some French citizens resorted to acts of low-intensity sabotage, but even the most passive acts of resistance were just as severely dealt with. Marthe remembered that:

> If the power or telephone lines were cut, it was the people who lived close by who were held responsible. They took someone away, a man or whomever, and sent them to Germany or just shot them.[36]

With individual civil liberties choked as they were, the Germans maintained tight control over the people who lived in the occupied northern area of France. In Graignes, the Rigault family could only accept the situation and adapt to their new, unpleasant life under German authority. Early that summer, a *Luftwaffe* airfield was established in the seasonally dry marshes near Graignes and soon German combat aircraft began filling the skies above the village on a daily basis. "From there they left to bomb England," remembered Marthe.[37] But the *Luftwaffe* lost the Battle of Britain and, when the winter months arrived, the marsh flats around the town flooded as they always had in the past. According to Odette, "All they (the Germans) saw was the water rising and rising, then the planes couldn't land there anymore, so they did it from June to the end of the year."[38] After the *Luftwaffe* abandoned the airfield, life in Graignes settled into a dull routine that was, thankfully remote to the dramatic and destructive violence that was visiting other European communities. "For years we waited for the Americans to arrive," Odette recalled.[39] During that wait, life in Graignes was, although not idyllic, at least peaceful and quiet. However, that peace and quiet would change dramatically early one Tuesday morning about four years later.

• • •

Like Harry Openheimer, Paul Le Goupil and Fernand François; Marthe and Odette Rigault had seen their lives changed forever. Such was the reality of life under Hitler's Germany. It was a reality where people were humiliated, excluded, deported and ultimately mass-murdered for their religious beliefs. It was a reality where the freedom of expression and the freedom of the press suffocated under the smothering weight of authoritarian rule. It was a reality that produced war orphans and refugees. This was the European continent that the men of the 507th Parachute Infantry Regiment were about to jump into. They would do so as a part of the righteous cause of correcting such injustices. They would do so to restore the peace and dignity of the people of France.

A pre-war picture post card showing part of the village of Graignes. (*Courtesy of the village of Graignes*)

5

Seize and Destroy

The operation that the 507th was about to be a part of would be massive and its objectives, intimidating. In addition to taking on a skilled and determined foe, Allied forces would be assaulting a heavily fortified coastline of concrete, steel, barbed-wire and land mines – an environment that favored the defender, an environment where the attacker was at a serious disadvantage. The relatively straightforward battle plan was divided into two operational components: Neptune and Overlord. Operation Neptune would consist of the movement of Allied naval and airborne forces across the English Channel immediately prior to the actual amphibious landing itself, which was code-named Operation Overlord. The Neptune half of the operational plan called for American and British airborne forces to secure the bridges and road networks on the flanks of the five invasion beaches in an effort to protect the amphibious assault from German reinforcements. The amphibious assault would be in the form of a *coup de main* over those beaches at dawn on D-Day.[1]

To prepare for the Neptune and Overlord components of the D-Day plan, intense training had become a fact of life for the Allied soldiers and sailors assembling at bases and camps throughout southern England. The paratroopers and glider infantry that were to be a part of the Neptune airborne operation gained valuable experience through exhaustive training. During this phase of the pre-invasion build-up, "the 507th practically lived in foxholes" due to the fact that it was almost constantly participating in field training exercises.[2] For the most part, these exercises were simulated jumps wherein small groups of paratroopers were driven in trucks to dispersed areas and dropped off. These simulations provided practice for the oh-so important skill of the night assembly and taught the men of the 507th that assembling 2,000 paratroopers in the dark was a very challenging thing to accomplish. This nocturnal activity

served as dramatic foreshadowing for what the regiment would soon be called on to do in Normandy. Then on May 12th, less than one month before D-Day, airborne training reached its climax with Exercise Eagle. This exercise involved a mass jump of the entire 82nd Airborne Division and it proved to be the true dress rehearsal for the airborne element of the cross channel attack.[3]

The men that were to be a part of the Overlord beach landings were receiving specialized instruction as well. During early 1943, the U.S. Army established a facility known as the Assault Training Center at Woolacombe Beach in northwest Devon where the men that would likewise make the tactical combat landing went through a specialized school of instruction.[4] But these men did not rehearse exclusively at Woolacombe Beach. Like their airborne counterparts, they also participated in large-scale training exercises, but the am-

The German *Schnellboote* was a heavily armed motor torpedo boat capable of great speed. To the Germans they were known as *S-bootes*, but to the Allies they were nicknamed E-boats. *(Courtesy of The National D-Day Museum)*

82nd Airborne Division paratroopers loaded into a C-47 for a practice jump. (*82nd Airborne Museum via Phil Nordyke*)

Pre-war view of the *S-11* showing its starboard torpedo tube. Because E-Boats carried the same powerful G7a and G7e torpedoes as the U-Boat fleet, they represented a very dangerous threat to allied shipping. This early type was later superseded by a modified design from *S-26* onward. (*Courtesy of The National D-Day Museum*)

The port side of a pre-war German E-Boat. On April 28, 1944 a group of E-Boats out of Cherbourg attacked the Exercise Tiger practice invasion fleet near Slapton Sands in Lyme Bay on the south coast of England. (*Courtesy of The National D-Day Museum*)

The starboard side of *S-14*. At Slapton Sands, the E-Boats attacked eight slow moving LSTs, sinking LST-507 and LST-531 and damaging LST-289. Tragically, 749 men of the U.S. Army 4th Infantry Division lost their lives in the attack. *(Courtesy of The National D-Day Museum)*

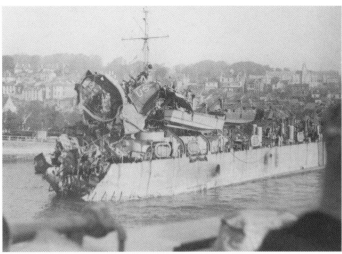

LST-289 returning to port at Dartmouth in southern England the day after the Lyme Bay disaster. *(Courtesy of The National D-Day Museum)*

phibious exercises in which they participated were conducted along the country's southern coast rather than in the fields of the English countryside. One of those pre-D-Day exercises, code named Exercise Tiger, met with disaster and produced circumstances that would have a direct impact on the 507th. On April 28th, two flotillas of German high-speed motor torpedo boats attacked the Exercise Tiger practice invasion fleet in Lyme Bay on the south coast of England. The enemy *Schnellbootes*, known as *S-bootes* to the Germans and as E-boats to the Allies, had sailed from Cherbourg ear-

lier that night and stumbled across the practice invasion fleet near a place called Slapton Sands. The E-boats penetrated the shipping convoy and then proceeded to attack its eight slow moving LSTs with torpedoes, sinking LST-507 and LST-531 and damaging LST-289. Tragically, 749 men of the U.S. Army 4th Infantry Division lost their lives as a result of the attack.[5]

The Exercise Tiger disaster near Slapton Sands had grave consequences on the planning for the coming invasion, which at that point was only five weeks away. To the Germans, the fact that the

Two LCVPs were used to tow LST-289 back to Dartmouth. *(Courtesy of Dr. James F. Tent)*

The starboard side of LST-289 as she enters port at Dartmouth after the Slapton Sands incident. *(Courtesy of The National D-Day Museum)*

Close-up view of the port side stern area of LST-289 showing the heavy damage she sustained during the E-Boat attack in Lyme Bay. Thirteen men died at their stations in the upturned 40mm gun tub located on the ship's stern. *(Courtesy of Dr. James F. Tent)*

Allies were conducting such a large amphibious training exercise at Slapton Sands represented an invaluable intelligence clue. They recognized that the topography of Slapton Sands was virtually identical to areas along the east coast of the Cotentin peninsula in Normandy, France. If the Allies intended to force a landing there, the perfect place to rehearse for such an operation was Slapton Sands, where the geography was practically identical. Correctly interpreting this as a sign that Allied Armies might be building up for an invasion in Normandy, the Germans quickly began to strengthen their presence in the area. One month later, an Allied intelligence report included a chilling statement that reflected the recently observed build-up of forces in Normandy:

> The recent trend of movement of German land forces toward the Cherbourg area tends to support the view that the Le Havre-Cherbourg area is regarded as a likely, and perhaps even the main, point of assault.[6]

Alert to the fact that the Cotentin peninsula was vulnerable and emerging as a "likely" target, the Germans prepared to defend against naval forces, amphibious landing forces and airborne forces. With the attack on the Exercise Tiger practice invasion fleet at Slapton Sands, the E-boat demonstrated that it packed a devastating punch. Since they obviously possessed the capability to inflict enormous amounts of damage to ships, the number of E-boats and the volume of E-boat patrol activity significantly increased in the waters between Cherbourg and Le Havre following the April 28th incident. Any large-scale movement of Allied ships across the English Channel in support of a landing operation would have to contend with the very real threat of devastating nightly E-boat attacks.

Franz Gockel, a private in *3rd Kompanie, Infanterie Regiment 726* of the German 716th Static Division, was one of the many defenders assigned to the WN-62 fortified bunker complex located at Colleville-Sur-Mer just above Omaha Beach. *(Courtesy of The National D-Day Museum)*

Above: This photograph, taken at low tide, shows the array of beach obstacles that was so typical along the Normandy coast before the invasion. Pictured are hedgehogs and timber ramps, as well as *Rommel's asparagus*. (*Courtesy of The National D-Day Museum*)

The German static divisions defending the beaches of Normandy also improved their defenses in the days and weeks immediately after the Slapton Sands incident. Franz Gockel, a private in 3rd *Kompanie, Infanterie* Regiment 726 of the German 716th Static Division, was one of those defenders. He was assigned to the WN-62 fortified bunker complex located at Colleville-Sur-Mer just above a stretch of beach that the Americans were already referring to as Omaha.[7] The infantry fighting positions and artillery casemates at WN-62 (WN stands for *Widerstandsnest* or 'resistance point') were in a commanding position on the high ground overlooking that beach. During the month of May, Gockel was personally involved in the strengthening of the defensive fortifications there:

Rommelspargel – or *Rommel's asparagus* – were one of a variety of different types of beach obstacles abundant in the beach defenses of the Normandy coast. As in the example pictured above, they could be topped with an anti-tank mine to make them even more dangerous. (*Courtesy of The National D-Day Museum*)

We constructed tank barriers on the beach at low tide from logs topped with Teller mines. Other beach obstacles were 'Czech hedgehogs' made from crossed iron beams, and 'Belgian Gates' from thick steel stakes. Running parallel to the waterline before us was a low wall made of water-worn stones enclosing the beach, and along the wall was laid a minefield for the purpose of protecting us from surprise attack during darkness. A tank trench had been dug between WN-62 and WN-61 and was protected with mines, and our position was protected with a tangle ring of barbed wire rolls.[8]

Above: View of one of the reinforced concrete artillery casemates of the WN62 Bunker complex on Omaha Beach. Note the beach at low tide in the background. (*Photo by the author*) Left: In addition to large numbers of beach obstacles, the Germans also buried millions of anti-tank and anti-personnel land mines behind the beaches in Normandy. (*Courtesy of The National D-Day Museum*)

After Slapton Sands, the beaches were becoming an even more inhospitable environment than they had been before.

In addition to the increased E-boat patrols and the expanded and improved beach defenses, the Germans also took special precautions to defend the Cotentin peninsula against airborne assault. Anti-aircraft artillery units were positioned throughout the peninsula and also to the west in the Channel Islands of Jersey and Guernsey where the 319th Static Division was stationed. Then in May, the 91st *Luftland* Division was transferred into the area. The 91st

A small sample of the anti-tank mines and booby-trapped artillery shells that were buried in Normandy by the German defenders. (*Courtesy of The National D-Day Museum*)

The other reinforced casemate at the WN62 bunker complex. German Pvt. Franz Gockel was stationed here on the morning of June 6, 1944. (*Photo by the author*)

The rear entrances to the casemates at WN62 were well protected by earthen traverses, evidence of which can still be seen at the site today. The 'Dog-Green' sector of Omaha Beach at Vierville-Sur-Mer is in the background to the west. (*Photo by the author*)

German infantrymen pose on a French Renault R-35 light tank. When France fell in 1940, a large number of Renault, Hotchkiss and Somua tanks were captured which the Germans later put into their own service. (*Courtesy of The National D-Day Museum*)

A French Renault R-35 light tank abandoned in a field after the fall of France in 1940. A number of R-35s were being operated by the *100. Panzer Ausbildungs und Ersatz Abteilung* when it was deployed to the Cotentin Peninsula in May 1944 as an element of the *91st Luftland Division*. *(Courtesy of The National D-Day Museum)*

was a specially trained and equipped "air-landing" division, the mission of which was to neutralize any vertical insertion of enemy forces by parachute and/or glider.[9] Composed of the *1057th Infantrie Regiment*, the *1058th Infantrie Regiment* and the *100. Panzer Ausbildungs und Ersatz Abteilung* (100th Tank Training and Replacement Battalion), the 91st Luft Division was under the command of 47 year old Generalleutnant Wilhelm Falley, whose headquarters was located near St.-Sauveur-le-Vicomte. The 91st was "an ad hoc, improvised unit" that had been hastily formed in 1944

and was consequently somewhat poorly equipped. As an example, the 91st Division's attached tank battalion (the *100. Panzer Ausbildungs und Ersatz Abteilung*) was not equipped with deadly and effective German-made Panzers like the Mk. IV, the Mk. V Panther or the Mk. VI Tiger. Instead, the battalion was exclusively equipped with 46 French-made Somua, Renault and Hotchkiss light tanks that had been captured from the French Army when Germany invaded in 1940.[10] The quality of equipment notwithstanding, the 91st would be the principal antagonist against which the 507th would ultimately struggle so violently in Normandy.

• • •

A French Somua S-35 light tank abandoned after the fall of France in 1940. The *100. Panzer Ausbildungs und Ersatz Abteilung* was operating a few S-35s at the time of the invasion. *(Courtesy of The National D-Day Museum)*

Another Renault R-35 abandoned along the side of a road in 1940. *(Courtesy of The National D-Day Museum)*

A French Hotchkiss H-38 light tank knocked out in 1940. The *100. Panzer Ausbildungs und Ersatz Abteilung* was also operating a number of H-38s at the time of the invasion. *(Courtesy of The National D-Day Museum)*

In addition to their functional value as beach obstacles, *Rommel's asparagus* could also be used to protect fields from being used for parachute drop zones or glider landing zones. The *91st Luftland* Division began placing *Rommel's asparagus* in the fields behind Utah Beach as soon as it arrived in the area in May 1944 and, by the time of the invasion much of the work had been completed. (*82nd Airborne Museum via Phil Nordyke*)

Field Marshall Erwin Rommel, the commander of German forces in Normandy, on an inspection tour of beach defenses. (*Courtesy of The National D-Day Museum*)

The *Pocket Guide to France* was an invaluable resource for the GIs who fought there. (*Courtesy of The National D-Day Museum*)

The arrival of the 91st *Luftland* Division in Normandy did not go unobserved. Allied aerial reconnaissance photographs detected the presence of the new unit soon after it moved into the area. In his 1978 book *On to Berlin*, Brigadier General Gavin described that, throughout the month of May, Allied intelligence was following a steady crescendo of German activity around St.-Sauveur-le-Vicomte. According to Gavin:

> German activity around that town had been increasing steadily. According to the calculation made by the division intelligence officer, St.-Sauveur-le-Vicomte probably housed a division headquarters plus division special troops, and possibly an infantry regiment besides. The Germans were stocking gas and oil dumps near the town, and quite a few gun emplacements were coming into view day by day in the air reconnaissance photos.

These reconnaissance photos also captured evidence of another, sobering development. The photos showed dozens of tiny holes in many of the open fields throughout the interior of the Cotentin peninsula. Allied photo-interpreters correctly recognized that the holes had been dug so that the Germans could plant a network of timber posts that they called *Rommelspargel* – or *Rommel's asparagus*. *Rommel's Asparagus* were so called because they basically resembled giant stalks of asparagus sticking up out of the ground and they were a frequently used type of the various defensive obstacles authorized by Field Marshall Erwin Rommel – the commander of the defenses in Normandy. When these obstacles were planted in a potential drop zone or landing zone, they could potentially wreak havoc on any paratroopers and/or gliders attempting to land there. The *Rommelspargel* holes observed throughout Norman farm fields that May triggered a dramatic change in the basic plan for the airborne element of Operation Neptune.

As of May 26, 1944, 82nd Airborne Division headquarters had completed all plans and preparations for the operation. Field and administrative orders had been published and distributed to all regimental and battalion commanders along with maps showing the details of the operational area. The plan called for the division's various regiments and attached support units to:

> Land by parachute and glider before and after dawn of D-Day west of ST. SAUVEUR LE VICOMTE: seize, clear and secure the general area ST. JACQUES DE NEHOU – BESNEVILLE – ST. SAUVEUR LE VICOMTE – BLANDAMOUR, and reorganize; seize and destroy the crossings of the PRAIRIES MARECAGEUSES north of LA SANGSURIERE, at ST. SAUVEUR DE PIERRE PONT; destroy the crossings of the OLLONONDE River in the vicinity of ST. Lô D'OURVILLE and block crossroads vicinity LE CHEMIN; prevent enemy forces moving north between ST. Lô D'OURVILLE and junction of DOUVE River with PRAIRIE MARECAGEUSES; and protect the south flank of VII Corps north of the same line.[11]

Had the 82nd Airborne actually carried out this "Plan A" the entire division would have dropped on top of the divisional head-

Map in the center of the
Pocket Guide to France.
(Courtesy of The National
D-Day Museum)

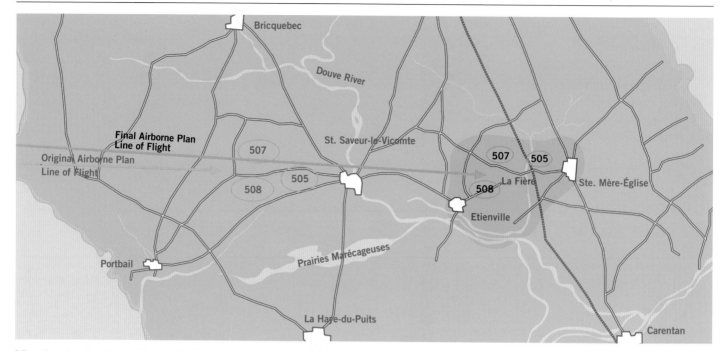

Map showing the 82nd Airborne Division's originally planned D-Day drop zones west of St. Sauveur Le Vicomte and the drop zones west of Ste.-Mère-Église that were ultimately used on June 6th. (*Map by Scott Carroll Illustrations*)

quarters of the German 91st *Luftland* Division at St. Sauveur Le Vicomte! This would have been a bloodbath for the 507th along with all the other units of the 82nd. But after the presence of the 91st had been detected by confirmed intelligence reports, Plan A was scrapped and rapidly replaced by a new plan. On May 26th, First Army Commander issued a revised battle plan that directed the 82nd Airborne Division to conduct its landings further to the east. This "Plan B" directed the 82nd Airborne to:

Land by parachute and glider before and after dawn of D-Day astride the MERDERET River, seize, clear and secure the general area NEUVILLE AU PLAIN – BANDIENVILLE within its zone; capture ST. MERE EGLISE; seize and secure the crossings of the MERDERET River, and a bridgehead covering them; seize and destroy the crossing of the DOUVE River at BEUZEVILLE LA BASTILLE and ETIENVILLE; protect the northwest flank of VII Corps within the Division zone; and be prepared to advance west on Corps order to the line of the

DOUVE north of its junction with the PRAIRIES MARECAGEUSES.[12]

Practically on the eve of the invasion, the entire division had thus been ordered to rewrite its battle plan completely. Since the revised battle orders shifted the division's drop zones and landing zones away from St. Sauveur Le Vicomte – away from the newly arrived 91st Division – the 82nd Airborne Division's operations section had to likewise revise its orders to the various units of the division. Accordingly, the 507th Regimental operations section thereafter adjusted its orders for the regiment's three battalions. When the mad scramble to get the job done was over, the 507th PIR would still be dropping on the Cotentin peninsula, but not on top of the 91st *Luftland* Division. The new insertion area for the 82nd Airborne Division would be in an area where it could block the eastward movement of the 91st *Luftland* Division rather than land on it. The regiment would be dropping on a new a drop zone far away from St. Sauveur Le Vicomte – a drop zone close to a little town named Ste.-Mère-Église.

6

"... a beautiful sight."

To the men of the 507th, the signs were beginning to come together – they were about to be a part of something big. In late May, Col. Millett pulled the regiment together and delivered a speech that did much to motivate them and "elevate" their morale.[1] Col. Millett said:

Men, several months ago I told you to put away your knives so you wouldn't get in trouble with them. I told you I would let you know when to get them out. Well men, get them out and sharpen them up, we have a big job ahead.[2]

That "big job" would be D-Day and as of late May, the 507th was in the final stages of preparing for it. During that time, every trench knife, bayonet and switchblade in the regiment was sent to a sharpener in Nottingham. He returned them all with a razor sharp edge and refused to accept payment.[3] Then, between May 24th and 28th, the men were issued specially modified M42 jumpsuits. Adopted in 1942, the M42 jumpsuit was specifically developed by the Army to be worn by airborne forces during jump operations. It consisted of a zipper front jacket and a pair of button-fly trousers, both of which were equipped with expandable cargo pockets. In anticipation of the Germans using poison gas to fight off the assault, the outer garments to be worn by those units spearheading the invasion were impregnated with an anti-gas chemical agent that would offer at least some protection from blister agents and irritants. Since they would be a part of the Normandy combat assault, the men of the 507th were issued such chemically treated M42s. In addition to this, some of the men that were designated to make the Normandy airborne drop had their M42s modified for added durability. In some cases, these modifications were done by the rigger section of the participating regiments, but in other cases the

jumpsuits were modified by units like the 320th Salvage Repair Company. This modification involved reinforcing the knees, elbows and cargo pocket bellows of the jumpsuit with pieces of tent canvas to reduce wear and extend the life of the garment. According to

Two men pose on one of the mobile service trailers of the 320th Salvage Repair Company in England in early 1944. The man at left is wearing the standard M1942 jumpsuit that was being issued to American paratroopers before the Normandy invasion. The man at right is wearing an M1942 jumpsuit that the 320th has reinforced. This modification was done to reduce wear and extend the life of the garment. (*National Archives and Records Administration 111-SC-314714*)

M42 jump jacket of the type worn by the men of the 507th during the Normandy operation. Note the 82nd Airborne Division patch and the M2 switchblade partially inserted into its placket pocket. The lower cargo pocket bellows, the left elbow and the right inner arm have been reinforced with pieces of tent canvas to reduce wear and extend the life of the garment. *(Collection of Tom Czekanski)*

M42 jump trousers of the type worn by the men of the 507th during the Normandy operation. The cargo pocket bellows and the knees have been reinforced with pieces of tent canvas to make the garment more durable. Canvas leg ties have also been added. *(Collection of Tom Czekanski)*

507th troopers leaving Tollerton Hall on May 28, 1944. The entire regiment was transported in civilian buses to the aerodromes at Fulbeck and Barkston-Heath near Grantham in Lincolnshire. (*National Archives and Records Administration via Jump/Cut Productions and Scott Carroll*)

Capt. Morgan A. Brakonecke of Regimental Headquarters Company/507th and another officer at Tollerton Hall near Nottingham on May 28, 1944. This image, taken from a piece of film footage, was filmed while the company was preparing to move to the airfield at Fulbeck. (*National Archives and Records Administration via Jump/Cut Productions and Scott Carroll*)

507th troopers boarding the buses at Tollerton Hall on May 28, 1944. (*National Archives and Records Administration via Jump/Cut Productions and Scott Carroll*)

Edward Jeziorski, these jumpsuits were "the lousiest, the coldest, the clammiest, the stiffest, the stinkiest articles of clothing that were ever dreamed up to be worn by individuals."[4] With such uniforms being distributed to the men, "it didn't require much of an IQ to figure out that the end of the beginning was upon us," remembered Bob Davis.[5]

On May 28th, the regiment's three battalions together with Regimental Headquarters Company were transported in civilian buses to and sequestered at a pair of aerodromes near Grantham in Lincolnshire. During the short drive, the men were apparently preoccupied with thoughts of what they were about to do. Clarence S. Hughart, a Pfc. in H Company remembered that, "on the way everyone was quiet; no one was talking or joking."[6] G Company's Lt. Johnny Marr recalled the situation:

507th paratroopers playing volleyball to pass the time at Fulbeck, Lincolnshire on June 4, 1944. 507th Regimental Headquarters Company and the 1st Battalion flew from Fulbeck. (*National Archives and Records Administration via Jump/Cut Productions and Scott Carroll*)

They moved us to the airfield under strict guard so that we could maintain the level of secrecy that was required of us and of course everybody cooperated to the hilt because they knew our lives might depend upon it.[7]

507th Regimental Headquarters and the 1st Battalion went to Fulbeck and 2nd and 3rd Battalions went to Barkston-Heath. Davis recalled what it was like at Fulbeck:

We were told that we were completely surrounded by barbed wire and that anyone attempting to leave would probably be shot, if not, spend the rest of their career in a jail cell somewhere. For obvious reasons, security was awfully tight.[8]

Chris Kanaras and the rest of the men of E Company/507th were sealed in at Barkston-Heath. They slept on cots in a hangar there and were closely guarded by U.S. Army Air Force personnel.[9]

At the various major airfields throughout southern England, all of the men of the 82nd Airborne were sealed in "tighter than a cork"[10] without access to telephones or outgoing mail as the division prepared to go to Normandy.[11] On May 31st the briefings began. Bob Davis recalled that, "following our initial briefing we knew where we were headed."[12] For the next five days, the officers and men of the regiment studied maps, aerial reconnaissance photographs and a mock-up sand table of Normandy. To Ed Jeziorski, June 1st through 3rd was one big "jumble" of maps, overlays, terrain scale models and mockups of DZs.[13] During this time, each of the regiment's companies received its specific mission objectives. Davis recalled that, "Upon learning our mission about four days before the jump, the tension grew by the hour, for we were in possession of top secret information unavailable to millions on the planet and the burden weighed heavily upon each of us to perform our part in a monumental task."[14]

When they were not being briefed, they worked on their equipment. At this point, they were promised that the regiment would be brought back to England after only about seven days of combat. "We were told we probably wouldn't be there more than a week," Davis remembered.[15] Before it was all over, the 507th would be in Normandy for thirty-five days.[16]

507th paratroopers carrying equipment to a waiting C-47 of the 306th Troop Carrier Squadron, 442nd Troop Carrier Group, 50th Troop Carrier Wing at Fulbeck, Lincolnshire on June 4, 1944. (*National Archives and Records Administration via Jump/Cut Productions and Scott Carroll***)**

507th paratroopers loading equipment onto a C-47 of the 305th Troop Carrier Squadron, 442nd Troop Carrier Group on June 3, 1944. (*National Archives and Records Administration via Jump/Cut Productions and Scott Carroll*)

507th paratroopers loading equipment onto a C-47 of the 305th Troop Carrier Squadron at Fulbeck, Lincolnshire on June 3, 1944. Note camouflage netting draped over the aircraft's freshly painted invasion stripes. (*National Archives and Records Administration via Jump/Cut Productions and Scott Carroll*)

507th paratroopers loading equipment bundles onto a C-47 of the 305th Troop Carrier Squadron, 442nd Troop Carrier Group at Fulbeck, Lincolnshire on June 3, 1944. (*National Archives and Records Administration via Jump/ Cut Productions and Scott Carroll*)

On June 3rd the men rigged their respective C-47s with the equipment bundles that would carry their heaviest gear. Ed Jeziorski and the men from his stick attached five para-packs to the undercarriage of a C-47 with the tail number Z-92422. Pack #1 contained Jeziorski's M1919A4 .30-cal. machine gun and four ammo cans of belted armor piercing .30-caliber ammunition. The other four bundles contained more small arms ammunition as well as an M2 60mm mortar. The men were also issued their field rations: three boxes of K-rations and three chocolate bars that the GIs referred to as "D-bars".

After a good breakfast on the morning of June 4th, the men learned that they would be jumping that night. They were told to take it easy and also to do whatever was necessary individually to prepare themselves for the jump. "I don't know one of us who didn't attend a religious service," Jeziorski remembered.[17] Because of the anxiety being produced by the prospect of soon being in combat, Cpt. John J. Verret, the regiment's chaplain, became a man in great demand in those hours immediately prior to the invasion. On June 4th, Jeziorski talked with Verret briefly. "He asked me if I was scared and I told him that I didn't think so," Jeziorski remembered.[18] The Chaplain then took Jeziorski by the hand, they both knelt down and said a little prayer together.[19] Meanwhile, some men checked and re-checked their main and reserve chutes while others sharpened their trench knives and bayonets. In the midst of this activity, thoughts turned to loved ones back home. Accordingly, some men took the opportunity to write letters while some manifested their emotions in other ways. For example, Jeziorski taped a photograph

of his fiancée to the inside of the liner of his M2 helmet because he was afraid that it would get lost or damaged in a pocket.

That afternoon, the men went through the arduous and tedious process of gearing up for the jump. Because of the weight of the equipment and the tightness of harnesses, they were far from comfortable. In an effort to reduce their discomfort, the men laid down on the tarmac alongside their C-47s and used their parachutes to support their backs.[20] After they had been there for some time, they received word that the operation had been postponed. The invasion

General Dwight D. Eisenhower, Supreme Commander of the Allied Expeditionary Force. (*Courtesy of The National D-Day Museum*)

Demolitions men are closely scrutinized by 507th Regimental Intelligence Officer Captain James A. Dickerson at Tollerton Hall shortly before D-Day. (*National Archives and Records Administration via Jump/Cut Productions and Scott Carroll*)

507th demolitions men taking a smoke break at Tollerton Hall shortly before D-Day. (*National Archives and Records Administration via Jump/Cut Productions and Scott Carroll*)

had originally been scheduled to begin on June 5th, but a storm had blown into the English Channel that weekend. Consequently, General Dwight D. Eisenhower, the Supreme Commander of the Allied Expeditionary Force, put the operation on hold hoping that weather conditions would improve. Like every other unit participating in the Normandy invasion, the men of the 507th had been prepared to go into combat the night of June 4th/5th when they received the word that they would have to wait. The news was received with mixed emotions within the regiment. Jeziorski observed that some of the men were relieved while to others it was a true "misery" to

be held over. "We were all very anxious to make a move one way or the other," he remembered.[21]

On June 5th, the men of the 507th repeated their activities from the previous day: checking and rechecking equipment, writing and rewriting letters home, and visiting and revisiting Father Verret. Early that evening, they were fed their last meal before the operation: steak and fries. "I knew right then that the time was near," remembered Pvt. Joseph A. Dahlia of Chicago, Illinois, "because the Army had never fed me steaks before."[22] Each evening at mealtime, Air Force personnel drove over to the airfield in a chow truck

507th medics preparing to leave Tollerton Hall on May 28th, 1944. (*National Archives and Records Administration via Jump/Cut Productions and Scott Carroll*)

A 507th paratrooper shows the unique assortment of weapons and equipment he will carry to Normandy. He has removed the butt stock of his M1A1 Thompson sub-machine gun and wears an improvised chest pouch to hold additional 30-round magazines for the weapon. (*National Archives and Records Administration via Jump/Cut Productions and Scott Carroll*)

to distribute dinner to the paratroopers since they were prohibited from leaving their airfields. When Chris Kanaras went up to the truck to get his chow on June 5th, one of the Air Force men recognized him from back home. Although the two men knew each other, they were not able to have an open conversation. In an effort to prevent security leaks at the airfields, Air Force personnel had been prohibited from speaking to paratroopers and vice versa. Because

of that rule, Kanaras could only give a quick nod before he moved on. After a few minutes, the man edged over to where Kanaras was sitting on the tarmac eating. Still standing, the man asked Kanaras if this was the big one. "What do you think?" was Kanaras's reply.[23] Although he could not really give any details about the operation, Kanaras did ask for a favor. "I asked him to write to my uncle and tell him that he had seen me."[24] For all Kanaras knew, it would be the last message that anyone back home would get from him.

He has also attached an M1918 trench knife to the right side of the horizontal foregrip of his M1A1 Thompson. (*National Archives and Records Administration via Jump/Cut Productions and Scott Carroll*)

Last but not least, he has tucked an M1911A1 .45-cal. automatic pistol between his improvised chest pouch and his M42 jump jacket. (*National Archives and Records Administration via Jump/Cut Productions and Scott Carroll*)

After dinner, the paratroopers at Barkston-Heath went back to the hangar, laid all of their equipment out on their cots and began checking and re-checking everything one last time before going out to the C-47s.[25] They also burned cork and then used the soot to blacken their faces and hands.[26] At approximately 8:00 pm someone yelled out that "Axis Sally" (known as the "Berlin Bitch" to the men) was coming on the radio. Many of the men gathered around to listen to her daily dose of propaganda. They were greatly sur-

prised when she said, "Good evening 82nd Airborne Division, tomorrow morning the blood from your guts will grease the bogey wheels on our tanks.[27] Shortly before 10:00 pm on June 5th, the men of the regiment loaded onto trucks that drove them out to the waiting airplanes. The cooks were left behind and had to stand guard duty. As the truck carrying Joseph Dahlia passed the front gate of the compound, he looked down and made eye contact with one of the cooks on guard. With tears in his eyes, the cook chased along-

In addition to his many weapons, this trooper also carries a pair of M1938 wire cutters, a Lensatic Compass in its pouch, a pair of M3 binoculars in the M17 leather case and an M7 rubberized assault gas mask bag which is attached to his leg. (*National Archives and Records Administration via Jump/Cut Productions and Scott Carroll*)

82nd Airborne Division paratroopers suiting up for the Normandy invasion at an airfield in southern England. (*82nd Airborne Museum via Phil Nordyke*)

507th Parachute Infantry Regiment officers at Tollerton Hall. Kneeling: (*left to right*) **Lieutenant Colonel Edwin J. Ostberg, Major Joseph P. Fagan, Lieutenant Colonel Arthur A. Maloney, Lieutenant Colonel Charles J. Timmes. Standing:** (*left to right*) **Lieutenant Colonel William A. Kuhn, Lieutenant Robert M. Hennon, Captain John J. Verret, Major Gordon K. Smith, Major Ben F. Pearson, Major George K. Vollmar, Major Charles D. Johnson.** (*Courtesy of Dennis and Barbara Maloney*)

507th Executive Officer Lieutenant Colonel Arthur A. Maloney at Tollerton Hall in early 1944. A 1938 graduate of the U.S. Military Academy at West Point, Maloney was a very popular and well-respected officer in the 507th. Command of the regiment would devolve to him in Normandy. (*Courtesy of Dennis and Barbara Maloney*)

side the truck briefly, begging Dahlia to trade places with him. Dahlia refused. For some reason, fate had chosen this cook to remain in England while Dahlia went off to participate in the liberation of France.[28]

When they arrived at their respective flight lines, rolls were called and then the men began the process of suiting-up for the jump. Their parachutes were waiting for them on the tarmac in neat rows next to each C-47.[29] The paratroopers conducted the usual equipment checks of their T-5s, then they began to gear up. It was during this part of the process that the Lt. Col. Arthur A. Maloney, asked the men that would jump in his stick to sign a piece of invasion currency. According to Bob Davis, each trooper was issued a few thousand francs worth of the currency prior to loading, to be used "to assist in avoiding capture in the event of failure to land at the predesignated drop zones."[30] Maloney took a 100-franc note, numbered it from one to eighteen and circulated it among the men preparing to load the waiting C-47.

Born in June 1914, Maloney grew up and went to Bulkeley High School in Hartford, Connecticut. After high school, he attended the U.S. Military Academy at West Point, graduating in 1938. In 1942, Maloney was assigned to the 507th as its regimental Executive Officer. During the regiment's training phase at Fort Benning and later in Nebraska, Maloney built a reputation for hard work and dedication. According to Paul Smith, "Art Maloney never missed a march, a run, a parachute drop or a field exercise – always on his own two feet – never in a jeep."[31] That was just the type leadership that earned the unending respect of his men. "He was the most fearless and effective leader I ever saw in all of my combat experience," Roy Creek recalled.[32] Maloney was a "big powerful figure of a man"[33] – six feet four inches tall and 240 pounds. With such a commanding profile and such powerful reputation, he was a man that seemed born to lead. Although the 100-franc note was numbered for eighteen signatures, only seventeen paratroopers signed it. The number one spot was left blank by the other troopers for Lt. Col. Maloney. But Maloney was not a man to put himself first on any list. In spite of the fact that he was the ranking officer of the stick and the stick's jumpmaster, Lt. Col. Maloney chose to leave the first space blank. Although he had no way of knowing it, within just a few hours command of the 507th would devolve to him.

• • •

The 100 Franc note that 507th Regimental Executive Officer Lt.Col. Arthur A. Maloney had the men of his stick sign while they were suiting-up at Fulbeck on the night of June 5, 1944. The signatures are as follows:

1. *blank*
2. William J. Miller, Jr.
3. Joseph F. Armstrong
4. Robert S. Davis
5. Rudolph R. Simek
6. Eric R. Gill

7. Stephen J. Kramer
8. John H. Summer
9. Clydis J. Patton
10. Henry B. Brant
11. John J. Verret
12. Bernard L. Gruseck

13. Perry V. McGhee
14. Jack Miller
15. Joseph O. Smith
16. Leslie H. Nicoll
17. Thomas P. Gallagher
18. Arthur J. Carzoli

(*Courtesy of Dennis and Barbara Maloney*)

Cases full of Gammon grenade fuses being prepared for the Normandy operation by 507th paratroopers at Fulbeck. (*National Archives and Records Administration via Jump/Cut Productions and Scott Carroll*)

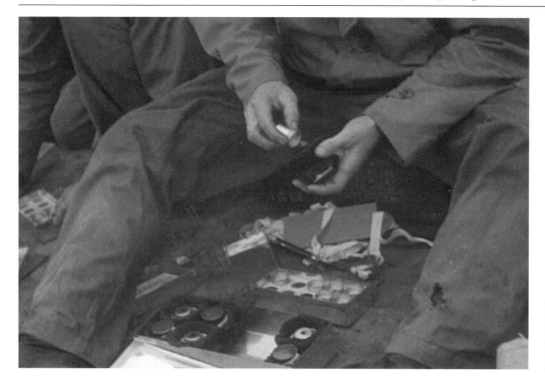

A 507th trooper assembling Gammon grenade fuses for the Normandy operation. (*National Archives and Records Administration via Jump/Cut Productions and Scott Carroll*)

The men of the 507th were heavily loaded with a number of specialized pieces of equipment for the Normandy jump. Pfc. Hughart recalled what he was carrying:

> For this jump I was fully loaded down with equipment – more equipment than I ever jumped with in my previous practice jumps. I was laden with grenades, an anti-tank mine, a beanbag shaped Gammon grenade, mussette bag, knife, M1 rifle, ammunition bandoleers, main and reserve chute.[34]

Since the nature of the mission of airborne forces involved the insertion of light infantry behind enemy lines, providing those forces with an anti-tank capability presented certain problems – especially in Normandy. Allied planners had every reason to expect that the fighting force that would, in all likelihood, face enemy armor first was the parachute infantry. But anti-tank guns were simply too big and heavy for parachute insertion and would have to be delivered to the battlefield by glider. However, if German armor managed to locate and attack parachute infantry units before the arrival of anti-

A Gammon grenade fuse assembly with plastic fuse cap in place. (*Photo by the author*)

A Gammon grenade fuse assembly with plastic fuse cap removed and ribbon streamer partly unwrapped. (*Photo by the author*)

tank guns, or if by some unforeseen complication those guns were destroyed or otherwise lost on landing, the results could be disastrous for the lightly armed paratroopers. Thus, the leadership of the Allied airborne divisions recognized that parachute infantry units would have to have their own lightweight anti-tank firepower. In American airborne units, the M1A1 "Bazooka" Rocket Launcher was one of the weapons issued to meet this need. But another anti-tank weapon was also distributed to U.S. parachute infantry units in time for the Normandy operation – the Type 82 grenade, also known as the Gammon grenade.

The Gammon grenade was developed by a British officer to meet the need for an alternative anti-tank weapon for airborne light infantry. It consisted of a plastic detonator fuse assembly attached to a cloth bag that could be stuffed with as much as 2 1/2 pounds of composition C-2 explosive (an early form of plastic explosive). Before throwing the weapon, the user first unscrewed and removed the plastic cap of the fuse body, which exposed a weighted ribbon streamer. While holding the streamer, the user would then throw the device which, when the streamer was pulled out of the fuse assembly in flight, would arm the grenade. Using the compound fulminate of mercury, the tumbler-type fuse would then detonate the explosive. Because it used a contact fuse that would go off with the slightest impact, the Gammon grenade was a dangerously sensitive weapon. Bob Davis of Regimental Headquarters Company/507th remembered that, "If you threw a Gammon grenade at a twig

The under side of a Gammon grenade fuse assembly with ribbon streamer partly unwrapped. (*Photo by the author*)

The Hawkins mine. (*Photo by the author*)

on a tree it would go off."[35] This sensitivity resulted in more than a few fatal accidents that gave the Gammon grenade a "rather dangerous" reputation.[36] One such accident occurred at Spanhoe airfield shortly before the men of Headquarters Company, 1st Battalion/505th PIR took off for Normandy. As one stick was boarding their C-47, a Gammon grenade carried by one of the paratroopers went off. The explosion set fire to the plane, wounded ten and killed three.[37] The 2 1/2-pound C-2 explosive charge of the Gammon grenade was capable of producing a blast comparable to a 105mm artillery round. This explosive force was enough to incapacitate enemy personnel, knock down the wall of a house or cripple a tank. As E Company commander Captain Roy Creek remembered, the Gammon Grenade "packed a terrific wallop."[38]

Everyone in Ed Jeziorski's stick jumped with a Gammon grenade, an M15 white phosphorous smoke grenade and two Mk. II fragmentation grenades. In addition to those explosive devices, some troopers carried the ten-pound Mk. IV anti-tank mine. For men armed with the M1 Garand rifle, they carried ten clips in their cartridge belts in addition to a pair of bandoliers each of which held an additional five clips for a total combat load of 160 rounds of rifle ammunition.[39] Although many paratroopers jumped into Normandy with their Garand rifles disassembled and stored in a padded case known as a Griswald bag, some of the men of the 507th did not. Jeziorski, for example, jumped with his M1 assembled and slung over his shoulder with the belly band of his T-5 parachute over it securing it in place.[40]

Chris Kanaras remembered the sequence of putting on his equipment for the D-Day jump. First he put on his M1923 ten-pocket cartridge belt with a canteen, an entrenching tool and Carlisle bandage pouch attached to it, all of which were supported by a pair

The primary American service rifle of WWII was the semiautomatic, gas-operated, 8-shot M1 rifle, popularly known as the "Garand" after its inventor, John C. Garand. Developed at the venerable government-owned Springfield Armory, the M1 rifle was adopted in 1936 and was chambered for the standard .30 caliber cartridge (".30-06"). It had a 24" barrel and weighed approximately 9 1/2 pounds. During World War II, Garands were manufactured at Springfield Armory in Massachusetts as well as at Winchester Repeating Arms Company in Connecticut. When the war ended in August 1945, just over four million M1 rifles had been produced. The semiautomatic action of the M1 gave hundreds of 507th paratroopers a firepower advantage that was often the difference between life and death. (*Bruce N. Canfield Collection*)

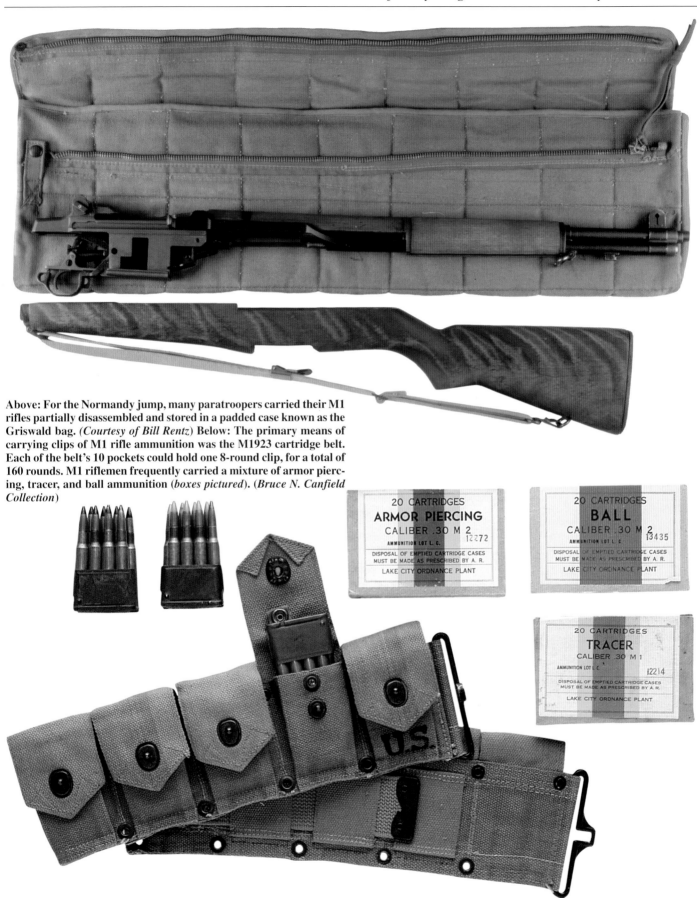

Above: For the Normandy jump, many paratroopers carried their M1 rifles partially disassembled and stored in a padded case known as the Griswald bag. *(Courtesy of Bill Rentz)* Below: The primary means of carrying clips of M1 rifle ammunition was the M1923 cartridge belt. Each of the belt's 10 pockets could hold one 8-round clip, for a total of 160 rounds. M1 riflemen frequently carried a mixture of armor piercing, tracer, and ball ammunition *(boxes pictured)*. *(Bruce N. Canfield Collection)*

Bayonet fixed on an M1 rifle. The bayonet pictured is an M1905E1 "Bowie Point" 16-inch bayonet that has been cut down to 10-inch length. This particular example was made by American Fork & Hoe in 1943. (*Bruce N. Canfield Collection*)

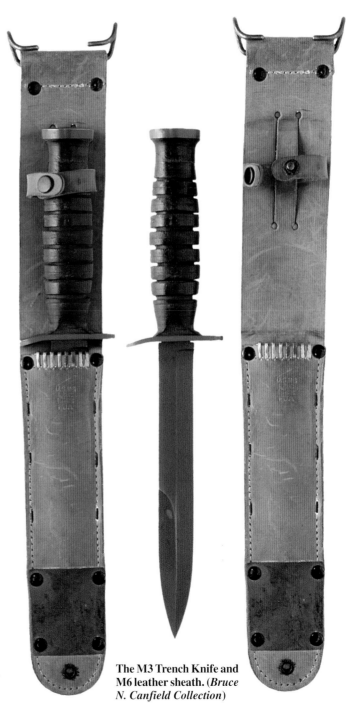

of M1936 suspenders. Then he strapped an M7 rubberized assault gas mask bag to his leg that contained an M5-11-7 gas mask. After that he put two M1 bandoleers across his chest "Pancho Villa" style,[41] attached a bayonet to his cartridge belt, and then strapped a knife to his right jump boot. When the men of the 507th dropped into Normandy, they carried a variety of edged weapons. To begin with, paratroopers armed with the M1 Garand rifle, like Kanaras, carried a rifle bayonet. The bayonet being used by front-line U.S. Army forces in mid-1944 was the ten-inch long M1, which replaced the 16-inch long M1905 bayonet. After it became evident that a bayonet as long as the M1905 constituted more of a liability on the modern, mechanized battlefield, the Army adopted a six-inch shorter version of the M1905 in April 1943. Contracts for the production of the new ten-inch M1 bayonet were issued to several civilian manufacturers including Utica Cutlery Company, Wilde Drop Forge & Tool Company and American Fork & Hoe. Because the military still maintained large inventories of the old 16-inch bayonet, thousands of M1905s were cut down to ten-inch length to meet the new requirements. These cut down M1905 bayonets were issued right alongside the new M1 bayonet.

507th paratroopers also carried a sturdy combat knife into the battle in Normandy. In late 1942, the Army had issued specifications for an individual fighting knife that ultimately led to the standardization of the M3 Trench Knife in early 1943. The weapon consisted of a 6_-inch dagger blade, a grooved leather handle and a steel pommel. Several companies produced the M3 during the war, including Camillus Cutlery Company, W.R. Case & Sons and PAL Blade & Tool Company. At first, the trench knife was issued with the M6 leather scabbard, but because the leather tended to wear out and deteriorate, it was ultimately replaced by a plastic scabbard designated the M8. Although the scabbards were equipped with belt hooks, photographic evidence shows that paratroopers frequently carried their M3s strapped to one of their jump boots so the weapon could be drawn quickly in the event of an emergency. The M3 Trench Knife was a useful, effective and popular weapon that was used by thousands of Americans from mid-1943 onward. After

The M3 Trench Knife and M6 leather sheath. (*Bruce N. Canfield Collection*)

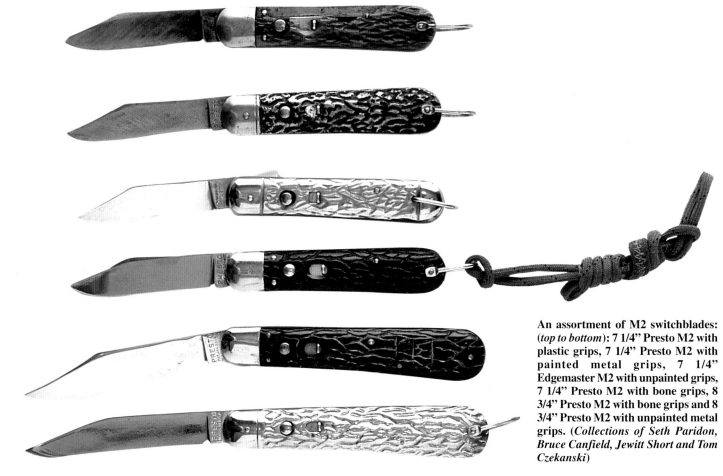

An assortment of M2 switchblades: (*top to bottom*): 7 1/4" Presto M2 with plastic grips, 7 1/4" Presto M2 with painted metal grips, 7 1/4" Edgemaster M2 with unpainted grips, 7 1/4" Presto M2 with bone grips, 8 3/4" Presto M2 with bone grips and 8 3/4" Presto M2 with unpainted metal grips. (*Collections of Seth Paridon, Bruce Canfield, Jewitt Short and Tom Czekanski*)

the end of the war in 1945, a U.S. Army Ordnance Department report commented on the effectiveness of both the bayonet and the trench knife in combat:

> Official records definitely establish that, in numerous instances, lives of service men were saved by reason of being armed with bayonets and trench knives....In combat theaters where terrain, weather or other conditions were favorable for enemy infiltration, it has been found that the bayonet and trench knife were the weapons most commonly used for disposing of enemy personnel...Experience has proven the possession of a trench knife was a great morale booster for the individual fighting man.[42]

In addition to their bayonets and trench knives, U.S. paratroopers also carried another knife as a backup – the M2 Switchblade.

A pair of unpainted 8 3/4" Presto M2s showing the closed and opened lengths. (*Collections of Seth Paridon and Jewitt Short*)

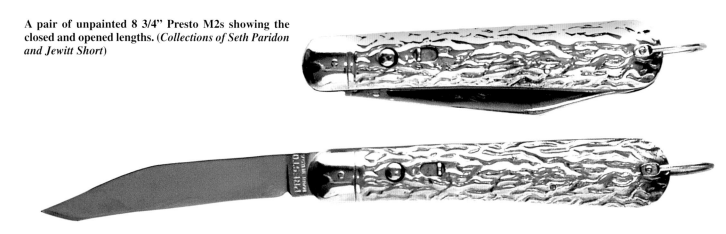

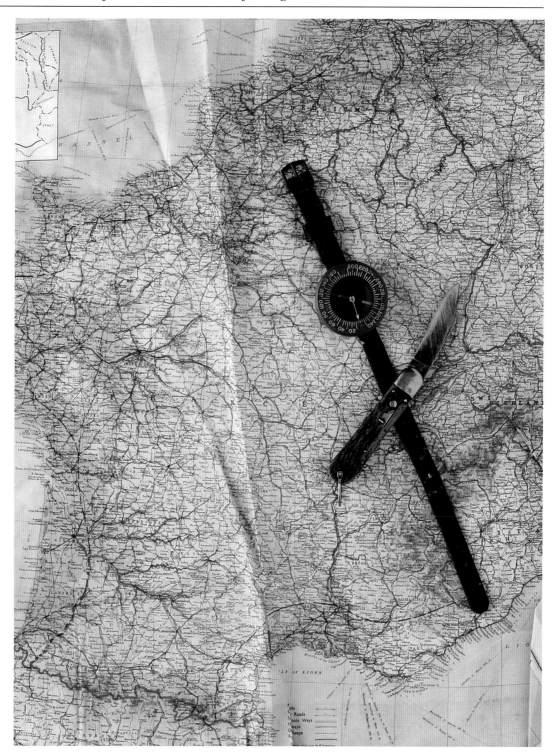

Three common items issued to U.S. paratroopers for the Normandy operation: a Presto M2 switchblade, a wrist compass and a silk map of France. *(Courtesy of Bill Rentz)*

First developed by Schrade Cutlery Company in 1940, the M2 was also manufactured by Presto and Edgemaster during the war. With a spring-actuated locking blade, the M2 was developed for use by airborne personnel as an emergency utility knife. M2s were produced in either 7 1/2" or 8 1/2" overall length and grips were made of either bone, metal (often painted black) or plastic with a simulated bone texture. The M1942 paratrooper's jump jacket was even equipped with a small easy to reach zip pocket on the upper placket that was designed specifically to hold the M2.[43]

In addition to his knife, bayonet and other equipment, Chris Kanaras also filled his pockets with two Mk. II fragmentation hand grenades, a Gammon grenade, an M15 white phosphorous smoke grenade and three D-bars (chocolate bars). At that point he put on his B-3 life jacket (or "Mae West") and then his T-5 parachute and

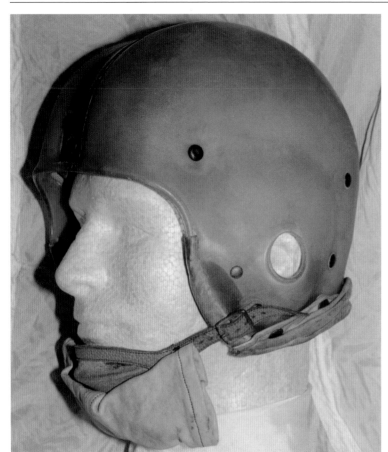

The Riddell football helmet was the original piece of headgear used in the early days of the U.S. Army airborne. *(Courtesy of Bill Rentz)*

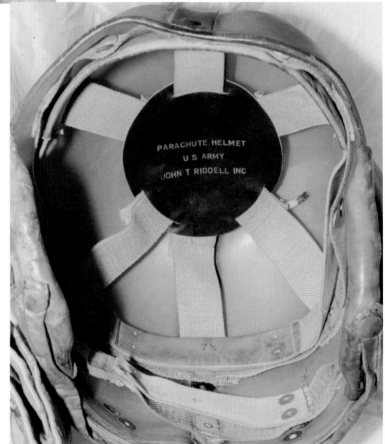

Designed and manufactured by John T. Riddell's Chicago based sporting goods equipment company, the Riddell helmet was not particularly well suited for the combat environment. *(Courtesy of Bill Rentz)*

To replace the Riddell football helmet, the U.S. Army adopted the M2 parachutist's helmet, which was basically a modification of the standard M1 steel helmet. (*Author's Collection*)

The M2 parachutist's helmet consisted of an outer helmet body, or "shell," made of tough Hadfield Manganese Steel, and an inner helmet liner made of either fiber or cloth laminate. (*Author's Collection*)

Detail view of the interior of an M2 parachutist's helmet liner. The liner pictured here was manufactured by Westinghouse and was made of a high-pressure molded resin-impregnated cloth laminate. M2 helmet liners were modified by the installation of a pair of inverted webbed cotton A-straps attached by rivets to the liner's inner suspension. A pair of buckles on the ends of the A-straps provided for the attachment of a chamois-lined leather-molded chin cup. (*Author's Collection*)

The inside of a fully restored M2 helmet showing one of the attachment points for the liner chin-strap, one of the inverted webbed cotton A-straps, and the helmet's liner chinstrap. (*Author's Collection*)

harness. Then he attached his M1936 musette bag to a pair of D-rings that allowed it to hang down over his crotch. The M1936 musette bag and suspenders were designed in such a way that after landing a paratrooper could remove the bag from in front of his stomach and reconfigure it as a backpack. Finally, he put on his AN 6513-1 reserve chute and he was ready to go.[44]

The final distinctive piece of equipment that paratroopers put on before the D-Day jump was the M2 parachutist helmet. When the U.S. Army adopted the new M1 helmet in 1941, the airborne was in its infancy and consequently had not yet developed the full spectrum of equipment suited for its specialized needs. In the early days of the airborne infantry, parachutists jumped wearing the Riddell football helmet designed by John T. Riddell's Chicago based sporting goods equipment company. Although the Riddell football helmet was effective in so far as it provided basic protection to the head of the parachutist, it was however not a piece of equipment suited for a combat environment. For that reason, the Army sought to adopt a more appropriate helmet to equip its growing airborne forces. At first the standard M1 helmet was tested, but it was quickly realized that it would not work. Although perfectly adequate for ground infantry forces, the M1 helmet was not at all suitable for use by airborne infantry. The primary flaw of the M1 was that it had a tendency to separate from the wearer as a result of the sudden powerful forces exerted by a parachute jump. To overcome the shortcomings of the basic M1 design, a modified parachutist version of the helmet was developed. This modified helmet was ultimately adopted in 1942 as the M2 parachutist's helmet.[45]

The M2 was largely similar to the standard helmet from which it was derived: it consisted of an outer helmet body, or "shell," made of tough Hadfield Manganese Steel and a helmet liner made of either fiber or cloth laminate. Despite the basic similarities, the M2's outer shell and liner were both specially modified for use by the airborne. First of all, the Hadfield Manganese Steel helmet shell was equipped with a pair of 'D' shaped loops, or "bales," to which the chinstraps were attached. The 'D' shaped bales of the M2 were made much larger than the bales of the M1 helmet so that the M2 shell's chinstraps could be rotated to the rear and fastened behind the nape of the wearer's neck. Additionally, both sections of the M2 shell's chinstraps were equipped with metallic male fasteners that could be snapped into a pair of corresponding female fastener eyelets in the helmet liner, thus securing the helmet shell and liner together to prevent separation. In addition to the pair of female snap eyelets, the M2 helmet liner was further modified by the installation of a pair of inverted webbed cotton A-straps attached by rivets to the liner's inner suspension. A pair of buckles on the ends of the A-straps provided for the attachment of a chamois-lined leather-molded chin cup. The modified features of the M2 provided a hel-

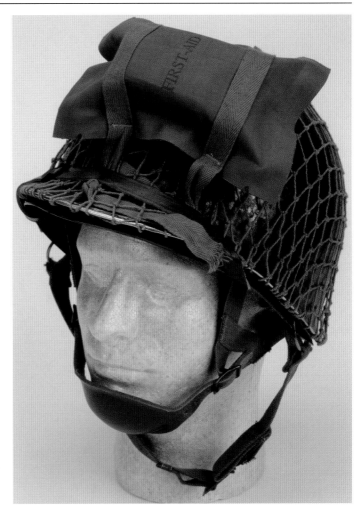

An M2 helmet suited out with the two standard extras that 507th paratroopers used for the Normandy operation: an airborne first aid pouch and a helmet net. *(Courtesy of Bill Rentz)*

met system that was held in place on the wearer not only by the chinstraps of the shell, but also by the chin cup assembly of the liner.[46]

Complete M2 helmets were the product of several wartime defense contractors. McCord Radiator and Manufacturing Company of Detroit, Michigan produced M2 steel helmet shells using Hadfield Manganese Steel stock purchased from Carnegie-Illinois Steel Corporation and Sharon Steel Corporation. Supplementing its production of M1 helmet shells, McCord manufactured approximately 148,000 M2 shells between 1942 and 1944. Three companies manufactured liners for the M2 helmet: Hawley Products Company of St. Charles, Illinois; Inland Manufacturing Division of General Motors; and Westinghouse Electric and Manufacturing Company. The Hawley Products liners were made of two layers of varnish impregnated fiber covered by a layer of olive drab colored gabardine. Approximately 43,000 Hawley Products fiber liners were converted for use with M2 helmets. The Inland and Westinghouse

This famous photograph depicts T-4 Joseph F. Gorenc of 3rd Battalion/ 506th Parachute Infantry Regiment of the 101st Airborne Division as he boards a C-47 at Exeter. Although Gorenc was not in the 507th, this photograph provides a priceless view of the typical combat load of an American airborne infantryman on D-Day. (*National Archives and Records Administration*)

C-47s and Horsa gliders lined up and awaiting the order to go to Normandy. (*82nd Airborne Museum via Phil Nordyke*)

liners, on the other hand, were referred to as "plastic" liners although they were actually made of a high-pressure molded resin-impregnated cloth laminate. Approximately 75,000 Inland and 30,000 Westinghouse "plastic" liners were converted for use with the M2.[47]

All of the men of the 82nd Airborne Division jumped into Normandy wearing the M2 parachutist's helmet. Unlike many of the other units that made the Normandy jump, the 507th did not make use of helmet markings to identify itself. Helmet markings for the regiment during the campaign were limited to painted rank insignia on the front of helmets worn by officers and painted white bars on the back of helmets worn by officers (vertical) and non-commissioned officers (horizontal). Although exact figures will never be known, surviving photographs of the men of the 507th indicate that the regiment was issued an assortment of fiber helmet liners and "plastic" helmet liners prior to June 6, 1944.

The heavy burden of extra, specialized gear more than doubled the body weight of many of the men. Frank Naughton would later recall that he weighed 325 pounds fully loaded for D-Day. Donald E. Bosworth was heavily loaded too. A Staff Sergeant in 1st Battalion/507th, Bosworth carried almost 150 extra pounds for the Normandy jump. He later recalled the full extent of it:

I weighed about 325 pounds. We were so heavy with all of the equipment, we had to help each other up. I weighed 180 pounds at that time (without the extra equipment).[48]

At Barkston-Heath, the 61st Troop Carrier Group was waiting. There, 72 Douglas C-47 Skytrains belonging to the group's four squadrons sat ready to carry 1,230 paratroopers of the 2nd and 3rd Battalions of the 507th to Normandy (approximately 61.5% of the regiment's total strength). At nearby Fulbeck, the 45 C-47s of the 442nd Troop Carrier Group were capable of carrying the balance of the 507th (an additional 770 paratroopers from 1st Battalion and Headquarters 507th).

By mid-1944, the men of these two Troop Carrier Groups had gone through just as much intense training as the paratroopers they were about to carry into battle. For these pilots and co-pilots, their military service had begun as much as two years earlier with primary flight training at such places as Napier Field in Dothan, Alabama or at Bennettsville Municipal Airport in Bennettsville, South Carolina.[49] This rigorous and competitive training cycle taught take-off, landing and basic flight maneuvering. In this phase, cadets learned how to get an airplane in the air and put it back on the ground in one piece through countless 'touch-and-go' approaches.

A Douglas C-47 in flight over western Nebraska in 1943. Adopted by the U.S. Army in 1940, the C-47 was a militarized version of the highly successful Douglas DC-3. The 507th was carried to Normandy on the night of June 5th/6th by 117 C-47s of the 61st and 442nd Troop Carrier Groups. *(Courtesy of the Knight Museum, Alliance, NE)*

C-47s in flight over southern England in mid-1944. *(Courtesy of Bill Rentz)*

From there, aviation cadets then moved on to receive instruction on such oh-so important flight fundamentals as spin recovery and cross-wind take-off and landing procedures. After a successful solo in primary flight training, a cadet moved on to the next level of flight instruction – advanced twin-engine training. For this phase, many of these cadets reported to Moody Field in Valdosta, Georgia. There the cadet pilot learned how to fly multi-engine aircraft at night and in inclement weather. It was also in advanced twin-engine training that cadets learned to solve challenging navigational problems during long cross-country flights. After successfully completing the twin-engine course, a cadet received his wings and his commission as a 2nd Lieutenant in the U.S. Army Air Force.

For these cadet pilots and co-pilots, advanced twin-engine training introduced them to the venerable Douglas C-47 *Skytrain*. During World War II, the U.S. military relied on the C-47 as one of its primary military movers. Development of the C-47 began in the 1930s with the Douglas "DC" series aircraft. The DC-1 flew in 1933 and was soon followed by the next aircraft in the evolution, the more powerful 14-passenger DC-2. In 1934 after only 193 DC-2s had been built, American Airlines asked Douglas to develop a new model with sleeping accommodations for international flights. Douglas responded with the DST – the Douglas Sleeper Transport. The DST could carry up to twenty-eight passengers for daytime flights or 14 for overnight flights using convertible seats as sleeper berths. Douglas also produced a version of the DST without the sleeper berths for non-overnight service: a 24-passenger aircraft known as the DC-3.

Making its first flights in December 1935, the DC-3 quickly established itself as a highly successful commercial airliner. Recognizing the great potential of such an aircraft, the U.S. Army requested that Douglas develop a modified version of the DC-3 suitable for military use. The Army specified a number of changes that transformed the civilian DC-3 into a military transport aircraft. First of all, the DC-3's engines were replaced with a pair of more powerful Pratt & Whitney R-1830 radial engines. Then, Douglas eliminated the twenty-four spacious airliner seats in favor of utility seating along the aircraft's bulkheads. Douglas also had to strengthen the floor of the aircraft so that it could bear the weight of the heavy cargoes it would be required to haul. Finally, the DC-3's narrow passenger-width door was eliminated in favor of large cargo loading doors. The Army adopted this militarized version of the DC-3 in 1940 as the C-47 *Skytrain*.

It did not take long for the C-47 to prove itself to be an enormously versatile tool capable of everything from delivering cargo, to towing gliders, to dropping paratroopers into combat. A fully assembled GPW (Jeep) or a 37mm anti-tank rifle could be carried by the C-47 and as a medical evacuation aircraft it could carry 14 stretcher patients and three nurses. For airborne operations, the C-47 was capable of carrying 18 fully equipped paratroopers. The C-47's pair of 1,200hp Pratt & Whitney radial engines made it possible to carry 10,000 pounds of cargo at a speed of 175 mph for up to 3,500 miles.

The U.S. government purchased 10,692 C-47s during the war at a cost of around $138,000 each. The Navy also flew the C-47

A C-47 of the 14th Troop Carrier Squadron, 61st Troop Carrier Group, 52nd Troop Carrier Wing taken at Barkston-Heath just before D-Day. The four parachute silhouettes painted just aft of the pilot's window represent the four combat parachute missions completed by this aircraft. Prior to the Normandy operation, the 61st flew two missions in support of the invasion of Sicily in July 1943 and two missions in support of the invasion of Italy two months later. *(Courtesy of Bill Rentz)*

"Available II", a C-47 of the 14th Troop Carrier Squadron/61st Troop Carrier Group, at Barkston-Heath just before D-Day. The 61st TCG carried the 2nd and 3rd Battalions of the 507th to Normandy. *(Courtesy of Bill Rentz)*

under the designation R4D. In addition to the U.S., several foreign nations used the C-47. The United Kingdom purchased 1,928 C-47 type aircraft that served in the RAF, RCAF and the RAAF. The C-47 was manufactured under license from Douglas in the Soviet Union as the Lisunov Li-2 and before Pearl Harbor the Japanese also licensed the aircraft for production as the Nakajima/Showa L2D. When production ended, Japan had built 485 L2Ds and the Soviets had built 2,000 Li-2s for a total worldwide production number of 13,177 C-47 variants.[50]

During its prolific World War II service career, the C-47 was only occasionally called the *Skytrain*. On a more frequent basis the C-47 was referred to with one of the many unofficial nicknames that it earned. To the British, Canadians and Australians, it was known as the *Dakota* and in U.S. Navy service, the *Skytrooper*. To most American service personnel though, the C-47 was simply known as the *Gooney Bird*. After receiving their wings, the fresh young pilots and co-pilots who had only recently been commissioned as 2nd Lieutenants then spent three or four additional months of training and familiarization with the *Gooney Bird*. That phase was inevitably followed by assignment to a Troop Carrier Squadron and then deployment overseas to become a part of the rapidly

"Starbuck", another C-47 of the 14th Troop Carrier Squadron/61st Troop Carrier Group, at Barkston-Heath just before D-Day. Note the L-4 Grasshopper flying above. *(Courtesy of Bill Rentz)*

Close-up view of the C-47 nicknamed "Sprag Wagon" – another 14th Troop Carrier Squadron/61st Troop Carrier Group aircraft. This photo was taken at Barkston-Heath just before D-Day and provides a nice detail shot of the C-47's pair of Pratt & Whitney R-1830 radial engines. *(Courtesy of Bill Rentz)*

Another 14th Troop Carrier Squadron C-47 at Barkston-Heath just before D-Day. This particular aircraft has a cartoon duck for its nose art and it was a veteran of the squadron's four previous combat missions. *(Courtesy of Bill Rentz)*

growing strength of the 9th U.S. Army Air Force. Sidney M. Ulan of Chester, Pennsylvania received his wings at Moody Field in March 1943 and, like so many other new troop carrier pilots, he was immediately assigned to the Troop Carrier Command. He recalled that, at the time, the Army needed pilots "to drop airborne troops in the invasion of Europe, so my entire graduating class was sent to the Troop Carrier Command."[51] Ulan started flying the C-47 at Bergstrom Field near Austin, Texas and was then transferred to Sedalia, Missouri where his Troop Carrier Group was formed. On March 1, 1944, Ulan's squadron departed Homestead Army Airfield in Florida, destination England. The squadron flew a circuitous route to ferry across the Atlantic Ocean. The first leg of the trip took the squadron from Florida to Puerto Rico. From there, they flew on to South America and then the long, lonely hop out over the open Atlantic to remote Ascension Island off the west coast of Africa. From Ascension, the squadron continued up through North Africa and finally on to a base in southern England where they joined the 9th Air Force.[52]

The 9th Air Force had been established in England in October 1943 under the command of Lt. Gen. Lewis Brereton with the spe-

The somewhat flamboyant nose art of "Pellican Pappy", a veteran C-47 of the 14th Troop Carrier Squadron/61st Troop Carrier Group at Barkston-Heath just before D-Day. *(Courtesy of Bill Rentz)*

cific mission of providing tactical air support for the Normandy invasion. To this end, the 9th AF was composed of the obligatory constituent elements of a tactical air force of the day: a Bomber Command, a Fighter Command, a Tactical Air Command and finally a Troop Carrier Command. Under the direction of Brig. Gen. Benjamin Giles, the mission of the 9th AF's Troop Carrier Command in connection with the Normandy operation was the movement of personnel and equipment from England to France.[53] For the pilots, co-pilots and ground crewmen of the 61st TCG and the 442nd TCG, much had to be accomplished to be ready to participate in the assault on fortress Europe. Resultantly, training schedules did not relax after arrival in England during February and March 1944.

Instead, the pace of training activities picked up as the 61st and the 442nd prepared to be a part of the coming Normandy operation.

Thus, when the men of the 507th arrived at Fulbeck and Barkston-Heath on the night of June 5th, their lives were placed in the capable hands of two groups of thoroughly trained military professionals. The 117 C-47s that waited for the men of the 507th thus represented much, much more than merely the product of American industrial capability. Having those aircraft sitting on the field that evening with full gas tanks and 117 well-trained flight crews standing by represented the incalculable bottom-line total of an enormous amount of human effort and energy. It had taken years for their families to raise and educate the young American boys

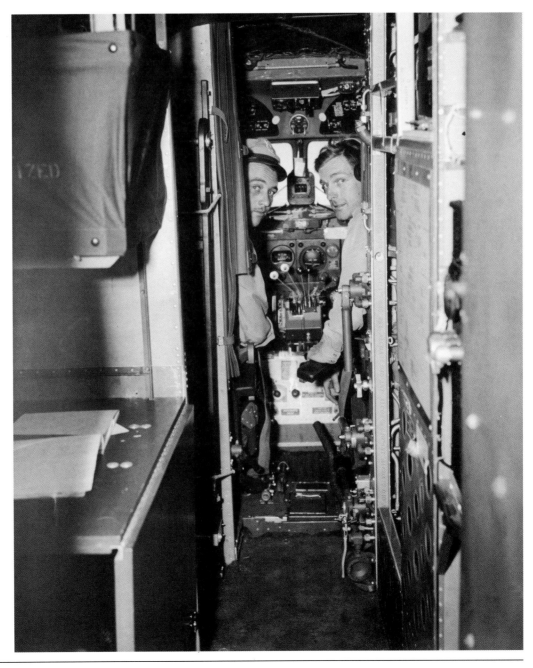

Interior view looking toward the cockpit of a C-47. *(Courtesy of the Knight Museum, Alliance, NE)*

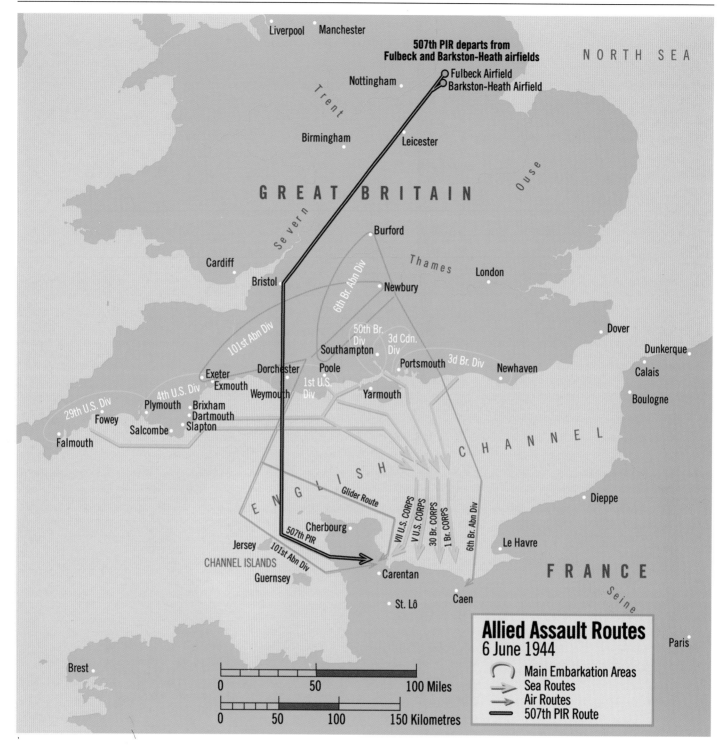

Map showing the route taken by the C-47s that carried the 507th to Normandy. The 61st Troop Carrier Group (consisting of 72 aircraft) flew from the airfield at Barkston-Heath and the 442nd Troop Carrier Group (consisting of 45 aircraft) flew from the airfield at Fulbeck. After take-off, the 117 C-47s formed up, turned to the southwest and flew out over the city of Bristol. The formations then turned due south for the flight across the English Channel. When they reached the Channel Islands, they turned to the east for the final approach to Drop Zone "T" near Ste.-Mère-Église. (*Map by Scott Carroll Illustrations*)

who were there to serve as pilots and co-pilots for the 507th that night. The U.S. government had picked up where their families, high schools and colleges left off, spending even more time and money turning these young men into 117 skilled flight crews. Their preparations during the weeks and months leading up to D-Day had been as comprehensive as was practical and possible. While these pilots and co-pilots had undergone countless hours of airborne training to prepare them for their mission, no training exercise could ever begin to simulate the trial by fire they were about to endure.

• • •

After being on standby from the night before, the men of the 507th were still tired and their nerves were once again being tested as they made their way to the C-47s at Fulbeck and Barkston-Heath on June 5th. But this time there would be no stand-down order, and the paratroopers went straight to work. Twenty-five year old New York native Sgt. Frank P. Costa of Headquarters Company, 3rd Battalion noticed that the eighteen or twenty paratroopers on the C-47 with him were "very serious."[54] The men showed no smiles, they made no wisecracks and they all appeared to be deep in thought. "I had a big lump in my throat," Costa remembered, "as the roar of the engines sounded loud and clear, ready to go."[55] Once on board his C-47, Pfc. Clarence Hughart made his way to an open seat and attempted to get some sleep during the flight. That is how many of the men dealt with the stress of the situation: some men slept, some men smoked and other men just talked. Hughart had made twelve previous jumps – Normandy would be number thirteen.[56]

Meanwhile at Fulbeck, the 507th paratroopers there received the final order to load the C-47s of the 442nd TCG. Helping each other up under the weight of their weapons and equipment, 770 paratroopers proceeded to board the 45 aircraft waiting there. As a part of C Company/1st Battalion, Ed Jeziorski was at Fulbeck and remembered the difficulty he experienced just getting into his C-47 with all of his equipment:

> When we finally loaded-up, there was an air force guy on each side of us and I remember them pushing us up the steps. We would have never been able to get up by ourselves.[57]

Once aboard the aircraft, Jeziorski took the precaution of swallowing two of the anti-motion sickness pills that the men had been issued for the operation and were being ordered to take. "I sure as heck didn't want to get sick up there," he remembered.[58] Such medication had never been distributed prior to any previous jumps. The pills were pure white cylindrical tablets about the size of a match head that produced a "happy glow" similar in effect to taking three double shots of whiskey on an empty stomach.[59] After taking the pills, Jeziorski settled in for the long flight to France. He would be the eighth man to jump in his stick. The first jumper would be the platoon leader for C Company's 2nd Platoon, Lt. Robert H. Parks. Jeziorski's Squad Leader, Sgt. Gregg Howarth, was just ahead of him in the number seven spot. Staff Sgt. Dominic P. Giacoletti, Jeziorski's Platoon Sergeant, would be the last man out.[60]

As ninety radial engines roared to life there at Fulbeck, Donald Bosworth took a seat in his C-47 and prepared for take-off. The forty-five Skytrains first taxied, and then began taking off one by one. Because they were so overloaded, the take-off run for each aircraft was much longer than normal. As a result, the C-47s seemed to roll and roll for the longest time before getting airborne.[61] The men were wearing watches with luminescent dials and could thus clearly make out the time in the fading light of the setting sun. It was ten minutes to midnight, and the 507th was in the air. After the C-47s lumbered up into the sky, they began circling the field as they formed up into a V or Vs formation. Then, the formations turned to the southwest and flew out over the city of Bristol before turning more to the south to fly out over the English Channel. That night, 850 C-47s took off from airfields in England, forming a massive air armada. Jeziorski's platoon leader, Lt. Bob Parks, had the best seat in the house to observe the scale of the air train bound for Normandy. As the troop commander and jumpmaster for his stick, Parks occupied a seat next to the door with a particularly good view of the outside. When he looked out that door, an amazing sight presented itself to him:

> The sea was calm, the moon was full, and as far as I could see were Vs of airplanes. It was the most impressive sight I had ever seen or have ever seen.[62]

Below the Skytrains, the silhouettes of the ships of the naval armada stood out in full relief as the moonlight reflected off the water.[63] Donald Bosworth was among the hundreds of men that observed the vast fleet of ships bound for Normandy. He later described what he saw:

> It was somewhat cloudy and the moon was shining as we were crossing the Channel. The moon came out from behind the clouds and we were able to look down and see all of the ships that were headed toward France. The ships were so numerous that it seemed you could walk from England to France, hopping from one to another. It was a beautiful sight![64]

7

"No turning back."

For the greater portion of the 507th, DZ "T" has only symbolic significance though. While it is generally well understood that the 82nd and 101st Airborne drops were badly scattered during the Normandy operation, it is not well known that the 507th was spread out over a greater area than any of the other parachute infantry regiments making the jump. While a few 507th troopers landed on the DZ, others landed in 101st drop zones. Elements of the 2nd Battalion landed far north of where they were supposed to – some came down near the village of Le Ham while one unfortunate stick of eighteen troopers landed north of Valognes just a few miles south of Cherbourg. Some troopers came down well to the east of the drop zone between Ste.-Marie-du-Mont and Hébert. A few men even ended up on the beach itself. Finally, ten sticks from 3rd Battalion landed twenty-five miles south of the DZ near the village of Graignes. In all, it is estimated that the regiment was spread-out over sixty square miles. Strangely, there was a positive element to this scattering. With such broad dispersion of landings, the German commanders on the scene were reporting that a much larger area was being attacked than was actually intended that night and they therefore concluded that a much larger force had been inserted into the Cotentin than actually had. With the magnitude of the airborne operation still an unknown quantity, the enemy reaction was slow and uncertain.[1] This bought time that the men of the 507th would need – time that would prove to be of decisive importance in the battles of the coming days.

The effect of the scattering was that the various elements of the 507th were not able to attack or defend as battalion or company-size units in the pre-dawn hours of D-Day. Regardless of what battalion they were assigned to, they fought with whomever they ran into that night.[2] Some 507th paratroopers stumbled across men from the 505th or the 508th and still others ended up fighting with men from the 101st Airborne Division. The dispersion of the 507th can be blamed primarily on a pair of factors: the regiment's late arrival over the drop zone, and the clouds.

As they approached Normandy, the 117 inbound C-47s carrying the regiment encountered the same disorienting cloudbank that the other regiments encountered earlier that night. The low, dense clouds broke up the formations of C-47s and set them off course moments before they flew into the punishing fire of the enemy's air defenses. Paul Smith, who was F Company commander at the time, could not see any of the other aircraft flying in formation with his. Hoping to get a better view, he ran forward and looked out the C-47's astrodome, but he could see nothing. "I could hardly even see the wingtips," he remembered.[3] Because of this, the C-47 formations began to drift further and further apart. With aircraft spread-out over a much wider area than had been planned, much of the 507th was already set-up to be misdropped. It did not help that the pathfinders had not been able to mark the drop zones as they were supposed to. Most of the pathfinders were misdropped as a result of the clouds and only two of the division's teams landed on their assigned drop zones.[4] When the pathfinders for the 507th landed, the enemy engaged them almost immediately. As a result, thirty-five 507th pathfinders were killed, wounded or captured that night. Had they been able to accomplish their mission, the C-47s carrying the rest of the regiment would have been guided in toward the drop zones. Instead, those C-47s approached unguided through obscuring cloud cover.

Then came the enemy ground fire. Because the 507th was based in an area of England two and half hours farther north than any of the other parachute regiments, it consequently had to contend with a longer cross-channel journey that made it the last to arrive over Normandy. The first paratroopers to jump that night – a planeload

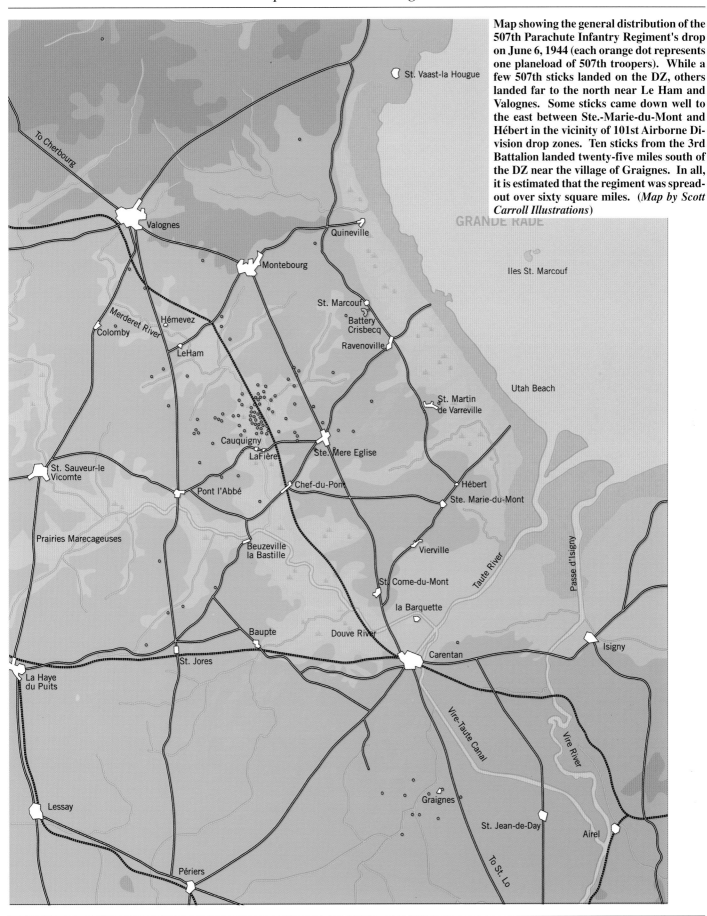

Map showing the general distribution of the 507th Parachute Infantry Regiment's drop on June 6, 1944 (each orange dot represents one planeload of 507th troopers). While a few 507th sticks landed on the DZ, others landed far to the north near Le Ham and Valognes. Some sticks came down well to the east between Ste.-Marie-du-Mont and Hébert in the vicinity of 101st Airborne Division drop zones. Ten sticks from the 3rd Battalion landed twenty-five miles south of the DZ near the village of Graignes. In all, it is estimated that the regiment was spread-out over sixty square miles. (*Map by Scott Carroll Illustrations*)

Above: F Company/507th in Alliance in 1943. *(Courtesy of the Knight Museum, Alliance, NE)*

Right: Captain Paul F. Smith was the company commander of F Company/507th at the time of the Normandy jump. When the C-47 carrying his stick ran into clouds on the approach to Drop Zone 'T', he ran forward and looked through the airplane's astrodome but could hardly even see its wingtips. *(Courtesy of the Knight Museum, Alliance, NE)*

One of the many German anti-aircraft guns that fired on the troop carriers on the night of June 5th/June 6th. *(Collection of The National D-Day Museum)*

Anti-aircraft guns like the one pictured here brought down twenty-one C-47s and damaged countless others on the night of June 5th/June 6th. *(Collection of The National D-Day Museum)*

of pathfinders from the 502nd Parachute Infantry Regiment, 101st Airborne Division – had jumped at approximately 12:15 am. The 507th, on the other hand, arrived over the area starting at approximately 2:30 am. Thus as the C-47s of the 61st and the 442nd came thundering in toward drop zone "T" to drop the 507th, German anti-aircraft gunners were ready. Aroused by the vertical envelopment that had been going on around them for nearly two hours, the anti-aircraft gunners produced a heavy curtain of fire. The bands of colorful tracers produced by the German anti-aircraft fire were so spectacularly impressive that it looked like the 4th of July.[5] Seated by the door of his C-47, C Company's Lt. Robert H. Parks "noticed an impressive fireworks display" outside.[6] He observed flashes of red, yellow, blue and white as they streaked past his troop carrier formation. "I admired the show until I realized what they were: anti-aircraft shells," he remembered.[7] Clarence Hughart remembered that, as his C-47 passed over the coast of Normandy and came under fire, he looked up at his Lieutenant and he was "white as a ghost."[8] No amount of training could have prepared any of the men in those C-47s for what they were flying into.

Sidney Ulan remembered that, "Suddenly, all hell seemed to break loose."[9] From the cockpit of his C-47, he had a front row seat for the spectacle:

> The sky was filled with red and green tracers, and searchlights beamed up at the planes just ahead of me. I could also feel the vibration of the flak coming up and shaking the plane. I realized that the flak suits we were told to wear might come in handy. I remember chewing gum, and the saliva in my mouth completely dried up from the fright. It seemed almost impossible to fly through that wall of fire without getting shot down, but I had no choice. There was no turning back.[10]

• • •

Meanwhile, just to the south of Ste.-Mère-Église, a group of German tank crewmen were awakened by the sounds of the anti-aircraft fire that was being directed at the approaching American troop carrier aircraft. They were men of the *1. Kompanie, 100. Panzer Ausbildungs und Ersatz Abteilung* (A Company, 100th Tank Training and Replacement Battalion), a unit that had only recently arrived in Normandy, having been deployed there attached to the 91st *Luftland* Division the month prior. The battalion had been formed just over three years earlier in April 1941 at Schwetzingen in the Rhineland and it served as a training unit for new tank crewmen. It transferred to Satory just outside of Versailles in the summer of 1942 and spent the next two years there performing light duties. Due to the fact that it was quite limited by the types of vehicles in its Table of Organization and Equipment, the battalion spent most of 1942, 1943 and early 1944 guarding the railroad

Shoulder flag worn by Pvt. William D. Bowell of Headquarters Company/507th during the Normandy campaign. *(Courtesy of William D. Bowell, Sr.)*

marshalling yards around Paris against sabotage. When the battalion was finally dispatched to the Cotentin peninsula, it was headquartered at the chateau at Franquetot and its various elements were widely dispersed in the area between Carentan, Baupte and Ste.-Mère-Église. During the weeks that immediately preceded D-Day, many of the battalion's 664 men had worked alongside French laborers in the frenzied installation of the large numbers of anti-landing *Rommelspargel* dotting the fields of the Cotentin. Roused from sleep that night, the men left their bunks to investigate the source of the noise and then proceeded to watch the tracers and explosions of the anti-aircraft barrage lighting the night sky.

Although the battalion had seen some very limited action against the *Maquis* before D-Day, it was of such low intensity as to be inconsequential in terms of practical combat experience. However, real combat experience was only hours away. While the young men of the *100. Panzer Ausbildungs und Ersatz Abteilung* watched the anti-aircraft fireworks that night, 6,400 paratroopers of the U.S. Army's 82nd Airborne Division were being inserted into the hedgerows and farm fields all around them. Among that 6,400 were the 2,004 paratroopers of the 507th Parachute Infantry Regiment who, like them, had not yet seen real combat either. Although it was unknown to them at the time, the men of the *Abteilung* would have their baptism of fire the next day at a village called Cauquigny in a desperate fight with paratroopers of the 507th. Although they

could not have known it then, the *Abteilung* would be decimated as a result of the battle that was just getting started that night to the north near Ste.-Mère-Église. In an effort to dismiss whatever anxieties were generated by his men watching the anti-aircraft spectacle, *1. Kompanie*'s commanding officer, *Oberleutnant* Weber said, "*Zirkus! Nicht für uns bestimmt!*" ("…it is only a circus display, not to worry").[11] Although Oberleutnant Weber could not possibly have known it, he had less than twenty-four hours to live.[12] Like Oberleutnant Weber, the 91st Division's commanding officer, Generalleutnant Wilhelm Falley, was in his last hours on earth as well. When he heard the early reports about the American airborne assault on the Cotentin peninsula, he made the mistake of rushing to return to his headquarters. On his way there, he would be gunned down in his staff car shortly after dawn on D-Day by 82nd Airborne Division troopers.[13]

• • •

The incredible intensity of the German ground fire created enormous problems for the pilots and co-pilots of the C-47s. Exploding anti-aircraft artillery shells not only peppered the thin skin of the Skytrains, but also produced turbulent shock waves that knocked the airplanes around in the sky. Sgt. Ed Jeziorski recalled the experience of being on one of the C-47s flying through this storm of bursting shells:

One of three 507th pathfinder teams that dropped thirty minutes ahead of the regiment's main serials in the pre-dawn hours of D-Day. Of the fifty-one pathfinders that jumped, only sixteen escaped injury. *(Courtesy of William D. Bowell, Sr.)*

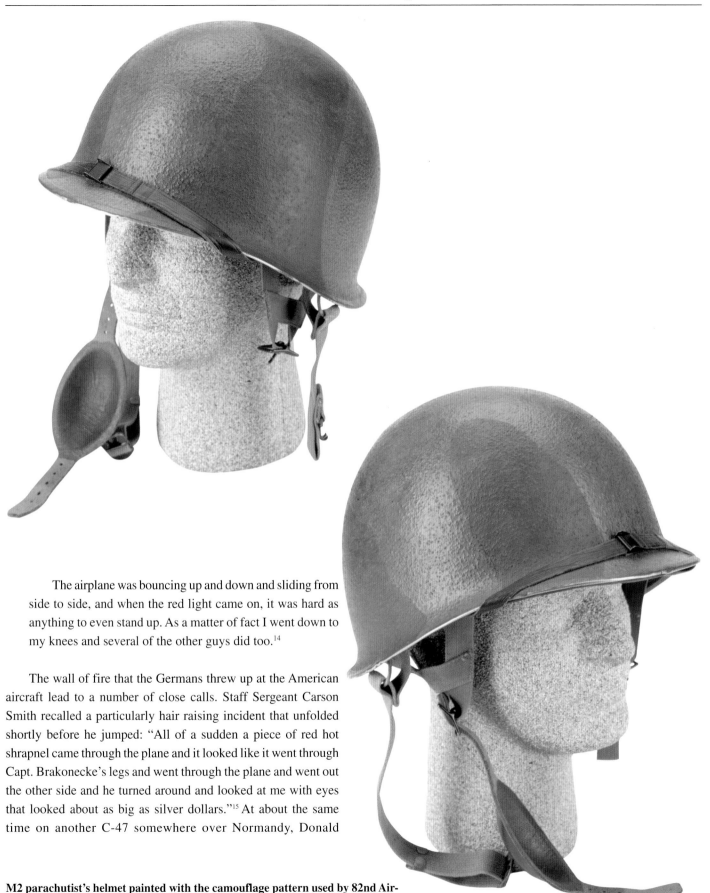

The airplane was bouncing up and down and sliding from side to side, and when the red light came on, it was hard as anything to even stand up. As a matter of fact I went down to my knees and several of the other guys did too.[14]

The wall of fire that the Germans threw up at the American aircraft lead to a number of close calls. Staff Sergeant Carson Smith recalled a particularly hair raising incident that unfolded shortly before he jumped: "All of a sudden a piece of red hot shrapnel came through the plane and it looked like it went through Capt. Brakonecke's legs and went through the plane and went out the other side and he turned around and looked at me with eyes that looked about as big as silver dollars."[15] At about the same time on another C-47 somewhere over Normandy, Donald

M2 parachutist's helmet painted with the camouflage pattern used by 82nd Airborne Division Pathfinders. *(Courtesy of Bill Rentz)*

Bosworth experienced something quite similar. His aircraft was inbound to the drop zone when suddenly "shrapnel went right through the plane, missing Lt. Law by a foot."[16] Bosworth went on to recall that "the pilot immediately gave us the green light to jump, even though we hadn't reached our drop zone."[17]

Just before arriving over the drop zones, the troop carrier pilots were supposed to throttle back to 90 mph and hold an altitude of approximately 800 feet while the paratroopers exited the aircraft. However, under the circumstances, such perfection was just not possible and the C-47s were resultantly moving much faster than usual when the paratroopers jumped. One major factor caused this – weight. 101st Airborne Division author and historian Mark Bando described the situation:

> The recommended safe maximum weight for a C-47 with cargo aboard is 27,900 lbs. Troop Carrier planes routinely flew ETO missions at 30,000 lbs. On the D-Day night drop, the C-47s were hauling equipment and overloaded paratroopers, which brought their weight up to as much as 34,000 lbs.[18]

E Company's Chris Kanaras recalled that the Troop Carrier pilots at Barkston-Heath were getting "upset" about the amount of equipment being loaded into the external bundles. On his C-47 alone, Kanaras recounted that the bundles were crammed with two M1919A4 .30-cal. machine guns, demolitions devices, boxes of ammunition, radios and rations.[19] Out of caution, the pilots and ground crewman of the 61st Troop Carrier Group made the 18 paratroopers of Kanaras's stick suit-up in full gear so that they could be weighed. They then combined the total weight of the troopers with the total weight of the bundles, and the sum was utterly shocking. In fact, the C-47 that carried Kanaras to Normandy was so overloaded that, even at full throttle, it bounced two times during its take-off run before it finally got up into the air.[20]

On a general basis in both the 82nd Airborne Division and the 101st Airborne Division, the C-47s that flew that night were heavier than they should have been. This increased weight had a strong adverse affect on the flight characteristics of the C-47s. Under normal loading circumstances, the aircraft were capable of maintaining stable flight at the relatively slow forward air speed of 90 mph.

The airborne infantry was such an elite unit that it was used to sell war bonds. (*National Archives and Records Administration***)**

However, the gross overloading of aircraft that occurred on D-Day increased the stall speed of the C-47s to the point that 90 mph was so dangerously slow that aircraft could potentially stall and then drop out of the sky. To compensate for the higher stall speed, Troop Carrier pilots were forced to drop their paratroopers at a forward air speed approximately twenty to thirty miles per hour faster than the ninety miles per hour speed of training jumps. Thus, the Troop Carrier C-47s were dropping their paratroopers at speeds of 110, 120 or even faster.

The Troop Carrier pilots also struggled with a number of other significant complicating factors during the Normandy operation. First of all, only about two out of every five Troop Carrier C-47s had a navigator aboard. This two to five ratio had never presented much of a problem during training exercises that were conducted in broad daylight under ideal conditions. But in the less than ideal, disorienting conditions of the Operation Neptune night drop, that ratio presented a major problem. Secondly, strict adherence to radio silence eliminated the possibility of the Troop Carrier pilots adapting and adjusting their plans to mitigate or overcome the problems encountered during the approach to the drop zones. The C-47s were not only prohibited from communicating with their bases back in southern England, but they were also prohibited from communicating from plane to plane when that may very well have helped the situation tremendously. Thirdly, twenty to thirty knot winds were blowing over the Normandy drop zones that night. Those winds generated sudden patches of turbulence that buffeted the C-47s and knocked many of them off course. Finally, the airspeed and altitude of the Troop Carrier C-47s was such that the pilots had only a very narrow window of opportunity to line up on their drop zones before they turned on the green lights.[21]

When the C-47 formations ran into that unexpected cloudbank over the 22-mile-wide Cotentin peninsula, they were at an altitude of 1,500 feet moving at 140 mph. Once they passed out of the clouds, the pilots had less than four minutes to orient themselves and make the necessary course corrections that would take them over the correct drop zone. Again, due to the gross overloading of the aircraft, the pilots could not slow their forward air speed to buy themselves more time to solve their unanticipated navigational problems. Another ever-present concern that was almost certainly in the mind of every pilot that night was that, if they hesitated too long to turn on the green light, they stood the chance of dropping paratroopers in the English Channel on the other side of the peninsula. Compounding this situation, the Troop Carrier pilots were under orders that no paratroopers were to be returned to England. Thus, if they could not get lined up over the drop zone on the first pass, they would have to turn around and fly another approach. Doing that would be enormously hazardous.

Obviously making a second approach to the drop zone areas on the Cotentin peninsula would mean flying back through the enemy's intense anti-aircraft defenses, but there was yet another danger. A total of 850 Troop Carrier C-47s were flying as a part of the Operation Neptune airdrop that night. Those 850 aircraft were all operating within the same airspace at night under combat conditions lit only by dim blue lights designed to be visible only from the behind. The traffic pattern for the Neptune drop ran from west to east over the peninsula. If a Troop Carrier pilot missed the drop zone on the first go around and decided to make another approach, he would be flying from east to west – in other words, against the flow of traffic in airspace where 850 airplanes were operating. Making a second approach would therefore be far more hazardous than the first approach. Despite the incredible quantifiable odds against them, a number of Troop Carrier pilots did make multiple passes over the peninsula in search of their appointed drop zones.

The C-47 carrying 507th Regimental Supply Officer Major Gordon K. Smith did exactly that on the approach to the DZ that night. Major Smith and Major Tommie Thompson had graduated from the University of Wisconsin together in 1938. By sheer coincidence, Major Thompson was the commanding officer of the 305th

Forty-seven year old *Generalleutnant* Wilhelm Falley, commanding general of the *91st Luftland* Division, and Major Joachim Bartuzat were both killed by 82nd Airborne Division paratroopers on D-Day. (*Collection of The National D-Day Museum*)

TCS, 442nd TCG at the time of the Normandy invasion and Major Smith was the jumpmaster on the airplane Thompson was piloting that night. At the pilot-jumpmaster briefing, Thompson had said, "Smitty, I will put you right in the center of your DZ."[22] But that was a promise that would be difficult to keep because, as Major Thompson approached the DZ on the night of June 6th, his C-47 drew so much anti-aircraft fire that he overshot the drop zone. Not wanting to let Smith down, Thompson executed a 180-degree turn, and made a second approach. The second time around, Thompson put all but two troopers on the DZ.[23] It seems almost miraculous that no midair collisions occurred as a result of the move.

Still another factor that must certainly have influenced the Troop Carrier pilots to turn on the green lights when they did was a desire to keep the paratroopers in the same area. That is to say that the pilots did not want to leave any paratroopers stranded on the ground without their full platoon, company or battalion to support them. The pilots must have realized that if they dropped the stick of paratroopers they were carrying far away from the other sticks being carried by other C-47s, those paratroopers would have a much more difficult time accomplishing their mission objectives. In other words, if a particular company of paratroopers was spread out over an unusually broad area, it would take a much longer time for that company of paratroopers to assemble on the ground, and would accordingly delay the completion of their mission. If a particular stick of paratroopers was dropped far enough away from the drop zone, linking up with other paratroopers and attacking an objective might not even be practical or possible. So those pilots knew that individual, isolated groups of paratroopers with limited firepower to defend themselves would be terribly vulnerable on the ground behind enemy lines. In small groups they would barely be able to defend themselves let alone overtake an assigned objective. Shortly before taking off from a base in southern England, one airborne officer lined up the pilots that would be carrying his unit to Normandy and gave them pointed instructions:

> I lined up all the pilots and I said I don't give a damn what you do, but if you're going to drop us in hell or if you're going to drop us on our zone, drop us all in one place![24]

The Troop Carrier pilots had to have known that the chances of making a successful second or a third approach to the drop zone were dismal. They obviously did not want to drop paratroopers in the English Channel. They obviously did not want to drop paratroopers far away from their assigned drop zones with little or no hope of assembling into contiguous companies, battalions and regiments. They obviously did not want to turn around and fly head-on into approaching C-47s to make another drop zone approach. To do

so would jeopardize their lives, the lives of the 18 paratroopers they were carrying and the lives of the men on the other C-47s with which they might potentially collide. For the pilots of the Troop Carrier C-47s, they had a difficult job to do under impossible circumstances that night.

• • •

With German fire lighting the sky, Lt. Johnny Marr described the anxious moments that passed immediately before receiving the signal to jump:

> We were anticipating the green light watching to the north all these flak guns. I can recall wondering, "when are we gonna get that green light? We gotta get it pretty soon or we're gonna get shot out of the sky."[25]

Throughout the 117 Skytrains carrying the 507th, those green lights began coming on at about 2:30am. In the C-47 carrying Sgt. Frank Costa, the red light came on at 2:25. The red light marked the four-minute warning before the jump. Costa remembered what happened next: "the Jumpmaster in his commanding voice told us, 'Stand up and hook up!" The paratroopers then attached their static lines to the anchor cable inside the aircraft, checked each other's equipment and then moved up close to the door. At 2:30 am, the red light went out, the green light came on and the Jumpmaster shouted, "Go!" and the men quickly exited the aircraft.[26] Edward Jeziorski recounted the particulars of what happened in his C-47:

> The green light came on, and Lieutenant Parks just yelled, 'Are you ready?!' And the answer was, 'Yes,' of course. And then came, 'Let's go,' and out the door we went.[27]

Captain Robert D. Rae of Service Company/507th remembered that, "The pilots were really trying to get rid of us – they put us out all over the place."[28] In some cases, C-47s began dropping much too soon. In other cases, the green light came on too late when the aircraft was not where it was supposed to be. As an example, earlier that night two C-47s from the 80th Troop Carrier Squadron carrying elements of the 101st Airborne Division had turned on their green lights much too late with the consequence that ten paratroopers from 1st Battalion, 502nd Parachute Infantry Regiment were dropped in the English Channel and drowned.[29]

As a result of the myriad of influences and circumstances affecting the Troop Carrier pilots that night, the men of the 507th were scattered. The scattered nature of the Normandy drop ultimately led to accusations that the pilots had behaved irresponsibly.

Nothing could be farther from the truth. The actions of these men seem far less irresponsible when the full dimension of the circumstances is considered and all of the facts are appreciated. On D-Day, there were "near-perfect drops, mixed drops, and totally disastrous drops."[30] The training exercises that the Troop Carrier Pilots had flown in preparation for the operation had not even approached the reality of what would be a hazing gauntlet of fire over the Cotentin Peninsula that night. Those circumstances made it impossible for the pilots to get their jobs done with the same level of precision that had been achieved in training. Although they have been somewhat criticized in the past, the Troop Carrier Pilots did the best they could have possibly done given the circumstances. While there were cases of disastrous misdrops on D-Day, there were also countless cases of pilots who went above and beyond the call of duty to make sure that the paratroopers they were carrying were delivered to their drop zone.

Sgt. Thomas J. Blakey jumped on D-Day with the 1st Battalion/505th Parachute Infantry Regiment/82nd Airborne Division and his opinion of the pilots and co-pilots is probably the most balanced opinion there is on this subject:

Those guys flying those planes had all they could handle. They had an airplane that had 18 guys in the back, and six equipment bundles. They were in formation, they were going in and out of clouds, they were getting shot at, they had no idea where they were, the Pathfinders hadn't worked, so they had no way of knowing what was going on and where they were. They were scared of running into each other because everybody was dodging. They had their hands full. So I can understand why they got to some place and said get 'em out, because they were going to be back over the channel before long. I never did hold it against any of those pilots.[31]

• • •

After dropping his stick of paratroopers, Sidney Ulan put his C-47 in a nose down attitude and leveled-off just above the deck to avoid ground fire. Flying just above the treetops at full throttle, Ulan's C-47 eventually passed over the beach and then came out skimming the water of the English Channel. The aircraft of Ulan's formation then climbed and formed up for the trip back to England. When he landed safely at Merryfield, Ulan inspected the outside of his C-47 and found several small holes in the skin of the airplane that had been produced by the German flak over the Cotentin peninsula. He breathed a sigh of relief because he had survived the

Sgt. Thomas J. Blakey jumped on D-Day with the 1st Battalion/505th Parachute Infantry Regiment/82nd Airborne Division. *(Courtesy of Thomas J. Blakey)*

ordeal. His participation in D-Day did not end there though. Early in the morning of June 7th, his squadron flew to Normandy again. This time Ulan's C-47 did not carry paratroopers but towed gliders instead. As he flew out over the Channel this time in broad daylight, he could see the immense armada of Allied ships stretching practically from coast to coast. He could even feel the concussion from the battleships firing at the German shore positions. After releasing the cable of the glider his C-47 was towing, Ulan looked back at the vast fleet and felt proud to have been a part of the invasion:

As I flew over the Channel, I was amazed at the sight of ships stretching from England to France, like a bridge across a wide river.[32]

8

Descent into Chaos

For the men of the D-Day assault force, stepping into combat would be a moment of dramatic finality, a moment wherein the mind of each man would have to make a singular, sober commitment to the enterprise at hand. As each paratrooper stepped out of his airplane that night, that step was as filled with irreversible finality as the moment that the ramps of the landing craft would begin dropping a few hours later. However for the airborne men, that step carried an entire added dimension of hazards and concerns that the men on the ground were free of. In addition to the traditional sober contemplations that dominate the minds of warriors going into combat, the men of the parachute infantry also had to make room for concerns about the dangerous practice of parachuting. Joseph Dahlia recalled what was going on in his mind right before he jumped that night:

> I was scared and nervous because I had so much equipment on me. I was afraid my equipment would be caught in the shroud lines or my chute wouldn't open.[1]

As if parachuting was not hazardous enough in and of itself, the men of the 507th also had to face the prospect of stepping out of their troop carriers into a night sky lit by tracers. The intensity of the incredibly intimidating barrage of enemy fire was such that the men were made acutely aware that they were about to enter a very inhospitable environment. The enemy fire was actually so thick and threatening that most of the paratroopers were anxious to get out of the easily targeted C-47s. On Donald Bosworth's aircraft for example, the group exit was so hasty that all eighteen men "jumped in eleven seconds."[2] On Joseph Dahlia's C-47, every trooper "went out the door as ordered – no one froze."[3] When Edward Jeziorski stepped out of his C-47, it seemed like the "whole world lit up"

right beneath him because of the spectacle of the anti-aircraft fire.[4] All around, tracers were streaming-up towards him and stitching their way across the silk of his open T-5. They were coming so close that he actually lifted his legs in an attempt to avoid being hit. Although it is not known how many men were killed by German ground fire, it *is* known that some were lost while descending to the ground under open parachutes – some because of what they were carrying. On D-Day, the demolition specialists carried large amounts of the explosive composition C-2. C Company's Lt. Bob Parks was no exception: "I had enough plastic explosive stuffed in condoms in my cargo pockets to level downtown Eureka."[5] Carson Smith carried explosives as well and recounted an especially chilling incident relating this very subject:

> The flak was coming up fast and I was standing there with forty pounds of TNT and Composition C-2 on my left hip, and five hundred pounds strapped under the plane to be dropped to us – it was a terrible feeling.[6]

The hazards of carrying these explosives became apparent to Carson immediately after he exited the aircraft. After his chute deployed, he heard a loud explosion. He turned his head to find out what had caused the noise and he saw the "tail end" of a flash. One of the men from his stick who had jumped after him had been blown apart when German fire ignited the demolition charge being carried on his hip.[7]

The murderous German fire soon began to bring down the C-47s too. Captain Paul Smith remembered that the enemy targeted the troop carriers even before they reached the French coast: "We started getting fire from the Guernsey and Jersey Islands."[8] Smith also recalled, "One of my platoons lost an airplane on the way in, it

One of the unlucky C-47s that was brought down by enemy fire over Normandy. (*82nd Airborne Museum via Phil Nordyke*)

crashed and burned and only a few people got out of it because they were near the door.''[9] Smith was referring to the fate of airplane No. 42-23638, a C-47A from the 14th Troop Carrier Squadron of the 61st Troop Carrier Group. No. 42-23638 was being piloted by 1st Lt. William R. Hitztaler when it took off from Barkston-Heath late on June 5[th][10], and it was carrying nineteen troopers of the F Company/ 507th platoon that was under the command of 1st Lt. Walter C. Heisler.[11] After take-off, No. 42-23638 formed up with other C-47s from the squadron and headed toward Normandy. When the formation passed over the west coast of the Cotentin peninsula, it began to draw heavy fire from an anti-aircraft concentration near Valognes, south of Cherbourg. The German fire was of such intensity that No. 42-23638 was soon hit. Bullets peppered the tail section and the left wing of the aircraft, damaging the left engine which immediately burst into flames.[12] Fed by burning high octane gaso-

line, the flames quickly spread across the wing from the leading edge to the trailing edge in one big plume that crept dangerously close to the point where the left wing root joined the fuselage.[13] Making the situation even worse, some of the cables to the aircraft's control surfaces were severed. Aware that No. 42-23638 had received fatal injuries, 1st Lt. Hitztaler ordered everyone to get ready to jump and 1st Lt. Heisler's F Company paratroopers went out first. Several of them had been hit by the bullets and fragments that bounced around indiscriminately inside the aircraft's troop compartment. In fact, one unfortunate trooper collapsed in the aisle from his grievous wounds, forcing his comrades to step over his lifeless body as they struggled to get out of the airplane. Once they were all out, the C-47's crew started jumping. For the Normandy mission, the crew of No. 42-23638 was made up of three officers (pilot, co-pilot, navigator) and two enlisted men (a radio operator

The scattered debris field at a C-47 crash site in Normandy. (*82nd Airborne Museum via Phil Nordyke*)

Detail of the tail section wreckage of the same C-47. (*82nd Airborne Museum via Phil Nordyke*)

Yet another C-47 crash site in Normandy. (*82nd Airborne Museum via Phil Nordyke*)

and an engineer). Co-pilot 2nd Lt. Stanley Edwards and flight engineer T/Sgt. Al Vezina bailed out together without incident, but they were captured by the enemy as soon as they hit the ground.[14] Navigator 1st Lt. John H. Hendry was next in line to jump. As he struggled over the body of the dead paratrooper, one last burst of anti-aircraft fire punched up through the floor of the fuselage. At that exact moment, Hendry heard the man behind him scream. He turned to see veteran radio operator S/Sgt. Orlo A. Montgomery as he collapsed with horrible wounds in his chest and stomach. "He was bleeding badly and seemed to be dying," Hendry remembered.[15] S/Sgt. Montgomery had flown with the squadron during the combat missions over Sicily and Italy. His luck ran out in the skies over Normandy. Unable to do anything for S/Sgt. Montgomery, Hendry threw himself out the door. With everyone out of the airplane who was not already dead, 1st Lt. Hitztaler climbed out of the cockpit through the escape hatch on top of the burning plane and pulled the ripcord on his chute as he fell away from it.[16] No. 42-23638 continued on for a few more miles and finally crashed in a field near the village of Saint-Joseph just south of Valognes. When the crash site was located later that month, the bodies of S/Sgt. Montgomery and a single 507th trooper were found in the wreckage. Of all of the plane's crew, Hitztaler and Hendry were the luckiest. They both reached the ground safely after their parachute jumps and they both managed to avoid being captured by the Germans. During the days that followed, both officers made their way back to Utah Beach whereupon they were returned to England and returned to the squadron.[17]

Ken Robinson was a radio operator with Regimental Headquarters Company. His C-47 experienced something very similar. "It was in between the Guernsey Islands that we got hit." One of the engines of the C-47 carrying his stick caught on fire as a result of the German AAA. When it became clear that the plane was going down, the flight crew prepared to jump with the paratroopers: "They climbed to about 1,500 feet which is higher than we usually jumped because the pilots and the co-pilots were going to get out as

This 82nd Airborne Division paratrooper had the misfortune of coming down in one of the many inundated areas of the Cotentin peninsula. Overloaded by the weight of weapons, ammunition and equipment, many of the troopers that landed in water could not struggle free and consequently drowned. (*National Archives and Records Administration*)

soon as we jumped."[18] Out of the 850 American C-47s that flew to Normandy that night, 21 were lost in combat.[19]

As the paratroopers in Carson Smith's stick approached the ground, they started receiving small arms fire from rifles and machine guns. When he landed, Smith found that water was backed-up everywhere. "It was such nice meadows that they knew we would use them for jump fields if we could, so they flooded them with water," he remembered.[20] He was among the lucky few who landed just beside the water and not in it. Pvt. Paul J. Mank was not so lucky. He was in Regimental Headquarters Company with Carson Smith and he landed in the same immediate area. "I landed in water up to my neck," Mank recalled, "and I tried to get to my feet and every time I tried to get to my feet the chute would fill full of air and then pull me and knock me down."[21] Weighed down with weapons, ammunition and extra equipment, most of the unlucky men that landed in even shallow pools, drowned. "We lost a lot of men in the water," Sgt. Smith remembered.[22]

• • •

Joseph Dahlia's jump went well. He got out of the aircraft intact and his main chute deployed correctly. During his descent, he noticed something below him. "As I was coming down I could see some movement on the ground," he remembered.[23] He braced himself for action and prepared to meet the enemy on the drop zone. When he landed, he was in a pile of manure in the middle of a cow pasture. The movement he detected had not been Germans at all, but only cows. On the ground, only eight men from his platoon managed to assemble. They wandered the Norman countryside until sunrise and then kept moving by dashing stealthily from hedgerow to hedgerow.

While running from one hedgerow to another later that day, Dahlia was shot by a sniper. The bullet ripped the gas cylinder and bayonet off of his M1 Garand rifle and ricocheted into his left hand, severing an artery and causing him to begin bleeding profusely. One of the other troopers in the group administered first aid and stopped the bleeding, but at that point Dahlia could do nothing to help them and, left with no choice, they moved on without him. Because his M1 had been rendered inoperative by the bullet strike, Dahlia was without a firearm to defend himself. All he had was a knife and four fragmentation hand grenades. After the others were gone, he wandered around for a bit longer and came to a farmhouse where the people took care of him. But, soon thereafter a pair of German soldiers came to the farmhouse looking for food. Instead of something to eat, they found Dahlia and promptly captured him. While being cared for by the Germans, he was operated on by an English-speaking doctor who had been educated at the University

of Chicago. The doctor ultimately amputated Dahlia's left index finger, sewed his thumb back on and removed the metacarpal bone. He was later transferred to the German prison hospital in Rennes, France, where he was liberated by the U.S. Army 8th Infantry Regiment on October 22, 1944.

• • •

Right before jumping, Chris Kanaras tripped the release levers that dropped the equipment bundles from his C-47. He then proceeded to step out the door and, as he fell away from the airplane, he could see the parachutes being pulled from the bundles in their racks underneath the fuselage.[24] "The opening shock of my chute was awesome," he remembered.[25] He had jumped at the low altitude of approximately three hundred feet, which did not give him much time in the air.[26] After only ten seconds, he hit the ground so hard that he was numb for the first few seconds. Kanaras was alone in the middle of a field and a German machine gun was nearby firing at the low flying C-47s. Evidently the German had not spotted Kanaras as he was descending, so he did not fire at him. He hastily retrieved the M3 knife from his boot, cut the suspension lines of his parachute and ran off the field to a ditch alongside a

Studio portrait of Pvt. Tony Guzzo of C Company/507th shortly after he completed jump school. *(Courtesy of Tony Guzzo)*

hedgerow. Once in the relative safety of the ditch, Kanaras unlocked one side of his reserve chute, unbuckled his chest harness and freed his M1 rifle. Realizing that he would not be able to move quickly with so much equipment, he dumped his gas mask and its waterproof bag, his first aid kit, his Mae West and musette bag. He had stripped down to just his rifle, ammunition and grenades. He checked his wrist compass and then headed off in the direction of the 1st Battalion/507th assembly area. Although he knew it was toward the south-southeast, he did not know that he had been dropped far from it.

Kanaras had moved about one hundred yards when suddenly he heard something moving behind him. He quickly rolled out of the ditch and waited for whatever it was to get closer. With his safety off, he pointed his M1 at the approaching obviously human silhouette, coiled his finger around the trigger and issued the challenge, "flash." Instead of getting the reply of "thunder" as he was supposed to, Kanaras instead heard, "It's me" from his old friend Pfc. Ezro Fontenella – who had been sitting next to him during the

Pvt. Guzzo poses with his parents in Columbus, Ohio, shortly after completing jump school. Guzzo would go on to earn the Distinguished Service Cross on the drop zone in Germany during the Operation Varsity jump. *(Courtesy of Tony Guzzo)*

flight across the Channel.[27] The two men walked toward the southeast for the rest of the night without encountering anyone else. The first indication that they were in the wrong place came a few hours after daybreak when a flight of six B-26 medium bombers flew by. Kanaras was able to identify the B-26s with ease because the Martin Aircraft Manufacturing plant where they were made was only fifteen miles from his parents' house. It was simple for him to recognize them because he was accustomed to seeing them buzzing around in the skies above Baltimore. To Kanaras, who knew that bombers were not supposed to be operating anywhere near the drop zones, this meant "big trouble."[28] The two men kept moving and at about noon they spotted a sign at a crossroads. Kanaras asked Fontenella to cover him while he ran down and inspected the sign. When Kanaras got close enough to read it, his stomach knotted up immediately. They were in Ravenoville and Ste.-Mère-Église was seven kilometers to the west. They were just over one mile west of Utah Beach and they were more than ten miles east of where they were supposed to be at Drop Zone "T". Although Kanaras and Fontenella had been badly mis-dropped, they were not the only 507th paratroopers to spend D-Day in close proximity to Utah Beach.

• • •

When Edward Jeziorski landed, he was close to the burning wreckage of a downed C-47. Silhouetted by the flames of the crash site, he was immediately taken under fire and pinned down by a nearby German machine gun – unable even to raise up.[29] His first instinct was to free himself of his parachute harness, but he encountered a great deal of difficulty doing so. He had strapped himself into his harness so snugly and pulled his adjustment straps so tight that he could not gather up enough slack to get the hardware unhooked. Every time he yanked on the harness attempting to loosen the straps, the German machine gunner would fire a burst or two at him. After struggling for a few futile minutes, he decided to abort the effort and cut himself free. Slowly and carefully, Jeziorski brought his right leg close enough up to pull his trench knife out of his boot. With sporadic bursts of machine gun fire still zipping just inches above him, he cut through the bellyband of his T-5 and all of the other lines and straps connected to it. When he finally struggled free of his parachute harness, Jeziorski rolled over into – as luck would have it – a little depression deep enough to allow him enough freedom of movement to get to his M1 rifle. He then pointed it in the general direction of the enemy machine gun and squeezed off a few un-aimed rounds. Apparently unnerved by the prospect of the enemy shooting back at him, the machine gunner stopped firing.[30]

Jeziorski was then somewhat free to move about. He was in a field – although he did not know where – and he was alone. With his M1 at the ready, he cautiously crept down along the length of a hedgerow. His progress was interrupted when he heard, "something or somebody coming through the underbrush."[31] As a precaution, he laid himself down in the prone position with his rifle pointing toward the unseen source of the noise. When it was close enough, Jeziorski called out with the password "flash." Another paratrooper then replied with the counter-sign: "thunder" and Pvt. Grover O. Boyce, Jeziorski's assistant gunner, stepped out of the darkness. Now that there were two men together, "It seemed like a better world all of a sudden."[32] Within a half an hour, Jeziorski and Boyce were joined by Pvt. Tony Guzzo and Pvt. Andrew Mander from the regiment's Medical Detachment. Together they continued moving through the night until they located a para-pack at about 4:00 am. The pack contained a single Browning M1919A4 machine gun and two .30-cal. ammunition boxes. "We really felt pretty good having that thing in our hands," Jeziorski remembered.[33]

Thus, shortly before dawn on D-Day, the 2nd Squad of 2nd Platoon, C Company/507th consisted of four men, four rifles and one machine gun with five hundred rounds of ammunition. Out of the 18 men that had jumped in their stick, only those four men managed to find each other that night. After wondering around the Norman countryside for several hours, the men finally formed a small defensive position around the .30-cal. machine gun along the side of a narrow road. "We didn't know where we were, but we knew that we weren't anywhere near where we were supposed to be," Jeziorski remembered.[34] Although the men were supposed to have been dropped on Drop Zone "T" near Amfreville, they had actually ended up one mile east of Ste.-Marie-du-Mont near the village of Hébert. They had landed 2 1/2 miles west of Utah Beach and 9 miles east of their drop zone. In other words, they were much closer to the beach than they were to Drop Zone "T".

At twilight, a German half-track started coming down the road toward their position. Jeziorski racked the bolt of his M1919A4, waited until the vehicle was within range, and then opened fire on it. The other three men also opened fire using their rifles. As the half-track continued moving at a high rate of speed, Jeziorski tracked it with the muzzle of the machine gun and continued to throw bursts at it. He would have followed the vehicle as it passed his position, but he could not continue to traverse the machine gun around. When he prepared his fighting position earlier that morning, he had been careful to dig the legs of the machine gun's tripod into the ground so that it would not bounce around during firing. Although that precaution guaranteed a more stable and consequently more accurate firing position, it was unfortunately too difficult to pick the weapon up and move it as the German half-track rolled past. Rather than just letting the half-track get by him, Jeziorski decided he had to do something. In desperation, he reached for his only Gammon

grenade, removed the cap and "heaved" it at the passing vehicle. There was a huge blast, but then the half-track revved its engine and kept right on moving. "I missed him by a mile," Jeziorski remembered.[35] As the enemy drove off, one of the other troopers managed to get off a few parting rifle shots, but it was not substantial enough to be fatal. Although their first encounter with the enemy had ended on an anticlimactic note, the excitement would soon continue.

Soon thereafter, the four men heard a firefight in progress nearby and began moving toward it. Jeziorski hefted the machine gun up onto his shoulder, Boyce picked up the tripod and together all four men moved out on the double. They quickly stumbled onto a small cluster of homes, selected a position, and hastily set up the machine gun again. A moment later, a German soldier stumbled out of one of the houses with his hands up attempting to surrender. Guzzo rose up and was moving cautiously toward the soldier to take him prisoner when suddenly the German's face just seemed to disappear – he had been shot in the head by one of his own men.[36] Jeziorski and the three other 507th paratroopers then proceeded to move quietly through the little village. They found that no one was left – Germans or civilians, but then they ran into a pair of 101st Airborne Division paratroopers. At once, the mixed group of men prepared to defend the village by cutting all communications wire, preparing fighting positions and erecting road blocks.

Then, without warning, one of the six men yelled, "Here come the Krauts!"[37] When Jeziorski looked up, he saw a squad of German soldiers advancing along a nearby stone fence. The Americans fired first. Garand rifles began popping and some of the Germans returned fire. After the first few shots had been exchanged, Jeziorski was ready with the machine gun and he thereafter fired a few bursts toward the advancing enemy. Then, a well-concealed German MG42 opened fire on Jeziorski's position. The two machine gunners traded bursts for a few tense moments as they both hurriedly tried to zero in on each other. Once Jeziorski had determined the location of the MG42 position, he simply walked his fire in on top of the gunner and then, "There wasn't any more noise from him."[38] The six men then backed off about two hundred yards from the village and kept moving. For Jeziorski, the rest of D-Day was one big blur of such brief, intense encounters. Time and time again they moved, running into one firefight after another. "It was just a constant scrap all day long," he remembered.[39] Throughout it all though, not one of the four paratroopers received so much as a scratch.

• • •

For Clarence Hughart, things began to go wrong even before he got out of his C-47. Struggling under the weight of his equipment, he experienced some difficulty even just working his way toward the door to jump. Then when the time came for him to exit the aircraft, he slipped. "As I stood in the open door and began to jump I lost my footing on the door's threshold."[40] Condensation had built-up in the C-47's doorway during the flight across the channel and the threshold was consequently slippery. Thus, right when Hughart needed firm footing the most, he did not have it. Because his feet shot out from under him, he did not snap sharply into a proper exit position like he was supposed to. That would have carried him swiftly away from the aircraft allowing his chute to deploy. "Rather than falling forward out the door, I was wedged in the door by my rifle," he remembered.[41] The men behind him began to shout, "Get the hell out of the plane!" When Hughart finally worked himself free, he fell away from the C-47 into the darkness of the night sky. The static line attaching him to the aircraft went taut, yanking out the T-5 parachute on his back. As the canopy quickly filled with air and snapped open, Hughart swung under it a few times – something the paratroopers referred to as an oscillation. Almost as soon as he stabilized under the open parachute, Hughart was on the ground. He regained his feet, gathered up his parachute and then cut himself free. He was one of the lucky ones that night that landed safely, but he was in an isolated field and all alone. "It was very dark and extremely quiet," he recalled.[42] With his Garand rifle at the ready, he cautiously began to make his way across that field. Then he stumbled onto the enemy.

With no warning, Hughart ran into a squad of German infantry crossing the same field. He described what happened next:

> I attempted to shoot at the first one I saw, but suddenly, I felt a searing pain in my leg. The next thing I knew I was surrounded by Germans pointing rifles at my head; I thought this was the end.[43]

The German soldiers swarming around him then proceeded to relieve him of his wristwatch and wallet. They were yelling at him, asking if he was an American. "I tried to stand up but my leg would not support my weight so my captors found a stick and tied it to my leg and carried me across a field," he recalled.[44] They took him to a waiting vehicle and "gently" laid him in the back on top of a few parachutes. From there, the Germans drove him to a command post where he was laid on a bed of straw where he remained for a few days. "I was diagnosed with a broken femur and was then moved to a German field hospital in Cherbourg."[45] For Clarence Hughart, the battle of Normandy was over. Although his 13th jump seemed to be rife with bad luck, he was actually quite fortunate to have survived the experience.

• • •

Clarence Hughart's aircraft was not the only one to have a man get stuck in the door during the D-Day jump. One C-47 carrying men of D Company/507th experienced the same thing and 1st Sergeant Barney Q. Hopkins was there to witness it. Each D Company stick included an appointed "pushmaster" to signal the first man to jump and insure that everyone was able to get out without getting snagged on anything inside the airplane. 1st Sergeant Hopkins was the "pushmaster" on his C-47 that night. As the airplane approached the drop zone, the jumpmaster (Lt. Lewis L. Harris) had the men stand up and hook up to the anchor cable. After conducting their equipment checks, Lt. Lewis gave the order, "Close-up, stand in the door."[46] When the green light came on, 1st Sergeant Hopkins tapped Lt. Lewis on the leg, and the lieutenant jumped followed in turn by several other paratroopers in the stick. Then suddenly, one man stopped in the door. The man had turned his M1 rifle horizontal and, because of this configuration, the muzzle and butt of the weapon jammed on either side of the door. The men crowding him from behind only exacerbated the situation. During jumps, the men would all push toward the door in an effort to get as rapid an exit from the aircraft as possible. The dividend of this practice was that the troopers would land closer together and would consequently have a swifter and more efficient assembly. However, with the men pushing from behind, there was so much pressure on the lodged soldier that he could not free himself. The three pushing men were neither aware that he was stuck in the door nor aware that he was pinned because of their pushing. While this was going on, tracers from the German anti-aircraft fire were zipping past the door. With each passing second of delay, the drop was becoming more and more dispersed and the troopers were getting further and further away from the DZ. Something had to be done. As the stick's "pushmaster," 1st Sergeant Hopkins reacted and quickly to correct the situation:

> I saw the problem and grabbed the lodged soldier by his shoulders and pulled him back, at the same time putting my right foot in the chest of the man behind him, and pushed the three men back. Consequently I straightened the lodged man's rifle and gave him a shove and a kick out the door.[47]

After that, the three remaining men followed him immediately out the door and Hopkins then jumped directly behind the last man out.

As soon as his parachute deployed, Hopkins became aware that someone on the ground was shooting at him. First he heard a rifle shot, then he heard the bullet "pop" as it sliced through the open canopy above his head. "I had descended just enough that my chute was where I had been a second sooner," Hopkins remem-

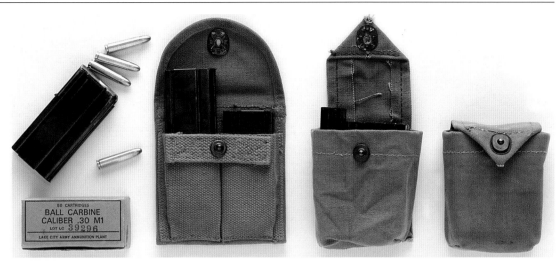

The M1A1 Carbine fired the .30-cal. Carbine cartridge from detachable 15-round box magazines. The weapon's magazines could be carried in the standard issue 2-cell magazine pouch (*left*) or in specially made rigger's pouches capable of carrying five magazines (*center* and *right*). (*Bruce N. Canfield Collection, photo by Scott Smith*)

The M1A1 Carbine was one of the weapons used by men of the 507th during the Normandy campaign. Derived from the standard M1 Carbine, the M1A1 was developed specifically for airborne use and was adopted in May 1942. It differed from the standard M1 carbine only in the design of the stock assembly, which featured a folding metal buttstock and separate wooden pistol grip. With the stock folded to the left side of the carbine, the weapon was much shorter and handier for airborne operations and the folding metal stock assembly only added about four ounces of weight. Inland Division of General Motors was the sole manufacturer of the M1A1 carbine and the firm turned out a total of 140,591 of the weapons. (*Bruce N. Canfield Collection, photo by Scott Smith*)

bered.[48] The German fired at him three times as he descended. After just a few moments in the air, Hopkins landed in a small orchard and his chute drifted over the top of a low apple tree. The German rifleman fired three more times at him when he was on the ground, but the shots were apparently aimed at the parachute canopy snagged across the apple tree because none even came close to Hopkins. He then cut himself out of his T-5 harness and proceeded to slip away from the area with his M1A1 Carbine, ammunition and grenades.[49] After the war, Hopkins described his predicament:

> Here it was, 2:35 in the morning, in enemy territory. It was quite dark, but not pitch dark, not sure where I was, and some 6 or 8 miles behind German lines.[50]

• • •

As soon as Lt. Bob Parks stepped out of his C-47, he felt his T-5 open and he instinctively checked his canopy. After confirming that everything looked "OK" with the parachute, he turned his attention to the ground where he would soon be landing. Then he felt a sudden jolt. "I looked up and the parachute was a rag waving in the wind," he recalled.[51] The propeller of a passing C-47 had chewed-up the canopy and Parks was falling under a streamer. Without missing a beat, he pulled reserve and, fortunately, the back-up chute snapped open. "I made one swing (oscillation) and landed on my back on a blacktop road," he recalled.[52] Once on the ground, he found an "unfriendly reception committee" was only forty feet away.[53] With bullets snapping all around him, he decided that discretion was the better part of valor, and took his chances by playing dead. A few moments passed and the firing died down with Parks still lying there in a fake lifeless state.

The M3 binoculars and M17 leather case that George Leidenheimer carried during the Normandy jump. *(Collection of The National D-Day Museum, photo by Jackson Hill)*

The M3 binoculars that George Leidenheimer carried during the Normandy jump. *(Collection of The National D-Day Museum, photo by Jackson Hill)*

Then, several enemy soldiers emerged from the dark hedgerows to take a closer look at what they thought was a dead American paratrooper. Describing his frustration, Parks remembered, "All the work and training we had gone through and I was caught like a mouse in a trap – no chance to get to a weapon to defend myself."[54] The soldiers gathered around him and were standing over him talking when suddenly, the sounds of someone approaching could be heard. It was another paratrooper walking down the middle of the road repeating the password "flash" at the top of his voice. "I couldn't believe my ears!" Parks remembered.[55] For a few random moments, the Germans did not move, but stared unbelievably at the approaching American that was about to walk right up on them. Then, one of the Germans shouldered his rifle and shot the man. With the enemy standing right over him, Parks continued to lie as still as he possibly could. "It has always bothered me that I had time to warn him but didn't," Parks recalled, "I have always wondered if he would have heeded a warning."[56] Sadly, the man was not killed by the German bullet, and he laid there in the middle of the road crying out for help.[57] After that incident, Parks did not feel any fear, but only "disgust and humiliation."[58]

Immediately thereafter, the enemy soldiers realized that Parks was not dead and quickly took him prisoner. His captors, who turned out to be members of a second rate Austrian Artillery unit, transported him to a nearby pillbox command post where he was interrogated. Parks was well treated during his time in custody and he has attributed that fact to what he believes was a desire on the part of the Austrians to turn themselves in:

I've decided over the years that I was saved to surrender to. Four men behind me in the stick that night were captured and sent back into Germany and there was no reason to keep me unless I was their ticket to safety.[59]

The fact that he was their only prisoner may also have been a factor. Parks was placed in the bunker with the other troops of the unit with one soldier specifically assigned to guard him. Strangely, the troops asked him if his condoms full of C-2 were sausages. During his brief captivity, no one gave him any "static" and his only real fear was boredom. Then on D+2 (June 8th), soldiers of the 4th Infantry Division moved into the area where the pillbox was located. A short skirmish ensued, which was punctuated by an American tank that fired a few blasts from its canon. The Austrian commander then summoned Parks forward and asked if he and his men could surrender without being killed.[60] "I assured them that they were perfectly safe," Parks remembered.[61] He was then sent out to negotiate terms with the 4th Division men, which he promptly did:

I spent the rest of the day with the tankers, accepted their help in disposing of some wine, which was of excellent quality, slept under their tank that night and caught a ride back to the remnants of the 507th PIR the next day.[62]

• • •

In the years immediately after World War I, John Taliaferro Thompson designed the .45 caliber sub-machine gun that would ultimately arm many of the men of the 507th in Normandy. The famous Thompson sub-machine, as it came to be popularly known, was first obtained by the U.S. Marine Corps in 1926, then by the U.S. Navy in 1928 and finally the U.S. Army in 1932. The model shown here, the M1A1, was developed for mass-production and was manufactured by Auto Ordnance Company of Bridgeport, Connecticut and Savage Arms Corporation of Utica, New York. During the war, Auto Ordnance produced 847,991 M1 Thompsons and Savage produced 539,143. *(Courtesy of The National D-Day Museum, photos by Scott Smith)*

Demolitions troopers of Regimental Headquarters Company/507th. Pfc. Paul Mank, who is seated second from the right on the front row, is holding an M1A1 Thompson submachine gun in his left hand. *(Courtesy of Dominique François)*

George Leidenheimer slept through practically the entire flight across the channel and awoke as his C-47 was approaching the peninsula. Red, green and blue tracers enveloped the plane as it closed in on the drop zone and bullets zipped up through the floor panels. Then the left engine was hit and burst into flames. Since he was to be the second man out the door after Lt. Alderton, Sgt. Leidenheimer saw the flames from the burning Pratt & Whitney R-1830 radial engine flash by the open jump door. The pilot then switched-on the green light and Lt. Alderton threw himself out the door with Sgt. Leidenheimer right behind him. "We jumped at what I estimate was less than three hundred feet, because I oscillated only once before hitting the deck," Leidenheimer remembered.[63] During his brief descent to the ground, a German machine gun fired a burst that barely missed him. When he landed with a jolt, he quickly retrieved his M3 trench knife and began to cut himself out of his harness. Right at the moment that he finally freed himself, the same machine gun fired a burst at him again. Startled, he accidentally dropped his knife and "hauled ass" down a road. The speed of his movement was somewhat impaired though by the heavy anti-tank mine he was carrying in his musette bag, but he continued to sprint nevertheless.

Leidenheimer had only gone a few strides when a German challenged him by shouting "Halt!"[64] With that, he jumped into the drainage ditch along the side of the road and dumped the anti-tank mine that was slowing him down without skipping a beat and took-off again, only faster this time. As he ran off, two Germans followed taking shots at him with their rifles as they ran. Leidenheimer was only seconds ahead of his pursuers when he came to an eight-foot fence that led to an open gate. He ducked through the gate, spun around and waited for the two enemy infantrymen:

The German soldiers were on the road in plain sight about twenty feet away. I should have killed them both, but we had been ordered not to fire until daybreak. So I fixed the bayonet on my rifle, expecting them to follow me. I knew that I could take them both since the gate was only wide enough to let one through at a time. However, they wouldn't leave the road and I got tired of waiting for them and left the area.[65]

Leidenheimer moved on and soon located another B Company man, Pfc. Richard Guscott. Although alive and conscious, Guscott was not in perfect fighting trim. On the way down during his jump he had oscillated into a stone wall and cracked several ribs. The result was that he was dazed and in pain. It was still dark and the strength of the enemy in the area was still unknown. Facing such an uncertain situation and concerned that Guscott would not be able to keep up because of his injuries, Leidenheimer hid him in a hedgerow and promised to come back for him after sunrise.[66] Soon thereafter, Leidenheimer located several other B Company men. The group then retrieved the contents of several equipment bundles and began preparing a defensive position around a former German dugout. "We set up two machine guns, a mortar, a case of grenades and plenty of ammunition," he remembered.[67] They were putting the finishing touches on their small perimeter when the sun rose on D-Day.

At that point, Leidenheimer told the rest of the men that he was going to find Guscott and set off in the direction of the hedgerow where he had left him only a few hours before. He moved cautiously with bayonet fixed and his Garand at the ready. He still had a fresh 8-rounds in the weapon because he had not yet fired it. For the first fifty yards everything was still, but then the quiet was shat-

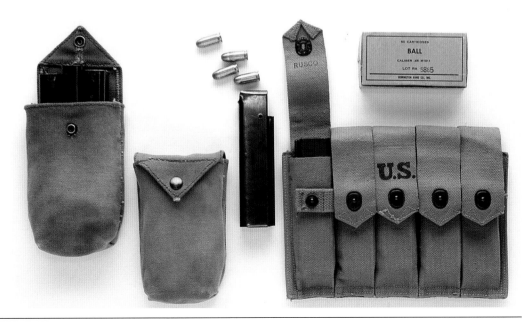

The M1A1 Thompson fired the .45-cal. cartridge from detachable 20-round and 30-round box magazines. The weapon's 20-round magazines could be carried in the standard issue 5-cell magazine pouch (*right*) or in specially made rigger's pouches capable of carrying four magazines (*left* and *center*). (*Bruce N. Canfield Collection, photo by Scott Smith*)

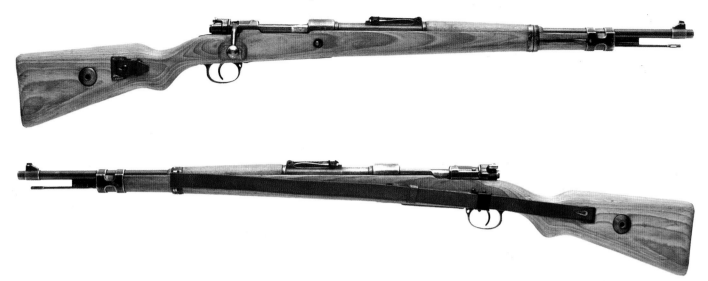

Above: The primary German infantry weapon at the time of the Normandy invasion was the Kar98k Mauser. This weapon was the World War II evolution of the old Model 1898 Mauser rifle, or Gewehr 98, that the German military adopted just before the turn of the 20th Century. The 43.6-inch long Kar98k was introduced in 1935 as a shortened carbine version of the 49.2-inch long Gew98. A manually operated bolt-action rifle, the Kar98k's internal box magazine could hold five rounds of the powerful 7.92x57mm Mauser rifle cartridge. After running out of ammunition for his M1A1 Thompson submachine gun, Captain Paul F. Smith, commanding officer of F Company/507th, picked up a Kar98k and carried it for the rest of the Normandy campaign. (*Author's Collection, photos by Scott Smith*)

Left: A typical Norman field dominated by typical Norman hedgerows. Fighting in the mazes of bocage in Normandy would become a common experience linking the antagonists who struggled there. (*82nd Airborne Museum via Phil Nordyke*)

tered when a German MG42 opened fire. Miraculously, the burst missed and Leidenheimer immediately hit the ground and began scanning the area for the machine gun that was trying to kill him. "I saw two 500-pound bomb craters in the middle of a large open field," he remembered, "and the machine gun's presence indicated that there was probably a squad of ten men in one of the two craters."[68] In case those ten men attempted to rush his position, Leidenheimer placed an extra 8-round en bloc clip on the ground right in front of him. That clip and the one already in his M1 would give him sixteen shots to fight off an enemy charge. He was looking toward the two bomb craters down the sights of his rifle when he heard a noise behind him. Leidenheimer spun around only to see a German Sergeant standing directly above him pointing the muzzle of an MP40 submachine gun at his head. The German Sergeant had the drop on the American Sergeant. "I stood and put my hands up, while nine Germans came out of the closer crater," Leidenheimer remembered.[69] Although it seemed like the war was over for him, George Leidenheimer's adventure was just beginning.

• • •

As the C-47 carrying Captain Paul Smith made its final approach to the drop zone, he prepared his men for the jump:

> I stood everybody up and had them hook up. Then I got in the door and I kept watching because I knew the Douve River was going to come up before the Merderet, and just about the time we got where we could see the Douve we ran out of this fog. By then, I didn't see any other airplanes. So I said, 'Let's go.' So we got out.[70]

Smith was the first man out the door in his stick. When he exited the aircraft, he was about eight hundred feet above the ground. After a "nice soft landing," Smith found that he was alone in a field beside a road eight kilometers north of the DZ. "I cut myself out of the harness and I didn't see a soul, nobody," he remembered.[71] Smith then moved in the direction of flight of the C-47 that dropped him, looking for other men from his stick. Although he found no one, he continued looking for the rest of the night:

> I began to doubt myself, so I started concentric circles. And I still didn't find anybody. About a half hour after dawn, I ran into a French farmer on the road, and I stopped him and almost scared him to death. And I asked him where I was, it took me a little time to find out but I was north of the DZ near a little town called Le Ham. And I said, "Where are the Germans?"[72]

These soldiers of the 325th Glider Infantry Regiment/82nd Airborne Division have set up a machine gun position at the base of a typical Norman hedgerow. Throughout the Normandy campaign, both sides used the mounds upon which hedgerows grew as defensive positions. (*82nd Airborne Museum via Phil Nordyke*)

The farmer replied by saying, "Les boches! Les boches! Les boches! Les Boches!" – indicating that the Germans were all around.[73] With the enemy so close by, it was almost a certainty that antagonists would ultimately meet in close combat. While it was still "rather early" on D-Day, Smith was involved in a few minor firefights that exhausted his ammunition supply.[74] He had jumped with an M1A1 Thompson submachine gun, but he carried only two magazines: one in the weapon and one in his musette bag. After he emptied both magazines, he was out of ammunition and there was no certainty that re-supply would reach him any time soon. For that reason, he decided to get rid of the Thompson. Not wanting a useful weapon to fall into the enemy's hands, he smashed it against a rock and replaced it with a German Kar98k Mauser.

Soon thereafter, Smith suffered a bayonet cut across his hand when he ran headlong into a German rifleman. "He was on the other side of the hedgerow and I was on this side and we kind of met in the middle," he remembered.[75] After the German soldier lunged with his bayonet, Smith wrestled with him briefly and then ended the struggle with the Kar98k Mauser rifle he had picked up earlier in the day.[76] Paul Smith had thus survived what would become the singular common experience linking the antagonists during the battle for Normandy. Beginning with the first paratroop drops on June 6th and continuing throughout the campaign, desperate fighting took place as Germans and G.I.s struggled through a battlefield dominated by what the French called the *bocage*. A century prior to the invasion, Honoré de Balzac left a vivid description of these hedgerows:

> The peasants, from time immemorial, have raised a bank of earth about each field, forming a flat-topped ridge, two meters

Gordon K. Smith, 507th Regimental Supply Officer. (*Photo by Jeff Petry*)

in height, with beeches, oaks, and chestnut trees growing upon the summit. The ridge or mound, planted in this wise, is called a hedge; and as the long branches of the trees which grow upon it almost always project across the road, they make a great arbor overhead. The roads themselves, shut in by clay banks in this melancholy way, are not unlike the moats of fortresses.[77]

Despite their appearance in reconnaissance photographs, Allied intelligence failed to recognize or appreciate the huge impediment that the hedgerows would obviously pose to the movement of fighting forces in Normandy. During the weeks and months preceding the invasion, photo-interpreters in England had spent countless hours poring over hundreds of photos that clearly showed the

hedgerows that were soon to become such a significant obstacle on the Normandy battlefield. But the photo-interpreters only analyzed images that were taken looking straight down on the bocage. From that perspective, the analysts had no reason to suspect that Norman hedgerows were any larger than the waist-high hedgerows of England. Consequently, the men of the 507th PIR – and all the other Allied ground forces for that matter – were sent to do battle in Normandy without being trained or even adequately advised of the impassable maze of growth that awaited them there.

Sgt. Donald Bosworth had an almost fatal encounter as a result of the hedgerows in Normandy. He had been sent to check out a farmhouse when, due to the thick growth of the bocage, he stumbled onto the enemy. Bosworth recounts what happened next:

I started to crawl over the hedgerow to get to the other side when suddenly I was face-to-face with two Germans, not more than four feet away. They were setting up a machine gun. It seemed like an hour before any of us moved.[78]

When the three men did react, they all reached for their weapons simultaneously. Bosworth pointed his Garand toward the two German soldiers and fired. Because his weapon was semi-automatic, he managed to shoot both men just as fast as he could pull the trigger. However, one of the Germans managed to get off a shot before being struck down by a bullet from Bosworth's rifle. That shot struck Bosworth in the right shoulder, throwing him backward. Although unconscious and wounded, he was taken to the basement of a nearby farmhouse where he spent the rest of the day.[79]

• • •

Gordon Smith (*third from left*) with three others paratroopers at Fort Benning in 1942. (*Courtesy of Gordon K. Smith*)

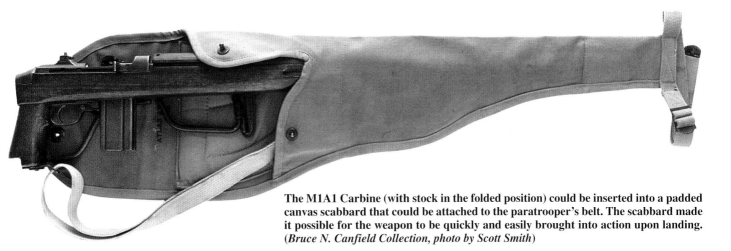

The M1A1 Carbine (with stock in the folded position) could be inserted into a padded canvas scabbard that could be attached to the paratrooper's belt. The scabbard made it possible for the weapon to be quickly and easily brought into action upon landing. (*Bruce N. Canfield Collection, photo by Scott Smith*)

After his University of Wisconsin classmate, Major Tommie Thompson, executed a 180 degree turn and made a second approach to the drop zone, Major Gordon K. Smith landed safely on the west side of the Merderet River. He soon found Sgt. Harmon R. Walters and then rounded-up eight other troopers, none of which jumped from his plane. In fact, some of these men were not even from the 507th. Smith and the small group of men then moved toward the west, in the direction of Gourbesville and Amfreville. As the regiment's S-4 Supply Officer, Smith was supposed to set up a re-supply drop area near there. Soon after the men moved out, they crossed the Merderet River bridge at La Gare northwest of Ste.-Mère-Église, two kilometers due west of Fresville. The group then passed the flooded area, got off the road and approached an apple orchard on some high ground.

As they entered the orchard, German riflemen took them under fire. With bullets zipping past them, all of the men made a dash for a nearby hedgerow, but Smith did not make it. While he was still running, a single German bullet struck his right arm. Because he was carrying his M1A1 Carbine at port arms, the bullet passed through his arm completely and lodged in his side. His men wasted no time, and quickly began to administer first aid. Sgt. Walters cleaned up his wounds and, as soon as he was done, Smith ordered the men to leave him. Aware that Smith was too badly wounded to carry away, they reluctantly followed the order and fell-back to the other side of the river.[80]

Alone and seriously wounded, Smith examined the hole in his side with his fingers and, with surprisingly little effort, retrieved the blood-soaked bullet that had created it. Although in great pain he was at least able to recognize that the bullet would make a great conversation piece, so he put it in the pocket of his jump jacket, intending to keep it. In agony, Smith then began to crawl on his elbows toward a nearby farmhouse, but he did not reach that destination either. While still many yards away and crawling, several German soldiers caught up to him. For him, the war was over right then and there.[81]

• • •

During the flight across the Channel, Bob Davis contemplated the seriousness of what he was about to do and how he would react:

I wasn't worried about my fellow troopers rising to the occasion, I was more worried about myself. I'd trained with them for a year and a half, we'd trained as a unit, and I knew these guys, and I had every reason to expect I could depend upon them.[82]

When Davis stepped out of his C-47 and into the night sky he was approximately six hundred feet above the ground. As was typical of all of the paratroopers that jumped at Normandy, Davis was

Gordon Smith leading a regimental review at Fort Benning in 1942. (*Courtesy of Gordon K. Smith*)

heavily loaded with approximately 85 pounds of equipment. He was carrying two Gammon grenades, several fifteen-round magazines for his M1A1 Carbine, K-rations, a life jacket, a gas mask and an SCR-500 radio.[83] Unlike most of the paratroopers in the regiment though, Bob Davis landed remarkably close to Amfreville. "In fact I landed, my whole stick fortuitously landed less than two hundred yards from Drop Zone "T", our pre-designated drop zone and perhaps 1,000 feet west of the flooded Merderet River."[84]

Davis and the other men in his stick came under fire as soon as they were on the ground. "The Germans had some light machine guns set up in the woods," he recalled, "We were surrounded pretty much by woods and hedgerows and we didn't know it at the time

because it was dark, it was almost pitch dark." Unable to get their bearings in the darkness and under small arms fire, Davis and the other men from his stick stayed close to where they had landed. "I crawled into a gully and the next thing I knew, I felt an itch in my boot. So I took the damn thing off, thought I had a mosquito bite or something, only to discover I'd been grazed by a machine gun bullet."[85] At daybreak, the German fire tapered off and the paratroopers at DZ"T" began to move around. In addition to men from the 507th, a few misdropped paratroopers from the 505th were there as well as the assistant division commander for the 82nd Airborne Division, 37-year-old Brigadier General James M. Gavin. In his 1978 book *On to Berlin*, Brigadier General Gavin described what happened during his D-Day jump:

The M1911A1 .45-caliber automatic pistol was the standard sidearm of U.S. forces in World War II. The original version of the pistol had been adopted before World War I and was still in service, although slightly modified, thirty years later in 1941. When the United States entered the Second World War, several commercial firms were given contracts for M1911A1 production. These included Colt, Union Switch & Signal, Remington-Rand and Ithaca. Hundreds of 507th paratroopers carried M1911A1s during the Normandy campaign. (*Bruce N. Canfield Collection, photo by Scott Smith*)

We were at about 600 feet, the green light went on, and I took one last precious look at the land below. A wide river was just ahead of us, plainly visible in the moonlight. Small arms fire was increasing. About three seconds after the green light went on, I yelled, 'Let's go,' and went out the door, with everyone following. I landed with what seemed to be pretty loud thud in an orchard. Among the trees were some grazing cows which kept munching quite contentedly – entirely unconcerned about what to me was a most momentous occasion.[86]

Gavin then went to work on the difficult task of organizing the mixed group of approximately 100 paratroopers that had assembled in his immediate vicinity in an apple orchard. This job was challenging because, as German fire sprang up around them, the paratroopers took cover in the hedgerows surrounding the orchard. Although it took some time, Gavin soon managed to establish a sem-

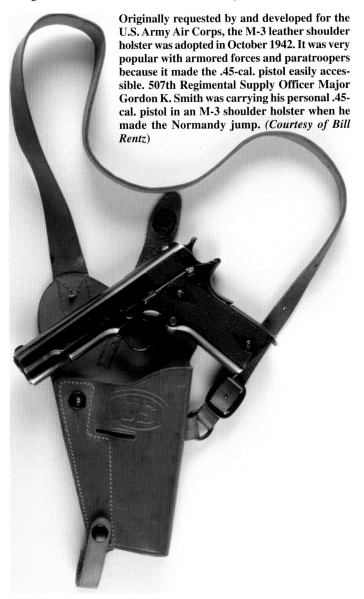

Originally requested by and developed for the U.S. Army Air Corps, the M-3 leather shoulder holster was adopted in October 1942. It was very popular with armored forces and paratroopers because it made the .45-cal. pistol easily accessible. 507th Regimental Supply Officer Major Gordon K. Smith was carrying his personal .45-cal. pistol in an M-3 shoulder holster when he made the Normandy jump. *(Courtesy of Bill Rentz)*

blance of order. He then directed some of the men to attempt to recover equipment bundles that had fallen into the 1,000 foot wide Merderet, but those attempts failed. The men experienced great difficulty groping around in the shoulder deep water of the flooded Merderet in their quest to locate the missing equipment. "Not only was the water deep, but since the swamp had been recently flooded there was thick swamp grass, knee-high, sometimes waist-high," Gavin remembered.[87] The combination of the deep water and tall grass made it impossible for Gavin's men to locate the sought bundles, and they resultantly came up empty handed.

All the while, enemy fire on the west bank was increasing. From his position Gavin could see a red light and a green light on the other side of the river. He knew that the green light was the assembly marker for the 508th PIR and the red light was the assembly marker for the 507th: both of which were obviously gathering on the opposite side of the river.[88] As that was the case, he decided that the most prudent course of action would be for the group to cross over to the east bank to join the rest of the division. Gavin and his paratroopers therefore began to cross with many of the men holding their rifles over their heads. After only a few minutes, the men found that the marsh grass made crossing the river an "exceedingly difficult" undertaking.[89] Gavin remembered that the grass "wrapped itself around our legs and seemed to pull us down."[90] To make matters even worse, German soldiers reached the west bank and began firing at the paratroopers while they were wading across. When the group finally reached a railroad embankment on the opposite side of the river, they turned southward and followed it. Gavin described the embankment in *On To Berlin*:

It was about six feet high, firm and dry, and we crawled up on it. Evidently the Germans did not have weapons capable of reaching that far. We reorganized, helped those who were wounded, and started a column down the railroad toward La Fière.[91]

Bob Davis remembered that, "Moving south along the railroad embankment offered us the route to one of our assigned missions: taking La Fière bridge and causeway."[92] Manoir de La Fière was a small settlement of stone buildings just west of Ste.-Mère-Église owned by M. Louis Leroux. Because of its strategic location astride the Merderet River, Manoir de La Fière was one of the 82nd Airborne Division's primary D-Day objectives. By an inconvenient stroke of bad luck though, twenty-eight German infantrymen had arrived at La Fière at 11:00 pm on June 5th to establish an outpost. Roused out of bed, M. Leroux was surprised by their arrival because strangely, no German soldiers had ever occupied the manoir before that night. Thus, as the men of the 505th and 507th were

Although it was adopted and manufactured during the First World War, the M1917 .45-cal. revolver also served the American military in the years that followed that conflict. Just over 300,000 M1917s had been manufactured by Smith & Wesson and Colt by the time production ended in 1919. With so many examples still in U.S. armories in 1941, M1917s were quickly handed out during World War II. In addition to an M1911A1 automatic pistol, Major Gordon Smith was also carrying an M1917 revolver when he jumped on D-Day. (*Robert J. Carr Collection*)

being flown across the English Channel in the early morning hours of D-Day, the Germans they would soon be fighting at La Fière were just beginning to settle in and prepare their defenses. Then, as hundreds of American paratroopers found their way out of the inundated area after the jump and started walking down the railroad embankment toward La Fière, those twenty-eight Germans were there waiting for them. The stage was set for battle.

· · ·

The German soldiers that caught up to Gordon Smith while he was attempting to crawl away after being shot immediately recognized that he was a major. They probably would have killed him had he been of a lower rank, but instead they took him prisoner. Their first order of business was to disarm their captive, so they took away Smith's M1A1 Carbine and his sidearms. He carried two M1911A1 .45 cal. automatic pistols: one for him, which was in a shoulder holster, and a second one that actually belonged to 507th Regimental Surgeon Major George K. Vollmar, which was in his musette bag. The third pistol was a Smith & Wesson M1917 .45 cal. revolver that Smith carried in a hip holster. After relieving Smith of these weapons, two of the Germans carried him to the side of the road and loaded him in a horse-drawn cart owned by a Frenchman who had just been passing by. The Germans then transported him to an aid station in nearby Gourbesville where he had a "most unusual" experience.[93]

A German doctor who spoke perfect English treated Smith at this aid station. While the doctor worked, he explained to Smith what had happened to him the year before in North Africa. There, the doctor had been captured by American forces and had been

allowed to treat some of his own wounded while a prisoner. The doctor was soon thereafter returned to his country in a prisoner exchange of German and American medical personnel. Smith recalled, "He told me that because of the treatment he had had prior to his return to the German Army, he would take the best care of me that he could."[94] The doctor had already operated on a 508th Corporal and, because of the severity of the wounds to that man's left arm, the doctor had been forced to amputate. However, the doctor pointed out to Smith that he had performed the amputation in such a way as to make it possible for a prosthesis to be attached. Shortly thereafter, the doctor operated on Smith's wounds.

When Smith revived after surgery, he was in a bed in a room with a German soldier on guard seated on a bench close by. The doctor stopped by to check on Smith a little later and, during the visit, informed him that the German guard was actually the rifleman who had shot him. The doctor then gave Smith a bottle of red wine, told him to drink it because he had lost a lot of blood and left the room. As Smith began to drink, he offered a swallow to the German guard, who gladly accepted. The two men then proceeded to polish-off the whole thing. "We handed the bottle back and forth until the wine was gone," Smith remembered.[95] For Smith, it was indescribably odd to be sharing a drink with the man who shot him, but he did it.

Late that night, the doctor visited again and asked Smith if he and the 508th Corporal (the amputee) wanted to be evacuated or placed in the aid station's cellar. Smith immediately chose the cellar, hoping that U.S. forces would soon break through to the town, liberating the hospital's patients. That hope quickly disappeared though when a highly agitated German Colonel came through the temporary ward soon thereafter and countermanded the cellar plan.

Smith and the 508th trooper were then placed on an ambulance and, fifteen-hours later, they arrived at a German hospital in Rennes:

> The other wounded and I were put on a bus. I was placed on the floor of the bus as I was still on a stretcher. After being taken on and off the bus at several stops over a period of several days, we ended up at an old French school that had been converted to a POW hospital.[96]

Although he ended-up in the same hospital in Rennes, Smith was destined not be as lucky as Pvt. Joseph Dahlia (who was liberated there in October). Instead, Smith was held at the hospital in Rennes until mid-July and was then removed to Oflag 64 in Poland where remained until the end of the war.[97]

• • •

After being captured by the German Sergeant with the MP40, George Leidenheimer was escorted to a small building where a group of American prisoners were being assembled. He found Pfc. Guscott there as well as Pfc. Louis Pfeifer of A Co. and about thirty other 507th men. Soon thereafter, a German Lieutenant who spoke perfect English came in and asked for everyone's names. After Pfc. Pfeifer gave his name, the Lieutenant asked him if he spoke German. Pfeifer lied and told him "no." The Lieutenant continued to work his way through the group of Americans until he got to Sgt. Leidenheimer. "When he got to me, I gave him my name, rank and serial number," he remembered.[98] The Lieutenant then noticed Leidenheimer's stripes and asked him how many paratroopers had jumped into France. Leidenheimer responded by saying, "Look, Bud, I told you my name, rank and serial number and that's all I'm gonna tell you."[99] Leidenheimer described what happened next:

> The German lieutenant looked at me, redfaced, clicked his heels and said, "Stand at attention when you speak to a German officer, and don't call me 'Bud'!" I refused to stand at attention and just glared at him with folded arms.[100]

Leidenheimer was trying to impress on everyone that they were to reveal only name, rank and serial number. The Lieutenant turned and spoke to the guards in German and then stormed out of the room. Leidenheimer sat down next to Guscott who was trying to light a cigarette. When the guard noticed what Guscott was doing, he stomped over and slapped the cigarette out of his hand and confiscated the pack.

The paratroopers were then taken outside and lined-up on a road. Then they began marching. As they marched, Leidenheimer slowly worked his way up to the front of the group to where his lieutenant was. He suggested to the lieutenant that they should attempt to overpower their guards and escape. There were forty Americans and only eight Germans, so the odds seemed to be in their favor. With the exception of one guard that kept prodding the paratroopers along with the muzzle of his MP40, the others were walking with their rifles slung. Defeated, the lieutenant said to Leidenheimer, "The war is over for us."[101] Leidenheimer decided right then and there that when the opportunity presented itself, he would escape alone.

The Germans led their prisoners through the streets of Valognes where the town's citizens got their first glimpse of American paratroopers. Leidenheimer had suffered a slight ankle injury during the jump that gave him a faint limp. As he made his way with the column of prisoners through Valognes and beyond, he purposely exaggerated that limp so that his German captors would think he was in much worse shape than he actually was. The prisoners were soon herded into the courtyard of a chateau where other paratrooper prisoners were gathered. Another German officer was there and began separating the men by division: the 82nd men were ordered to one side of the courtyard and the 101st men were ordered to the other. The officer was walking from man to man, inspecting shoulder patches when he noticed Leidenheimer, who was putting on his best "theatrical limp." The officer asked him if he was wounded and Leidenheimer replied saying, "I think I broke my ankle on the jump."[102] Since he appeared to be injured, the officer told him to sit against the outer wall of the chateau's barn, and Leidenheimer promptly did so. What the officer did next was almost too good to be true.

"He directed more 82nd guys in my direction," Leidenheimer remembered, "and I soon realized that I couldn't see the guards and they couldn't see me!"[103] With dozens of men standing in front of where he was sitting, Leidenheimer thought quickly and decided that now was his best chance to escape. "I crawled into the doorway of the barn and pulled an old wooden butter tub, some rakes, shovels and hoes over me," he remembered.[104] Afraid that his bright red 82nd Airborne Division patch would be too easily spotted, Leidenheimer ripped it from the shoulder of his uniform. At that point, he remained as still and quiet as possible. Moments later, there was a commotion outside and Leidenheimer heard the officer say that any prisoner attempting to escape would be shot. Then the German officer announced that the prisoners were going to be fed. "I was so hungry I was tempted to postpone my escape," Leidenheimer recalled.[105] Toward dusk the Germans began counting excitedly: they had obviously discovered that one of the prisoners was gone. They counted and recounted the prisoners in the courtyard and then began looking for the missing man. "One German came into the barn and seemed to look directly at me, but he left without seeing me," Leidenheimer remembered.[106] Obviously, it was George Leidenheimer's lucky day.

Just after dark, he decided that the only way out was to sneak past two guards posted near the barn. "I crawled out on an open lawn, taking what seemed like ages to get to a four-foot wooden picket fence next to a tree," he remembered. He started climbing that fence and then one of the guards appeared and came within ten feet of him. But, the guard did not spot Sgt. Leidenheimer because his head and shoulders were obscured by the tree's foliage. "He turned and continued walking his post so I dropped down and moved toward town, scaling several stonewalls that divided the apple orchards," Leidenheimer recalled.[107] Soon he was in the rolling French countryside and he was no longer a prisoner.

At dawn on June 7th, all was quiet as Leidenheimer entered a churchyard. He found an unlocked door leading into the one of the church's small outbuildings and quietly entered. He was still hungry from not having eaten at all the previous day, so he was more than glad to see a table with a bottle of wine and a half loaf of bread on it. "I finished them quickly before I realized it was probably the host and wine for Mass," he remembered.[108] He then began to explore the rest of the church grounds, starting first with the church building itself. He descended a set of stairs into the basement and there found a room full of sleeping children and two nuns. As soon as he entered the room, the two nuns bolted upright in bed and stared at him in disbelief. At that point, Leidenheimer made his first mistake of the day when he said, "Je suis Americain!" The two nuns looked at each other, and then began to chatter away in French assuming that he could understand them. He was then in the uncomfortable position of having to interrupt them to say, "No parlez Français."[109] With that, one of the nuns left and returned a few min-

utes later with the priest and a man who could speak English. Sgt. Leidenheimer then explained to the translator that he had escaped from the Germans and that he was in need of a place to hide. "Sergeant, if they find you here, they'll kill all of us," was their response.[110] Leidenheimer thanked them and started to leave the church grounds. He had not gone far when the French translator caught up to him and offered a place to hide. The Frenchman then led Leidenheimer to the barn in the back of the churchyard and showed him where to conceal himself. "He was preparing to leave when I told him, "Mangez!" Leidenheimer remembered.[111] A few minutes later, the Frenchman returned with a sandwich and a bottle of milk, which Leidenheimer quickly consumed. Finished with his meal, Leidenheimer climbed up into the hay loft and went to sleep.[112]

He was awakened at 2:00 that afternoon by the sound of aircraft overhead – a group of eight P-47s were attacking German tanks parked in a wooded area nearby and Leidenheimer had a front row seat for the show. Each plane carried a pair of 500-pound bombs, which they began dropping on the target. The first plane dropped its bombs far away from Leidenheimer's barn, but the first bomb from the second plane gave him a close call. "The third bomb blew all the shingles off the roof of my building," he remembered.[113] The Thunderbolts dropped the rest of their bombs and then flew away. At sundown, which was 11:00 pm that time of year, the Frenchman returned to the barn to give Leidenheimer instructions. Pointing at a map, he showed the Sergeant how to get to the closest American lines. Just as he was about to leave, Leidenheimer asked the man if he had any kind of weapon that he could take. When the man shook his head, Leidenheimer asked him if he could take a hatchet he had seen in the churchyard and the man nodded in the affirmative. With a hatchet as his only weapon, Leidenheimer stepped out into the uncertainty of the night. He then came to a road that turned out to

LA NORMANDIE – « La C. P. A. »
10. Environs de SAINTE-MÈRE-ÉGLISE – Le Pont de la Fierre

be the N-13. It was busy with traffic; German command cars, motorcycles and trucks kept passing and Leidenheimer had to wait for a gap in the traffic to cross. He then moved on and began to follow the Cherbourg/Carentan railroad line to the south toward Ste.-Mère-Église.

When the sun rose on D+1, Leidenheimer was still walking and he was still alone. By

Postmarked July 1908, this post card shows the Merderet River bridge at La Fière. The photograph was taken from a position on the west side of the bridge facing east toward Ste.-Mère-Église. (*Courtesy of Yves Poisson*)

then, he was hungry again and decided to ask for food at a farmhouse just off the railroad tracks. He waited outside the house until a man emerged. "I called him over and showed him the American flag on my shoulder, made an eating motion with my right hand, and he invited me in and gave me a bowl of hot cream of wheat," Leidenheimer remembered.[114] The farmer then mentioned that other paratroopers were hiding in the woods nearby and Leidenheimer was soon joined by three other 82nd troopers. The four paratroopers then discussed how they could go about sneaking their way back to American lines. But first it was decided that they would carry out a special mission and destroy a 150-foot German radio tower that was located nearby. The Resistance was supposed to have done the job the week prior, but they lacked the proper explosives.

So later that night, the three other troopers slit the throats of the two radio operators while Leidenheimer rigged the tower with C-2 explosive and proceeded to blow it down. That night, the French threw a party to celebrate the successful completion of the mission and then gave the Americans a place to sleep. In the morning, a French boy took their canteens so that he could fill them at a nearby chateau as a courtesy. This chateau was reputed to have the best water in all of Normandy. Soon after he left, the boy returned and excitedly told the Americans, "boche, boche!" – the enemy was at the chateau.[115] Unfortunately, the paratroopers badly needed that fresh water, so they talked it over and decided to go after it even if the Germans got in the way. With the decision made, Leidenheimer turned to the French boy and said, "Show me boche."[116] The boy

As in the U.S. Army, the firepower of the German infantry squad also included a highly effective pistol caliber submachine gun – the MP40. It fired the 9x19mm Parabellum pistol cartridge from a 32-round detachable box magazine and was equipped with a folding metal butt stock. Between 1940 and 1944, German manufacturers produced over one million MP40s, which were issued to every branch of German military service. Sgt. George Leidenheimer of B Company/507th carried a captured MP40 for many days during Normandy campaign. (*Seth Paridon Collection, photo by Scott Smith*)

then led the troopers to the barn outside the chateau where ten German soldiers were eating and smoking. Leidenheimer and the other troopers simultaneously threw hand grenades in among the enemy soldiers. "The Germans were not well trained, instead of rolling on the ground, away from the grenades they jumped up," Leidenheimer remembered.[117] Those that were not killed outright by the blast, quickly surrendered. "I ordered the Germans who could move, to drag the wounded ones into the courtyard," Leidenheimer remembered, "and we went through their pockets and took their sardines."[118] At that point, Leidenheimer finally replaced his hatchet with an MP40 submachine gun that he confiscated from one of the Germans. He felt that the MP40 was one of the finest weapons of the war and he was glad to have one.

For the next few days, the four paratroopers continued their journey to make it to American lines. The cycle of staying in one place during daylight and moving only after dark was time consuming and frustrating though. After a few days, some of the men were frustrated by their slow progress and felt that they had no choice but to attempt moving in broad daylight. "I told them that was a bad idea, but agreed to try it," Leidenheimer remembered.[119] The first morning of their daylight attempt, the four troopers had gone less than a quarter of a mile when they heard someone whistling. All of them froze as the person drew closer and closer. Leidenheimer described what happened next:

> A German was walking on the path on the other side of a tall hedgerow. There was a wide metal farm gate at the end of our field. We knew when he walked past the gate we would be in his full view. He walked almost past the gate, but at the last minute, he looked at us.[120]

Before any of the troopers could move, the German shouted "Americans!" at the top of his voice and ran off. Leidenheimer ran back to the others and sarcastically asked, "So, how do you like traveling in the daytime?"[121] They all knew that they were deep trouble and that more Germans would soon come to look for them. They knew that they could not just stay where they were. One of the men suggested that they should hide in a close by hedgerow, but Leidenheimer overruled that idea – that would be the first place the enemy would look. Instead he led them to a field a few hundred yards away and together they all hid among 18-inch high stalks of wheat. Throughout the rest of the day, they could hear the Germans yelling back and forth as they hunted for the four paratroopers. Since the option of moving during daylight was no longer practical, they waited for dark. When dark came, Leidenheimer ordered the men to get ready to move – they were going to keep searching for American lines. "Suddenly, the area lit up like daylight – the Americans

were sending up parachute flares and continued to do so until morning," he remembered.[122] Knowing that they could be shot by either side if they were silhouetted by the flares, the troopers decided to stay right where they were. They remained there throughout that night and the following day. They attempted to move again that next night, but flares went up again. In all, the four lost paratroopers remained in the same spot in the wheat field with no food or water for more than seventy-two hours. The men were hungry and because of sleep deprivation, they were beginning to hallucinate. Since they had no shelter, direct sunlight baked them each day, making their thirst a terrible ordeal. The situation grew more and more desperate with each passing hour.

No flares went up on the third night when they moved. They then made their way to a road and continued on their southward trek. Shortly after they started walking on that road, Leidenheimer stepped in a water filled rut along the side of the road. When he realized what it was, he dropped to his knees, pushed the scum aside on the surface of the water and started drinking.[123] When the others realized what he was doing, they started drinking from the rut too like hogs at a trough. After filling their bellies with the putrid water, the men continued on and climbed a hill that looked safe to settle in for the night to get some sleep. The next morning, June 18th, they could see smoke rising from the chimney of a nearby farmhouse. "One of us should go over there and get some food," Leidenheimer suggested.[124] When the men simply stared back at him and made no response to the suggestion, he decided just to do it himself. He went up to the house and, when the farmer came outside, Leidenheimer asked him for food and directions. The Frenchman gave him three large pancakes and pointed him in the direction of American lines. He rushed back to the men and they started out for American lines as soon as they finished eating. Shortly thereafter, the troopers were walking slowly down a path between two apple orchards when they spotted an American soldier at the end of the path guarding it with a .50-cal. machine gun. Leidenheimer slung his MP40 around to his back and slowly walked forward with his hands clearly visible. When the soldier spotted the paratrooper approaching his position, the American soldier yelled halt and began asking him questions like "Who are you?" and, "What state were you born in?"[125] When Leidenheimer had answered those questions to the soldier's satisfaction, he was instructed to approach the position. The soldier kept his .50-caliber machine gun trained on the paratroopers the entire time as they approached and then, when he was convinced that they were Americans, he let them pass. After being captured, escaping and wandering around behind enemy lines for several days, Sgt. Leidenheimer was finally behind American lines. A few hours later, he was reunited with the men of B Company/507th.

9

To Cross the Merderet

After his jump, 2nd Battalion Commanding Officer, Lt. Col. Charles J. Timmes landed on the west bank of the Merderet, just to the east of Amfreville. As a result of the general state of disorder caused by the misdrops, Timmes did not know where the rest of the regiment was. Also, he was without a radio to communicate with regimental HQ, so he could not coordinate his movements with Col. Millett. He organized the men on hand – a force of about thirty paratroopers – and then moved toward Amfreville to join an attack that could be heard already in progress (this was Col. Millett's attack that is discussed in detail in Chapter 12). However, German defenders in the village repulsed that attack, forcing Timmes to withdraw. He pulled his force back to the apple orchard northeast of Le Motey where General Gavin had landed and spent his first hours on the ground.[1] At the orchard, Timmes established a defensive perimeter with the flooded Merderet river basin at his back.

Under normal conditions, the Merderet is little more than a narrow, meandering creek. But the river's condition was far from normal in June 1944, and it was swollen to many times its normal size. This had been the case for the most part ever since the Germans closed the locks at La Barquette in 1943.[2] In fact, as a result the Merderet was less of a river than a huge shallow lake a kilometer wide by ten kilometers long. The virtually impassable inundated

The locks at La Barquette near Carentan. Because these locks had been closed in 1943, the Merderet River was less of a river than a huge shallow lake a kilometer wide by ten kilometers long.

Aerial photograph of the Utah Beach landing area looking toward the west across the Cotentin peninsula. The flooded Merderet River can be seen at the top of the photograph.

area produced by the flood-stage river separated the Amfreville/Motey area on the west bank from Carentan, Chef-du-Pont and Ste.-Mère-Église on the east bank. The swollen condition of the river introduced a frightening problem into the American situation on the Cotentin Peninsula. With infantry and mechanized units of the U.S. Army VII Corps pouring across Utah Beach, the road networks leading from the beach into the interior carried inestimable strategic value. The American plan called for first the establishment, then the expansion of the Utah beachhead, followed by the drive toward Cherbourg. To do this, the personnel and vehicles flooding Utah Beach would need somewhere to go. With the Merderet and the Douve both in flood stage, the movement of VII Corps was severely restricted.

In the Utah Beach area only a scarce few elevated roadbeds, or 'beach exits', allowed passage through the marshy areas to the firm ground of the interior that could lead to Cherbourg. Securing these beach exits was the objective of both American Airborne divisions on D-Day. For the 82nd Airborne Division, its three parachute infantry regiments had each been given mission objectives in the Ste.-Mère-Église area. In his 1994 book *D-Day June 6, 1944: The Climactic Battle of World War II*, Dr. Stephen E. Ambrose described the mission tasking for the forces in the Utah Beach objective area:

> At Utah, the 4th Infantry was to cross the beach, establish control of the coast road, and move west along the causeways to the high ground inland, ready to wheel to the right to drive for Cherbourg. The 101st Airborne would land southwest of

Ste.-Mère-Église to secure the inland side of the causeways and to destroy the bridges in the vicinity of Carentan while seizing others to protect the southern flank of Utah. The 82nd Airborne was to land west of St. Sauveur-le-Vicomte to block the movement of enemy reinforcements into the Cotentin in the western half of the peninsula.[3]

According to this plan, the 505th Parachute Infantry would take the town of Ste.-Mère-Église itself as well as the eastern ends of the Merderet River crossings at Chef-du-Pont and La Fière. By dropping near Amfreville, the 507th would be in a position to capture the western ends of those two river crossings and the 508th would capture the Douve River crossings to the southwest. These river crossings had to be taken to prevent Rommel from carrying out his plan to destroy the Allied landing where it would be the most vulnerable – on the beaches.[4] Failure to secure the river crossings would almost certainly result in VII Corps first being backed up and isolated on the beach, and then destroyed piecemeal by German armored reinforcements. For that reason, taking Ste.-Mère-Église, Chef-du-Pont, La Fière and a little village named Cauquigny intact was of the utmost importance. Ambrose described that importance in *D-Day*:

> The 82nd had hoped to take La Fière and Chef-du-Pont during the night, then spend the day attacking westward to secure the line of the upper Douve River, but in the event the division had a terrific daylong fight for the two positions.[5]

• • •

The M1A1 rocket launcher, also known as the "Bazooka," was a 54-inch long, 18-pound weapon that fired a 2.36-inch high explosive rocket capable of penetrating light armor. When Lieutenant Louis Levy's ten-man patrol outposted Cauquigny at noon on D-Day, they carried one M1A1 to defend against enemy vehicles. (*Robert J. Carr Collection*)

After establishing his paratroopers in defensive positions at the apple orchard, Lt. Col. Timmes decided that the Cauquigny had to be defended. With his finger pointing out Cauquigny on the map, he turned to Lieutenant Louis Levy and said, "Take ten men, move south, dig in around this church and make sure that your fire positions are sited to cover the west end of the causeway."[6] Levy picked his ten men and took off immediately to establish the outpost as he had been ordered. For the most part Levy's crew was lightly armed: one man carried an M1A1 Thompson submachine gun, one carried an M1918A2 Browning Automatic Rifle (a.k.a. "BAR") and the rest carried M1 Garands.[7] However, they also toted the extra firepower of a number of Mk. II fragmentation hand grenades and a single M1A1 "Bazooka" rocket launcher.[8] The *bazooka* was a 54-inch long, 18-pound weapon that fired a 2.36-inch high explosive

rocket capable of penetrating light armor and it would be needed in the event that German armored vehicles appeared.

At Cauquigny an elevated causeway stretched five hundred yards across the inundated Merderet basin to the settlement of La Fière on the east bank. Holding Cauquigny, La Fière and the causeway stretching between them would give the U.S. Army VII Corps back at the beach the open artery over the swollen river it needed. The La Fière causeway was thus one of the most important strategic objectives in Normandy. At 11:30 am, Lieutenant Levy's patrol ran into Lieutenant Joseph Kormylo of D Co./507th. Kormylo was leading a group of twenty 507th troopers who were armed with rifles and a single Browning M1919A4 .30-cal. machine gun. The two Lieutenants had a quick conference and Levy decided that the best course of action would be for everyone in Kormylo's group

Aerial view of the La Fière causeway looking toward the west. La Fière manoir is in the foreground with the causeway extending across the Merderet River to Cauquigny beyond.

Photo of the La Fière causeway taken with the river in flood stage. This photograph was taken from just a few feet beyond the La Fière bridge looking west toward Cauquigny. (*82nd Airborne Museum via Phil Nordyke*)

except for the machine gun crew to move north to the orchard and join Timmes. Lt. Kormylo asked for permission to accompany the patrol to Cauquigny and Levy agreed and everyone continued on. When the patrol arrived around noon, Cauquigny was found to be clear of the enemy. Although the Germans had previously prepared defensive positions there, strangely no enemy soldiers had as yet deployed to occupy those positions. After setting up their weapons, the men broke out rations and started lunch. While they were eating a Frenchman appeared out of nowhere and gave the men milk and cider. All was quiet and everything seemed to be going perfectly according to plan.

• • •

After jumping, G Company Commander, Captain Floyd B. "Ben" Schwartzwalder landed on the north end of the inundated

The east side of the main house at La Fière manoir. Twenty-eight German infantrymen arrived here at 11:00 pm on June 5th to establish an outpost and paratroopers of the 82nd Airborne Division spent the first half of D-Day running them out of it. (*82nd Airborne Museum via Phil Nordyke*)

Manoir La Fière today. (*Photo by Heidi Stansbury-Paridon*)

Opposite: The barn at Manoir de la Fière today. (*Photo by Heidi Stansbury-Paridon*)

The west side of the main house at La Fière manoir. *(Photo by author)*

The south side of the main house at La Fière manoir. An MG42 machine gun firing from the second floor window harassed paratroopers of the 82nd Airborne throughout the morning on D-Day. *(Photo by author)*

area. From there, he and a group of about 45 other paratroopers moved south along the double tracks of the Cherbourg/ Ste.-Mère-Église railroad until they reached the road leading to La Fière at

dawn. From there, the La Fière manor was only eight hundred yards to the west. Realizing that his force's assigned sector was on the opposite bank at Amfreville, he decided to move it across the Merderet basin via the La Fière Bridge and causeway. Outside of La Fière, Schwartzwalder's group ended up fighting alongside the 505th PIR and Colonel Roy Lindquist's 508th PIR. By the time Schwartzwalder's force arrived, paratroopers had been exchanging fire with German defenders at Manoir de La Fière for several hours. That firefight had begun before dawn when an MG42 held up Lieutenant John J. "Red Dog" Dolan's A Company/505th Parachute Infantry. Although A Company's sole D-Day objective was to seize the La Fière bridge, the German fire forced the company to halt and then withdraw. The twenty-eight German soldiers who had arrived to occupy the manoir at 11:00 pm on the 5th were not going to give up without a fight. Since La Fière was one of the 82nd Division's primary D-Day objectives, those 28 Germans had to be driven from the settlement.

With the arrival of Dolan's men followed then by Schwartzwalder's and others, what was developing at the La Fière manoir that morning was a fight in which several units were simultaneously converging on an uncertain situation without the benefit of a briefing or proper communications. Each American element entered the situation piecemeal rather than as a part of a cohesive coordinated attack. In his 1962 book *Night Drop*, the Army's chief historian General S.L.A. Marshall described the lack of coordination in the early phase of the battle:

> Parties of fighting Americans were already pressing toward the same target from all directions, and at least one of them had already closed on it, engaged and shed blood. Not

Bullet damage to the east side of the main house at La Fière manoir. *(Photo by author)*

one was coordinated with any other, and none early sensed the presence of other Americans fighting in the vicinity. Of this lack of concert came much of the bitter hardship and unnecessary loss.

After making contact with the enemy, Dolan's 505th troopers, led by 1st Lt. George W. Presnell, attempted to flow around the obstacle by maneuvering around to attack the right or north side of the manoir. In doing so, they ran into more small arms and machine gun fire. In his 1999 book *No Better Place to Die*, Robert M. Murphy of the 505th PIR described the situation:

> By 0800 the action around the manoir was getting intense. It was the full-fledged beginning of the four-day continuous, vicious battle, likely the worst killing ground in the Normandy Airborne battle zones.[9]

Schwartzwalder's force of 507th troopers joined the fray soon thereafter. Having grown to a size of eighty men, the group continued down the Cherbourg/Carentan railroad until reaching the Ste.-Mère-Église/Amfreville road at daybreak on June 6th. Schwartzwalder had the men cross over and enter the fields on the south side of the road. Once in the fields, they began moving cautiously toward the manoir. But moving in that terrain was not without its complications – complications that would play a significant role in the confusing and uncoordinated fight that was developing. In *Night Drop*, S.L.A. Marshall provided a vivid description of this terrain:

The ground to the immediate south and east of the manoir buildings – a terrain partly pasture, partly orchard and partly truck garden – is extremely irregular. The side road cutting in through the manoir and used principally in servicing the establishment is bounded on the north by several large knolls, shaped not unlike the kitchen middens of Florida or the tells of the Middle East. The complex is crisscrossed by hedgerows. It was through these small hillocks and their surrounding hedges that Schwartzwalder made the first bid of the morning to seize the eastern end of the causeway.[10]

After moving only a short distance, the group came under fire from a German machine gun in the manoir – one of the same machine guns that had stopped Dolan's 505 paratroopers earlier that morning. In an attempt to outflank that gun, Schwartzwalder ordered his platoon leader for 1st Platoon, Lt. Johnny Marr, to take four men and try to make their way around to the south side of the manoir grounds. Marr quickly put his scouts out and started moving. He had landed on the east side of the Merderet River at 2:38 that morning. When he recovered from his parachute landing fall configuration (or PLF as the paratroopers referred to it) he was in water up to his chest – he had landed in the inundated area. Marr was about two miles east of Drop Zone "T" and there were no other members of his stick anywhere around. The reason for that was that the pilot had misjudged the terrain below him and overshot the drop zone. By the time he signaled the paratroopers to begin exiting the aircraft, it was already too late. Marr remembered, "We didn't get the green light until we were well past the Gourbesville DZ and over the water." The last man out of Marr's airplane that night was Cpl. Johnnie R. Nichols. When Nichols hit the ground, he was only a short distance from Utah Beach and was quickly captured by the Germans. Because he jumped well before Nichols, Marr had much better luck and landed very close to the Cherbourg/Carentan railroad embankment. Even in the dark of night, he could faintly make out the silhouette of the embankment and the power lines that ran along it. Since it was the closest dry land, he began sloshing his way toward it like so many other paratroopers that night. When he reached the embankment, he turned to the south and followed it in the direction of La Fière. That is when he linked up with Captain Schwartzwalder and the balance of the G Company men in the area.

Lt. Marr decided to approach the manoir by leading his team along the hedgerow closest to the river. As they moved down the length of that hedgerow, gunfire broke out all around them. "Why we weren't all killed, I'll never know," Marr remembered.[11] Deciding that it was "too hot" there, he yelled "Follow me!" to the men and dashed back down the length of the hedgerow to look for another route.[12] The five men then started toward the stone wall along the road to the bridge. But first they had to cross a small open field area to get there. As they did this, a German machine gun opened fire on them from only ten yards away. "They let us get that close," Marr recalled.[13] When the burst from the MG42 rang out, they were near a cattle fence on the southeast side of the manoir and T/5 Gaspar A. Escobar and Corporal Harold M. Lawton immediately went down – both shot through the legs. Despite his wounds, Escobar was nevertheless able to open up with his M1A1 Thompson submachine

An M15 White Phosphorous Smoke grenade recovered from the battle area at La Fière manoir. *(Photo by author)*

Bullet damage to the central post of the spiral staircase inside the main house at La Fière manoir. Clearly, the bullet traveled through the small window visible in the background. *(Photo by author)*

gun, firing wildly into the machine gun position as he fell. At that moment, a German soldier raised himself up with a cocked arm to throw a stick grenade toward the paratroopers. Corporal Lawton, who was wounded too, shouldered his M1A1 carbine and drilled several rounds into the German in rapid succession. The enemy soldier did not die immediately though, and stood there staggering and struggling to get rid of his grenade. Then Corporal Lawton and Private Marion Parletto each threw Mk. II fragmentation hand grenades in on the enemy position simultaneously. The explosion that followed killed three German soldiers and knocked out the machine gun. Despite this success though, the five point men were still in trouble. After the grenade explosions, Sub-machine gun fire from an unseen MP40 began to sweep the ground where the men were laying prone. Realizing that their position was untenable, Marr ordered a pull back and then tended to Corporal Lawton. Since Lawton had sustained two bullet wounds to the legs, Marr picked him up and carried him several hedgerows back to the main body where Schwartzwalder and the rest of his force were waiting.

When Marr reached Schwartzwalder, he reported that the machine gun had been destroyed. At about that time, Colonel Lindquist

with a group of men of the 508th PIR arrived on the scene as did Capt. Arthur Stefanich, company commander of C Company/505th PIR. By then, General Ridgway himself had directed Lindquist to seize the La Fière bridge,[14] so he etched out a very simple and straightforward battle plan: he wanted the 505 to continue pressuring the manoir from the north, he wanted the 508 men to come down the center (the Ste.-Mère-Église/Amfreville road) and he wanted Schwartzwalder's 507th troopers to continue pressuring the Germans from the south side. Unfortunately, inter-unit communications were not functioning optimally and A Company/505th PIR did not receive word of the organized effort. The result was that they continued fighting throughout the rest of the morning without knowing that they were being supported.[15]

With a minimum of coordination, these units continued to converge on the objective until elements of the 505 and the 508 began to enter the manoir grounds through the backyard. Soon thereafter, Lt. Dolan and 505th regimental Commanding Officer Colonel Ekman were standing in the driveway discussing the next move when suddenly approximately twelve Germans started firing out of the second floor windows of the manoir homestead.[16] There was some

Live Gammon grenade recovered from the battle area at La Fière manoir. *(Photo by author)*

Live ordnance recently recovered from the battle area at La Fière manoir. An M9A1 Anti-tank rifle grenade *(top),* **five Mk. II fragmentation hand grenades** *(center)* **and two M15 White Phosphorous Smoke grenades** *(bottom).* *(Photo by author)*

Another live Gammon grenade discovered recently near La Fière manoir. *(Photo by author)*

sporadic return fire lasting approximately ten minutes, then a white flag was waived out of one of the windows. A young 508 trooper then stepped forward into the open to take the surrendering Germans into custody. After only a few steps though, a shot rang out and the trooper fell dead. Although it may seem like it, he was probably not the victim of treachery but of misunderstanding. It is likely that not all of the defenders in the manoir were in on the surrender attempt and that the 508 trooper was shot by a German who did not know that a white flag had been presented. Miscommunication notwithstanding, heavy small arms fire erupted from all directions as soon as the man was killed. One of the A Co./505 men advancing with Dolan fired an M1A1 Bazooka rocket launcher, and a 2.36-inch rocket slammed into the stoutly built stone house. Then a 508th PIR Sergeant by the name of Palmer darted through the front door and emptied a full magazine from his M1A1 Thompson sub machine gun up through the floorboards of the second story. What was left of the German force surrendered at that point and the battle for the Leroux manoir at La Fière was over.

In the aftermath of the battle, M. Leroux, his wife and three children emerged from the wine cellar of the farmhouse. They had sought shelter there when the fighting began just after sunrise and then spent the next six hours listening to the furious battle going on all around them. As soon as the family came out of the cellar, First Sergeant Ralph Thomas of the 508 spoke with M. Leroux and convinced him that it would not be safe for them to stay at La Fière.

With the situation across the river at Cauquigny still unknown, continued enemy activity was certainly not a remote possibility, but practically a guarantee. M. Leroux agreed and the family departed that afternoon for a friend's farm nearby. The decision to leave would ultimately prove to have been a wise one because, during the next three days and nights, the fighting would only get more intense at La Fière. By the time that the Leroux family would return to the manoir after the battle, nearly half of the front of the farmhouse would be gone – the result of the heavy fighting yet to come.

• • •

At 1:45 pm, Capt. Schwartzwalder ordered his contingent of 507th men to cross the La Fière Bridge and proceed to the church at Cauquigny with Lt. Marr's composite platoon as the point element. Accordingly, Marr put his scouts out and the squad began to move forward. The scouts were Pfc. Johnie K. Ward and Pfc. James L. Mattingly. Lt. Marr remembered that, "The scouts got across the bridge, Ward was in the lead about a hundred yards up when Mattingly crossed the bridge."[17] As he moved cautiously out onto the open causeway and began to advance toward Cauquigny, a German defender concealed along the north side of the road just past the bridge rose to fire his Kar98k Mauser: Pfc. Mattingly had walked right up on an unseen MG42 machine gun nest. Miraculously, the shot missed and Mattingly spun around, leveled his Garand at the German and pumped eight rounds into him. After the eighth round, the en bloc clip pinged out of Mattingly's rifle and the bolt locked in the rear position. Mattingly dropped the now empty weapon, threw himself to the ground and tossed a hand grenade in on the MG42 crew. After the debris from the explosion settled, four badly wounded Germans in the north nest surrendered and five others concealed in a well camouflaged position on the south side of the causeway did likewise. Lt. Marr personally witnessed Pfc. Mattingly's conduct. "I was absolutely paralyzed watching this guy work," he recalled.[18] Mattingly then picked up his empty M1 and herded both groups of Germans together and lead them back toward the manoir at bayonet point. It was all over in fifteen seconds. General S.L.A. Marshall later recounted that, "In this way, the Merderet causeway was first taken by the enterprise of a solitary American rifleman."[19] Mattingly was ultimately awarded the Silver Star for what he did there that day. "It was the best piece of individual soldiering I've ever seen," Marr later recalled.[20]

Schwartzwalder's G Company had thus been an important component of the assault on the La Fière Manoir – the assault that secured the east end of the causeway. Then, Mattingly had singlehandedly routed the concealed Germans defending the causeway itself and Lt. Levy's recon patrol from Timmes's Orchard had con-

The Merderet River bridge at La Fière manoir. *(Photo by author)*

firmed that the west end was clear of the enemy. The La Fière causeway was now in American hands and the way had been paved for unfettered movement from one side to the other. Bob Davis was there when the paratroopers overran the manoir and then moved on toward the causeway. When his group of paratroopers crossed the bridge soon thereafter, there was no resistance and there were no Germans on the other side at Cauquigny. That situation, however, would soon change. Davis and his group would soon retrace their steps and return to La Fière.[21]

Since the situation on the west side of the causeway appeared to be secure, Schwartzwalder led his force of eighty paratroopers across the now secure causeway to link up with the small force at Cauquigny. With the 505th and 508th holding the east bank and with Levy's patrol holding the west bank, to Schwartzwalder the

82nd Airborne Division communications center near La Fière. (*82nd Airborne Museum via Phil Nordyke*)

Top: 82nd Airborne troopers passing a knocked-out Sherman tank in Normandy. (*82nd Airborne Museum via Phil Nordyke*) **Above: 507th paratroopers marching down a hedgerow-flanked road in Normandy shortly after D-Day.** (*Collection of The National D-Day Museum*)

situation at the causeway seemed well under control. That is when Schwartzwalder made a critical decision. He left Lt. Levy and eight men to guard Cauquigny and then led his force of eighty off on the west bank to look for Lt. Col. Timmes – a move that would soon cause the Americans to lose their western bridgehead, a loss that would lead to one of the more dramatic battles of the entire Normandy campaign.

• • •

Immediately after the conclusion of the fighting at the manoir, Colonel Lindquist began organizing the defenses for the bridge-head at La Fière. Since the manoir had been the specific D-Day objective of the 1st Battalion/505th PIR, and since General Gavin had instructed him to organize a reserve force, Lindquist turned things over to the battalion commander of the 1st Battalion/505th, Major Frederick Kellam. At about the same time that Schwartzwalder's force moved through Lt. Levy's squad at Cauquiqny, Kellam's 505 men went to work making preparations to receive the full weight of an enemy counterattack. Sergeant William D. Owens, a squad leader in the 505th PIR, described those preparations:

We placed our antitank mines right on the top of the road where the Germans could see them, but could not miss them with their tanks. We placed our two bazooka teams where they had a good field of fire.[22]

Four 505thmen made up the two bazooka teams: John D. Bolderson, Gordon C. Pryne, Marcus Heim, Jr. and Swedish-born Lenold Peterson. They occupied the pits that James Mattingly had cleared earlier in the day. The bazooka on the left (south) side of the causeway was twenty-five yards ahead of the other.[23] The 505 men even pushed a disabled German ammunition truck into the middle of the causeway to act as one final obstacle. Last but not least, a 57mm anti-tank gun was positioned directly at the bend in the road on the east side of the Merderet overlooking the causeway. Through much strenuous toil, the weapon had been recovered from a wrecked glider by men of B Co./307th Airborne Engineer Battalion and dragged to La Fière. The 57mm gun had actually been hauled up to the scene at 8:30 that morning, but could not be used in the assault against the manoir. Although sidelined during that battle, it would ultimately figure rather importantly into the battle that was about to take place. It was the afternoon of D-Day and the paratroopers at La Fière were bracing for the attack that they expected would soon come. They would not have to wait long.

10

"hold at all costs"

At the time of the Normandy operation, Roy Creek was E Company Commander in Lt. Col. Timmes's 2nd Battalion/507th. Creek had taken an ROTC commission in the U.S. Army after graduating from New Mexico State University in 1940 with a degree in agriculture. He volunteered for the parachute infantry soon thereafter and in July 1943, he was assigned to the 507th. During the flight across the channel, most of the men in Creek's stick slept. "As the formation passed the northern end of Guernsey Island the pilots notified the jumpmasters that they were twenty minutes out," he remembered.[1] Since Creek was the jumpmaster for his stick, he began waking up the other paratroopers so that they could begin getting ready to jump. A few minutes later, the red light by the door came on and Creek shouted "Four minutes!" to his men. He turned back to the door and could just make out the west coast of the peninsula and a heavy cloud bank which was beginning to reduce visibility.[2] When the pilot hit the clouds, his visibility was obscured right at the moment he needed it most. He must have wandered off course during those precious minutes of zero-visibility because when the airplane flew out of the clouds on the other side, the pilot made a number of dramatic course corrections. "We were banking all over the place," Creek remembered.[3] When visibility returned, the pilot evidently realized that he was in the wrong place because he turned his C-47 around 180 degrees and made a second drop zone approach. Since the planned drop zone approach had been from the west to the east, when the pilot reversed course to try it again, he was flying from east to west. Once the pilot had reoriented himself and the final course correction was done, he turned on the red light to signal the paratroopers to prepare to jump. Creek then turned to the men of his stick and issued the pre-jump series of orders: "Stand up! Hook up! Check equipment!" When the red light turned green, Creek shouted, "Let's go!" and jumped through the door.

Commanding Officer of E Company/507th PIR, Captain Roy E. Creek. *(Courtesy of Roy E. Creek)*

Captain Roy E. Creek leading E Company/507th PIR on parade. *(Courtesy of Roy E. Creek)*

His chute snapped sharply as it deployed correctly and then the night got very quiet as the C-47 flew off into the distance to the west. As Capt. Creek approached the ground, he could see that he was about to land in what looked like a "beautiful flat meadow."[4] When he hit though it was not a meadow at all – Capt. Creek had landed in water over his head. He reacted quickly by drawing his "razor sharp" M3 trench knife, and cutting his way out of his parachute harness. Once free, he struggled to get his head above water to take a gasp of air. After moving to a depth where he could at least touch the bottom, he proceeded to wade over to the nearest dry ground.[5] This was Creek's first thorough soaking of the day. Two more would follow. As the first man to jump in his stick, Creek had landed near the bridge at La Fière. The rest of his stick either landed in the inundated area or in the vicinity of Amfreville. In a night of many misdrops, Creek's pilot dropped his stick with remarkable accuracy after his 180 degree course correction. Although Capt. Creek landed in the inundated area to the east of Amfreville, some of the men from his stick that jumped after him actually landed on

Drop Zone "T". Although his identity is not known, that was one Troop Carrier pilot who certainly deserves to be commended for doing his duty under the most difficult of circumstances.

Once on the ground, Capt. Creek was only able to locate one other paratrooper from his stick because the others ended-up on the west bank of the Merderet inundated area. Practically all of those men were quickly captured. He soon found himself in a disorganized assembly area with a mixed group of lightly armed 82nd paratroopers. "There was no tactical unity, no supporting weapons, just a group of invaders who were wondering what had happened to all of their thorough planning," he remembered.[6] Soon they started to hear voices, but Creek could not tell if they were Germans or Americans. Alert and cautious, he crouched behind a tree, pointed his M1A1 Thompson sub-machine gun into the darkness and barked the challenge word: "Flash." He was supposed to get the reply "Thunder", but what he heard instead was, "Flash hell! This is Colonel Maloney!"[7] With only fifty men present, Lt. Col. Maloney assigned Creek to take charge of the group and organize a defensive perimeter while he attempted to contact the regiment with the only radio available; a waterlogged SCR-300.[8]

Since Lt. Col. Maloney did not know the whereabouts of Lt. Col. Timmes, Creek and the paratroopers with him were placed under the command of 1st Battalion CO, Lt. Col. Edwin J. Ostberg. At about 9:00 am on D-Day, Lt. Col. Ostberg and Creek Company forded the inundated Merderet to join Brigadier General Gavin on the east bank of the river near La Fière. It was Creek's second D-Day soaking. "As we waded in water sometimes chest deep, we were fired on by snipers," he remembered.[9] The German sniper fire was ineffective though, evidently due to the long ranges involved. Extreme range and inaccuracy notwithstanding, being under fire was an unnerving experience. "One couldn't help being concerned about the shots splashing water in his face," Creek remembered.[10]

By the time Ostberg's and Creek's force reached Brigadier General Gavin's CP, Lt. Levy's small force had occupied Cauquigny and elements of the 505th, 508th and 507th had taken La Fière.

German Kar98k Mauser equipped with telescopic site. A German sniper armed with a weapon such as this harassed Capt. Creek and his men as they crossed the Merderet River inundated area on D-Day. *(Collection of Seth Paridon)*

With both sides of the causeway in American hands, the situation seemed under control. Upon reporting in, Gavin directed Lt. Col. Ostberg to take his paratroopers south along the Cherbourg/Carentan railroad to Chef-du-Pont to seize the town and bridge across the Merderet "whenever it would be feasible."[11] Lt. Col. Maloney went with the group as its ranking officer. Ostberg would use Creek's lightly armed company to get the job done. "There were about one hundred men altogether equipped only with what they could carry: rifles, carbines, sub-machine guns, three machine guns and grenades of various types."[12] The force moved south along the railroad embankment until it reached the outskirts of the city.

In an attempt to overwhelm any enemy resistance swiftly, the paratroopers raced through the town toward the bridge with Lt. Col. Ostberg in the lead. A West Point graduate of intense dedication to duty, Ostberg had a reputation as an aggressive officer. He was known for rushing headlong into the most dangerous situations. "He was absolutely fearless," Creek remembered, "He would absolutely disregard his own personal safety at his own risk and peril."[13] By 10:00 am Ostberg's force "had reached the railroad station of

Chef-du-Pont without any opposition."[14] Ostberg dispatched one of his squads to clear the area to the northeast of the station and then led the remainder of his force southwest toward the bridge over the Merderet. Having as yet encountered no enemy resistance, it surprised the paratroopers when they suddenly drew fire from several buildings simultaneously. "Houses lined both sides of the road leading to the bridge," Creek recalled.[15] In short order, four paratroopers were hit by small arms fire from those houses and the rest of the force quickly sought cover. The swift momentum of the advance had been lost and Ostberg's men spent the next two hours clearing the western portion of the town building by building.

At the end of that two hours' fighting, the German defenders had fallen back toward the bridge. "We knew the bridge had to be taken before the Germans could organize their defense so we made a semi-organized dash for it," Creek remembered.[16] As the column of paratroopers moved through the outskirts of the town, they passed a large two-story creamery and proceeded on toward the bridge on the double. There they found German infantry dug in on both sides of the road in defensive positions – they were too late. The Ameri-

Aerial view of Chef-du-Pont showing the Merderet River Bridge. The creamery is at far right.

A German anti-tank gun abandoned in Normandy.
(Collection of The National D-Day Museum)

cans proceeded to clear "the eastern side of the bridge by overrunning the positions along the shoulders of the road."[17] Lt. Col. Ostberg, still leading from the front, then pressed on to the bridge and was moving across it when a shot rang out. He collapsed near the edge of the bridge and tumbled off into the Merderet – his fearlessness had caught up with him. The men behind immediately dove off to either side of the road seeking cover and some began to return fire. When Ostberg was shot, Captain Creek was three hundred yards back down the column on the other side of the creamery. Upon learning the news, he rushed forward and, with one other trooper, sprinted down to the riverbank where they spotted Ostberg floating in the water. The two men then hurriedly waded out and pulled him to shore (Creek's third soaking of the day). Luckily, he was not dead. Ostberg would live to fight another day, but for the duration of that battle he was out of action.

As the second highest-ranking officer present, Roy Creek was the next in line of command. Consequently, he immediately took control of the situation. He found that the force of paratroopers was in a very difficult position. Ostberg had extended the group out from the town along the causeway approaches leading from the creamery to the Chef-du-Pont Bridge. With the bridge approach flooded on both sides, Creek's men were woefully exposed and had nowhere else to go. "No one could hope to attack successfully or withdraw along these causeways without a preponderance of supporting fires – something we did not have," Creek remembered.[18] The volume of enemy rifle and artillery fire soon picked up, making the paratroopers' position near the bridge almost untenable. Then the crisis worsened when Lt. Col. Maloney received word from Gavin that he was to return to La Fière to help contain the crumbling situation there. Maloney did so immediately, taking a large

A pre-war view of the Merderet River bridge Chef du Pont. *(Courtesy of Dominique François)*

number of paratroopers with him and leaving Roy Creek with only thirty-four men. The punishing German artillery fire quickly reduced that strength to a mere twenty.

Just when it seemed that the situation could get no worse, an observer at the creamery spotted an ominous sight. A window on the second floor of the building provided a commanding view of the area surrounding the bridge. From that window, one of the paratroopers observed an estimated company-sized force of German infantry maneuvering around to the left rear of Creek's exposed position. It seemed that the grossly outnumbered paratroopers occupying exposed positions on the east side approach to the bridge were about to be outflanked. At about that same time, Creek received a message from Brigadier General Gavin to hold Chef-du-Pont at all costs. According to Creek, "It was pretty obvious that it couldn't cost much more."[19]

Then, as if by divine intervention, a flight of C-47s passed over the battle area dropping bundles of weapons and equipment. "One bundle of 60mm mortar ammunition dropped right in our laps," Creek remembered.[20] Luckily, the paratroopers had carried an M2 60mm mortar with them and the weapon was quickly brought into action with the healthy supply of M19A2 high explosive rounds that had fallen from the sky. Then a Waco glider lumbered in and

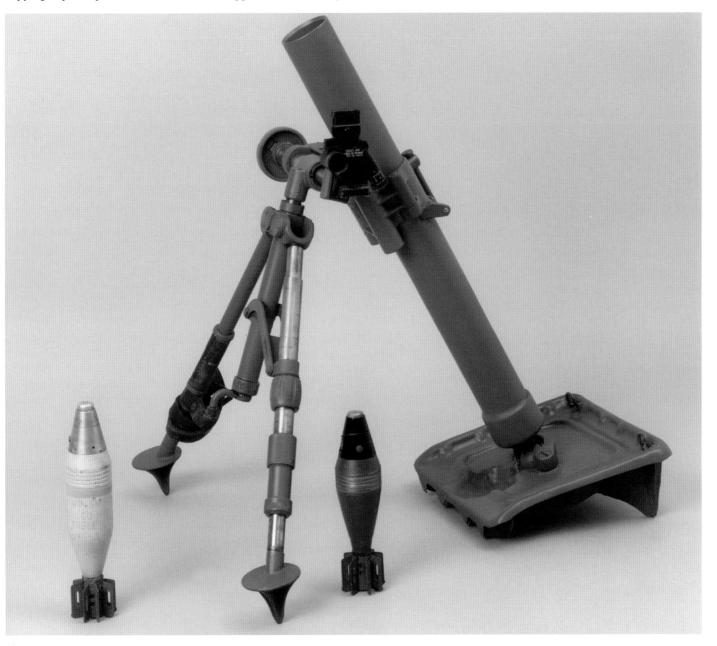

During the battle to capture Chef du Pont, the 507th force being led by E Company commander Captain Roy Creek depended on the supporting fire of an M2 60mm mortar like this one. At a critical moment in the battle, an equipment bundle containing 60mm ammunition fortuitously landed in the middle of Captain Creek's position. (*Robert G. Segel Collection*)

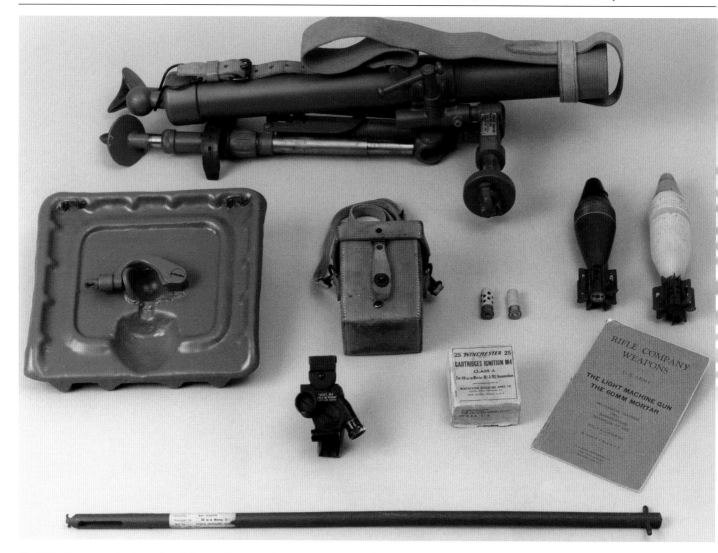

The M2 60mm mortar is pictured here with its various accessories: to the right of the base plate is the M4 leather carrying case for the M4 optical sight, two rounds of M4 ignition cartridges, an M19A2 High Explosive round, an M302 White Phosphorous round, a box of 25 M4 ignition cartridges, a 1941 manual, M4 mortar sight and an M9 cleaning staff. (*Robert G. Segel Collection*)

skidded to a landing near Creek's position. Inside that glider was a 57mm anti-tank gun that was quickly hauled up to Creek's position near the bridge and placed into action against the German artillery across the marsh. Fire from that 57mm gun immediately suppressed the German artillery fire and, after a few salvoes, scored a direct hit. With the German gun on the other side of the Merderet out of action, Creek's chances improved significantly.[21] Thirty minutes later, another godsend materialized when reinforcements arrived from La Fière in the form of one hundred paratroopers. Together with the recently arrived reinforcements, Creek's men organized strong defensive positions on both sides of the road and prepared to make one last attack to capture the bridge. Creek recounted the final stage of the battle vividly:

We opened fire with every weapon we could get into position, including our 60mm mortar. On a prearranged signal, all fires lifted and ten men and one officer stormed the bridge and went into positions on the western approach to guard the causeway. Five Germans made a run for it down the deathtrap causeway and were immediately shot down. That did it. The battle was over. The bridge was ours and we knew we could hold it.[22]

The southern bridge across the Merderet had thus been secured and the decisive battle for control of Chef-du-Pont had been won. Further to the north at La Fière, the drama was only about to begin.

Two 507th paratroopers talking with soldiers of the 90th Infantry Division near the body of a German KIA in Normandy. Note that the two troopers are using segments of T-5 parachute as improvised camouflage helmet covers. The paratrooper facing the camera has also "liberated" a 9mm Browning Hi-power pistol. *(Courtesy of Mark Bando)*

11

No Better Place to Die

Aware of the dire importance of what was at stake at the La Fière crossing of the Merderet inundated area, the Germans had already dispatched forces on the west bank to counterattack toward Cauquigny and the American bridgehead beyond. Soon, elements of the *1057th Infantrie* Regiment and the *.100 Panzer Ausbildungs und Ersatz Abteilung*, both a part of the German *91st Luftland* Division, appeared west of Cauquigny, bearing down on the causeway. Brigadier General Gavin remembered that, "From then on the German forces attacked aggressively and increased in strength."[1]

As Lt. Levy was finishing his lunch, a group of thirty-nine paratroopers from the 508th PIR arrived at Cauquigny. The platoon-size group was a composite of several small groups of men that had landed on the west bank. These new arrivals had not yet participated in any fighting and were quickly absorbed into the defensive positions around the church. Levy had placed the machine gun so that its field of fire covered the western bank of the inundated area and the bridge and he deployed riflemen around it.[2] The bazooka team had been set up in such a way that it covered the road leading off to Amfreville; any vehicle coming down that road would drive into its field of fire. Feeling secure with these preparations, Levy had sent a runner back to Timmes's Orchard that afternoon with the message: "We have secured the bridgehead."[3]

No sooner had Levy sent that message though than his situation underwent some major changes. Of course shortly thereafter, Capt. Schwartzwalder's group of eighty paratroopers had moved through Levy's line, paused briefly and then moved off toward Timmes's Orchard. When Schwartzwalder departed Cauquigny, he took most of the composite 508th group with him, including the Bazooka team. Not long after Schwartzwalder's departure, Col. Lindquist had personally crossed the causeway to get an appraisal

of the situation. There he had found Lt. Levy's small, lightly armed force guarding the western bridgehead. Lindquist had thereafter returned to La Fière and ordered B Co./505th to move across the causeway and reinforce Levy.[4] "B Company" was actually the polite designation that had been given to an "ill-armed and motley medley" of approximately forty "strayed artillerymen and headquarters hands."[5] Lindquist had dispatched them to Cauquigny with the hopes that they could prove useful in the event of a counterattack. As fate would have it, they were just leaving La Fière when the expected counterattack started.

•••

At that exact moment, the defenders at Cauquigny were beginning to hear something. Although at first very faint, each person gradually became aware that a far-off noise was growing louder with each passing second. "Then rose the staccato chorus of an unmistakable and spine-tingling rumble," recounted S.L.A. Marshall.[6] For the paratroopers at Cauquigny, their worst nightmare was bearing down on them from the west – tanks were approaching. What the men could hear was the engine noise of the Renault R-35 and Hotchkiss H-35 light tanks of *1. Companie* of the *100. Panzer Ausbildungs und Ersatz Abteilung* coming from the west from the le Motey/Amfreville area. The *Abteilung* had collected and assembled during the evening of June 6, 1944 to form a roadblock on the N803 running from Baupte to Carentan. After sunrise, the unit was sent piecemeal to various spots around the Cotentin. In the afternoon, *1. Companie* was ordered to attack American parachute forces known to be present in the vicinity of La Fière.

With enemy tanks approaching, Levy was not content to wait for the enemy to roll over him, so he turned to Lt. Kormylo and an unidentified private and said, "Come on along with me."[7] Levy then ran down a sunken lane flanked by tall hedgerows on the boundary of the church property that ran perpendicular to the main road to Amfreville. As they moved, Levy said to Kormylo, "Maybe we can swing around their left and get in a few licks before they know what has hit them."[8] Levy lead the men down the sunken lane and stopped short of its intersection with the Amfreville road. He then directed the other two to move up close to the intersection to engage the enemy. "If it gets too rough, run, and I'll cover your retreat," he advised them.[9] Lt. Kormylo and the unknown Private crept down the hedgerow alongside the lane until they were within one stride of the open road.[10]

By then, the roar of the German tanks had grown deafening. The three paratroopers shouldered their weapons and aimed at the intersection. Kormylo saw the tanks first as they began to cross in front of him. Then a small group of German infantry appeared and obliquely crossed his front as they surged ahead of the tanks. Kormylo and the unknown Private both opened fire with their M1s simultaneously and the enemy infantry began to fall. After each man had fired a complete clip of 8 rounds, they both sprang to their feet and dashed back past Lt. Levy's position. Through the leaves of the hedgerow, Levy observed a group of Germans setting up an MG42 just short of the intersection with the sunken lane. He knew that if they succeeded, they would be able to rake the Cauquigny churchyard with machine gun fire to support their advance. Unhesitatingly, Levy drew a Mk. II fragmentation hand grenade from his pistol belt, pulled the pin and lobbed it toward the gun. The grenade landed directly on target and exploded, wounding the

members of its crew. As the three wounded Germans lay where they had been thrown by the explosion, Levy ran out onto the open roadway and finished them off with his M1 rifle.[11] He then turned and fired a few rounds at the lead tank before extracting himself and falling back to the concealment of the sunken road.

At that point, the tanks began shelling the church and causeway as the supporting infantry moved up to the last hedgerow and began laying down intense small arms fire. Bullets zipped and ricocheted across the graves in the little cemetery around the chapel leaving damage that is still visible there today. By then, only six paratroopers were left occupying the churchyard. At the forward position with Levy, Kormylo and the unknown Private, the bank of the hedgerow was too tall and the shrubbery too thick for exchanging effective rifle fire, so the fight quickly broke down to an exchange of hand grenades at five yards range. They threw several, and the Germans replied with several of their own. However, the three lightly armed and outnumbered paratroopers did not stand a chance against the overwhelming German force swarming into them. Suddenly a German soldier attempted to push through the hedgerow close to Lt. Kormylo's position while he was firing towards the tanks with an M1A1 Carbine. As the German struggled to penetrate the natural growth, the Lieutenant thrust the carbine's muzzle against the German soldier's helmet and proceeded to empty an entire magazine into the man's skull. The Germans were getting closer with each passing minute and the situation was getting more desperate.

Since the three men had succeeded in slowing the Germans down at the intersection as had been the intention, and since they were in peril of being overrun at any moment, the time had come for them to pull back to the churchyard at Cauquigny. Kormylo lead the way and yelled out, "Come on, let's get the hell out of

The 20-pound M1918A2 Browning Automatic Rifle – referred to as the BAR by GIs – was the U.S. Army's squad automatic weapon during World War II. (*Robert J. Carr Collection*)

The bitter fighting around the church at Cauquigny left damage that can still be observed there today. *(Photo by author)*

here!"[12] Lt. Levy went with him and the two Lieutenants made it to the churchyard wall unscathed. The unknown Private, however, was killed before he could get there. As they continued to roll towards the church and bridgehead, a bazooka rocket slammed into the lead Hotchkiss and it burst into flames. No one knows where that rocket round came from though. When the first tank was hit, Pvt. Orlin Stewart was occupying the roadblock that had previously included the only bazooka at Cauquigny. When the mysterious bazooka round hit the Hotchkiss, he rose from his concealment and ran toward the intersection firing his BAR as he went. Just as he got there, two other tanks came around the bend in the road and began to pass the burning tank. Stewart leapt into a roadside ditch. He could see the two tanks clearly as they advanced toward him, clearing the final bend in the road before the bridge. They were only thirty yards away when a Private and a First Sergeant crawled down the same ditch and prepared to toss grenades at the tanks as they passed. The

unknown Private and a First Sergeant uncapped several Gammon grenades and waited for the two tanks to pull broadside to their position. With Stewart providing covering fire from his BAR, the two men hurled the grenades as soon as the tanks were alongside the ditch.[13]

The explosions of five Gammon grenades then rang out and the two tanks clanked to a stop right in front of the ditch, disabled and in flames. The crew of one of the tanks attempted to bail out, but a well-placed fragmentation hand grenade killed two of them before they could get away. A third crewman, sheltered from the hand grenade blast by the steel of the crippled tank, dashed out from behind his cover and began to run back in the direction of Amfreville. Without hesitating, Stewart finished him with a burst from his BAR. Then, another tank came around the bend in the road followed by a column of supporting infantry. The defenders there at Cauquigny were at that point grossly outnumbered and almost out of ammunition. The survivors followed the only escape route available to them and retreated back to Timmes's Orchard. There, they joined a group that, prior to their arrival, consisted of twenty-one officers and one hundred and twenty men. After catching a quick breather, Levy and Kormylo talked out a quick postmortem of the battle in which they had just participated. Both men agreed that, had there been a full dug-in rifle company there, the enemy would not have been able to capture Cauquigny. Had there been a full rifle company there, the enemy would have been stopped before the causeway. As destiny had it though, there was no great

More bullet damage in the churchyard at Cauquigny. *(Photo by author)*

defensive victory at Cauquigny on the afternoon of D-Day. Instead, the bridgehead had been lost in a skirmish that had lasted from start to finish no more than ten minutes.[14]

• • •

Although dramatic events had just played themselves out around the churchyard, an equally dramatic yet tragic episode occurred simultaneously on the causeway itself. When the counterattack struck, the men of B Co./505th were only just beginning to reach Cauquigny. At about the same time that German infantrymen were in the process of sweeping past the church, B Company's two leading squads were arriving at the western end of the causeway. Those first two squads were turning off to the south to begin digging in when the tanks began shelling the church and causeway. For the remaining men of B Company – those that were not yet on the firm ground of the west bank – this was a death sentence. The tanks proceeded to shell the causeway behind them to cut off their

line of retreat. Then machine guns brought forward by the attackers prevented the stragglers from moving off to the right of the axis of advance (the north side of the causeway). In *Night Drop*, S.L.A. Marshall described what came next:

It was too late to advance, retreat or deploy. The men broke to the left and individually tried to wade, crawl and swim back through the marsh. But Germans and their weapons were thick on the western bank and were flailing the marsh with fire before the Americans had time to vanish into the rushes and reeds. Many of the fugitives were shot dead while wading in the muck next to the west shore; more of them, wounded, struggled on, only to die by drowning in the river; if any escaped, report was not made of it.[15]

As soon as the Germans developed their hold on the western terminus of the causeway, mortars and artillery fire began falling on the Americans still occupying La Fière on the east bank. "They

Tanks of the *100. Panzer Ausbildungs und Ersatz Abteilung* (**100th Tank Training and Replacement Battalion**) **on the La Fière causeway on June 10, 1944. These tanks were knocked-out by paratroopers of the 505th Parachute Infantry late in the day on June 6th.** (*National Archives and Records Administration via Jump/Cut Productions and Scott Carroll*)

were throwing everything in the world at us," remembered Carson Smith.[16] In an attempt to weaken the American force on the west bank, the Germans pounded La Fière with deadly and effective fire. Of the experience, Bob Davis would later recall the artillery with vivid detail: "We had a lot of respect for the German 88, I'll tell you that."[17]

At about 5:30 pm, the German force that had earlier overrun Cauquigny started across the causeway toward La Fière where the men of A Co./505th were waiting. The enemy advanced quickly with two more Renault tanks, trailed by a large infantry force. "We let them come on in," remembered Sergeant William Owens.[18] The first tank moved ahead until it was forty feet short of the line of anti-tank mines stretching across the road. There it halted while the crew evidently considered options about how to proceed. With the vehicle at a dead stop, it was a perfect target. The tank commander then opened his hatch and stood up in the turret to take a look at the situation. With the tank commander in full view, the defenders at La Fière opened up and three things happened simultaneously. First, Pvt. Clarence Becker fired a long burst from his .30-cal. machine gun that killed the tank commander. Second, both M1A1 Bazookas rang out and a pair of 2.36-inch rockets hurtled toward the target at 275 feet per second. The rockets struck the tank's comparatively thin armor and exploded. Thirdly, the 57mm anti-tank gun on the hill fired and the hapless vehicle erupted into a blazing inferno.[19]

With the first tank hit and burning, the other tank then attempted to navigate around the line of anti-tank mines by steering off to the side of the causeway. Lenold Peterson then sprang from his concealed pit and ran forward with his bazooka. He fired four rockets into the turret of the tank as quickly as he could load the weapon, but nothing happened. Then he scored an effective hit right where the turret meets the body and followed that with a direct hit that shattered the tank's bogey wheels. Peterson then ran forward and put a rocket into the rear of the vehicle. Unaware of the extent of the damage to the bogeys, the driver put the vehicle in reverse and attempted to back away from the area. It was then that Peterson fired one last rocket that set off the vehicle's fuel tank and incinerated the crew.[20] "Then they tried to get the infantry through to knock us out," Sgt. Owens remembered.[21] A company-sized force of German infantry had advanced out onto the causeway behind the tanks, but because of Peterson's effective bazooka fire, their protection had been stripped away. Although these same Germans had quickly overwhelmed Lt. Levy's force, the wide-open causeway in front of La Fière offered none of the concealment that the hedgerows at Cauquigny had. The German infantrymen were consequently easy targets for the paratroopers on the high ground on the east bank of the river. Concentrated fire from the paratroopers' M1 rifles and especially their .30-caliber machine guns tore viciously into the

infantry exposed on the open road, decimating them. What was left of the German force fell back to Cauquigny. A stalemate had developed at the La Fière causeway and the next two days would pass with German and American forces locked in a life or death struggle to break it.

• • •

The next morning (June 7th) the Germans attacked La Fière in force again. It began at 8:00 with a crescendo of 120mm mortar and 88mm fire as well as machine gun fire that targeted the paratroopers at the manoir. "They really clobbered us," Sgt. Owens remembered.[22] Then, just as they had the day before, more tanks and infantry appeared on the causeway. The two tanks of this renewed assault advanced as far as the wreckage of the tanks that had been knocked out the previous day. With its path blocked, the lead tank first slowed and then stopped. Back at the heights above La Fière, the 57mm anti-tank gun barked and the lead tank instantly burst into flames. It rolled a few more feet until it was even with the old truck that the paratroopers had dragged out to block the road. When it finally coughed, lurched and squeaked to a stop, it blocked the progress of the other three tanks moving down the causeway. The motionless tanks became a steel shield for the advancing German infantry, providing a measure of protection on a roadbed that would

A derelict Hotchkiss H-38 light tank of the *100. Panzer Ausbildungs und Ersatz Abteilung* on the La Fière causeway after having been knocked out by 82nd Airborne Division paratroopers on D-Day. *(Courtesy of Dominique François)*

otherwise have been nothing short of a deadly gauntlet. Exploiting the opportunity of cover provided by the tanks, the enemy infantrymen quickly dashed forward one by one as far as the knocked-out lead tank. Incoming mortar fire picked up on the exposed American positions at that point and the Germans took advantage of that supporting fire to creep to within thirty-five yards of the forward defensive positions at the La Fière Bridge.

At point blank range, the enemy tossed grenades and poured a relentless fire into the paratroopers using Mauser rifles and MP40 sub-machine guns. Dolan's A Company/505th men at the foot of the bridge were exposed to the full weight of the German assault, and the combat grew to a ferocious intensity. "We gave them everything we had," Sgt. Owens later recalled.[23] A quiet punch-drill operator from Detroit, Owens was conspicuously brave in fighting off the German thrust. He first began firing into the ranks of onrushing German infantry with a Browning M1919A4 .30-cal. machine gun. It was such a target-rich environment that the .30-cal. machine gun he was using built up so much heat that it quit firing. He then picked up a nearby M1918A2 Browning Automatic Rifle and turned its firepower on the enemy. When he exhausted the BAR's ammunition, he found another .30-cal. machine gun that was not being used in a nearby position. The two men that had been using the weapon had both been killed by an artillery round that landed close to their fighting position. Owens took up the weapon and discovered that its tripod was missing. Undaunted by this, he simply rested the barrel shroud of the weapon on a pile of dirt and opened fire. Although the volume of fire generated by Sgt. Owens' determined stand inflicted numerous casualties on the enemy, the enemy was likewise taking a heavy toll on the American platoon. Casualty after casualty mounted until the Germans had reduced it to just fourteen men capable of fighting. "I don't know how it was possible to live through it," Owens remembered.[24] With mortar rounds exploding all around them and with the German assault force poised to overrun their positions, the situation for Dolan's paratroopers at the La Fière Bridge looked grim. Without a radio to communicate with Lt. Dolan, Sgt. Owens sent a runner back up to the manoir to report his squad's situation and ask for orders. The runner returned after only a few minutes with a note to Owens from Dolan that read, "I know of no better place to die than this."[25]

But then the brutal attack mysteriously ended. As if by divine intervention, the German infantry that had advanced almost to the bridge melted back toward Cauquigny in a fighting withdrawal. A strange quiet soon settled over the battlefield and shortly thereafter the Germans asked for a truce to remove their wounded. Sgt. Owens described the gruesome scene: "I moved to where I could get a good view of the causeway and I estimated that I could see at least two hundred dead or wounded Germans scattered about."[26] It took the enemy nearly two hours to remove their casualties and then they disappeared from sight. A single platoon of American paratroopers had broken the back of the final German attempt to capture the bridge at La Fière.[27]

Afterward, the artillery fire from the west bank resumed although it was less intense than before. The shelling continued after dark and then later that night the Germans made an attempt to move one of the knocked-out tanks. At approximately 2:00 am the defenders at La Fière began hearing movement on the causeway. First, they registered the unmistakable sounds of another tank approaching and they consequently began preparing to defend against a night attack. Then, by the sounds coming from out of the dark night, the paratroopers could tell that the new tank was attempting to push the disabled tank out of the way to clear the causeway. The paratroopers correctly realized that if the Germans could move the disabled tank blocking the causeway they would be able to send armor across under the cover of darkness to sweep through La Fière and perhaps even push on toward Ste.-Mère-Église. "I knew if they succeeded we would be through," Sgt. Owens remembered.[28] Owens then took a couple of Gammon grenades and in the pitch darkness crawled to within approximately thirty yards of the enemy tanks. "The first grenade I threw missed and hit the disabled tank instead of the one that was trying to move it." The force of the exploding grenades apparently intimidated the German tank crew because they soon thereafter beat a hasty retreat. "The Germans didn't take any more chances, they put the tank into reverse and moved back," Owens remembered.[29] They would not be back again after their abortive attempt to move the disabled tank. From that point forward, no more German tanks or infantry would set out onto the causeway itself. "They never tried to get across again after they raised the Red Cross flag," Sgt. Owens remembered.[30]

The counterattacks on June 6th and 7th constituted the Germans' serious bid to drive the 82nd Airborne Division back toward Ste.-Mère-Église. Those counterattacks had failed, consuming the Germans' available military resources in the process. The enemy still had the manpower to defend Cauquigny, but because the paratroopers put up such a remarkable fight, the German ability to launch any further offensive thrusts toward the defenders at La Fière had been exhausted. Although the paratroopers had survived the German onslaught, the situation at the causeway remained a stalemate and the great, decisive battle was yet to be waged.

12

Stabbing Westward

As of sunrise on D-Day, 1st Sergeant Barney Hopkins had located and teamed up with a handful of other troopers including D Company commander Captain Clarence A. Tolle. The men were moving in the direction of the 507th assembly area near Amfreville when, at about 9:00 am, they met up with a group of about two dozen 507th troopers being lead by Colonel Millett. After a brief discussion with the new arrivals, Millett decided to take the group into Amfreville with Captain Tolle, Hopkins and five other D Company men on point. As the 507th men cautiously entered the village, they suddenly drew gunfire from a group of four Germans. The enemy soldiers fired just a few shots and then broke and ran. With that, Captain Tolle turned to Hopkins and said, "Go get 'em."[1] Hopkins and two other paratroopers took off like a bolt of lightning in pursuit of the fleeing soldiers, catching up to them at a nearby barn. As the three paratroopers approached the barn, the Germans ran again. Rather than letting them get away, Hopkins shouldered his M1A1 Carbine and shot three of the Germans, killing them as they fled. The other two paratroopers killed the fourth German. Having completed that assigned task, the three men then moved back to rejoin the others. When they were only about fifty yards away from his position, Captain Tolle rose up a little and called out to Hopkins. At that moment, a German machine gun fired a long burst and four bullets exploded into Tolle's chest. Hopkins, who was watching as it happened, ran over to his Captain and pulled him into a ditch along the side of the road. Moments later, Captain Tolle died in that ditch in Barney Hopkins's arms.[2]

The men knew where the machine gun burst that killed Captain Tolle had come from – a building at the end of the street with a large red cross painted on it. Hopkins led them to an "obscure" position across the street from the building in question and the men prepared to attack. One of those men, Corporal Karl Kuhn, was armed with an M1 Garand rifle that was equipped with an M7 grenade launcher. Once in position, Hopkins ordered Corporal Kuhn to put a rifle grenade through the second story window. Kuhn then retrieved a grenade, mounted it on the M7 grenade launcher on his Garand and fired it right through the window that Hopkins had indicated. The paratroopers waited for an explosion, but nothing happened. It turns out that, in his excitement, Kuhn had neglected to pull the grenade's safety pin before firing it. "Pull the pin and put another one in there," was Hopkins's reply.[3] Kuhn did it right this time and the rifle grenade exploded on target. Following the explosion, three Germans came running out of the building's ground floor. Hopkins was ready for them and shot and killed all three with his carbine as they spilled out into the street.[4]

Not knowing the strength of the enemy in the village, Hopkins decided that the prudent thing to do would be to return to Colonel Millett's position. When they did, they carried Captain Tolle's body with them. Colonel Millett decided that the enemy strength in Amfreville was too great for the small force he had on hand to get into a house-to-house fight. He therefore decided to withdraw and pulled the men back to a sunken road about eight hundred yards west of town where they set up defensive positions. While there, a few more paratroopers from various units joined them. By that time, the group numbered approximately forty men.[5]

• • •

After sunrise on D-Day, Paul Smith stumbled across a small group of paratroopers being lead by 507th Regimental Operations Officer, Major Ben F. Pearson. Throughout the day the size of this group grew as it absorbed other small groups of paratroopers. The day was spent searching for Col. Millett and in small firefights with the Germans. All that night, the group moved west and ended up near the Gourbesville-Ettienville highway at daybreak on D+1 (June 7th). Although the group only had one radio that worked, contact was established with Col. Millett's people that afternoon. A runner was then sent to guide Smith and Pearson's group to the 507th regimental CP where they found Col. Millett with a group of paratroopers, which had by then grown in number to about 120. Pearson's men then joined Millett's defensive perimeter.

While organizing the enhanced defensive line, Captain Smith and 1st Sergeant Hopkins found themselves deployed at the northern end of the perimeter along a "well-traveled" sunken dirt road.[6] The two men were surveying the situation there and improving their fighting positions when they heard a vehicle approaching. Every paratrooper deployed in the vicinity of the well-traveled road took cover and went to the ready with their weapons. Moments later, a motorcycle sidecar appeared carrying two Germans. Holding their fire, the paratroopers let the motorcycle get close. When it was practically on top of them, Hopkins, Smith and the others released a flurry of bullets that killed both Germans. The motorcycle sidecar careened off into the ditch at the side of the road and stopped about fifteen yards from Hopkins. "To be sure the two Germans would not oppose us any further, I went down to them and shot them again, to make sure they were dead, with Captain Smith giving me coverage while out there," Hopkins remembered.[7]

After the incident, Smith and Hopkins discussed what had happened and concluded that the motorcycle was an advanced party scouting ahead for some other force. This suspicion was confirmed during their conversation when the sound of another approaching vehicle became audible. The troopers made ready again. Then an open-topped German command car carrying a driver and three officers approached the position. Smith and Hopkins were hidden in a hedgerow bordering the road only fifteen feet from the middle of the road. Just as they had with the motorcycle, the paratroopers held their fire until the command car pulled abreast of their position, and then they opened fire. With the driver mortally wounded by the opening broadside, the car swerved, ran off the road and turned over on its side. Hopkins made sure the four Germans were dead using his M1A1 Carbine.[8]

Smith and Hopkins talked again and concluded that the two vehicles they had just dealt with were the advanced party for a larger force that would be on top of them sooner than later. Smith then prepared a trap to deal with that anticipated eventuality. First, the paratroopers covered the motorcycle sidecar and the staff car with some brush to conceal them. Then Corporal Kuhn was placed in a hedgerow overlooking the road and instructed to load an anti-tank grenade onto his grenade launcher. Smith then placed five paratroopers on each side of Kuhn for protection. While Smith and

Hopkins were still organizing it, the trap was sprung. Less than ten minutes had elapsed since the destruction of the staff car when a convoy of seven German vehicles approached the waiting ambush.

When it was even with his position, Corporal Kuhn fired the anti-tank grenade into the hood of the lead vehicle. The truck's engine compartment exploded into flames and the other six vehicles came to a grinding halt behind it – right in front of the waiting 507th men. Then the paratroopers opened fire on the vehicles with their M1 rifles, carbines and submachine guns. Germans began spilling out of the vehicles only to be mowed down by a curtain of concentrated small arms fire. A dozen or so Germans were killed in an instant and another dozen or so promptly surrendered. The paratroopers then emerged from the hedgerows to inspect the vehicles of the convoy and to take control of their prisoners. One of the troopers called for the 1st Sergeant to come quick and Hopkins ran over to the second truck in line. The paratroopers had found several boxes of German occupation currency, all in 1,000-franc denominations. There was such a large quantity that it was likely a division payroll. Assuming the money to be worthless, Hopkins told the men that they could do whatever they wanted with it. "Many of my soldiers stuffed hand fulls in their pockets," he remembered.[9] Those 1,000-franc notes proved to be very useful for starting campfires and even as toilet paper in the weeks to come.

• • •

Millett's perimeter remained under constant attack all that day and night and was later reinforced when Captain Allen W. Taylor, H Company Commander, arrived with an additional one hundred men just after dawn on D+2 (June 8th).[10] Throughout that day, attacks on the position increased in intensity. Barney Hopkins recalled that, "The Germans attacked us three times that day, a different place each time and we suffered several casualties."[11] As that was the case, Col. Millett decided to pull back to the east, toward the Merderet in search of a more easily defensible position. After sunset, the force prepared to move out toward the Merderet, finally getting underway around midnight. Made up of 250 Americans and 90 German prisoners, the column was large and unwieldy. 1st Sergeant Hopkins, who was with the rear guard, described how challenging it was to move the big column:

> We were just about surrounded by Germans, so we moved out in single file so we could slip through German lines. When we detected an enemy patrol, we stopped to let them pass. Our men were dead-tired, not having slept or eaten very little in the past three days. As a result, when we stopped, having to wait ten or fifteen minutes for the German patrol to pass, various

men would doze off. This broke up our line and we fragmented into various size groups.[12]

Soon after turning northeast toward the Amfreville-Gourbesville highway, the head of the column began to draw fire from a pair of MG42s. With his force at a dead stop and under fire, Millett decided that the best thing to do would be to back away from the German machine guns rather than assault them head-on in the dark. Captain Paul Smith and another officer threw hand grenades and fired on the MG42s to provide covering fire for the head of the column as it started to back up. The almost zero visibility of

the pitch-black night, the dense vegetation of hedgerows and the broken ground fragmented the large force even more. The head of the column separated from rest with the result that a group of 507th troopers that included Col. Millett was, shortly thereafter, captured by the enemy. Paul Smith soon found himself in command of 150 paratroopers and all 90 of the prisoners. Despite the setback, he kept what was left of the column moving toward the Merderet.

Just after sunrise, a sudden explosion blew the point man into the air. Although at first it seemed obvious that the man had stepped on a land mine, closer investigation proved otherwise: the Gammon grenade in the left cargo pocket of his jumpsuit trousers had actu-

ally caused the explosion. When 1st Sergeant Hopkins got there, he found that the man's leg had been nearly blown off by the grenade. The troopers that rushed to his aid did what they could; they put a tourniquet on the leg, treated it with sulfa and bandaged the entire wound. They gave the man some sulfa pills and a canteen of water, then wished him well and left him in a nearby hedgerow. "There was no way to do better, we were fifteen miles behind the German lines," Hopkins remembered.[13] Obviously the Gammon grenade could be a very dangerous device.

After a temporary delay in dealing with the injured man, Captain Smith's column continued to the east. At approximately 8:00 am, the column encountered considerable enemy fire from a group of stone houses about 1,000 yards northeast of Amfreville.[14] At that point, 1st Sergeant Hopkins was advancing with a group of about twenty troopers when a German machine gun in one of the houses pinned them down with accurate fire. The only way for Hopkins to keep the group moving was by laying down suppressing fire with his carbine while the men crawled forward. The German gunner would keep his head down while Hopkins fired off a fifteen-round magazine, then when Hopkins went to change magazines the German would open up on the paratroopers again. At first Hopkins was able to get away with this and he repeated the cycle a few times. But then the German machine gunner figured out where he was and began firing burst after burst toward him. Hopkins had taken up a position underneath an apple tree with branches that extended all

the way to the ground. As soon as the German zeroed-in on the tree, he proceeded to spray bullets at it, cutting all of the leaves off of the branch a few inches above Hopkins's head. When two of those bullets passed through the fabric of the shoulder of his jump jacket, Hopkins decided that it was time to move to another spot. He rolled over and over to his left about ten feet, jumped to his feet and dove headfirst through a break in a hedgerow. Once on the other side, the two-foot high mound upon which the hedgerow had grown protected him from the German machine gun fire.[15]

As soon as Hopkins caught his breath, he looked around to determine where he should go next. That is when he spotted a German dugout bunker fifty yards up the hedgerow. He could see a machine gun protruding out from the bunker's slit and he could see three Germans inside. Lucky for him, they were not looking toward him, but out toward the open field. Hopkins then crawled quietly to within ten feet of the dugout and threw a Thermite grenade in through its back entrance. When the grenade exploded, it threw burning Thermite all over the men inside. Hopkins shot all three Germans as they ran out.

While Hopkins was attacking the dugout bunker, his men were working their way closer and closer to the house with the machine gun in it. Although the gun was still a formidable impediment to movement, the men continued to creep around its flanks. Soon, one man got close enough to the structure to toss a Gammon grenade inside. The explosion that followed reduced the enemy's fire, but

Opposite: Map showing the route followed by the 1st Battalion/325th Glider Infantry Regiment in crossing the Merderet inundated area on the night of June 8th/9th. The battalion successfully negotiated the swollen river, engaged in a brief exchange of gunfire with Germans at the "Gray Castle" and, after linking up with the 507th paratroopers at Timmes's Orchard, assaulted Cauquigny at daybreak. (*Map by Scott Carroll Illustrations*)

Soldiers of the 325th Glider Infantry Regiment pose in front of a Horsa glider at an airfield in southern England on June 5, 1944. The men of the 325th were destined to struggle alongside their 507th comrades throughout the fight for the La Fière causeway during the first three days of the invasion. (*82nd Airborne Museum via Phil Nordyke*)

Medics of the 325th Glider Infantry Regiment relaxing next to their Horsa glider before boarding it for the flight to Normandy. (*82nd Airborne Museum via Phil Nordyke*)

did not silence it. Then, D Company's Pvt. Joe Gandara jumped to his feet and charged the position (although he had not been ordered to do so). His courage inspired the other men around him to follow, and the position was quickly captured. 1st Sergeant Hopkins rejoined his men immediately thereafter and was at the house when, just a few minutes later, a sniper's bullet killed Gandara. After the campaign, Gandara was recommended for the Medal of Honor for leading the charge on the house where he was ultimately killed, but the recommendation was not approved.[16]

Continuing on under Captain Smith's direction, the men moved out again in the direction of the Merderet. Shortly thereafter, the

group approached a field bordered by hedgerows. Captain Smith directed the men to hold their positions while he and 1st Sergeant Hopkins scouted forward to assess the terrain situation and to locate a route to the river. They then moved ahead about seventy-five yards while the rest of the men waited to be called forward. Smith and Hopkins were moving down the length of a hedgerow on their left when they spotted a German machine gun crew directly ahead of them setting up their weapon. "They saw us about the same time we saw them," Hopkins later remembered.[17] The two paratroopers immediately dove for cover in an indentation in the hedgerow to their left whereupon 1st Sergeant Hopkins leaned out and opened fire. His fire pinned the Germans down and made them take cover as well. But no sooner had Hopkins started firing than his M1A1 Carbine jammed. Captain Smith was just behind him against the hedgerow when the jam interrupted the fire suppressing the machine gun crew. Without missing a beat, Smith leaned out to the right and began firing his captured Mauser at the German gun crew. Due to his position against the bank of the hedgerow, the muzzle of Smith's Mauser was barely 12 inches away from Barney Hopkins' head. His shots neutralized the enemy soldiers and deafened Hopkins's right ear. After extracting themselves from that exchange, they returned to the group and continued moving and finally reached the riverbank not long thereafter. Captain Smith then led the force to a field and established a defensible perimeter backed up to the Merderet. In the morning, Smith attempted to contact Col. Millett without success. He did however reach Lt. Col. Maloney who was, in the absence of Col. Millett, acting Regimental Commanding Officer. Lt. Col. Maloney, who was on the east bank of the river, directed Smith to hold his position on the west bank. Soon thereaf

325th Glider Infantry troops fully loaded for D-Day. Note the gliderman armed with the M1A1 "Bazooka". (*82nd Airborne Museum via Phil Nordyke*)

Men of the 325th Glider Infantry at "stack arms" in front of the Horsa gliders that will take them to Normandy. (*82nd Airborne Museum via Phil Nordyke*)

ter, a Lieutenant Colonel from another regiment walked into Smith's perimeter and delivered the news that Col. Millett had been captured. He also described that, earlier in the morning, he and his men had spotted a large number of German reinforcements moving toward Smith's position. As the ranking officer on the scene, the Lieutenant Colonel took command of Smith's paratroopers and ordered the entire group to cross over to the east bank of the Merderet. Despite Smith's vigorous objections to the move, the Lt. Col. overruled him and the group abandoned its position leaving only the force at Timmes's Orchard to stand against oncoming German reinforcements on the west bank.

• • •

By D+2 (June 8th), Lt. Col. Timmes was well aware of his force's tenuous position. With reinforcements from the German 91st Division swarming the hedgerows throughout the area, Timmes made one last bid to contact the regiment. He directed Lt. John Marr and Pfc. Norman Carter to cross the Merderet and establish communications with friendly forces on the east bank. With the help of directions provided by a French farmer,[18] Marr and Carter located a stone road that, although only knee deep in water, had gone unused up to that point. The two men proceeded to slosh their way across the secret ford, which delivered them to the Cherbourg/Ste.-Mère-Église railroad embankment north of La Fière on the other side of the swollen river basin. Lt. Marr and Pfc. Carter then followed the railroad embankment south and soon encountered fellow paratroopers. They were then loaded onto a jeep and were being

driven toward the 82nd Airborne Division Command Post when they spotted General Ridgway, Commander of the 82nd Airborne Division. Marr and Carter reported the situation on the west bank to Ridgway who then set a new plan in motion.

It was decided that Lt. Marr would lead Maj. Teddy H. Sanford's 1st Battalion/325th Glider Infantry Regiment across the submerged stone road to the other side of the Merderet. The 325th had come in by glider beginning at 7:00 am on D+1 (June 7th) and had not as of yet been committed to heavy action. According to the plan, the 325th would attempt to reinforce the friendly forces isolated on the west bank and to attack south toward the western terminus of the La Fière Causeway at Cauquigny. Simultaneously, Col. Millett's force

Glidermen of the 325th loading onto a Horsa at an airfield in southern England on June 5, 1944. (*82nd Airborne Museum via Phil Nordyke*)

325th men inside a Waco CG4-A glider before D-Day. (*82nd Airborne Museum via Phil Nordyke*)

325th men inside a Horsa glider before D-Day. (*82nd Airborne Museum via Phil Nordyke*)

C-47s towing Waco CG4-A gliders carrying the 325th Glider Infantry on the way to Normandy. (*82nd Airborne Museum via Phil Nordyke*)

A Horsa glider after landing in a Norman farm field. Although a British-made glider, this Horsa carried Americans to Normandy. (*82nd Airborne Museum via Phil Nordyke*)

would move to the southeast to join the perimeter at Timmes's Orchard and attack south alongside the glider infantry. That night, Sanford's battalion successfully negotiated the swollen river crossing and engaged in a brief exchange of gunfire with Germans at the "Gray Chateau" – a stone castle dominating the surrounding river valley just to the north of Timmes's Orchard. A small detachment from the battalion remained behind to neutralize the German force in the chateau and the rest of the battalion continued on, although much delayed by what had happened. Thereafter they linked up with the paratroopers at Timmes's Orchard and prepared to assault Cauquigny at daybreak. June 9th was destined to be a fateful day at the La Fière causeway.

But the plan ran into problems from the start. Col. Millett's column became disorganized in the darkness before reaching the orchard. When the column broke up into fragments, it was not able to join the dawn attack. Although lacking the additional firepower of Millett's paratroopers, the men of 1st/325th nevertheless began their assault before first light. Moving south from the perimeter at Timmes's Orchard, the battalion at first advanced steadily toward the north side of Cauquigny against sporadic resistance, but as the sun began to rise, the defenders quickly organized themselves. The German counterattack that followed overwhelmed the inexperienced glidermen by sheer numbers. In *No Better Place to Die*, Robert Murphy described the situation with 1st Battalion/325th: "The night attempt to infiltrate across the marsh and turn to the south was ambitious for the untried unit."[19] German infantrymen swarmed out of the hedgerows around Cauquigny and smashed into the men of 1st/325th. The numerically superior German force quickly pushed the 325th back with torrents of small arms fire from Kar98k rifles and

MP40 sub-machine guns. Consistent with their preferred method of attack, the Germans used their riflemen and sub-machine guns to lay down a sustained base of covering fire while they maneuvered their most devastating infantry weapon into position: the awesome MG42 machine gun. With concentrated automatic weapons fire directed at them, the 325th could not maintain the momentum of the advance.

The weight of the German counterattack was so great that the battalion faced certain annihilation. For that reason, the 325th began a strategic withdrawal: pulling back toward the semi-prepared defensive positions at Timmes's Orchard in an effort to avoid disaster. This put one platoon from the 325th GIR's C Company in a particularly disadvantaged position. This platoon had penetrated an outer perimeter of defending riflemen and machine guns during the first phase of the assault, and was still moving toward Cauquigny when the German counterattack struck like a sledgehammer. The direct result of its far forward position was that the platoon was cut off as the rest of 'C' Company fell back to the north. Pinned-down, the isolated platoon of glidermen sought cover in a shallow roadside ditch from which they began returning the enemy's fire.

The platoon's position in this ditch was far from perfect though because it was about to be exposed to direct gunfire from the German riflemen flowing around its flanks. The enemy was approaching from the left, from the right and from the front. At any moment, the enemy would have them surrounded and they would all be dead. By the time that the men of the platoon realized this, it was almost too late. Their only hope was to fall straight back to the orchard without delay, but there was one complicating factor that interfered with that move – and it was a major one. As was the case in count-

This Horsa overshot its landing zone and punched through a hedgerow bordering a narrow road. (*82nd Airborne Museum via Phil Nordyke*)

less other firefights during the Normandy Campaign, the hedgerows limited options. In order for the platoon to fall back toward Timmes's Orchard, each man would have to filter through a break in the hedgerows, forty yards to the rear of the shallow roadside ditch. It was obvious to the men that, because the Germans had so many men and weapons in the area, any movement toward that break in the hedgerow would be greeted by a swarm of bullets. The situation had become absolutely critical for the small band of glider infantry.

Pfc. Charles N. DeGlopper was one of those men. A 23-year-old native of Grand Island, New York, DeGlopper was big: 6-foot, 6-inches tall, 240 pounds with size 13 feet. He had the perfect bulky and powerful stature for hefting the considerable weight of the weapon he carried; the 19.4-pound Browning Automatic Rifle. Where such a heavy weapon would have exhausted a soldier of slighter build, DeGlopper could carry the BAR with relative ease. The only problem was that his size also made him a perfect target. Detecting the danger associated with making a dash for the break

Like so many others, this Horsa glider crashed on landing in Normandy. (*82nd Airborne Museum via Phil Nordyke*)

Another unlucky Horsa glider that broke up on landing in Normandy. Note the damaged Jeep at left. (*82nd Airborne Museum via Phil Nordyke*)

American glider infantrymen killed when their Horsa glider crash-landed in Normandy. Glider operations in World War II were very hazardous and consequently carried a high human toll. (*82nd Airborne Museum via Phil Nordyke*)

in the hedgerow, Pfc. DeGlopper volunteered to support the withdrawal of the platoon with fire from his BAR. He obviously reached the sober realization that the only way his comrades stood a chance was if someone were to draw the enemy's fire while they made their escape. Unhesitatingly assuming that responsibility, DeGlopper shouted to the others to go and that he would cover them. After that he went to work:

> Scorning a concentration of enemy automatic weapons and rifle fire, he walked from the ditch onto the road in full view of the Germans, and sprayed the hostile positions with assault fire.[20]

Shoulder firing his BAR in the open, the big 23-year-old instantly attracted the enemy's attention. German fire was directed at DeGlopper from several different sources and within moments, he was hit. Ignoring his wound, he remained on his feet and continued firing at the enemy. Then, DeGlopper was hit by German bullets again and began to stumble. Although he dropped to one knee, he steadied himself and then amazingly still found strength enough to load a fresh twenty-round magazine into his BAR and then level at the enemy one last time. Weakened by his grievous wounds, he continued to fire burst after devastating burst at the Germans while the men of his squad fell back through the break in the hedgerow whereupon they continued fighting from a more advantageous position. While still kneeling in the middle of the road, DeGlopper was finally killed outright by concentrated gunfire. By drawing the enemy's fire, he had saved the lives of all of the men of his squad. In the spot where DeGlopper made his stand, his comrades later found the ground "strewn with dead Germans" and the many ma-

A rifleman of the 325th Glider Infantry Regiment aims his M1 Garand over the top of a typical Norman hedgerow. (*82nd Airborne Museum via Phil Nordyke*)

Glider infantrymen of the 325th man a Browning M1917A1 heavy machine gun in a defensive position in a Norman hedgerow. (*82nd Airborne Museum via Phil Nordyke*)

A gliderman of the 325th mans his Browning M1919A4 light machine gun in a defensive position overlooking a Norman field. (*82nd Airborne Museum via Phil Nordyke*)

chine guns and automatic weapons that DeGlopper had single-handedly knocked out of action. DeGlopper was posthumously awarded the Medal of Honor for what he did that morning near the La Fière causeway. It was the only Medal of Honor received by a soldier of the 82nd Airborne Division during the Normandy campaign.

Repulsed in the dawn attack, the 1st/325th GIR withdrew back to Timmes's Orchard and the Germans remained in their positions around Cauquigny. Although the American force on the west bank at the orchard was one battalion stronger thanks to the 325th, that

The awesome MG42 machine gun was one of the most destructive infantry weapons of the Second World War. MG42s concealed in the hedgerows around Cauquigny and Amfreville would lay down devastating firepower throughout the fight for the La Fière causeway. (*Collection of The National D-Day Museum*)

The famous "Gray Castle" north of Timmes's Orchard and Cauquigny. Soldiers of Maj. Teddy H. Sanford's 1st Battalion/325th Glider Infantry Regiment attacked German soldiers occupying this chateau in the pre-dawn hours of June 9th. (*Photo by author*)

Pfc. Charles N. DeGlopper of C Company/325th Glider Infantry Regiment. During the abortive pre-dawn assault on Cauquigny on June 9th, DeGlopper sacrificed his life to cover the withdrawal of the men of his squad. For this action, he was posthumously awarded the Medal of Honor. (*National Archives and Records Administration 111-SC-313653*)

force was nevertheless three miles behind enemy lines and vulnerable to being overrun at any minute. With the causeway still in enemy hands, there was no way to get relief to the orchard. The situation had taken on a desperate dimension. "We could not lose a moment in forcing our way across and rescuing the troops on the other side, and the German strength was obviously building steadily," remembered Brigadier General Gavin.[21]

When word of the failure of Maj. Sanford's attack on the west bank reached General Ridgway, he ordered a direct assault across the La Fière causeway. He appointed Brigadier General Gavin to coordinate the attack and selected the 3rd Battalion/325th Glider Infantry to serve as the spearhead. By that time, the 90th Infantry Division was ashore and its artillery was available to support the assault. Gavin was also given about one dozen M4 Sherman medium tanks of Lt. Col. D.G. Hupfer's 746th Tank Battalion to support the infantry. To coordinate the supporting fires, Gavin and the 90th Division's ranking artillery officer, Brigadier General John M. Devine, crawled down to a position overlooking the La Fière Bridge. From that vantage point the two officers "had a direct view of the causeway and the buildings, houses and barns, that were occupied by the Germans." Gavin pointed out the areas on the west bank of the river from which the 82nd had been drawing fire and Brigadier General Devine noted those designated areas as targets for his guns.

The tactical plan for the assault was as straightforward as it could be: the divisional artillery would commence a preliminary bombardment at 10:30 am; the supporting fires would lift after fifteen minutes; then the infantry would charge in. The Sherman tanks were lined up a few hundred yards behind Gavin's observation post

155mm howitzers of the 345th Field Artillery Battalion provided the punch behind the bombardment that preceded the attack across the La Fière causeway on June 9th. (*82nd Airborne Museum via Phil Nordyke*)

A 155mm howitzer firing from a camouflaged position near La Fière. Weapons such as this provided invaluable fire support on the morning of the June 9th battle for the causeway. (*82nd Airborne Museum via Phil Nordyke*)

and the 90th Division's artillery – 155mm howitzers of the 345th Field Artillery Battalion – were further to the rear.

At 10:30, everything opened fire "with a tremendous explosion" that Gavin later described in vivid detail:

> Dust and smoke and flames seemed to cover the far shore. Soon Germans in a bad state of shock, their faces covered with dust, and blood trickling from their mouths, began coming across the causeway with their hands up.[22]

Up to that point, the Germans had only been opposed by rifle, machine-gun and mortar fire. They knew that the Americans were planning a push across the causeway and consequently they had reinforced the regiment on the west bank with additional mortars and artillery. However, the heavy artillery concentration that came crashing down on them that morning came as a great shock. Gavin was confident that, because of the incredible volume of supporting fire, enough of the 325th men could make it across the causeway to establish a bridgehead on the west bank. But just to be safe, Capt. Robert D. Rae's composite company of 507th paratroopers was designated to serve as the follow-up reserve force in the event that things turned ugly for the 325th. As it turned out, it was prudent for Gavin to give this responsibility to Bob Rae.

• • •

Like so many of the other paratroopers that jumped at Normandy, Captain Rae spent the first night alone and lost. "I ended up over in the 101st area, which was quite a ways away from where I was supposed to be."[23] He landed southeast of Ste.-Mère-Église and he was in combat almost immediately after landing. "I was lying on the ground, I hadn't gotten up yet and the machine guns started firing, firing right over me and I could tell they were just over me because I could hear the bullets going through the leaves of the hedgerows."[24] Rae slipped away from the gunfire and wandered the countryside alone until sunrise, looking for other paratroopers. "I just started walking right down the center of the fields. I figured if I stayed in the center they couldn't bushwhack me," he recalled.[25]

Soon after sunrise, Rae finally stumbled onto a handful of 82nd Airborne Division men and together they moved in the direction of the sound of a nearby firefight. Rae knew that the source of the firing he could hear had to be American paratroopers engaging the enemy. "I said let's go over there and help them."[26] Leading his men toward the sound of the guns, Rae found that the fighting was taking place around a small farmhouse. "Just about the time we came out of our cover – which was a hedgerow – four or five Ger-

Robert Dempsey Rae of Service Company/507th as a Lieutenant in 1943. Rae jumped into Normandy as a Captain on D-Day and met his destiny three days later on the La Fière causeway. *(Courtesy of Albert "Bud" Parker)*

mans came running out the back door. They didn't know we were there, so it was like shooting fish in a barrel."[27]

After that brief fight, Rae and his handful of paratroopers moved off to continue searching for the rest of the 507th. At that point, Rae's main concern was figuring out where they were. "When I landed I knew I wasn't where I was supposed to be," he recalled.[28] Obviously, getting his bearings had become something of supreme importance:

> We found a young man and his wife and two little children…I couldn't talk to him so I took out my map and pointed to me and then to the map. He knew exactly where I was so he showed me where.[29]

With that, Rae and his men proceeded to a nearby 101st Airborne Division collection point where a group of American paratroopers from both divisions had assembled:

> I rounded up exactly ninety paratroopers, all 82nd Airborne, and lined them up in columns of twos. So we headed off. We walked all the way to Ste.-Mère-Église without any incident at all. No problems.[30]

After arriving at Ste.-Mère-Église, Rae learned that the 507th had moved into defensive positions along the Merderet River just to the west of town. With his group of ninety men, Rae then proceeded toward the Merderet and reported to Lt. Col. Maloney. But Maloney was in a difficult position: Col. Millett had been captured,

Antique postcard showing the marketplace in Ste.-Mère-Église. *(Collection of The National D-Day Museum)*

Street scene in downtown Ste.-Mère-Église. *(Collection of The National D-Day Museum)*

the regiment he was now supposed to lead was spread out all over the Cotentin peninsula, and he was left with an assembled total strength that was closer to the size of a battalion than a regiment. He then organized all of the 507th troopers on hand into three groups, each the approximate size of a company. Maloney appointed the three ranking officers on hand to lead these provisional "companies." Those three men were Headquarters Company's Captain Morgan A. Brakonecke, E Company's Captain Roy E. Creek (who had supervised the capture of Chef-du-Pont the day before) and Captain Rae. Dubbed Brakonecke Company, Creek Company and

Rae Company, these provisional units were then fed into the defensive line around La Fière. Maloney deployed Rae Company's men in the furthest forward defensive positions near the bridge where they relieved what was left of the platoon from Lieutenant Dolan's A Company/505th that had taken such a beating in the morning counterattack on June 7th. There, at the foot of the stone bridge at La Fière, Rae Company remained for two days under the almost constant artillery and mortar fire of the strong German forces on the west bank. As the preliminary bombardment against Cauquigny opened on the morning of June 9th, Rae Company was about to meet its destiny.

An antique picture postcard showing the road to Carentan in Ste.-Mère-Église. *(Collection of The National D-Day Museum)*

This is what Ste.-Mère-Église looked like when Capt. Rae entered town late in the day on June 6th. (*82nd Airborne Museum via Phil Nordyke*)

Lt. Col. Arthur A. Maloney – the man who led the 507th during the battle at the La Fière causeway. (*Courtesy of Dennis and Barbara Maloney*)

13

"... you've got to go."

During the preliminary artillery bombardment on the morning of June 9th, the 3rd Battalion/325th Glider Infantry was poised at the line of departure to spearhead the attack across the causeway. Their commanding officer, Lt. Col. Charles A. Carrell, only stayed with the battalion long enough to issue assault orders to his officers. When General Gavin asked him to come forward for more specific instructions immediately prior to the attack, Carrell said "I don't think I can do it!" Gavin then demanded to know why he could not. "I'm sick," was Carrell's response. General Gavin lowered his voice to a whisper and said to Carrell, "OK, you're through."[1] The commanding officer of the 325th GIR, Col. Harry L. Lewis, then appointed the regiment's S-3 officer, Major Arthur W. Gardner, to lead the attack in Carrell's place.[2] After Lt. Col. Carrell asked to be relieved from leading the assault, Gavin was nervous about how the 3rd/325th would perform. Shortly before the attack kicked off, Gavin called Lt. Col. Maloney and Capt. Rae aside to give them orders. Maloney and Rae were "both men he trusted"[3] and he wanted them to be prepared to act in the event that things turned ugly for the 3rd/325th. He designated Capt. Rae's composite company of 507th paratroopers as the follow-up reserve force. As it would turn out, Gavin was prudent in giving this responsibility to Bob Rae. "He said now Rae, I want you to stay exactly where you are because you're the one that's going to have to support the 325th if they falter."[4] Gavin was very careful to articulate exactly what he expected Rae to do: "I want you to get all your men lined up and get all the ammunition you can get a hold of and I want you to attack when I tell you you've got to go."[5]

At 10:30 am, the six heavy howitzers of the 345th Field Artillery Battalion and the 75mm guns and .50-cal. machine guns of A Company/746th Tank Battalion opened with the fire that subjected the Germans on the opposite bank to the heaviest pounding they had yet seen.[6] The 325th had been promised a smokescreen to obscure their advance along the causeway, but because there were no white phosphorous shells available, that smokescreen never materialized. The result was that the exposed glider troops began to draw German fire as they approached their jumping-off point for the attack. When the battalion turned the last bend in the road near the manoir, German machine gun fire instantly swept over it from the west bank. In reaction, men threw themselves into the roadside ditches seeking cover. Much to their shock and dismay, the bodies of 507th troopers killed by the relentless artillery fire lay in those ditches with them.[7]

The 3rd/325th attack was to be led by G Company, followed by E Company and then F Company. As the vanguard of the thrust, Captain John Sauls's G Company was at the head of the road column during the battalion's approach to La Fière. When his men walked into the beaten zone of the enemy's machine gun fire, he immediately sought another avenue to approach the jump-off point. Sauls reconnoitered to the left (south) and found a low stone wall running along the south side of the road at an oblique angle to the bridge and causeway. Since the wall offered protection almost all the way up to the bridge, it was exactly what G Company needed. When the time of the attack arrived, the G Company men would have to leave the protection of the stone wall and advance in the open across the causeway just as that badly mauled German company had attempted to do two days earlier.

Throughout the minutes during which Sauls maneuvered his company into position, German machine gun fire continued to ricochet all around the grounds of Manoir de La Fière. As the G Company men moved down along the protected side of the stone wall, they had to dash across a 7-foot-wide gap that had been produced by the explosion of a German shell. Evidently having observed

In addition to the big guns, the 82nd Airborne Division's mortars also contributed to the preparatory bombardment on June 9th. In these photos, 81mm mortar teams of the 325th Glider Infantry fire to support the attack. (*82nd Airborne Museum via Phil Nordyke*)

A 325th 81mm mortar team in the Norman bocage. The man kneeling with the glasses is Colonel Harry L. Lewis, commanding officer of the 325th Glider Infantry Regiment. (*82nd Airborne Museum via Phil Nordyke*)

German casualties near La Fière. (*82nd Airborne Museum via Phil Nordyke*)

An unfortunate victim of the American preparatory bombardment on the morning of June 9th. *(Courtesy of The National D-Day Museum)*

movement there, the enemy began placing automatic weapons fire into the gap. The machine gunning was of such intensity that it "beat like hail" on the wall and nearby road.[8]

As the artillery bombarded Cauquigny, men of the 82nd Airborne Division's own combat engineer unit – the 307th Airborne Engineer Battalion – went to work on the various obstructions and debris littering the causeway. One platoon of the 307th began clearing the anti-tank mines that had been put down by the paratroopers on June 6th. The other platoon focused its efforts on attempting to move the three knocked-out German tanks sitting abandoned on the roadbed. Since the derelict tanks could potentially impede the progress of American vehicles attempting to advance across the causeway, they had to be moved. The airborne combat engineers

worked throughout the fifteen-minute-long artillery concentration as outgoing American artillery rounds screeched over their heads and German incoming mortar and artillery rounds landed dangerously close to them. In all of the noise and confusion of the moment, the engineers missed one of the anti-tank mines on the embankment – an error that would ultimately produce unfortunate results.

Then at 10:45 am, the American mortar and artillery fires lifted and the 325th's charge began. Captain Sauls, turned to his men and shouted, "Go! Go! Go!"[9] Taking the lead, Sauls was followed by Sergeant Wilfred Ericsson and Lieutenant Donald Wason. Realizing that the only chance of driving the Germans from Cauquigny was with the momentum of a swift attack, Captain Sauls began his

German prisoners lined-up along a road in Normandy. When the preparatory bombardment lifted on the morning of June 9th, dazed and disoriented Germans emerged from their positions at Cauquigny and stumbled toward American lines to surrender. *(Courtesy of The National D-Day Museum)*

sprint across the five hundred yards of exposed causeway. As he and his men moved off of the bridge and down onto the raised macadam roadway, the Germans unleashed murderous fire. At first, 7.92mm bullets from MG42 machine guns sliced into the glidermen as they ran. Then, German mortar and artillery fire began to crash down around them with devastating effect. The concentrated artillery, mortar and small arms fire lead many survivors of the action to characterize it as the "hottest" sector they experienced during the war. General S.L.A. Marshall later wrote that, "No American charge into enemy country was ever pressed home by so few men."[10]

Miraculously, Captain Sauls, Sergeant Ericsson and Lieutenant Wason made it all the way across the causeway followed by the lead squad. At that point, a thoroughly winded Captain Sauls turned to urge his men forward and only then noticed that just a few had followed. Rather than having the full company on the opposite side of the causeway, "scarcely thirty men had come over with him to close with the enemy."[11] The reason for that related to that 7-foot gap in the stone wall back at the manoir. Moments after Captain Sauls lead off the attack, Private Melvin L. Johnson of G Company was shot through the head by a German machine gun bullet as he passed in front of the gap. His lifeless body collapsed in the middle

of the gap right in front of his shocked comrades. The rest of the men behind him (practically all of G Company) were supposed to follow Sauls, but Private Johnson's violent death stunned the men and made them hesitate. This hesitation produced congestion that held up the rest of the battalion's advance with the result that no one else jumped off for the attack.

Nearly ten minutes passed during which the men of the 325th remained motionless behind the stone wall. Then Lieutenant Frank E. Amino, seeing the problem, took the initiative and ran forward along the stone wall exhorting the crouching glidermen forward. Amino yelled, "Let's go on and kill the sons of bitches," as he darted across the gap in the wall and proceeded down onto the causeway.[12] Then the men finally began moving forward toward the open causeway. Sauls and the lead squad all managed to make it over to the other bank largely because the preparatory bombardment had not yet lifted when they stepped off. As they sprinted across the causeway, the enemy's fire was suppressed by the American fire support. However, the guns ceased fire shortly before Amino got the rest of the company moving. Thus, as the rest of G Company crossed, the enemy's fire was not suppressed and an intense barrage was loosed at the glidermen.[13] Lacking cover to shield them from bullets or

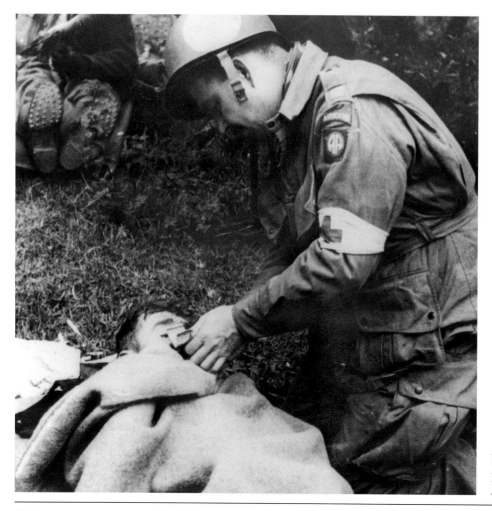

An 82nd Airborne Division medic treats a wounded man during the fighting in Normandy. (*82nd Airborne Museum via Phil Nordyke*)

fragmentation, they began to fall, and the causeway was soon littered with the dead, the dying and the wounded. In *No Better Place to Die*, Robert Murphy described the scene: "There were soon twenty to thirty casualties strung out along the road while more men slowly crossed over, picking their way over the fallen."[14]

As the gliderman stumbled forward, stepping over the casualties scattered along the road, the assault began to bog down and lose its momentum. The German machine gun fire was of such intensity that many of the men gave in to the tempting instinct to seek shelter. They threw themselves down on the edges of the elevated road where they found at least some measure of protection from the enemy fire. Despite this seemingly hopeless situation, a few of the men attempted to continue the assault to join Captain Saul's force on the west bank. Some of the glidermen got up from where they had sought shelter, but they were quickly mowed down by German automatic weapons. When a heavy weapons section attempted to dash forward, they too were sprayed with 7.92mm bullets from the MG42s hidden at Cauquigny.[15] Seeing so many men gunned down evidently shook the resolve of those men still alive along the flanks of the causeway and consequently the momentum of what was left of the 325th assault sagged even more.

At that point, one of the 746th Tank Battalion M4 Shermans back at La Fière joined the battle. It rolled forward from the heights above the manoir, crossed the bridge and moved down onto the causeway in an attempt to support the stalling glider infantry assault, but it accomplished nothing. Just a few moments after passing over the bridge, it had to steer off the shoulder of the road embankment to avoid one of the derelict German tanks. While so doing, the Sherman rolled over the one anti-tank mine that the 307th Airborne Engineers missed. When the mine exploded, it disabled the Sherman and wounded seven men who were in the immediate vicinity. Thus, as the latter elements of the 325th moved from La Fière toward Cauquigny, they had to contend with a host of obstacles on the causeway. In addition to the now derelict Sherman and the scattered casualties, the knocked-out German Hotchkiss tanks still sat on the causeway past the bridge, which made for an environment of multiple obstacles that exacerbated the developing congestion. This congestion was forcing more and more of the glider infantry to the ground along the roadside.

In the wake of G Company's advance, E Company/325th joined the general confusion on the causeway. Since the shocking death of Private Johnson at the gap in the stone wall stalled the spearhead of the advance for ten minutes, E Company's advance was likewise delayed. When it finally began to cross the causeway, German fire "seriously depleted" E Company's numbers.[16] The men that survived the sprint across the Merderet deployed to the right side of the main road as they reached the west bank. 507th paratroopers actually provided valuable supporting fire for the E Company men

Wounded 82nd Airborne Division paratroopers being evacuated to an aid station during the fighting in Normandy. (*82nd Airborne Museum via Phil Nordyke*)

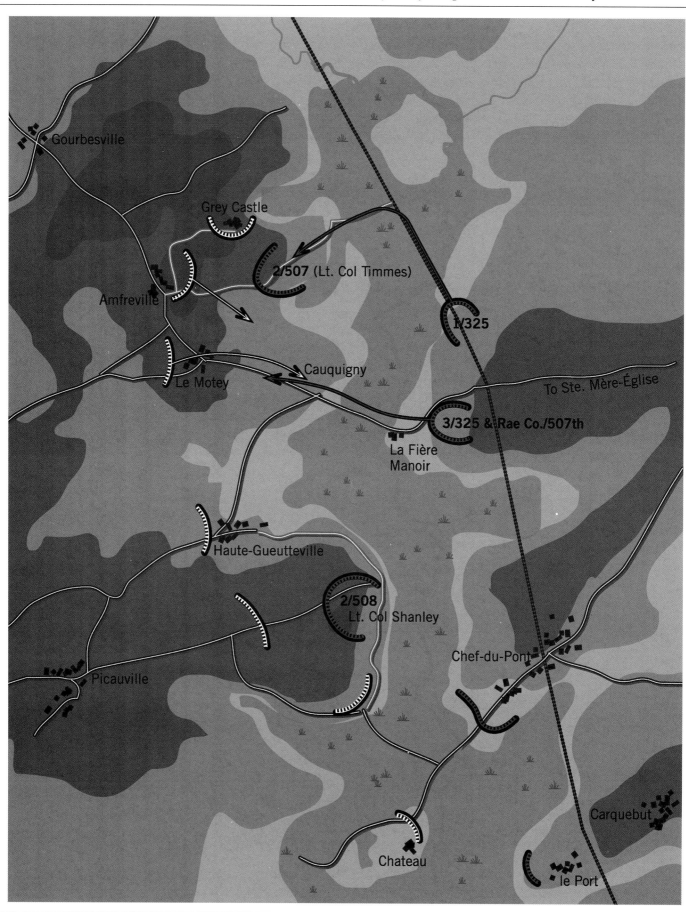

as they closed with the enemy. From their trenches on the eastern shore, the 507th troopers directed accurate rifle and machine gun fire on the German positions at Cauquigny with deadly accuracy. This fire was of such intensity that the remnants of E Company/ 325th were greeted by Germans eager to surrender.

Captain Sauls's men took a few prisoners too when they reached the west bank. Some G Company men proceeded straight up the main road and others "disappeared into the fields and among the hedgerows" as they maneuvered to engage the enemy. Lieutenant Wason was killed as he single-handedly assaulted the machine gun nest that had devastated G Company while crossing the causeway. Sergeant Ericsson and a few riflemen peeled off from the rest of the men and scouted down a trail along the riverbank in an effort to smoke out the Germans directing enfilading fire along the causeway. They pitched hand grenades over hedgerows and more than a dozen Germans emerged with their hands up. The prisoners were sent back toward the causeway and into American captivity. In the minutes that followed, more grenades were thrown and more German soldiers surrendered. The 325th had established a tenuous bridgehead.

A bridgehead is the area immediately around the terminus of a bridge that is held by an attacking force. It is very similar in concept to a beachhead in so far as a beachhead is the first foothold of an assault on enemy-held territory. Similarly, a bridgehead is the first foothold of an attacker on the far side of a bridge. The plan of the 325th GIR attack that day called for first establishing, then expanding a bridgehead at Cauquigny. Success there would cement the American hold on the La Fière causeway. Although few in number as a result of the gauntlet of fire encountered while crossing the causeway, the G and E Company glider infantrymen had nevertheless managed to establish the bridgehead. F Company/325th, under the command of Capt. James M. Harney, then started across the causeway. Like those that had preceded it, F Co./325th suffered very heavy casualties. It had originally been conceived that F Company would simply be mopping up the remains of the German defenders in Cauquigny, but that did not happen in the end. Instead, most of the men of F Company foundered amid the wrecked vehicles on the causeway. General S.L.A. Marshall described what happened to F Company in *Night Drop*:

There was no real excuse for them. They had simply goofed off at the first opportunity. Harney tried to get them ahead by booting them in the pants. Also, he cursed them a little. But it did no good; "They reacted as if they had their brakes set." He thought to himself that if he tarried to argue with them, in the end no one would move. Then anger filled him, and he pulled away from them, attended by a few personal retainers from his headquarters group.[17]

Capt. Harney's men got across the causeway relatively intact and, what was left of the small group, then attacked directly up the main road in an effort to deepen the bridgehead. They did not get far though and were forced to join those elements of G Company and E Company fighting in the hedgerows around the village. The three heavily depleted companies of the 325th were holding ground in savage, close-quarters fighting, but they needed help. They needed reinforcements to join the continuing effort to develop the American perimeter at Cauquigny and they needed to be re-supplied as well. By then, nearly an hour had passed since the attack began, during which the glider infantrymen had been locked in almost constant life or death exchanges of small arms fire with the enemy. Such a sustained volume of fire meant that the small force of 325th men on the west bank was beginning to run low on small arms ammunition and hand grenades. If they were going to maintain their tenuous hold on that bridgehead, they were going to need ammunition and they were going to have to be reinforced.

"The 325th was a good outfit, and they fought good, no question about it, but you could tell it wasn't going to be long before we were going to need to give them some help," Bob Rae remembered.[18] Back at La Fière, it was not apparent that any elements of the 325th had made it to Cauquigny. With no radios to communicate the details of the developing battle, Captain Sauls could not report his progress back to General Gavin. Gavin could only assess the situation based on what he could see – which was not encouraging. He could see the knocked-out Sherman tank, he could see dozens of motionless soldiers crouching along the road embankment seeking cover and he could see dozens of dead and wounded men sprawled out in the middle of the causeway. But that was all he could see. He could not see the small groups of G, E and F Company men struggling to hold a bridgehead. The reality of the situation was that more men were needed immediately in Cauquigny to keep pressing the attack forward before the enemy could regroup and counterattack. The American force on the west bank was just too small to hold for much longer. Although the reality at Cauquigny was indeed a critical situation, it seemed absolutely disastrous to General Gavin back at La Fière. To him, it seemed that the 325th GIR's attack had stalled and that the entire battalion was about to retreat. With such a small group of men struggling to hold the west bank bridgehead, that assessment was actually quite accurate. The situation had reached a turning point and a decision had to be made. That is when General Gavin turned to Bob Rae and said, "All right, you've got to go.[19]

Opposite: Map showing American and German positions in the vicinity of the La Fière causeway during the battle there on June 9, 1944. (*Map by Scott Carroll Illustrations*)

14

Into the Mouth of Hell

Cannon to right of them, cannon to left of them, cannon in front of them volleyed and thundered; Stormed at with shot and shell, boldly they rode and well, into the jaws of Death, into the mouth of Hell, rode the six hundred.

— from *Charge of the Light Brigade*, by Alfred Tennyson

Immediately after Gavin told him to go, Capt. Rae shouted to the ninety paratroopers of his company, "Follow me!"[1] He then pressed the safety selector of his M1A1 Carbine, moving it into the *fire* position and began his dash toward the bridge and into the mouth of hell. "We came running out there like a bunch of Indians raising Cain, firing all our weapons," Rae remembered.[2] The company streamed across the bridge in two columns with Rae in the lead at a full sprint. Just past the bridge, they had to stop. S.L.A. Marshall described the scene in *Night Drop*:

> Stragglers had knotted up around the ruined vehicles just beyond it (the bridge). The solid wall of blackened steel and human flesh stretched from waterline to waterline, barring the way.[3]

With Rae Company stalled there before the congested causeway, a German artillery round slammed into the embankment nearby and four 507th troopers were thrown to the ground seriously wounded. When the round hit, Rae's runner Pvt. Richard Keeler hit the dirt out of instinct. Unfazed by the explosion, Rae picked Keeler up and said, "Now listen son, if you're going to get it, you'll get it, so you just keep walking this road with me."[4] Rae's words evidently had an inspirational impact on Keeler because he immediately began going from man to man, pulling them to their feet and exhorting them to continue the advance. Keeler then organized a flying "wedge" of about eight men and bulldozed forward through the huddle of men lying amid the wrecked tanks.[5] Once the passageway had been opened, it stayed open and the traffic on the causeway began moving at last. Because of this, medics were finally able to get down to the causeway to evacuate the litter patients, a move that relieved the congestion even further.[6] As this

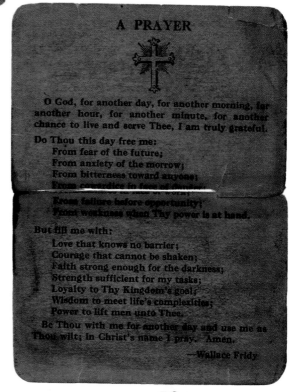

121   PSALM CXXI.

1 I TO the hills will lift mine eyes,
   from whence doth come mine aid.
2 My safety cometh from the Lord,
   who heav'n and earth hath made.
3 Thy foot he'll not let slide, nor will
   he slumber that thee keeps.
4 Behold, he that keeps Israel,
   he slumbers not, nor sleeps.

5 The Lord thee keeps, the Lord thy shade
   on thy right hand doth stay:
6 The moon by night thee shall not smite,
   nor yet the sun by day.
7 The Lord shall keep thy soul; he shall
   preserve thee from all ill.
8 Henceforth thy going out and in
   God keep for ever will.

The Truth of the Matter

MY LOVER is sweet,
   My lover is kind.
A man like him
   Is hard to find.
He doesn't argue
   Over a trifle.
My moods and whims
   He doesn't stifle.
He doesn't forbid,
   He doesn't insist.
My sympathies
   He doesn't enlist.
He doesn't coax,
   He doesn't plead.
He gives me full rein—
   So much indeed
That somehow or other
   I always do
Exactly the thing
   That he wants me to.

A PRAYER

O God, for another day, for another morning, for
another hour, for another minute, for another
chance to live and serve Thee, I am truly grateful.

Do Thou this day free me:
   From fear of the future;
   From anxiety of the morrow;
   From bitterness toward anyone;
   From cowardice in face of danger;
   From failure before opportunity;
   From weakness when Thy power is at hand.

But fill me with:
   Love that knows no barrier;
   Courage that cannot be shaken;
   Faith strong enough for the darkness;
   Strength sufficient for my tasks;
   Loyalty to Thy Kingdom's goal;
   Wisdom to meet life's complexities;
   Power to lift men unto Thee.

Be Thou with me for another day and use me as
Thou wilt; in Christ's name I pray. Amen.

—Wallace Fridy

Capt. Rae carried these items in his pockets when he led his composite company across the La Fière causeway on June 9th. *(Courtesy of Albert "Bud" Parker)*

Opposite: Pvt. Edward J. Jeziorski was a .30-cal. machine gunner in C Company/507th at the time of the invasion. On June 9th, he was the third man behind Capt. Rae while crossing the La Fière causeway. *(Courtesy of Edward J. Jeziorski)*

Capt. Rae wore this shoulder flag on his M42 jump jacket throughout the campaign in Normandy. After the war, he continued to carry the flag every day until April 1982. *(Courtesy of Albert "Bud" Parker)*

was happening, Gen. Ridgway, Gen. Gavin and Lt. Col. Maloney moved down onto the causeway too and began urging men to move forward and join the assault. Ridgway set a calm example while Gavin moved from man to man saying, "Son, you can do it."[7] Maloney also shouted words of encouragement to his men with his deep, bellowing voice. Earlier that morning, a German artillery round had landed close to him, hurling a fragment into his M2 helmet. The fragment punctured the Hadfield Manganese steel of the helmet, sliced through the comparatively soft skin of the helmet's liner and gouged a deep wound in the side of his head.[8] The wound was serious enough that he could have honorably called himself out of action because of it. But Arthur Maloney was not that kind of leader. If he could still think, he could still command. He had a medic bandage his head and he found another helmet to replace the one that was punctured by the German shell fragment. Thus as men observed his hulking form moving about on the causeway, they saw his face streaked with blood and they were motivated by the example of his toughness.[9]

Capt. Rae was also carrying this letter from his mother when he led his company across the La Fière causeway. (*Courtesy of Albert "Bud" Parker*)

Carson Smith and the rest of the men of Brakonecke Company, started across the causeway right behind Rae Company. Smith later recalled what it was like to run directly into the German fusillade:

> It was really rough going across that bridge. You couldn't see a thing because there was so much dust and gun smoke and artillery shells and just about everything you could think of coming from across firing all on that road.[10]

Despite the intensity of the German fire, Bob Rae's determination drove him onward – toward the enemy. From his command post back at La Fière, General Gavin watched what happened. After the battle, he described what he had seen:

> Captain Rae placed himself at the head of the company and led the assault directly into the concentrated rifle, machine gun, mortar and artillery fire of the enemy.[11]

As he sprinted down the first one hundred yards of the causeway, Rae had to steer around the derelict tanks and the bodies of the dead and wounded men of the 325th. Advancing further and further out onto the road, Rae had to dodge fewer and fewer obstacles, but he drew closer and closer to his antagonists. Half way across, he saw German prisoners with their hands held high crossing toward La Fière. Rae paid little attention to them because of what the enemy was throwing at him. The column was beginning to draw heavy rifle fire from German troops deployed along the edge of the marsh south of the road and those bullets were tearing into the humanity on the causeway, indiscriminately injuring American paratroopers and retreating German prisoners alike.

Ed Jeziorski was the third man in the left column on the left hand side of the causeway during Rae Company's charge. According to him, the air was alive with a "continuous whine" of German bullets.[12] He was running as fast as he could carrying his Browning M1919A4 machine gun on his left shoulder and an ammunition can held in his right hand.[13] His assistant gunner, Pvt. Grover O. Boyce, was directly behind him carrying the machine gun's tripod and more ammunition. The wall of German gunfire was so intense that, to Jeziorski, it sounded like "a million mosquitoes in a confined space."[14] As they advanced, a 507th lieutenant turned around and shouted, "Come on, you paratroopers, let's go!"[15] At that exact moment, Jeziorski saw the man drop to the ground – struck down by the enemy's fire.[16] Throughout it all, the men of Rae company never faltered, never hesitated, and stayed right with the man that was leading them. The unrelenting intensity of the German rifle and machine gun fire lead Captain Rae to conclude that no other

A pair of 507th troopers pose with a Browning M1919A4 light machine gun. In this photo, the weapon is being fed by a white cloth belt of .30-cal. ammunition. *(Courtesy of Gordon K. Smith)*

force had yet reached Cauquigny intact to engage the enemy there, so he kept driving his men forward with bullets zipping past dangerously close to him.[17]

Moving targets being harder to hit than stationary ones, Rae Company's momentum challenged the German gunners and made it difficult for their fire to achieve full effect. Despite this, the concentration of German bullets was bound to take its toll. Even with a rapid paced advance, some of Rae's paratroopers fell. However, the rest kept coming as fast as they could. "How we got through that I don't know," Ed Jerziorski remembered.[18] The 507th's Regimental S2 officer, Lieutenant J.H. Wisner, described the scene as, "..an escalator, two streams of men on the inside trying to run forward and on the outer side, streams of wounded trickling back."[19] Throughout it all, Bob Rae was right out front, leading his men onward. In one of his pockets, Rae carried a photograph of his mother. On the back of that photograph, Mrs. Rae had written the words "Put me in your pocket for luck." In another pocket, he carried a copy of the XXIIIrd Psalm, which read:

I to the hills will lift mine eyes, from whence doth come mine aid.
My safety cometh from the Lord, who heav'n and earth hath made.
Thy foot he'll not let slide, nor will he slumber that thee keeps.
Behold, he that keeps Israel, he slumbers not, nor sleeps.
The Lord thee keeps, the Lord thy shade on thy right hand doth stay:
The moon by night thee shall not smite, nor yet the sun by day.

The Lord shall keep thy soul; he shall preserve thee from all ill.
Henceforth thy going out and in, God keep forever will.

Through the storm of bullets, it certainly seems that someone was protecting Bob Rae that morning. Unfazed by the men being struck down all around him, he continued on unscathed. He maintained his all-out sprint toward Cauquigny only slowing to motivate men stalled along the sides of the causeway embankment to get up and follow. Rae urged them forward by shouting, "Get up, get moving," as he passed.[20] His bold leadership example was exactly what was needed to reverse the stagnant, demoralizing situation and countless glidermen rose to their feet to follow the 507th assault. According to General Gavin's account, Captain Rae "…moved with such speed that he carried his men across the bridge, reorganized and pressed his initial advantage and overran the enemy positions."[21] Against incalculable odds, Rae reached the opposite bank at the end of his 500-yard dash. When Captain Rae and his paratroopers arrived, the Americans on the west bank were attacking or defending as separate units with no cohesion in a largely disorganized fight for survival. The situation was made all the more serious by the fact that pockets of German defenders were intermingled among pockets of American attackers scattered among the hedgerows. Rae was enough of a true professional soldier to know that, under such circumstances, there had to be some central directing authority among the Americans at Cauquigny. For that reason, Rae voluntarily yielded command of the situation to Capt. Harney by saying, "Now what do you want me to do?"[22] Harney replied with an on-the-spot battle plan:

82nd Airborne Division paratroopers crossing the La Fière causeway on June 10th, the day after the big battle. (*National Archives and Records Administration via Jump/Cut Productions and Scott Carroll***)**

Pvt. James Schaffner of the 325th Glider Infantry Regiment poses in front of the east side of the heavily damaged Roman-Catholic church at Cauquigny. This photo was taken in the afternoon on June 9th after the battle had already flowed toward Le Motey. (*82nd Airborne Museum via Phil Nordyke***)**

Take all the men now moving on the left side of the road, regardless of unit, go by the trail leading left and try to make contact with George Company's left flank. When you find them, advance west to the high ground and take up a defensive position.[23]

With that, Capt. Rae and his people took off to make contact with the remains of G Company's left flank. Moments later while Harney was giving out more instructions, two machine gun sections made it to Cauquigny. He sent one of the weapons off to the right to join a small group of 325th men and then sent the other section to the left support Rae Company. Since he was hefting the weight of one of those M1919A4 machine guns, Ed Jeziorski had not been able to fire as he crossed the causeway. Instead, he and Pvt. Grover Boyce (his assistant gunner) had concentrated on getting to the other side as quickly as possible. Under Captain Rae's

direction, Jeziorski and Boyce kept moving and in seconds they came to a fork in the road. Jeziorski remembered what happened next:

As we came to that fork, 150 yards ahead of us there was an MG42 on the left-hand side of the road and this guy opened up on us and when he did, Boyce dropped the tripod and we set-up the gun right on the road.[24]

With Boyce providing covering fire with his rifle, Jeziorski dropped the pintle of the M1919A4 into the tripod, opened the weapon's top cover, placed a cloth belt of .30-cal. ammunition into the feedway, closed the cover and racked the bolt. He then opened fire on the MG42 from right there in the middle of the road.[25] It only took a few well-placed bursts to silence the German gun. In fact, one of Jeziorski's bursts struck the German machine gunner

Pvt. Schaffner (*left*) and Pvt. Gerald W. Arnold (*right*) of the 325th Glider Infantry Regiment pose on the west side of the Roman-Catholic church at Cauquigny on June 9th. (*82nd Airborne Museum via Phil Nordyke*)

JAMES M. GAVIN
25 ACORN PARK
CAMBRIDGE, MASSACHUSETTS 02140

March 31, 1981

Mr. Albert N. Parker
2496 Hyde Manor Drive, N.W.
Atlanta, Georgia 30327

Dear Mr. Parker:

Thank you for your letter of March 19. Certainly
it is good to hear from a son-in-law of Captain Robert Dempsey
Rae.

As you know, he was with me on D-Day in Normandy,
and for quite some time thereafter. He did an outstanding
job and in Normandy, in particular, in a very dramatic action
he took part of a battalion of glidermen, who were about to
retreat, into an attack into the German positions. He succeeded and held his position against heavy German counterattacks.

I am sending you herewith an autographed copy of
On To Berlin, and also a photograph which I have autographed
to your father-in-law.

Sincerely,

James M. Gavin

Photograph mailed separately

Letter written by Jim Gavin in 1981 to Mr. Albert "Bud" Parker describing Capt. Rae's actions at the La Fière causeway on June 9, 1944. *(Courtesy of Albert "Bud" Parker)*

right in the neck.[26] "When we passed that position a little bit later, the guy's body was in the hole and his head with his helmet on it was next to the hole - I had taken his head off," Jeziorski remembered.[27] After knocking out the MG42, Jeziorski, Boyce and the remaining Rae Company paratroopers continued to advance toward the village of Cauquigny. Suddenly, a German reserve force arrived from the direction of Amfreville and began to deploy. These Germans had not arrived on foot, but on bicycles. As the approximately one hundred bicycle infantrymen wheeled up to the battle area, the remains of Rae Company opened fire. "We hit them just as they were getting off their bicycles," Jeziorski remembered.[28] Fire from the paratroopers quickly decimated the Germans and their bicycles were left littering the area. Pvt. Andrew Manger, a medic assigned to C Company/507th, used one of those bicycles for days thereafter to carry his medical supplies.[29]

For the defenders, the situation went rapidly out of control and they were driven from their positions. As the Germans began to fall back toward Amfreville and Le Motey, the paratroopers of Rae Company and glidermen of the 325th pursued them. Cauquigny had been recaptured and the La Fière Causeway was once again in American hands.

Soon, enemy fire on the causeway itself dissipated significantly, allowing reinforcements to advance against virtually no opposition. Heavy weapons sections were able to move up to Cauquigny intact to lend support to the forces stabbing westward. General Ridgway personally supervised the clearing of the knocked-out tanks from the area around the bridge. Then at about noon, the Sherman medium tanks of the 746th Tank Battalion that had been at La Fière moved up in column and began across, sweeping the west bank with fire from their 75mm guns and Browning .50-cal. machine guns as they advanced. With the causeway an open artery, almost immediately Americans began to flood across it in such volume as to be unstoppable. Four Jeeps towing trailers full of ammunition dashed across, delivered their valuable payloads to the Americans in Cauquigny and then returned to La Fière for more.

The American bridgehead perimeter that had been so close to collapsing barely an hour earlier was by that time expanding. With the causeway road open to traffic, supplies and reinforcements began flowing across in volume. By then, the enemy had no hope of containing the penetration or neutralizing the bridgehead. For the Germans, it was too late. There would be no further counterattacks at Cauquigny and the Germans would never again threaten to check the development of the Utah beachhead. The pivotal battle for the La Fière causeway had been won, but fighting still raged on around Cauquigny.

• • •

This phase of the fight took on an especially desperate dimension because the enemy was so very close at hand. In what can only be characterized as an intense slogging match, paratroopers and glider infantry struggled against the Germans for every foot and every hedgerow. According to Robert Murphy, "It was bullet for bullet and life for life and the enemy had to be shot in their foxholes one-by-one during the advance."[30] The Germans were so near that even General Ridgway had a bit of a close call. After reaching the Cauquigny end of the causeway, Ridgway was discussing possibilities with two officers when Pfc. Kenneth Lynn appeared leading a group of 25 German prisoners. Only moments before, Lynn had captured the Germans a mere one hundred feet from where Ridgway stood.

Close quarters notwithstanding, the Germans were being driven away from Cauquigny. Bob Rae organized his column of 507th men, pushed out from Cauquigny and began driving the enemy back toward the strategically important crossroads of Le Motey. As the column approached the hamlet, they came under "fierce" artillery fire, but a few nearby buildings provided the men some protection from the incoming 88mm rounds. With artillery crashing in along the road over which his men had to advance, Captain Rae halted the column having suffered six casualties. With his remaining 21 able-bodied paratroopers, Rae slipped back away from the target area in search of a tank to radio for fire support to cover the advance.[31] At exactly 1:00 pm, Rae ran into General Ridgway and Col. Harry L. Lewis, commanding officer of the 325th GIR, at the Cauquigny church. At that point, Lewis gave Rae the following instructions: "You will set up your force in the vicinity of the church and serve as general reserve."[32] Rae's group waited there as the reserve element until, later in the afternoon, Colonel Lewis came back to him saying, "I am being counterattacked on both flanks and I need more men on the fire line."[33] To that Rae replied, "Be specific – where do I put my men?"[34] Lewis then told him to take his troops forward, find a hole in the line and plug it.[35]

Although the Germans had been driven from Cauquigny, they were still making things very difficult for the Americans. "The enemy still seemed to have an inexhaustible supply of mortar and artillery rounds," remembered General Gavin.[36] As ordered, Captain Rae pulled his men back to the vicinity of the church as a precaution against a possible counterattack. At that point, an element of Rae's force was able to make contact with Colonel Timmes's beleaguered 507th troopers. After the attack across the causeway overran Cauquigny, the German force that had been besieging Timmes's Orchard for the past four days began a strategic withdrawal. In stark contrast to the bloody competition that had been going on since D-Day, it had become strangely quiet at the orchard. In *No Better Place to Die*, Robert Murphy described that, "Rae just walked in to Timmes's position without any enemy in sight."[37]

Shortly before 9:00 pm General Gavin inspected the bridgehead at Cauquigny personally. He could tell that the situation was clearing because he could hear no rifle fire. Although he found things to be somewhat stable with glidermen and paratroopers digging-in for the night, he knew that the bridgehead could easily collapse in the event of a nighttime attack. He rationalized that it would be far better to keep up the pressure on the Germans than to let them reorganize for a counterattack. So he ordered everyone to prepare to attack to the west including headquarters personnel, regimental clerks and ranking officers. Le Motey had still not been occupied and to him it seemed like the right time to strike deeper into enemy territory, so he sought out Lt. Col. Maloney and Captain Rae. Maloney, despite his size, had not received a scratch during the

assault across the causeway – neither had Rae. Rae was bent over digging a foxhole as the last hints of daylight were fading from the sky when Gavin found him. "Let's move," Gavin said, "I want you to take your men and go forward."[38] Rae asked, "How far do you want me to go?" in reply. "Go to town!" was Gavin's response. With that, Rae assembled his men and led them back toward Le Motey just as he had early that afternoon. The paratroopers made it all the way to the village, this time "meeting no opposition en route, finding no Germans there."[39] By the time that the sun had finally set on June 9th, Rae and his men were deployed in and around Le Motey. That night, a pocket of German troops remained in the hedgerows just to the west of Cauquigny, but when they pulled out at dawn, the bridgehead battle concluded.

• • •

82nd Airborne Division paratroopers receiving awards from Major General Omar N. Bradley in La Haye-du-Puis in July 1944. Capt. Rae is next in line and is about to receive the Distinguished Service Cross he earned on the La Fière causeway on June 9th. *(Courtesy of Dominique François)*

La Fière was a hard-fought victory for the 82nd Airborne Division. As a result of the determination of the Germans to capture the causeway and the equal determination of the Americans to repel them, La Fière has been called one of the most vicious battles of the entire Normandy campaign.[40] At the beginning of the June 9th battle, Rae Company numbered ninety men. When the company pulled back to La Fière manoir the next day, only sixty officers and men were left. Gen. S.L.A. Marshall later wrote that La Fière was, "probably the bloodiest small struggle in the experience of American arms."[41] Although the battle cost the Army 60 killed and 529 wounded, what it won was something of infinite and inestimable importance to VII Corps – freedom of movement. Capturing the La Fière Causeway made it possible for the troops and vehicles back at Utah Beach to move inland, toward other objectives on the Cotentin Peninsula. Robert Rae personally witnessed this – the product of his efforts – the morning after the battle when the 90th Division moved through Le Motey to continue the drive westward. The fact that the day after the June 9th battle the 357th Infantry Regiment could move up from the invasion beachhead and pass over the Merderet River unmolested was the most poignant validation that could have been hoped for.

The men of the 82nd Airborne Division had been asked to re-open the causeway and they had done it. Robert Rae's 507th PIR paratroopers played a significant part in that victory. The intense enemy fire had devastated each of the three rifle companies from 3rd/325th that attempted to cross the causeway with the result that only a small number of glidermen were on hand to hold the bridgehead. Forced to bear the full weight of the German defenders, that small force suffered heavy casualties and quickly began to run low on ammunition. Under those circumstances, the glider infantrymen were just incapable of holding on against an organized counterattack, let alone developing the bridgehead. At that critical moment in the battle when disaster began to loom-up out of the developing crisis, Bob Rae's company of 507th paratroopers helped turn the tide. The ground that Bob Rae had helped to win then became "the springboard for the further pursuit and destruction of the German armies to the west."[42] In a 1989 letter to Mr. Albert "Bud" Parker (Bob Rae's son-in-law), General Gavin described his recollection of Captain Rae's contribution:

> He did an outstanding job, and in Normandy in particular, in a very dramatic action he took part of a battalion of glidermen, who were about to retreat, into an attack into the German positions. He succeeded and held his position against heavy German counterattacks.[43]

Although instances of individual heroism were common during the battle for the La Fière causeway, some were exceptional. For unhesitatingly charging headlong into the valley of death on June 9th, Robert Rae was awarded the United States' second highest award for valor – the Distinguished Service Cross. The following month in an awards ceremony in La Haye-du-Puis, none other than General Omar N. Bradley, Commander of the U.S. 1st Army, pinned the DSC on Capt. Rae. General Gavin personally wrote the citation:

> Captain Robert D. Rae, 01288948/507th Parachute Infantry, United States Army. For extraordinary heroism in action against the enemy on 9 June, 1944 near Ste. Mere Eglise, France. Elements of a Division were ordered to establish a bridgehead across the Merderet River to relieve isolated groups of the Division which had been holding fast on the other side of the river. Attainment of this objective involved a frontal assault across the bridge and over the river against heavy enemy fire. One company started the attack and was pinned down by the full force of the enemy fire. In order to maintain the momentum a composite company under Captain Rae was ordered to pass through the unit that was pinned down. He moved with such speed that he carried his men across the bridge, reorganized and pressed his initial advantage and overran the enemy positions. The courage and leadership displayed by Captain Rae reflect great credit on himself and were in keeping with the highest traditions of the Armed Forces.

15

Graignes

Far to the south of any of the airborne drop zones, a small village named Graignes became the center of a great deal of activity not long after midnight on June 6th. Located six miles south of Carentan, Graignes was situated on high ground overlooking a marshland that surrounded the village on three sides. At the time of the invasion, Graignes consisted of about two hundred widely dispersed buildings. These were mostly private homes, a few businesses, a grocery-café, a girls' school and a boys' school. The most striking and imposing of all the structures though was the village's XIIth century Roman Catholic Church which was prominently visible throughout the surrounding countryside.[1] The citizens of the village were accustomed to the type of simple life so typical among the rural farming communities of Normandy. They had been largely bypassed by the war with Germany and even the occupation that followed had only slight impact on their everyday lives. However, the war's full fury descended on them in the early morning hours of D-Day in the form of the American airborne assault. The parish priest at Graignes, later recorded what was going on around the village in those first hours when the invasion was just beginning:

> The night of June 5th was a terrible one. From the town, especially from the belfry of the church, one could perceive in the distance, in the direction of St. Mairie-du-Mont reddish lights and artillery fire. The air was filled with airplanes that striped the night sky. The German artillery units in Carentan fired without stopping. Planes were dropping bombs and the distant explosions shook the earth. Others were leading gliders and dropping parachutists over the region.[2]

Opposite: Map showing the location of the village of Graignes and the marshes that surrounded it at the time of the invasion. (Map by Scott Carroll Illustrations)

A pre-war view of the XIIth century Roman Catholic Church in Graignes. (Courtesy of The National D-Day Museum)

At approximately 1:00 am, the Rigault family was suddenly awakened by the sound of low-flying aircraft. The planes continued to pass over their farm in Le Port St. Pierre for twenty minutes or so, then quiet settled back over the area.[3] Everyone in the house was up by then: Marthe, Odette, their father Gustave, their mother Marthe and their two-year-old little brother, Jean Claude. They all knew that something was happening and they suspected it was the beginning of the Allied invasion that they had been waiting for since 1940. Shortly thereafter, Lucie Mauduit (a family friend) knocked at the Rigault's front door. Lucie was not alone though. She was with an American paratrooper – the first of many they would inter-

act with during the coming days. The man was quickly led into the dimly lit house. Since the Rigault's had no electricity, they depended on candles and a fireplace to illuminate the home. Fearing that someone would be able to see what was going on inside the house, particularly the Germans, Gustave quickly draped blankets over the windows, after which the first attempts at communication began. To M. Rigault, this move was absolutely necessary because the farm was most certainly under surveillance by the Germans.[4] Using an English-to-French dictionary, the paratrooper explained what was happening. "He told us that thousands of Americans were coming here to rescue us," Marthe remembered.[5] The family knew right then and there that the invasion had indeed begun.

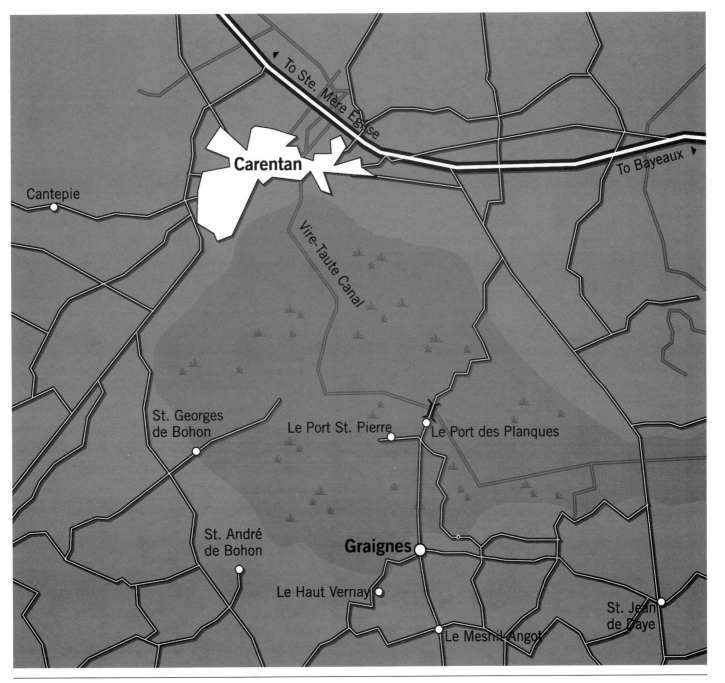

The Rigault family farm's main house in Le Port St. Pierre near Graignes. Paratroopers of the 3rd Battalion/507th Parachute Infantry repeatedly sought shelter at the Rigault farm throughout the dramatic sequence of events played out in the area. *(Courtesy of Odette Lelavechef)*

The paratrooper then produced a large map and asked the family to tell him where he was. The map generally covered the area from just north of Ste.-Mère-Église south to Carentan as well as the east coast of the Cotentin peninsula. It did not however cover the vicinity of the Rigault farm or nearby Graignes – which were well below the lower edge of the map. Gustave Rigault indicated that fact to the paratrooper. "Then he understood that he did not land at the right place," Marthe remembered.[6] The paratrooper stayed only a short time, about one hour, during which time the Rigaults gave him something to eat and a cup of coffee. Before he departed, the trooper gave Marthe and little Jean Claude some much-appreciated chocolate. Marthe remembered the gift, "It was so nice that I could never forget it – at that time we could not find any here."[7] M. Rigault then went outside alone to make sure that there were no Germans anywhere nearby and, with the coast clear, the lone paratrooper left.[8]

Soon, the lone paratrooper's promises were confirmed when more Americans drifted down out of the sky to land in the marshes around Graignes. The village priest described that activity as well:

Towards 1:30 in the morning, a glider landed in the large swamp between the village and the road to Tribehou, containing a jeep with supplies and a team of men. Later, around 2:20 am, a wave of aircraft approached Graignes at a very low altitude and dropped close to two hundred parachutists into the swamps of the community and neighboring areas. Soon they were heading for Graignes.[9]

Staff officers of the 3rd Battalion/507th Parachute Infantry: (*left to right*) Lieutenant H.E. Wagner, Captain L.D. Brummitt, Lieutenant Colonel William A. Kuhn, Lieutenant E.F. Hoffman and Lieutenant G.M. Dillon. *(Courtesy of William D. Bowell)*

The parachutists that the priest spoke of were from the 3rd Battalion/507th Parachute Infantry Regiment and, just after 2:00 am on June 6, 1944, fate placed them there in the marshes around Graignes. The episode that would unfold in this obscure little village over the course of the next five days stands as a remarkable example of the undefeatable human spirit encountered with such frequency as to be common during the Second World War. Over the course of the next five days, each of these paratroopers would do his duty where fortune had placed him, but the people of Graignes would likewise demonstrate the highest level of commitment to the cause of the liberation. Seemingly unafraid of the consequences of their actions, they would choose to support the Americans – a choice that would provoke the full fury of German retaliation. They, alongside some of the paratroopers, would be the victims of a shocking act of brutality that would leave thirty paratroopers and thirty-two civilians dead, and a village in ruins. But in the momentous battle for Normandy, the story of the Graignes tragedy would end up somewhat overlooked. In its minute detail though, it is one of the most dramatic yet tragic stories of indomitable human courage and sacrifice that would come out of the battle for Normandy.

• • •

Normandy was 1st Lieutenant Frank Naughton's twenty-sixth parachute jump. When he threw himself out of the door of his C-47 that night, he was about five hundred feet above the ground. Jumping from so low an altitude allowed only a few seconds of hang time under his open canopy and then he was on the ground. "We landed fifteen to twenty miles from where we were supposed to," he recalled, "and I landed in the water up to my shoulders."[10] A few hours before sunrise on D-Day, twelve planeloads of paratroopers from the 507th were scattered throughout the inundated area south of Carentan. They were supposed to have dropped sixteen miles to the north at drop zone "T" near Amfreville, but instead they ended-up in the vicinity of the village of Graignes. Theirs was the worst misdrop of any airborne unit on June 6, 1944. After sunrise, several small groups of these men slogged their way out of the marsh, gravitating toward the small agrarian community whose XIIth century church was silhouetted against the rising sun.

Sergeant John Hinchliff was serving in Headquarters Company, 3rd Battalion with Frank Naughton at the time. Like Naughton, he landed in the flooded area near Graignes, but he was very lucky. He landed in water that only came up to mid-thigh. Other troopers were not so lucky. "We lost a lot of troopers because they got tangled up in their parachute risers and drowned," he remembered.[11] Once on the ground, Hinchliff and his 17-year-old assistant gunner, Pfc. Patrick Sullivan, began searching for the equipment bundle containing their Browning M1919A4 .30-caliber machine gun and its ammunition. Because of their heavy weight, machine guns and machine gun ammunition were not carried individually during the jump. Instead, they were loaded into equipment bundles that were dropped at the same time that the paratroopers exited the troop carrier aircraft. Hinchliff described the scene:

> The two of us found the equipment bundle, we found the machine gun and adequate ammunition, and we didn't know where to go or what to do because we were many miles from our drop zone. But we saw in the distance, on the horizon, a cross and a steeple so we figured that had to be high ground and so we made our way towards that and dawn was just breaking when we entered the village of Graignes.[12]

• • •

Shortly before dawn, the Rigault family heard someone in their back yard and then came a knock at the door. Suddenly, they heard a man's voice speaking in perfect French say, "Don't be afraid, open the door."[13] It was Cpl. Benton J. Broussard of Headquarters Company, 3rd Battalion/507th. Cpl. Broussard, a French Canadian by birth, had a fluent command of the French language that would be of great value over the course of the next few days. Odette Rigault remembered that, "He spoke French very well!"[14] M. Rigault opened the door and Cpl. Broussard with several paratroopers immediately checked the house for Germans. Twelve-year-old Marthe remembered that, "There were Americans everywhere: in the kitchen, in the bed rooms – the courtyard was full of them."[15] According to nineteen-year-old Odette, they could not even close the door for all the Americans.[16] In all, about one hundred 507th paratroopers took refuge at the Rigault house before dawn on D-Day.

At the time of the invasion, Marthe's and Odette's parents owned some cows that had to be brought in and milked every morning at about 7:00 o'clock. Although it was not yet 7:00 am, M. Rigault sent Odette to do the chore early on D-Day because he correctly estimated that fighting would erupt at first light. "When dawn comes," he had said, "there's going to be trouble."[17] Odette then left the house with Marthe following, and the two girls had to step around paratroopers on their way out of the yard. They walked down to where the cows were grazing near the edge of the inundated area and went to work. "Our house was right in front of the marsh, and we could see for several kilometers," Marthe recalled.[18] Unfortunately prying eyes somewhere out in the marsh were watching and could see the two Rigault girls as well as the large number of paratroopers walking about in the farmyard. After they had been there only a few minutes, bullets suddenly slammed into the ground right at Odette's feet.[19] At first, the girls did not realize what was happening, but when several more bursts of fire struck the ground near them, they ran for their lives. Once the girls were sheltered from the incoming fire, one of the paratroopers took Odette by the arm and told her that they had to get out of there. A German machine gun crew hidden somewhere nearby was responsible for the attack, proving that the Rigault family farm had become a battlefield. Cpl. Broussard was close by and, speaking in French, added, "You'll see – I'm going to kill that guy over there – I'm going to slit his throat!"[20] The girls then returned to the house and, upon arrival, Marthe ran straight down into the cellar to hide. "I was terrified," she recalled.[21] For Marthe and Odette, war had come to their backyard. Unfortunately, this incident would not be the last brush with death the two girls would endure during the fighting around Graignes. Because the Rigault farmhouse was so prominently visible and consequently vulnerable along the edge of the marsh, M. Rigault decided to move the family temporarily to his father's house one hundred yards inland from the marsh. They would be safer there.

Later in the day, Gustave Rigault and a family friend named Isidore Folliot, along with Marthe and Odette took boats out into the marsh to look for some of the airborne equipment that had landed there. When they would spot one of the equipment bundles, they would row over to it, heave it aboard the boat and then row it back to shore. When they reached shore, their cargo was then carried up to and hidden in a barn on the farm. This process was repeated multiple times during the afternoon to the point that the barn was practically overflowing with ammunition and other airborne equipment.

• • •

Throughout the morning of D-Day, small groups of exhausted and thoroughly soaked 507th paratroopers filtered into the village of Graignes and generally assembled at the XIIth century stone church. Father Albert Leblastier, the Parish Priest, or *Curé*, of Graignes, was there to welcome them. More than just the community's spiritual leader, Father Leblastier was also a valued and much sought after counselor of every facet of collective existence in the village.[22] Parish records described the reception he extended to the Americans:

> The soldiers were greeted warmly. Some of them, drenched and wet, shivered and rattled their teeth. Very quickly a flow of sympathy and confidence established itself.[23]

By 10:00 am, twenty-five paratroopers under the command of Capt. Leroy D. Brummitt had gathered in the village. Considering what they had been through, the small group of troopers was surprisingly well armed. In addition to their personal weapons, the men had five M1919A4 .30-cal. machine guns and two 81mm mortars. As a precaution, Capt. Brummitt put out perimeter security to serve as an early warning in the event that the enemy approached the village. Two hours later, more 3rd Battalion men arrived. Led by Major Charles D. Johnson, the group also included Capt. Richard H. Chapman, 1st Lt. Elmer F. Hoffman 1st Lt. Earcle R. "Pip" Reed and Capt. Abraham Sophian, Jr., the battalion's surgeon. After discussing the situation with Capt. Brummitt, Major Johnson took control of the 507th men assembled in the village. He felt that, moving the force toward the American airborne units fighting to the north was an impractical idea because the 82nd and 101st Division drop zones were just too far away. He therefore decided that

Marthe and Jean Claude Rigault in their father's small boat in Le Port St. Pierre near Graignes. Note the inundated condition of the marsh behind them. *(Courtesy of Odette Lelavechef)*

Boats in an inundated area around Le Port St. Pierre near Graignes. Troopers of the 3rd Battalion/507th Parachute Infantry landed in this marsh shortly after 2:00am on D-Day. *(Courtesy of Odette Lelavechef)*

the best course of action would be to keep the force in Graignes where it could potentially interfere with the lines of communication connecting Carentan to the rest of occupied France. Capt. Brummitt disagreed and argued that the force should attempt to reach the regiment's objective area to the north. Brummitt remembered the situation:

> In my capacity as Battalion S-3, I formulated a tentative night march plan to go through the flooded swamp area, through which we had waded finding it to be waist to chest deep, or alternatively to go around the surrounding coast line to Carentan, link up with the U.S. force there and continue to the 82nd Division area. The plan had its negative aspects: 81mm mortars would have to be spiked, ammunition destroyed and various other equipment abandoned. Additionally, the swamp appeared to include canals of unknown depth, requiring us to swim a short distance or requisition two or three of the small fishing boats observed nearby for ferry use in accommodating the heavy equipment and non-swimmers. I considered our Battalion mission to be critical, overriding these obstacles and worthy of our best effort. I presented the plan to Major Johnson, who rejected it curtly.[24]

Major Johnson felt that the troopers should stay-put and organize a defensive perimeter to await a link-up with ground forces coming across the landing beaches.[25] As the ranking officer present, Johnson's decision was final: Graignes would be defended.

"That decision entailed an on-the-spot reorganization of our specialist personnel into provisional infantry fire teams reinforced by machine gun and mortar platoons," Captain Brummitt remem-

bered.[26] The Americans immediately began preparing defensive positions, and the village became a hive of activity. Soldiers started digging-in around the town's perimeter, cutting fields of fire, installing communications and otherwise making ready to receive a counterattack. The mortar platoon dug-in around the cemetery and sent a detachment to occupy the church belfry as an observation post. From that vantage point, the observer enjoyed an unobstructed view of the network of roads and trails leading to the village from the west and southwest. The view would make it possible to adjust fire on any enemy force attempting to the approach the village from any direction. Although the rear area of the village was a seemingly impenetrable marsh, it too was covered by firepower. The main road leading uphill to the church was also covered by riflemen located strategically along its flanks. Last but not least, anti-tank mines were positioned along the village's major road approaches. In short, all routes into Graignes were covered by rifles, machine guns, mines and mortars. There was no way in that was not covered by fire. While these defenses were being prepared, Major Johnson established his Command Post at the boys' school.[27] Graignes had become the Alamo of Normandy.

Throughout this digging-in process, troopers continued to arrive in Graignes. At approximately 5:30 pm on D-Day, a large group of Headquarters Company personnel entered the village with 1st Lt. Elmer F. Farnham, 1st Lt. Lowell C. Maxwell and 1st Lt. Naughton.[28] With them were eighteen men from B Company, 501st Parachute Infantry Regiment, 101st Airborne Division being led by Capt. Loyal K. Bogart and 1st Lt. George C. Murn. Although he was B Company Commander, Capt. Bogart had sustained injuries that made him unable to execute the full responsibilities of that leadership role. He had been wounded by fragmentation in both legs while still in his C-47 during the approach to the drop zone. Despite of his wounds, Capt. Bogart jumped with his stick anyway only to be wounded again on the ground. When Bogart reported-in at Graignes, he insisted that he was capable of making a worth-while contribution to the force and asked for something to do. Maj. Johnson responded by placing him in charge of the central switch-board at the command post. The remaining B Company, 501st men were given a sector on the line.[29] By the end of D-Day, a mixed group of ninety Americans had assembled in Graignes. That night, more men entered the village, and by the end of the following day (D+1), the group had grown in size to 182 (12 officers and 170 enlisted).[30] In addition to the greater part of Headquarters, 3rd Battalion/507th PIR and the group of 101st troopers, others served on the line there as well. A glider pilot ended-up in the village along with a C-47 pilot and two soldiers from the 29th Infantry Division that had landed at Omaha Beach on the 6th.

• • •

On the morning of June 6th, M. Alphonse Voydie awoke to find American paratroopers in the field behind his house. When he was informed that more paratroopers had assembled at the church in town, he quickly rushed to the scene to establish contact with them. He felt he had a responsibility to do so because, at the time, he was the village's acting mayor. The official mayor, who had been an elderly man, died the week before the invasion and the villagers had appointed Voydie to serve in his place on an unofficial provisional basis. By the time that he got to the Americans on D-Day, Maj. Johnson had already begun the process of preparing defenses around the village. Voydie and Johnson met and discussed the situation with Cpl. Broussard serving as the translator. At first, Maj. Johnson requested information about the general layout of the area as well as German troop movements. Without hesitating, Voydie and several other villagers told him everything they could. Then Johnson also asked about having use of a boat to retrieve the equipment bundles that had landed in the marshes around the village because his men were going to need the ammunition and heavy weapons they contained. Finally, Johnson asked about the food situation. He faced the very real and immediate problem of having only a very limited supply of rations for his force. Also, since the misdropped band of troopers would almost certainly not be re-supplied any time soon, Johnson was genuinely concerned about how he was going to feed his people. Voydie wanted to help the paratroopers, but he realized that coming up with enough to feed 182 hungry young men several times a day was not something that he could manage alone or even with the help of a few people. He recognized that such an effort, as well as the effort to recover the equip-

ment bundles, would require the cooperation and assistance of the entire Graignes community.

For that reason, Voydie called a meeting for the next day, June 7th. All heads of the family had to attend by order of the (acting) mayor. As Odette Rigault later recalled, the purpose of the meeting was "to give instructions to each head of the family what needed to be done for the Americans."[31] During the meeting, which was held in the XIIth century church, Voydie appealed to the citizens of Graignes to place all the resources of the village at the disposal of the Americans. His impassioned plea was successful because at the meeting's conclusion, there was a unanimous decision to help the paratroopers. This decision was not entered into lightly though, as it carried grave implications. They all knew that if the Germans caught them assisting the enemy, the punishment would be harsh. This was not a perceived fear based on intuition, but very real and based on proof. By the summer of 1944, the Germans had demonstrated their willingness to carry out harsh sentences time and again in their merciless crack-downs on the Resistance (such as the incident at Chateaubriant in late 1941). Despite this, the people of Graignes elected to be active participants in their own liberation. With a sober appreciation for the consequences of their actions, they mobilized with as much energy and dedication as the paratroopers in their midst.

After the meeting, Voydie mobilized the women of the village in an effort to procure, prepare and distribute food for the Americans. Since the paratroopers would soon exhaust the supply of light rations they had carried with them to Normandy, something had to be done quickly. The proprietor of the village café-grocery, 50-year-old Madame Germaine Boursier, was therefore recruited to organize an effort to provide meals to the paratroopers. Her assistance to the Americans actually began during the pre-dawn hours of June 6th when several paratroopers landed in the marsh near her home. She took the cold, drenched men into her home and offered them food from her café. From that point forward, Madame Boursier set the standard for aiding her liberators. Under her direction, the women of Graignes began cooking on a round the clock basis so they could serve two meals each day. Using her establishment as the base of operations, Madame Boursier even supervised and coordinated the transportation of meals out to the soldiers occupying the many dispersed observation positions guarding the village and the approaches to it. "Madame Boursier was our Mess Sergeant," Frank Naughton remembered.[32] With almost two hundred extra mouths to feed, high demands were placed on the existing food supplies. The challenge of collecting food in sufficient quantities was, to say the least, daunting, but Madame Boursier was industrious and resourceful. She organized a makeshift food drive to collect milk, fruit and meat for the men. When that effort failed to provide a sufficient amount, she had to travel outside of the village at night in a clandestine effort to contact her suppliers and convince them to fake or misrepresent the amounts of food she was gathering. This was an especially difficult obstacle because everyone in occupied France was still restricted to receiving food based on ration cards. Madame Boursier then had to conceal the extra food that she managed to gather in her horse-drawn cart in order to sneak it back in to Graignes. She also depended on friends like Renee Meunier who created imaginary reasons that justified unauthorized travel outside of the village to do the same thing.[33] Fulfilling this mission even required some of the women to make the trip over mined roads by horse-drawn cart to the nearby German-held village of St.-Jean-de-Daye to obtain additional bread.[34]

Voydie also had to deal with the issue of the equipment bundles in the marshes around the village. The paratroopers could not conduct a thorough search of these inundated areas without dangerously exposing themselves to enemy observation and possibly enemy fire. The civilians however, could move around in the marsh without attracting German suspicions. So teams of men, women and even children were soon hauling wagonloads of valuable salvaged equipment back to the Graignes perimeter. They recovered much-needed machine guns and mortars – weapons that would make the positions around the village far more defensible. They also recovered large quantities of ammunition that they thereafter delivered into the hands of the American defenders. These scavenging parties were so successful that the Americans soon had an abundance of ammunition and weapons with which to defend the village.[35] According to 1st Lt. "Pip" Reed, "We never did recover the full complement of heavy weapons, but we certainly had more ammunition than we thought we could ever use."[36] Frank Naughton remembered that, "We probably had some of the 101st Airborne's ammunition containers."[37]

But even before Alphonse Voydie called the meeting that organized this effort, some recovery activity had already begun. Marthe, Odette and Gustave Rigault along with Isidore Folliot began pulling items out of the marsh the day before (on D-Day). While Gustave and Isidore were recovering equipment, the girls recovered the silken T-5 canopies that littered the area. "We went to look for parachutes so we could make dresses," Odette remembered.[38] What they recovered, they stored temporarily in the Rigaults' barn. When Gustave received word of the (acting) mayor's meeting the next day, he wasted no time and set out for Graignes. Not long after his departure, a paratrooper came back to the Rigault farm to retrieve the ammunition and equipment being stored in their barn. Odette was there and described what happened next:

> He asked my mother if we could transport the ammunition that was in our place, from the barn in question. So naturally my mother said, "Well yes, we'll do it – we're not going to refuse." And I said, "I want to go." I was already 18 at the time. I called for our horse and cart and the American soldiers loaded up the cart, and I left with my parents' horse and my parents' cart to transport the ammunition 4_ kilometers to the church. There were two roads. I took the road that ran along the marsh so as not to find myself with the Germans, since they were still moving about. So I went 4 kilometers like that with all the ammunition, my cart full of it.[39]

Odette used sacks of feed and fertilizer and mounds of hay to conceal the contraband cargo that she was hauling to town. Frank Naughton described what she did:

> I remember this young lady bringing in weapons concealed under a load of hay. She left right under the Germans' eyes, and she drove that into our perimeter.[40]

Odette Rigault used this horse and wagon to carry the paratrooper's ammunition and equipment from Le Port St. Pierre to Graignes on June 7th. *(Courtesy of Odette Lelavechef)*

When Odette was entering town with her horse-drawn manure cart full of ammunition, she ran into her father, who was leaving. He was walking back to the family farm after having just left Voydie's meeting. At the same moment, some villagers appeared with the warning that Germans were approaching. Odette remembered what happened next:

> There I was with my horse and my cart full of ammunition. Papa told me, "Get out of the cart. Get out of the cart. Give it to them." There were two Americans walking with me, one in front and one behind. So he said, "Leave them and they'll tie up the horse and we'll find them again later." He said the Germans were approaching from all sides. So I left with my father.[41]

Father and daughter then returned to the family farm together and Odette's cartload of ammunition was distributed among the American defenders. That ammunition was put to good use during the next three days.

The paratroopers spent the days between Thursday the 8th and Saturday the 10th consolidating their positions around the village and staying alert for enemy activity. Each morning patrols went out, each evening they came back in, all the while defenses back in the village were improved. Captain Brummitt described it:

During the ensuing days, the officers and men proved beyond a doubt that they were elite troops of the highest order. They went on both reconnaissance and combat patrols, mined the key Graignes bridge, manned outpost and perimeter defense positions set up with final protective fires, targeted gaps with pre-planned mortar fires and established wire and radio communications throughout the position.[42]

For practically all of Major Johnson's daily patrols, Graignes resident Charles Gosselin served as scout and navigator. Since his intimate familiarity with the local area had proven to be of decisive importance in certain critical situations, Gosselin's services were in great demand.[43]

With so much activity going on around the village, there were bound to be close calls. At one point, the men of a recon patrol operating to the east of Graignes barely avoided contact with an enemy patrol by submerging themselves in the marsh. Also, some of Johnson's other recon parties observed a dramatic increase in enemy traffic on the north-south road two miles west of the village. The Americans were perceptive enough to recognize that the Germans they were seeing on that road were moving back and forth to the battle area in and around Carentan to the north. The inevitability of this intensifying situation was that contact with German forces had become unavoidable. This resulted in a series of small firefights that confirmed for the Germans that American forces were indeed

An 82nd Airborne paratrooper talking with two French children. Throughout the Normandy campaign, American paratroopers and French civilians interacted extensively. At Graignes, that interaction was extensive. (*82nd Airborne Museum via Phil Nordyke*)

in Graignes. The Germans reacted to the developing situation by sending more and more patrols out with each passing day.[44] In addition to this increased frequency, each day these patrols came with greater and greater firepower.[45] Once the Germans knew the enemy was there they began probing the American positions around Graignes in an effort to identify the strong and weak points of the perimeter. But each of these probing reconnaissance attacks was beaten back by the mortar and machine gun fire of the well-organized American defenders.[46]

On Saturday, June 10th Major Johnson ordered 1st Lt. Naughton to take the demolitions squad to destroy the bridge at Le Port Des Planques. Located a few kilometers north of Graignes, the bridge spanned the Vire-Taute Canal and was so situated as to provide the enemy with a potential attack route through the marsh to the village. Since the enemy's intensifying reconnaissance patrols had been probing various approaches to Graignes during the previous two days, Major Johnson decided that blowing the bridge would hamper their ability to assault the village perimeter. Lt. Naughton assembled the demolitions squad and some support personnel in Graignes and then led the group north toward Le Port Des Planques. They covered the ground without incident and, upon arrival, went to work. Naughton then turned to one of the NCOs and asked how long it would take to wire the bridge. "It'll take 30-minutes sir," was the reply. He immediately ordered Sgt. Frank S. Costa and Pvt. David E. Purcell to cross to the north side of the bridge to cover the approach while the blasting charges were being set. "We double-timed to that other side of the bridge where I set-up my BAR and Purcell took up a position with his carbine," Costa remembered.[47] With the demolitions men busily working, Costa and Purcell kept a nervous vigil on the road ahead of them. At first everything was quiet for the two guards alone on the far side of the bridge, but then the situation changed. Only a few minutes after they had taken up their positions on the north side of the Vire-Taute Bridge, Costa and Purcell spotted a force of about thirty Germans marching around the bend in the road a few hundred yards in front of them. "I told Purcell to go back and inform Lt. Naughton that the Germans were fast approaching," Costa recalled.[48] He then checked the ammunition supply for his BAR and sighted-in on the enemy. As the Germans got closer and closer, Costa tracked them with the weapon, but did not fire – he wanted them to get nice and close before he let them have it.[49]

When the Germans were five hundred yards from the bridge, Costa opened fire. As soon as the bullets from his first burst struck, German infantrymen scattered in every direction. These infantrymen were experienced though and continued to advance with concealment along the sides of the road. As Costa laid down fire, Lt.

Naughton's demolitions men continued to prepare the bridge for destruction. With the staccato of BAR fire in the background, the demo men attached explosives and laid wire that ran back to a detonator at Naughton's position. By then, Costa was the only man left on the north side of the bridge. He was fighting a solitary crusade against Germans who were determined to overrun his position and capture the bridge intact. Just then, Purcell signaled him to fall back to the south side. "I picked up my BAR and ran across the bridge with the Germans no more than two hundred to three hundred yards away," Costa later described.[50] Although bullets were slicing the air all around him, Costa beat the odds and made it across unscathed. As soon as he was safe on the south side of the Vire-Taute canal, Lt. Naughton yelled to everyone: "The bridge is ready to go!"[51] He waited until the Germans were on the bridge and then gave the order to detonate the charges, blowing the bridge "sky high."[52] The blast killed countless soldiers and the remaining Germans fell back. The paratroopers continued to exchange gunfire with the enemy as they withdrew and then when the shooting died down, Naughton took the men back into Graignes to report the action to Maj. Johnson. With the northern approach to the village closed, the Germans shifted their efforts to the west.

That afternoon, a mechanized patrol approached a defensive position that was manned by some of 1st Lt. George Murn's B Company, 501st men. They let the patrol get close, then opened fire killing two to four of the enemy and capturing one motorcycle sidecar. That night, outposts reported hearing a great deal of activity in the same vicinity and contact was made with the Germans several times. In one of those firefights, the paratroopers ambushed a convoy, killing one enemy soldier. When the troopers searched the dead German's pockets for intelligence papers, they discovered some documents that revealed him to be assigned to a reconnaissance battalion of an armored division – an ominous sign of what the Americans were up against.[53] Knowing that such a German force was out there in the hedgerows to the west of Graignes sent a wave of nervousness through the Americans. As a consequence, that night was spent on a full alert with officers conducting almost constant inspections of the perimeter. Prior to that night, the paratroopers at Graignes were confident that American units from the invasion beaches or the 101st Airborne would get through to them before the enemy could launch any kind of serious attack against their perimeter. However, the crescendo of enemy activity around the village throughout the 8th, 9th and 10th seemed to indicate that they could not expect relief to arrive before the Germans. To the American paratroopers and the French civilians clustered around that XIIth century church, it appeared that the moment of truth was drawing near.

16

Ten to One

The next morning (June 11th) was a great contrast to the previous night's activity. There was no sign of the enemy and all was quiet on this the first Sunday since the invasion began. That being the case, Major Johnson gave permission for the men to do something for the first time in Normandy: attend mass. "We went in small groups," remembered Lt. Naughton, who arrived at the church just after 8:00 am.[1] Marthe and Odette Rigault went to mass that morning as well. An unexpected casualty of the previous day had been their father Gustave, who suffered a sudden heart attack. In his time of need, M. Rigault was cared for by a 507th medic and, by Sunday morning, his condition had improved. Nevertheless, he was not well enough to attend services with his family as he did every

Sunday. For that reason, he remained at home with his wife and the two girls – Marthe and Odette – went to church alone. By previous arrangement, Cpl. Benton Broussard walked out to the family farm to escort the two girls into town for ten o'clock mass. They left their house at about 9:30 am and arrived as Father Leblastier began right on time. It would be the last service over which he would officiate.

At about the same time that the parishioners and the Americans were assembling just before the start of ten o'clock mass, two paratroopers went out to bury the German reconnaissance soldier that had been killed the night before. They moved out of the village and were on their way to a field south of Graignes when they drew

The XIIth century Roman Catholic Church in Graignes as it looks today. (*Photo by the author*)

German small arms fire. Although neither man was wounded, the fire that drove them back was unusually heavy compared to previous days. Captain Brummitt, who heard the firing, rushed to the scene and quickly determined that a large German force was approaching Graignes from the south. He reinforced the southern flank and prepared to receive the weight of a direct attack. He would not have to wait long.

Meanwhile back in the church, the firing rudely interrupted Father Leblastier, who was ten minutes into the liturgy.[2] At first he continued, but then half way through the service, a Mrs. Bazire burst into the church with a warning. Odette remembered that Mrs. Bazire was yelling, "Hurry! Hurry! The Krauts are coming! The Germans! Save yourselves, the Krauts are coming!"[3] In all truth, a German patrol had indeed managed to penetrate to within two hundred meters of the church, causing what amounted to a panic among the assembled parishioners and soldiers. Marthe remembered that, "Everybody started to run away but they started shooting, so we had to stay inside the church."[4] Sgt. Hinchliff was one of the people attending Mass that morning and he remembered what he did after the firing began: "I stepped out the door (of the church) and ran over to my machine gun position, a couple hundred yards from the church."[5] For a short while, soldiers from both sides dashed around seeking cover among the various buildings in the town center in an intense, albeit brief, firefight. Automatic weapons fire ricocheted around the stone structures of downtown Graignes as attacker attempted to overrun defender and defender attempted to repulse attacker. Throughout this, all of the villagers assembled for Mass had

to huddle inside the nave of the church just to stay out of the way of the hundreds of bullets flying in all directions outside. Marthe and Odette sought shelter by hiding behind the stone altar.[6] Throughout the attack, one of the paratroopers told the civilians what was happening outside. He also told them that they should all remain inside where he could protect them.[7] "We couldn't get out – if the Germans had gotten into the church, we would have all been shot to death," Odette remembered.[8]

The assault, which lasted only ten minutes, had been a poorly organized, uncoordinated, piecemeal effort during which the paratroopers inflicted heavy casualties on the attacking force.[9] Frank Naughton remembered that, although the attack did not succeed, "Nevertheless, it did provide us a sample of firepower that was available to the Germans, even if in using it they exposed themselves unnecessarily by failing to use covered approaches."[10] After the brief fight, Major Johnson ordered all available personnel to man the defensive line around the village. He correctly recognized that the morning attack had only been a probing action and that another assault would soon follow. Some of the parishioners in the church decided to accept the risks and leave the village during this lull, but they ended-up being sucked into a very ugly reality of war. Marthe described what they were forced to do:

Those who were able to get out were captured by the Germans because, since the Americans were doing a lot of injuring and killing, the Germans needed help loading all their dead and wounded into the trucks. The French people had to help them.[11]

A wagon being used to collect German dead in Normandy. During the June 11th battle at Graignes, trucks and wagons could be seen moving from collecting point to collecting point picking up casualties caused by the American paratroopers in the village. *(Collection of The National D-Day Museum)*

From the belfry of the church, trucks could be seen moving "from collecting point to collecting point" picking up the dead German soldiers that the French villagers had been forced to gather up.[12] All of the work that the paratroopers put into preparing fields of fire to cover avenues of approach had paid off, and the Germans sustained very high casualties. The defenders had used supporting mortar fire with devastating results and the crossfire produced by machine guns with interlocking fields of fire had been likewise highly destructive. Although firepower repulsed them in round one, the Germans did not give up and round two was about to begin.

At about 2:00 pm, the Germans commenced a punishing mortar bombardment of Graignes. This preparatory fire was swiftly followed by a second infantry assault against the flanks of the defensive line around the village. This time the attackers moved so swiftly that the perimeter was almost breached at one point. However, Capt. Brummitt quickly shifted forces to meet the threat, and the line held. Once again, the paratroopers' supporting fires were decisive in holding off defeat: scores of enemy infantry were caught in the crossfire of the multiple machine guns defending the village center and accurate mortar fire also inflicted heavy losses. During this second attack though, the paratroopers and the citizens of Graignes began to suffer their first significant casualties. The church sanctuary was thereafter transformed into an aid station as the wounded were rushed there to receive medical attention from Capt. Sophian. His selfless devotion to his comrades would soon cost him his life. In addition to them, several villagers assisted the best they could in caring for the injured men. Father Leblastier was a study in serenity and confidence throughout it all and did everything he could to comfort the soldiers, as did Father R. P. Louis Lebarbanchon, a Franciscan priest posted to Graignes on temporary assignment. Cheerful, poised and highly intelligent, Father Lebarbanchon's warm spirit had managed to overcome the language difference, producing a harmonious environment that strengthened the linkage between his parishioners and the American paratroopers.[13] Alongside the two priests, the rectory's two housekeepers, eighty-year-old Eugenie DuJardin and Madeleine Pezeril, also provided as much valuable assistance as they could. Although it was well staffed, this makeshift aid station lacked proper supplies and was quickly stretched well beyond its modest means.

An uneasy quiet fell over Graignes following the second attack. During this lull, Major Johnson pulled his outposts back to the defensive line in the village and assessed his situation. He found that, after the morning's two major assaults, ammunition was be-

3rd Battalion/507th surgeon Capt. Abraham Sophian, Jr. He stayed behind to care for the troopers wounded during the June 11th battle and was murdered by soldiers of the *17th SS Panzergrenadier Division* in the aftermath of the battle. (*from the 507th yearbook, collection of The National D-Day Museum*)

ginning to run low. The remaining small arms ammunition and mortar rounds were then redistributed among the defenders to provide each position with an even supply. At the same time that this was taking place, villagers distributed food and water to the beleaguered defenders. Then, an unnerving sound was heard rising from the maze of hedgerows surrounding Graignes. What was clearly the sound of heavy vehicular movement announced that the Germans were bringing in reinforcements. Carentan, ten kilometers to the north, was under direct threat of falling into American hands, and the Germans were massing their forces in the area to prevent it.[14] But the strength of their hold on Carentan was largely dependent on the security of their lines of supply to the city. The pocket of resistance at Graignes was threateningly close to those lines of supply and was, consequently, a pocket that had to be eliminated.

Since the observed evidence indicated that Graignes was about to be the target of a major attack, Major Johnson sent all of the civilians away. After almost nine hours of confinement in the church during the day's fighting, Marthe and Odette were both "ready to leave."[15] Marthe remembered that, "At 7 o'clock pm Major Johnson told us that we should go home because they did not have enough

ammunition for the night and the night was coming."[16] According to Odette, "He told us that we had to try to get out if we could, but if we did and we came across some Germans, then we must certainly not tell them that they [the Americans] were there."[17] French speaking Cpl. Benton Broussard, who had escorted the girls to church that morning, was not able to escort them on their trek back home. "Cpl. Broussard could not come with us of course but he promised that he would come back to see us," Marthe remembered.[18] The girls said goodbye to Broussard there at the church, unaware that they would never see him again or that he had less than twenty-four hours to live.

Marthe and Odette then left on what was to be a treacherous trip home to the family farm in Le Port St. Pierre. "It was just the two of us with three, almost four, kilometers to go," 12-year-old Marthe recalled.[19] When they were one hundred yards away from the church, the girls started running because, "…there was shooting from everywhere."[20] But they had to slow down soon thereafter as they approached the paratrooper's outer defensive perimeter. "Then we met three soldiers who told us that a little further down they had planted some mines and that we had to be really careful

The 36-pound Browning M1919A4 .30-cal. machine gun. Colt, Buffalo Arms and the Saginaw Steering Gear Division of GM manufactured 389,859 M1919A4s before production ceased in 1945. Sergeant John Hinchliff of Headquarters Company, 3rd Battalion/507th used this type weapon during the defense of Graignes. (*Robert J. Carr Collection*)

not to walk on them," Marthe recalled.[21] "We told them good bye, it was very sad," she remembered.[22] Then both girls proceeded to step over the three rows of mines and made their way out of the village. The next few kilometers passed without incident, but then when they were only five hundred yards from home they ran into more potential danger. When they rounded the last bend in the road before the farmhouse, there suddenly appeared ninety German soldiers marching right toward them. "We were very afraid," Marthe remembered.[23] The pack of Germans was being led by a neighbor and family friend named Isidore Folliot. He had encountered the Germans as they were fleeing south, away from Carentan and he purposely guided them along a road that led them as far away as possible from the Americans in the village. "They didn't know what was happening in Graignes," Marthe remembered.[24] After speaking briefly with Isidore, the girls continued on toward their house. "When we were in front of the Germans, they looked at us but they did not ask anything," Marthe recalled.[25] Despite the close call, the girls arrived safely at their home around 8:00 pm.[26]

• • •

Meanwhile back at Graignes, the signs were getting more and more ominous with each passing hour. Through his binoculars, 1st Lt. "Pip" Reed could see two German 88mm guns setting-up and digging-in on a farm located just a few kilometers away on the heights of nearby Thieuville. Reed realized that, once those guns were in position, high explosive 88mm rounds would begin falling on the American positions in the village. He also realized that the primary observation post in the church's belfry would surely be a target of incoming rounds. For that reason, he rushed there without delay to warn the two men manning the position, one of which was 1st Lt. Elmer Farnham:

> I went up to the belfry to coax Farnham and another observer to abandon their position because of imminent enemy artillery fire. Farnham wanted to stay and I left the belfry and returned to my machine gun.[27]

Farnham then made an unsuccessful attempt to direct and adjust mortar fire onto the two 88s before they could commence firing, but fate would not have it. The mortars that Farnham was attempting to direct were firing at extreme range and consequently could not reach their intended target with any degree of reliable accuracy. The result was a futile effort that did little more than consume precious ammunition. At about 7:00 pm, when the Germans were finished setting-up, the 88s opened fire on Graignes. Incoming rounds swept across the boys' school, the town square and the

church. As shells landed all around the church, "Pip" Reed looked up at the belfry just in time to see a shell score a direct hit on it. Sgt. Frank Costa was watching at that exact moment too and saw the steeple "literally blown off."[28] The enemy shell ripped through the observation post, killing Lt. Farnham and his assistant observer.[29] But Farnham was not the only officer to lose his life to those 88s. When the bombardment began, Maj. Johnson was at the bedside of 1st Lt. Lowell C. Maxwell, who had become violently ill since arriving in Normandy on Tuesday the 6th. While the two men were talking, one of those 88mm rounds tore into the command post and exploded, killing both Johnson and Maxwell instantly.[30]

This artillery barrage proved to be the beginning of the final assault against the Americans at Graignes. The Germans had apparently learned valuable lessons over the course of the morning and afternoon attacks, because this renewed thrust was even more determined and savage than the ones that had preceded it. After a thorough "softening up" of the target by the mortars and the 88s, the infantry moved in for the *coup de grace*. It was immediately obvious that this assault force was at least twice as large as the assault force from the afternoon battle.[31] This time, the Germans used cover wherever possible to mask their approach to the village. With the observation post in the belfry destroyed, it was no longer possible to use long-range mortar fire against the approaching enemy. The mortar crews consequently cranked the elevation mechanisms of their tubes to the maximum for extreme short-range work. They then attempted to use their mortar rounds to stop the German infantrymen that were already closing ranks with the defensive perimeter in the village itself. This did not succeed in driving the attackers away. However, an early breech of the line was repulsed during the final glow of fading daylight by a pair of M1919A4 .30-cal. machine guns that produced a crossfire on one of the principle approaches to the village center.[32] But soon, darkness settled over Graignes and, although the day was done, the fighting continued on into the night. Even though the paratroopers were running out of ammunition at an alarming rate, they were nevertheless able to fight off repeated assaults before it was clear that they would not be able to hold on much longer. The confused nature that the fighting took on after dark was such that men from both sides were firing wildly at each other, and soon the number of paratrooper casualties was rising as a result.

From their parent's farm four kilometers away in Le Port St. Pierre, Marthe and Odette could hear the rumble of the intensifying firefight in Graignes. Though they could not see anything, they knew what was going on in Graignes and they were anxious about the outcome. For them, it was an agonizing wait to learn of the fate of the paratroopers, so many of whom they had befriended during the last six days. The sounds of battle made it impossible for them to sleep. Then at about 11:00pm, the girls saw something that made their hearts sink – a sight which Marthe later described:

> We saw the red flares signaling for help go up from the church. Since the Americans were out of ammunition, they could no longer hold off the enemy.[33]

By the time the Germans made the final thrust into Graignes that night, the defenders had been reduced to a few isolated pockets of resistance spread out around the village. In most cases, men were

beginning to run out of ammunition. As that happened, the enemy was quick to exploit the situation by overrunning the outer perimeter and moving into the streets of the center of the village. Those points of the line that were not overrun, were cut off from communication with the command post and the aid station. The enemy was present in such large numbers that they swept through the outer ring of defenses so quickly that some of the defenders were simply bypassed. This is exactly what happened to Sgt. Frank Costa, Pvt. James Klingman and Pvt. Edward T. Page. They had been assigned to a foxhole by the marsh guarding the rear of village. The three

The M1 81mm mortar with an M49 (TNT) high explosive round and an inert practice round. The weapon weighed 136 pounds and was capable of accurate fire at a maximum range of 3,290 yards. The 507th paratroopers that defended Graignes used effective fire from two 81mm mortars to fight off two German attacks against the village on June 11th. (*Robert G. Segel Collection*)

men were aware of the bombardment and they could hear a large volume of small arms fire coming from the area around the church, but they had no idea that the Germans were swarming over the center of the village. As that occurred the American tactical situation in Graignes fell apart at the seams once and for all.

The defenders had done everything in their power to hold out, but they were simply too disadvantaged by the overwhelming numerical superiority of the enemy and they were also out of ammunition. With Major Johnson dead, command of the force at Graignes devolved to Capt. Brummitt – the man who had opposed defending the village to begin with. To him, there were only two possibilities: stay in Graignes and be killed or escape into the marsh and live to fight another day. He wasted no time and very wisely chose the only option that carried the possibility of saving lives; he ordered the men to withdraw. With that, paratroopers began slipping away from the village and into the night. Pvt. Harvey Richig was one of those men and he remembered what happened there at the bitter end of the battle:

> We had to evacuate our positions when our ranks were decimated and ammunition expended. We were told by our officers to disassemble our crew-served weapons, pair off, and try to make it to Carentan or Ste.-Mère-Église as best we could.[34]

When word of the withdrawal order reached Sergeant John Hinchliff and his assistant gunner Pfc. Patrick Sullivan, they were still at their Browning .30-cal. air-cooled machine gun. Unlike most 507th troopers in the defensive perimeter around Graignes at that point, they both still had some ammunition left. "We had to disperse, we had no choice but to move or else we'd get killed," Hinchliff remembered, "So we had to leave our wounded and our dead and Captain Sophian."[35]

When Capt. Brummitt issued the order, Captain Sophian was at the aid station and was in no position to evacuate. He was the ranking physician present and he was treating a number of non-ambulatory wounded men. Since there was no possibility of carrying the wounded out through the marshes, Sophian realized that it was inevitable that they would all fall into German hands. He must have feared that, in German hands, the wounded men might not receive the immediate attention of a suitably trained surgeon. For many of them, immediate attention was a life or death question at that point. Sophian must have assumed that if he remained, he would be able to continue treating his patients. He also had to have known that staying behind would almost certainly mean spending the remainder of the war as a prisoner, or perhaps worse. Thus, he was faced with the most important decision of his life: the choice between duty and self. But the situation in Graignes was spinning out

An 81mm mortar and its accessories. (*from top, left to right*) **M1 81mm mortar tube, M49 (TNT) round, practice round, M4 mount in folded position, traverse mechanism, M14 leather carrying case for M4 sight, baseplate, box of M3 ignition cartridges with two loose rounds, M4 sight and two World War II 81mm technical manuals.** (*Robert G. Segel Collection*)

of control so rapidly that Sophian had no such luxury as time to weigh options. He had to make a snap, on the spot decision. Without hesitating, he chose to stay behind to care for his wounded comrades – he chose duty. He was not ordered to do it; he did it of his own free will. It was a decision that would cost him his life.

As Capt. Brummitt's evacuation instructions circulated among the other Americans, they began slipping away from the village almost immediately. In some cases only in pairs, and in other cases in larger groups, paratroopers began escaping from Graignes. Capt. Brummitt and a group of about twenty troopers slipped away into the marsh to the west of the village with German riflemen shooting at them as they went. Lt. Naughton could hear breaking glass and shouting back at the church as he left the village. His group of twenty-three troopers had no 81mm mortar rounds and no .30-cal. ammunition left. He then got them out by leading them in an all night forced march to the southeast. Lt. "Pip" Reed got out with a small group of men as well. Sergeant Hinchliff and Pfc. Sullivan got out too. As soon as they were directed to withdraw, Hinchliff hefted the considerable weight of his machine gun and its tripod and ordered Sullivan to grab the weapon's remaining ammunition: one last can of 250 rounds of belted .30-cal. cartridges. Then together the two men dashed off down the hill toward the marsh. "I knew we had suffered severe losses when I saw that my assistant and myself were the only two troopers in the vicinity," Hinchliff remembered.[36] When the two men reached the bottom of the hill near the edge of the marsh, Hinchliff realized that in his haste to evacuate, Sullivan had inadvertently left the machine gun's ammunition back at their original position. "I asked him to cover me while I ran back to get it," Hinchliff recalled.[37] He dropped the machine gun and his M1A1 Carbine and left them with Sullivan "in order to avoid any encumbrance."[38] Then he started back to the defensive position that they had occupied only minutes before.

When Hinchliff reached the former position, he leaned down to pick-up the ammo can at the same moment a German stepped from one of the 81mm mortar positions behind a nearby hedgerow and opened fire with an MP40 submachine gun. "I quickly grabbed the ammo and ran a zig-zag pattern down the hill with bullets fly-ing all around me, fully expecting to get hit at any moment," he remembered.[39] At the bottom of the hill, he threw himself through the opening in the hedgerow where he had left Sullivan to cover him only moments before. "I get to the bottom of the hill and I dove head first over the hedgerow thinking Pat would take him on, but Pat was gone," he remembered.[40] Much to his surprise, Sullivan and the machine gun were both gone. However, Hinchliff's M1A1 Carbine was still right where he had left it, so he snatched it up, swung the muzzle around and opened fire on several German soldiers who were pursuing him. Although Sullivan was nowhere in sight, Hinchliff knew that he could have only picked one direction for his escape due to the fact that the marsh restricted movement in all others. "I grabbed the ammo, my carbine and personal belongings and retreated in that direction," he remembered.[41] The Germans who had been firing on him had by then spread out and started to chase him. For that reason, Hinchliff found it necessary to, drop to a firing position and fire on his pursuers from time-to-time. After a while, the Germans gave up the chase. "It was beginning to get dark," he recalled, "and seeing no Germans, I then realized that I had successfully evaded them."[42] Hinchliff then continued along the probable route that Sullivan had taken until, later in the evening, he caught up to him. Soon thereafter, both men joined the group being led by Capt. Brummitt.

In the end, the escape of elements of the American force at Graignes would be the only positive element to a story with an otherwise tragic ending. After the Americans evacuated and the Germans captured the village, something terrible happened. Elements of *Generalmajor der Waffen-SS* Werner Ostendorff's 17th SS Panzergrenadier Division had conducted the final assault on Graignes. When the *17th SS* attacked, it was with a regimental sized force of approximately 2,000. The odds were literally ten to one in the Germans' favor. Despite those odds though, the 182 paratroopers defending Graignes inflicted an estimated five hundred killed and seven hundred wounded on the Germans during the course of the fighting on the 10th and 11th. The stubborn and determined American defense that gave the 17th such high losses brought on a vicious and brutal reprisal.

17

"We lived only to save."

On Monday morning (June 12th), Odette Rigault ventured out from the family farm for the first time since the Germans overran Graignes. "My father told me, 'Go see if your grandfather needs anything,' so I left, thinking I would end up at my grandfather's," she remembered.[1] On the way there, she saw a soldier coming toward her with no helmet on. He had no weapon and nothing in his hands. "So I said to myself, 'Boy, he's going to get shot," she recalled.[2] Although she did not speak any English, Odette nevertheless attempted to warn him in French by saying, "Oh! There are Germans everywhere, everywhere!"[3] Odette then led the man to the barn where her family had stored the ammunition on D-Day. That same morning little Marthe overheard their grandfather talking to a stranger outside of the house. When he came back inside, Marthe asked whom he had been speaking with. "He said that it was an American soldier who wanted to stay at the house, but my grandfather was afraid and told him to leave," she recalled, "he said we would all be shot if he stayed.[4] Marthe then ran after the soldier and, when she caught up with him, she motioned for him to follow her back to the farm. She then deposited him in the barn and went back out looking for more Americans.

Shortly thereafter, she encountered a scout from the group of paratroopers being led by Lt. Frank Naughton. Like so many other 507th troopers, Naughton and his group of approximately twenty men had evacuated Graignes in the closing moments of the battle and had then spent the entire night wondering through the marsh until they were "absolutely exhausted." After the war, Naughton described this difficult experience:

> It was three feet of water and every hundred yards or so, six or eight feet of water because of the drainage ditches. It was a

The barn on the former Rigault family farm in Le Port St. Pierre near Graignes. Pat Costa, Frank Naughton and several other 3rd Battalion/507th paratroopers sought shelter here after Graignes was captured by the 17th SS on June 11th. *(Courtesy of Odette Lelavechef)*

grueling experience with these soldiers. We'd lost a couple nights' sleep anyway and were on meager rations and we were out of ammunition for all practical purposes.[5]

At first, neither Marthe nor Odette mentioned to their parents that they were hiding paratroopers in the barn. Their father had already suffered one heart attack since D-Day and they did not want to put him through any additional stress. They knew that he might not be able to cope with the anxiety associated with harboring Americans at a time when the Germans were sure to be searching high and low for them. Besides, they would only be hiding a small group of the soldiers for a short period of time. Or so they thought - before long, the Rigaults' would have a barn full troopers. Throughout the day on June 12th and 13th, paratroopers continued to emerge from the swamps and proceed to the Rigault farm. They were all 507th men who had been at the barn on D-Day and returned hoping that the Rigaults' would help them again. "Oh, it was a joy to find them like that," Odette remembered, "…after the battle with

"X" marks the hayloft where Sgt. Pat Costa and twenty other 3rd Battalion/507th troopers hid for five days after the fall of Graignes. *(Courtesy of Odette Lelavechef)*

all the dead they left behind, to find each other again - It was comforting."[6] According to Odette, "The only thing we wanted was to save them, so we put them in the barn and I said I would bring them something to eat."[7]

As the number of 507th troopers increased throughout the day on the 12th, it was becoming more and more difficult for Marthe and Odette to keep their parents in the dark. Later in the day, Odette had no choice but to reveal the secret to M. Rigault:

All of a sudden, my father spotted two soldiers coming from the marsh. So he said, 'What are we going to do? Where are we going to put them? Where are we going to hide them?[8]

At that point, she told him that there were already others hiding in the barn. Knowing the situation, M. Rigault threw all of his support behind the mission of protecting the 507th men.

Lt. Naughton's group remained at the barn for just a few hours on June 12th. Just after noon, they were joined by a group of approximately sixty troopers being led by Capt. Brummitt, who was anxious to get the force out of the area and join the rest of the regiment. The combined group remained at the Rigault farm until dusk, at which time they were taken north in boats. At dawn on June 13th, they got out of the boats, continued their journey on foot and arrived in Carentan that evening.

• • •

At the break of dawn on June 12th, Sgt. Costa, Pvt. Klingman and Pvt. Page were still in their foxhole in a field by the marsh guarding the rear of Graignes. Having been bypassed by the night's fighting, they were unaware of the fact that the Germans had taken the village. They were aware that a battle had been fought because they had heard its intense roar, but they were not aware that it had ended with a German victory. After sunrise though, it did not take long before Costa noticed Germans digging-in on the other end of the field in the direction of the village center. As soon as he put two and two together, Costa woke up Klingman and Page. "It looks like the Germans captured the village," he said to them.[9] With that, Klingman and Page shook themselves awake. Costa then instructed Page to move to a point where he could look into the village and report back what he saw. "After a while, Ed (Page) returned with the information that the village was teeming with Germans and there must be a thousand of them," Costa recalled.[10] The three men agreed that they would have to withdraw from their position and attempt to get through to American lines, but they also agreed to wait until after dark to avoid detection. They waited until nightfall, but when it arrived they still thought that movement would be too risky. They were hoping that Americans might break through to them. "We also hoped that the Germans would leave, but that was wishful think-

Left: The XIIth century Roman Catholic church in Graignes as it appeared after the battle. (*Courtesy of the village of Graignes*)

Another view of the ruins of the church. Note the damage to the belfry area (upper left) where 1st Lt. Elmer Farnham and another observer were killed by a direct hit from a German 88mm round. (*Courtesy of the village of Graignes*)

Photographs showing the sanctuary of the XIIth century Roman Catholic church in Graignes before the battle and after the battle. (*Courtesy of the village of Graignes*)

ing," Costa remembered.[11] They then delayed their departure again and waited through yet another night.[12]

The next morning, Tuesday, June 13th, Costa, Klingman and Page were still in their foxhole and the Germans were still in Graignes. Pvt. Page wanted to leave right then, but Pvt. Klingman wanted to wait for nightfall. "We knew the longer we waited the weaker we would be," Costa remembered.[13] The three troopers had been without food or water since Sunday evening, so by Tuesday morning their strength was rapidly declining. Desperate from thirst and hunger, they decided to withdraw from the position and try to find a sympathetic farmer who could supply them with food and drink.[14] Pvt. Page knew of a nearby farm and, with a minimum of effort, managed to locate it. One of the men then knocked on the door and a frightened French woman answered. They asked her for food and also for information about the fate of the Americans who had been defending Graignes. The woman went to her refrigerator and brought each man a pancake and some cider, which the hungry troopers gladly accepted. She then gave them directions to Carentan and the three men began walking in that direction. When necessary, they moved through fields, but they generally stayed near the hedgerows as much as possible so as not to be too conspicuous.[15]

About an hour into their walk to Carentan, the three troopers heard someone approaching on a nearby road flanked by hedges. They all immediately went to the ready in preparation for an encounter with the enemy. Then, fifteen-year-old Jean Rigault (Marthe and Odette's cousin) stepped through an opening in the hedgerow and told the three Americans to follow him. At first they were a little suspicious; "We had him lead the way, thinking that if he was leading us to slaughter, he'd be the first to go," Costa remembered.[16] But the young Frenchman turned out to be a great asset because he knew his way around. He led Costa, Klingman and Page directly to the barn on the Rigault family farm where ten other 507th troopers were hiding in the hayloft. "Needless to say how happy we were to see each other and know we were alive," Costa remembered.[17]

Americans continued to trickle in to the Rigault farm throughout the day on the 12th and 13th. With each new arrival, Marthe and Odette took them to the barn with the others. The number finally reached the total of 21 paratroopers – all of them 507th. The sudden appearance of these 21 houseguests put a strain on the family's food situation. Just as the village had to resort to creative ways of feeding the troops the week before, the Rigault family had to do the same beginning on June 12th. However, the situation at the farm that began on June 12th was more dangerous because there were Germans all over the area by then and they were actively searching for the Americans that had fought at Graignes. This meant that the family could take no chances whatsoever on being discovered. If the Germans found them hiding Americans, they would be killed. So they took every possible precaution to keep their mission a secret.

The family feared that German observers were watching the farm constantly, so a considerable amount of energy went into presenting the outward appearance of every day life as usual on the farm. Even mealtime was a covert mission. When Odette took each daily meal out to the paratroopers in the barn, she had to be very careful when she did so. She did not want it to look as if she were carrying food for twenty-one people because that would certainly arouse the suspicion of any observer. For that reason, she created a brilliant subterfuge:

> When we brought them food to eat, I had a bucket in each hand. I would bring it to them, as if I were going to feed the animals, you know. I had buckets on either side, then I would cough. That was the signal. I went, "Uh!", a little sound like that and they would go and get their mess kits and pass them through a hole in the back. And then of course everyone went back to their hiding spots.[18]

Because they could not go into the village to purchase anything from Mme. Boursier's grocery, the Rigaults' were severely limited in terms of the food they had available. Despite this, the family was nevertheless able to provide the paratroopers with chicken, vegetables, cider and chocolate milk.[19]

For the men cooped-up in the barn, the days passed with no excitement whatsoever and the men had little to look forward to except the meals that Odette surreptitiously delivered each day. They had to be very careful not to make any noise, so they could not move around much and they could not speak in normal tones. They could not even look forward to a cigarette break because their supply was exhausted. Sgt. Costa recalled a semi-comical moment that occurred during one of those days in the hayloft in connection with this subject:

> The boys were dying for a cigarette. One of the men had one left. He lit the cigarette took a deep drag and passed it to the others. This was one time I was happy I never smoked. It was just like the movies only real. It was sad and at the same time funny to see eleven men taking a deep drag, holding the smoke in their mouths, reluctant to let it out. It was like taking their last breath, hanging on for dear life.[20]

As time crept by hour after hour, boredom set in and everyone involved lost all concept of time. The circumstances of their confinement and inactivity were such that they were only barely aware of the difference between day and night. For Odette, the focus of her life had shifted to carrying out the mission of taking care of the twenty-one American paratroopers hidden in her parents' barn. "We were living, but we no longer had any notion of the passage of time – we lived only to save these people and wondered what would become of them," she remembered.[21]

The Rigaults' and the Americans were hoping that a breakthrough would occur and that Allied forces from the north would move into the area around Le Port St. Pierre and Graignes. As long as they believed that such a possibility existed, there was no need for the Americans to risk venturing from their hiding place in the barn. The fact that the 101st Airborne captured Carentan on the 12th hinted that such a breakthrough might happen, so everyone waited and hoped for the best. Disappointingly, Tuesday the 13th brought no news of an advance from Carentan. When the situation remained unchanged on Wednesday the 14th as well, it began to sink-in that the 101st was simply consolidating its position around Carentan and that a breakthrough might be days, if not weeks away. Odette remembered that, "It reached a point where we had to decide, we wouldn't be able to keep hiding them like that; and as for them, they wanted to leave."[22]

The 14th also brought a very dramatic close call. That morning, Mme. Rigault was on her way out to the barn with milk for the paratroopers when she saw German soldiers approaching the farm. There were approximately thirty of them, probably evacuees from Carentan. The Americans had spotted them as well and were preparing for a firefight. Mme. Rigault called up to the paratroopers and asked them not to shoot. She told them that she would "try to do something" if they came any closer.[23] She then closed the barn doors and walked toward the approaching Germans. They were preparing to cross a flooded marsh area on foot when she got to them. She warned them that the water was "very deep" and pointed out a boat one hundred meters away that could carry them across. They asked her to point them in the direction of St.-Jean-de-Daye and St. Lô and when she did so, they moved on. Mme. Rigault had thus diverted the enemy away from the farm and diffused what could have been an explosive situation.[24]

If anything, that close call convinced everyone that the situation was getting far too risky. The Rigaults and the twenty-one paratroopers therefore reached the conclusion that the best thing to do would be for the Americans to attempt to reach Carentan. However, they would not be able to use the roads because they were sure to be choked with groups of Germans moving south from there. Wading through the marsh area immediately to the north of the Rigault farm at Le Port St. Pierre was not a viable option for the 507th men either because, first of all, it would be very hazardous and, secondly, it would take too long. In other words if the paratroopers set out on foot just after sunset, they could not possibly make it to Carentan by sunrise. Being caught out in the open marsh in daylight in an area swarming with enemy troops was certainly no option at all. The only reasonable possibility was therefore moving the Americans to Carentan at night by boat via the shallow canals that crisscrossed the marshy inundated area north of Le Port St. Pierre.

That conclusion having been reached, Gustave Rigault began looking for a boat that could do the job. On the evening of Wednesday the 14th, he told the paratroopers that he had found a boat for them and that they were to leave as soon as possible. "He explained the route to take in the canal and also where to make turns," Sgt. Costa remembered, "It seemed quite complicated."[25] At that stage, M. Rigault did not plan to accompany the Americans on the journey, so they said their goodbyes and set out on their own. After only about twenty minutes, they were obviously getting nowhere because they kept turning down dead ends. Making matters worse, they noticed that the boat was beginning to leak. Since the circumstances seemed to be working against them, they decided to turn back before they got lost or they were spotted by the enemy.[26] Sgt. Costa described what it was like when they got back to the farm:

> M. Rigault couldn't believe it when he saw that we had returned. We told him that we would have to get someone familiar with the canal to get us through, since we were in German territory. It was imperative that a knowledgeable person was needed to get us back safely.[27]

Rigault said, "Well, we're going to have to work something out," and agreed to see what could be done to arrange for a guide.[28] The paratroopers then went back out to the barn and up to their old familiar hayloft.

The next day, Thursday, June 15, 1944, the troopers were in the hayloft waiting for M. Rigault to arrange for a guide. According to Sgt. Costa, the Rigault family was "getting apprehensive" because German patrol activity around Le Port St. Pierre was increasing with each passing day.[29] "They knew the Germans were not far away and if they were caught harboring us they would all be shot," he recalled.[30] Then that afternoon two Germans arrived at the farm on a motorcycle sidecar. The paratroopers in the hayloft readied their weapons as quietly as possible as the Germans conducted a cursory search around the farmhouse. Then both Germans approached the barn, opened the barn door and entered. As the two Germans searched around on the ground floor, twenty-one well-armed Americans were right above their heads with fingers on triggers. "We were ready to blast them," Sgt. Costa remembered.[31] The two Germans generally rifled-through everything on the ground floor and then, miraculously, they turned and left the barn. Luckily, they

Graignes was not the only war crime committed against 507th paratroopers during the Normandy battle. This image, extracted from a
reel of film, depicts the recovery of seven 507th paratroopers at the
village of Hémevez. (*National Archives and Records Administration via
Jump/Cut Productions and Scott Carroll*)

A graves registration detail recovers the bodies of the 507th paratroopers buried at the village of Hémevez in late June 1944. (*National Archives and Records Administration via Jump/Cut Productions and Scott
Carroll*)

did not even bother to check the loft. As they drove off, 21 Americans breathed a collective sigh of relief. If they had been forced to
kill the two Germans, the shooting would have quickly brought
more Germans to the farm. If that had happened, the Americans
and the Rigault family would probably not have survived.

That afternoon, M. Rigault went to the hayloft to explain to the
Americans that he had found a young man who had volunteered to
lead them to Carentan that night by boat. He then introduced Isidore
Folliot's son Joseph with the words, "This man will be able to take
you through the canal to the American lines."[32] The Americans then
began preparing for their departure. Before leaving, Mme. Rigault
offered each man coffee with Calvados. Then, the Americans offered thanks and their final farewell to the family whose warmth
and hospitality had saved their lives. As they stepped out of the
house for the last time at 10:00pm, twelve-year-old Marthe gave
each trooper a flower, which she tucked in the pockets of their jump
jackets.[33] Joseph then led the troopers down to the water's edge
where a bigger boat was waiting. This new boat was seven or eight
meters in length and was used to carry construction materials like
bricks and sand.[34] To the paratroopers, Joseph seemed to be "very
well versed" and "experienced" at what he was about to do.[35] "He
told us to get into the boat and lie down flat," remembered Sgt.
Costa.[36] Once the Americans were all loaded, Joseph began moving. Costa described what it was like:

> During the trip, passing the German lines and entering into
> the American lines, flares were going up at regular intervals.
> Some small arms fire could be heard and we remained calm.[37]

The paratroopers made no noise during the trip. The only sounds
came from Joseph's paddling and the far off gunfire. Then, Pvt.
Carlos J. Hurtado broke the silence in a rather loud tone of voice
and said, "Hey Costa, I'm getting all wet!"[38] Just like the night before, the troopers were in a leaky boat. Costa, who had by then been
wet for the past half hour, snapped back at Hurtado saying, "You
better shut-up or you'll get us all killed."[39] By that time, the boat
was a third full of water. Then just after midnight, Joseph pulled
over to the bank and said, "We're OK now, get off here and follow
the path for about one hundred yards and you will be in American
territory."[40] The paratroopers were indebted to Joseph. He "knew
his job well" and they wanted to do something to thank him.[41] Costa
then asked all of the troopers to give him their invasion currency
and he attempted to give it all to Joseph, who was reluctant to accept the gift. The troopers insisted, and he gratefully took it. "We
were sorry we couldn't give him more and thanked him, then wished
him the best and went on our way," Costa remembered.[42] Joseph
then went right back in the direction he came, returning to Le Port
St. Pierre at 3:00 am.

For the troopers, the most dangerous part of the journey was at
hand. They had to cover unknown ground in pitch-blackness and
then enter a heavily defended perimeter in a combat zone. When an
American sentry challenged them, they knew they were home. They
were taken into Carentan where they told their story and, before
sunrise, they were on trucks bound for Ste.-Mère-Église. When they
arrived there, the twenty-one exhausted 507th troopers laid down
in the street in front of 82nd Airborne Division Headquarters. To
these men, it was an incredible relief to be in friendly territory finally after eleven days. "Words cannot describe the anxiety of what

The 507th paratroopers murdered at Hémevez surrendered after a brief firefight with the Germans and then, after being disarmed, they were each executed by a rifle bullet to the back of the head. (*National Archives and Records Administration via Jump/Cut Productions and Scott Carroll*)

One of the unfortunate 507th paratroopers executed at Hémevez. After the crime was committed, French civilians buried the men in the church cemetery. (*National Archives and Records Administration via Jump/Cut Productions and Scott Carroll*)

a soldier goes through trying to make it back to friendly lines," recalled Sgt. Costa.[43]

Although Sgt. Costa was starving when he arrived in Ste.-Mère-Église, he was far too tired to eat and promptly fell asleep. He woke up the next morning to the smell of C-ration pork and beans cooking. Without delay, he drank a couple of canteen cups of coffee and then ate his first hot meal since coming to Normandy. "Being without food for most of the eleven days, that was a treat I shall never forget," he recalled.[44] Later in the morning, the 21 men were able to take showers and then they were issued new uniforms. After that, they were taken by truck to Lt. Col. Maloney's command post where they were reunited with the other men from the 3rd Battalion that were lucky enough to make it out alive. Those twenty-one men were the last Graignes survivors to make it back. Their eleven-day trek behind enemy lines had been an incredible ordeal that they were truly lucky to have survived.

Not everyone that was at Graignes was so lucky though. When the battle ended, the atrocity began and those that could not flee were quickly caught-up in the fury of the enemy's brutal reprisal. At the end of the June 11th battle, the 17th SS stormed the church and found Capt. Sophian's aid station. They promptly forced the Captain and all of the wounded outside where they were made to line-up against a wall. There were nineteen American survivors in all. Ominous though that was, nothing happened to the men at that moment because the Germans evidently did not want anyone to witness what they were about to do. At some point immediately after that though, the men were divided into two groups and marched away from the church. One group was marched off to the south and the other was marched down to the edge of a shallow pond behind

Madame Boursier's café. At the edge of the pond, the SS murderers bayoneted the helpless, wounded men and threw them into the water one on top of the other. Some of them were not even dead when they were pushed in. They were later found there all huddled together and the French later buried them.[45] The other group of 507th paratroopers was forced to march four kilometers to the south to a field near the village of Le Mesnil Angot. There the wounded men were forced to dig a pit. As soon as the pit was complete, the SS murderers shot each one of them in the back of the head and dumped their bodies in the pit one on top of the other.

When Allied forces finally liberated the area the following month, French civilians were quick to report the details of the atrocity. The U.S. Army responded to the reports by sending in teams that recovered the remains of the paratroopers at Graignes and

A medical corps Captain searches for identification on the body of one of the Hémevez victims. (*National Archives and Records Administration via Jump/Cut Productions and Scott Carroll*)

(Manche) 9388 & 5723

28 June 1947

Manche 9388 & 5723

28 June 1947

N A R R A T I V E

Investigation of these two cases in the village of Graignes resulted in ascertaining that during the period 6-12 June 1944 witnesses saw a total of nineteen (19) dead American paratroopers.

The mayor of Graignes, Mr Voydie, declared that ten dead American paratroopers had been removed from the village during the period 13-20 July 1944 (see statement). Mr Voydie further stated that if any paratroopers had fallen in the fields the farmers would have found them because the swamps in this area are mowed every year.

The mayor of Mesnil Angot, Mr Poullain, stated that he saw nine dead American paratroopers and that during the period 30 June to 4 August 1944, American troops removed these dead (statement attached).

Two more statements were obtained, one from Miss Meunier and one from Mrs Lereculey. These two women could not shed further light, except for the possibility that these nineteen dead American paratroopers might have been removed to the U.S. Military Cemetery of Blosville.

/s/ James A. Hoovler
JAMES A. HOOVLER
1st Lt., Inf.
Investigating Officer

T R A N S L A T I O N

I, the undersigned, Mr Voydie Alphonse, Mayor of Graignes declare:

After the departure of the American soldiers in the night of 11-12 june, I went at the village on the 12th in the morning. I removed 5 bodies from the pool located in Mrs Boursier's farm, three from the church, those three bodies were killed by the Germans, 2 other bodies were found in the fields. I put those bodies in a field but the Germans did not permit me to bury them. Then I had to evacuate. The American troops liberated the comunity on 13 july. I came back on 20 July.

Contrarily at what Mrs Lereculey said, the bodies of the 10 American parachuters were removed between the 13 and 20 July and not at the beginning of August.

Besides that if paratroopers had parachuted down in the swamps, their bodies should have been found when mowing grass, therefore it is possible that several paratroopers landed straight in the main canals and streams, but bodies should have floated at the surface of the water.

/s/ Voydie

Translated by:
/s/ J. Leseigneur
J. Leseigneur

The narrative report and translated personal statements of four eyewitnesses to the Graignes atrocity. These documents were prepared in June 1947 when the incident was being investigated by the Army. (*Total Army Personnel Command, Freedom of Information Act Office*)

T R A N S L A T I O N

I, the undersigned, Poullain Jean, Mayor of Mesnil Angot, declare:

On June 12, 1944, I saw 9 American parachutist prisoners of the Germans, they took them in a field and killed them. A few days later I saw these bodies in a hole. The Germans ordered us to evacuate on 30 June 1944, we came back on August 4, during that time the 9 parachutist bodies were removed by American authority, but I could not say were they were taken to.

/s/ Poullain

Translated by:
/s/ J. Leseigneur

Manche 9388

Manche 9388 & 5723

T R A N S L A T I O N

I, the undersigned, Miss Meunier Renee, Schoolteacher at Graignes, declare:

On June 6, I saw the American paratrooper D. J. Wellis member of the 507 PAR COHT Inf, Hq Co., The American troops stationed here from the 6 to 11 of june. At this date there had a fighting between American and Germans, the Americans were obliged to retreat toward Carentan in the night of 11 to 12 June.

I have no knowledge of soldiers having parachuted in the community on 8 and 11 june.

On 12 June, I was prisoner of the Germans, I saw 11 American prisoners, the Germans took them at Mesnil Angot and killed them. They were removed by American authority and buried at Blosville. I know that 5 bodies were removed from the pool located at Mes Boursier's farm.

/s/ Meunier

Translated by:
/s/ J. Leseigneur

T R A N S L A T I O N

I, the undersigned, Mrs Denise Lereculey-Boursier, residing at Vieux Bourg, at Graignes, declare:

On June 11, 1944 the Germans shot 5 American paratroopers in a field, near our farm. An interpreter who was working with the American troops said that he heard the German officer giving the order to shot them. Then, they throw them in the pool located in our farm. the grave digger Mr Lenormand, and the Mayor Mr Vodis removed 5 bodies from that pool, but the Germans did not permit to bury them in the cemetery. They digged a hole and they put the 5 bodies in it. At the beginning of August 1944 the American troops removed these bodies.

In the night of 11-12 june the Germans burned several bodies in a field located near the farm, in April 1945 officers came on investigation, and went on the place where the bodies were burnt, and they say that they recognized human bones.

/s/ Lereculey

Translated by:
/s/ J. Leseigneur

Mesnil Angot. In Graignes, the French had buried the five troopers that were found in the pond, but they also later found three dead paratroopers in the church and another two dead troopers in a nearby field.[46] In Mesnil Angot, the bodies of the nine murdered soldiers there were exhumed from the pit into which they had been so anonymously dumped.[47] There were nineteen victims in all.[48] The bodies of the murdered paratroopers were then transferred to a temporary cemetery in Blosville and subsequently removed to the American Cemetery in Colleville-Sur-Mer where they were each given the honorable burial they deserved. With them died the exact details of what happened during the last horrifying moments of their lives. Although only their murderers know the full details of the crime, the evidence does provide us with a faint hint of what the full measure of their agony was. For these men, the end was neither merciful nor quick for their murderers wanted to torture them. Their murderers wanted there to be a long, slow build-up to the bayonet in the back or the bullet in the head. For these men, their last conscious memories were either standing in front of a pond or kneeling in front of a pit that they had been forced to dig. Never forget, each one of those men volunteered to be there. Never forget that several of them lied about their age just so they could be there. Never forget that one of those men, Capt. Abraham Sophian, was not even wounded. He chose to stay behind intending to help the men whose lives he probably had to watch being brutally extinguished by war criminals.

Sadly, the murder of the paratroopers was only the beginning of the atrocity at Graignes. While one group of the Germans led the twelve Americans off to summary execution, others began systematically rounding-up French civilians suspected of assisting them. At about the same time, a group of SS men proceeded to the church rectory seeking revenge. They knew that the church's belfry had been used throughout the battle as an observation point. They knew that the accurate and devastating mortar fire that had been controlled by the observers in that belfry had killed and wounded hundreds of their comrades. Consequently, they sought to make an example out of the people at the church whose interaction with the Americans had permitted those casualties to happen. The Germans burst into the rectory, dragged Father Leblastier and Father Lebarbanchon into the courtyard and shot them both to death. Father Leblastier's body was riddled with bullets while a single bullet to the back of the head ended Father Lebarbanchon's life. The Germans then discovered eighty-year-old Eugenie DuJardin and Madeleine Pezeril, the rectory's housekeepers. Overwhelmed with fear, the two ladies had been cowering in their beds ever since the beginning of the final assault. The Germans shot both women in their beds.[49]

Meanwhile, a total of forty-four villagers had been rounded-up and were under interrogation by the Germans as suspected collaborators. They were held captive and threatened with execution if they did not turn in the names of any and all villagers who actively assisted the Americans. However, the camaraderie within this group was such that not a single one of them turned in a single name. In fact, none of them revealed the prominent role that Alphonse Voydie played in the Graignes drama. What they told the Germans instead was that the mayor had died shortly before the invasion, which was of course true. They simply neglected to mention that Voydie had been named the provisional mayor. Had the Germans known that Voydie had been the catalyst of organization that he was, they would have executed him too. But in the end, no one was sold out to the enemy and the people of the village maintained perfect loyal fidelity to their patriotic spirit at all times.

The villagers' refusal to cooperate only exacerbated the Germans' fury. Many of the detained citizens were immediately sent south to nearby Le-Haut-Vernay where they were forced to help remove the hundreds of Germans who had been killed or wounded in the day's fighting.[50] This lasted practically the entire night. Then the next morning (June 12th) the Germans began ransacking every house in the village. During their searches, furniture was overturned and rifled-through and valuables were plundered. Many of the villagers that had fled the previous night's attack attempted to return to their homes on the morning of the 12th only to be turned away on the outskirts of town. Machine guns that had been set-up at several strategic approaches presented an uninviting sight to the exhausted villagers. On Tuesday the 13th, the Germans attempted to destroy the evidence of the atrocity. They poured gasoline over the bodies of Father Leblastier, Father Lebarbanchon, Eugenie DuJardin and Madeleine Pezeril and then set them on fire. The ensuing blaze burned out of control, destroying 66 homes, the boys' school, Mme. Boursier's café and the XIIth century church. Another 159 homes and other buildings were damaged either as a result of that fire or the fighting. Before the June 11th battle and the German retaliation that followed, the village of Graignes had consisted of just over two hundred dispersed homes and other structures. Afterward, only two houses survived unscathed.[51]

Graignes was forever changed by the battle and atrocity that took place there. In addition to the significant collateral damage that the village suffered, human lives were likewise affected. The twelve American paratroopers, the priests and the rectory's housekeepers were not the only lives lost at Graignes. In addition to those deaths, eighteen paratroopers and twenty-eight villagers were killed during the battles of June 11th. After the war, the ruins of the church were turned into a memorial where the names of the dead are forever enshrined.

Gustave Rigault (*left with pitcher*) and Isidore Folliot (*right with broom*). Isidore was killed by German machine gun fire on June 17th while looking for American rations among the equipment bundles in the marsh area north of Graignes. (*Courtesy of Odette Lelavechef*)

• • •

The harsh German response did not end with the executions in town and at Le Mesnil Angot. In the days following the June 11th battle, the Germans searched the area around Graignes for the American force that they presumed had escaped from the village. When they came up empty-handed day after day, the Germans grew suspicious that local citizens were assisting the Americans in their efforts to evade capture. It was at that point that patrol activity intensified, leading ultimately to that close call at the Rigaults' barn on Thursday, June 15th in which the twenty-one paratroopers hiding there were almost discovered. When Joseph Folliot returned from taking those paratroopers to Carentan late that night, he did not return the boat to the exact position it had occupied before. It was an unfortunate oversight and the Germans apparently noticed it, because they began to watch the area around Le Port St. Pierre even more closely than they had before. To underscore their seriousness on the matter, the Germans notified the people living in the area that the movement of boats would not be permitted. "We no longer had the right to move any boats," Odette remembered, "we couldn't even get in a boat."[52] For whatever reason, Isidore Folliot did not respect the German dictate. He had helped Gustave Rigault in collecting parachute bundles beginning on D-Day and had continued to do so off and on during the days that followed. On June 17th, he took a boat out to look for American rations among the equipment in the marsh and, unbeknownst to him, a machine gun team was watching. Odette recalled what happened:

He was cut in half by machine-gun fire because he got in a boat and he went to search for supplies. They saw him with a pair of binoculars. They fired a burst from the machine-gun

that cut him in half. Our mother took care of him all night long, but he died of blood loss. We wrapped him in a parachute and we buried him, poor Isidore.[53]

Clearly the Germans were willing to use force to prevent the French from engaging in any activity that that could even remotely benefit the Americans. But not even this heavy handedness was enough to satisfy the Germans, and they would soon take an even more dramatic step to prevent interaction between French civilians and the U.S. Army forces in the area.

Several days later, the Rigault family received an unexpected, rude awakening. At 6:00 am, a German squad arrived at the farm and a soldier came to the door with a gun and informed the family that they had twenty minutes to get out. Because of widespread Allied bombing in support of the expanding beachhead, the Rigault house was full of neighbors whose homes had been damaged or destroyed. "We were sleeping on the floor," Marthe remembered.[54] The order applied uniformly to everyone in the house and the German warned that if they were not all out in the dictated time, they would be shot. "We had to leave just like that, without even an apron…just leave immediately," Odette remembered.[55] They quickly gathered some clothes and left the house as they had been instructed. It was thus that the Rigault family became war refugees. During the course of the next two months, Marthe, Odette, their mother and father, their grandfather and their little brother Jean-Claude, would be forced to travel sixty kilometers from their home at Le Port St. Pierre near Graignes. They traveled on foot by day and stopped at night where they slept in barns. They walked so far that they even wore out shoes. "I was walking barefoot because my shoes were rubbing the skin off my toes," Odette remembered.[56] The column of refugees was being led by German soldiers and was

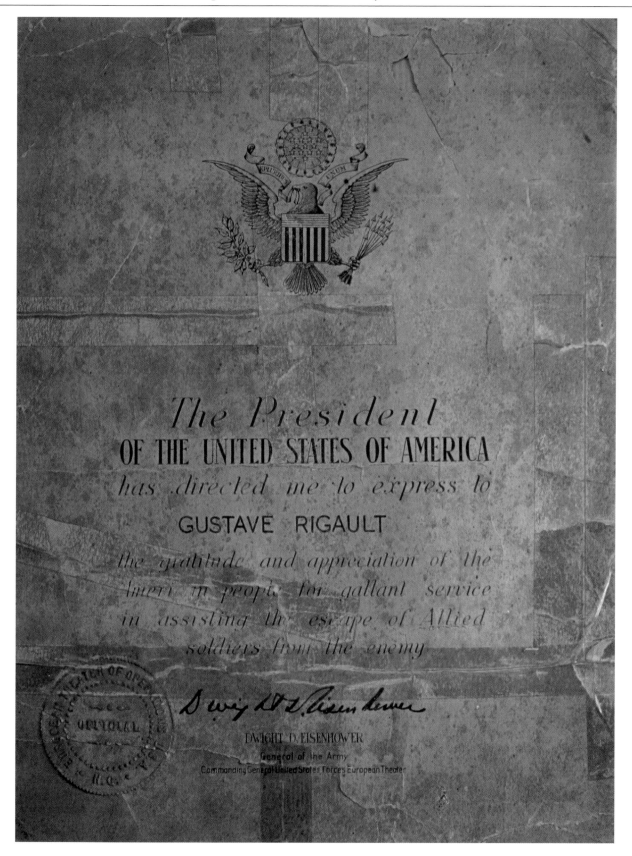

Certificate of appreciation signed by General Dwight D. Eisenhower and presented to Gustave Rigault for "assisting the escape of Allied soldiers from the enemy." *(Courtesy of Marthe His)*

Left: The Rigault family poses with two GIs after Le Port St. Pierre and Graignes were liberated in July 1944. The boat in the photo was the one that they used to recover airborne equipment bundles from the marsh on D-Day. *(Courtesy of Odette Lelavechef)*

Below: Edouard and Odette Lelavechef married on October 6, 1945, which is when this photograph was taken. Odette's wedding gown was made from the white silk of the 507th reserve parachutes that she and her sister recovered from the marsh near their family farm on D-Day. *(Courtesy of Odette Lelavechef)*

consequently vulnerable to air attack. On multiple occasions American combat aircraft attacked the column of refugees, mistaking it for a military convoy. In each of these cases, the Germans fired back at the attacking aircraft and Marthe, Odette and the family were forced to throw themselves into roadside ditches for shelter. "There were many times when our lives were in danger," Marthe remembered.[57]

When the Rigault family was finally allowed to return to Le Port St. Pierre in August, they were lucky to find that their house had escaped destruction. Although looters had helped themselves to some of the Rigaults' personal belongings, the family's possessions were still largely there and the house itself was largely undisturbed. However, most of the silken T-5 parachutes that Marthe and Odette had recovered from the marsh just after D-Day were gone. Odette was pleased though to find that a few T-5s she had hidden in the barn had not been discovered by the thieves. She had plans for that silk. Despite their two months of suffering as displaced persons, the Rigaults were nevertheless very fortunate people. Unlike many, they still had a home and, most important of all, they had survived. The Rigault family resumed their normal lives after the temporary interruption that D-Day brought them. They went back work on the farm and Marthe, Odette and their little brother Jean Claude continued growing up. Immediately after the war, Odette's relationship with Edouard Lelavechef blossomed into an engagement and the couple married on October 6, 1945. The wedding gown Odette wore that day was made out of the white silk of 507th parachutes.

18

"Here's your ticket - goodbye."

Even after the dramatic battles at Chef du Pont, La Fière, and Graignes, the 507th continued to fight in Normandy. By June 12th, the various scattered elements of the 507th had finally assembled into what was left of the regiment's organic battalions and companies. On D+7 (June 13th), the regiment moved to a forward assembly area west of the Merderet River in preparation for a coordinated attack to the west. At 9:00 the following morning, the 3rd Battalion attacked German positions around the village of Renouf followed by an attack by the 1st and 2nd Battalions on the village of La Bonneville. The day after that (June 15th), the 1st and 2nd Battalions continued to attack to the west and were hit by a German counterattack that included tanks. However, all ground gained was held until the 505th Parachute Infantry Regiment passed through the 507th to continue the westward advance. The regiment suffered 192 casualties in combat on June 14th and 15th.[1]

Up to that point, the regiment was under the command of Lt. Col. Arthur A. Maloney who had been serving as the *de facto* regimental commander after Col. Millett's capture. Following the battles at Renouf and La Bonneville though, Lt. Col. Maloney was unceremoniously replaced by Col. Edson D. Raff, the man that had led the first American Airborne operation of the war in North Africa in 1942. Maloney, who had done such an exceptional job as a stand-in regimental commander for ten days, was placed in command of the regiment's 3rd Battalion. Maloney's incalculable contribution during the confused and desperate battle at La Fière was later acknowledged by his being awarded the Distinguished Service Cross. With Maloney commanding the 3rd Battalion, Raff put Major Ben F. Pearson in command of the 1st Battalion and retained Lt. Col. Charles J. Timmes as 2nd Battalion Commander. On D+10 (June 16th) the 507th was moved south by truck across the Douve River to relieve the 508th Parachute Infantry Regiment in static positions

in the vicinity of the village of Francquetot. Two days later, on June 18th, Maj. Pearson's 1st Battalion crossed a branch of the Douve River to seize the village of Vindefontaine and the strategically valuable crossroads immediately to the west of it. When the battle ended the next day, the battalion had suffered thirty-four casualties in carrying out the mission. By June 23rd, the entire regiment was on line at Vindefontaine and ready to continue the advance west.

At about the same time that Cherbourg was being captured toward the end of June, the U.S. 1st Army under the command of General Omar N. Bradley formed the new VIII Corps and placed it under the command of Major General Troy Middleton. Although it was overdue to be relieved from combat, the 82nd Airborne Division was given to Middleton for a major attack to cut off the Cotentin peninsula – an attack that would include the 507th. VIII Corps launched the drive on July 3rd and, on the 4th of July, 2nd Battalion/507th attacked and seized the village of La Fauvrerie in coordination with elements of the 325th Glider Infantry Regiment. With the 2nd Battalion holding the village as a reserve force, the 1st and 3rd Battalions then began to advance with the 325th toward the highest point in Normandy – La Poterie Ridge or *Hill 95*. On July 5th Maloney's 3rd Battalion assaulted and captured the eastern end of the ridge and Timmes' 2nd Battalion assaulted and captured the western end. But the Germans were dug-in along the center of the ridge in defensive positions that turned-out to be difficult to neutralize and sporadic fighting continued on *Hill 95* throughout the 6th and 7th. On the morning of July 8th though, the 3rd Battalion attacked and captured the saddle of the ridge in what was to be the final combat action of the 507th Parachute Infantry Regiment in the Normandy Campaign.

On July 12th, the 507th was relieved on the line and pulled back to the vicinity of Utah Beach. After their baptism in combat,

The troopers of B Company/507th pose for a group photograph near Utah Beach on July 11, 1944 shortly before the regiment returned to England. B Company suffered eighty-four combat casualties in Normandy. *(Courtesy of George H. Leidenheimer)*

the men were exhausted and ready to rest and reorganize. By then, they were a "sorry looking" bunch according to T/5 Bob Davis:

> Our jump suits had been chemically impregnated against gas attack and they were stiff, dirty, I mean we looked like hoboes. Many of us hadn't had the opportunity to shave, most hadn't had a shower, we had been subsisting principally on K-rations since D-Day.[2]

While they waited for a transport to take them back to England, the men were issued new uniforms. However, they were not issued new M-42 jump suits, but "plain" olive drab wool uniforms of the type issued to non-airborne personnel. The reality was that the men of the 507th were being stripped of anything that could identify them as being an airborne unit. Their new olive drab uniforms carried no insignia of any kind and their jump boots were taken away and replaced with non-airborne footwear. According to Bob Davis, this was done "so that we would appear to all in Britain, including possible enemy spies, that we were new recruits from the States."[3] On July 15th, the 507th moved down to Utah Beach and the men boarded an LST that took them back to England. "They pulled the nose right on the beach, opened up the front and we boarded the ship through the nose," Davis remembered.[4] On the night of June 6, 1944, it had taken 117 C-47s to transport the 2,004

men of the regiment across the English Channel to Normandy. At the end of their thirty-five days in combat, a single LST was all that was needed to transport what was left of the 507th back to southern England. By then, combat attrition had reduced the regiment to approximately seven hundred men. B Company alone suffered more than 62% casualties: 136 paratroopers from that company jumped

A 1943 photograph showing 507th troopers in the Black Hills of South Dakota: (*kneeling*) Sgt. William L. Tippett, Pvt. William McDade, Pvt. William H. Witt, (*standing*) Pvt. Stanley Drapala, Cpl. Walter L Choquette and Pvt. Chester J. Parker. Witt, Parker and Choquette were all killed in Normandy. Choquette was murdered at Graignes. *(Courtesy of William D. Bowell)*

on June 6th and yet only 52 were left to board the LST on July 15th. The regiment's combat baptism in Normandy had taken a heavy toll.

After the men of the 507th disembarked from that LST at Southampton, they boarded a train that took them back to Tollerton Hall. "We arrived there at 1:00 am, and although it was supposed to be a secret, the whole city turned out to welcome us," Sgt. George Leidenheimer remembered.[5] His girlfriend Sheila Purdue was there and the two had an emotional reunion. One of Sheila's girlfriends was with her and asked where her boyfriend T/5 Lou Francis was. Leidenheimer had to break it to her that Lou had been killed by machine gun fire in Normandy. She left in tears.[6] As the men moved back into their pyramidal tents, some decided that a celebration was in order and made a "bee-line" for the medical office in search of "medicinal alcohol."[7] They had managed to get their hands on

some concentrated orange juice and were determined to blend it with the alcohol to make "ersatz" Screwdrivers.[8] After thirty-five days in combat, they were ready to unwind and a little celebration with alcohol and orange juice offered their first opportunity to do so. "We were all tensed up and we wanted to relax and this is one way of doing it," remembered Bob Davis.[9]

The next morning, Col. Raff had what was left of the entire 507th assemble on the regimental parade ground to announce that everyone had been granted nine days leave.[10] Cheers and whistles greeted the news and the men immediately scattered to the four corners of the United Kingdom. Some men went to London to spend their nine days partying while others sought only peace, quiet and solitude. John Hinchliff was one of the men who just wanted to relax. As soon as he found out that he had nine days to do with however he pleased, he cleaned-up, put on a clean shirt and left the

Sgt. John H. Fessler of G Company/507th was killed in action near Amfreville on June 10th. *(Courtesy of Harry Fessler)*

Master Sgt. William D. Fessler was serving in the U.S. Army Air Force when he visited his brother's grave in Normandy later in the summer of 1944. *(Courtesy of Harry Fessler)*

regimental camp at Tollerton Hall. Hinchliff then proceeded directly into Nottingham to a "nice looking" little cottage he had seen there before going to Normandy. He specifically recalled seeing a sign on the front of the cottage that said "Rooms for rent" so he went up to the door and knocked. A little old British lady answered and he said, "I'd like to rent a room."[11] The little old lady then informed him that she did not allow women or drinking on the premises, to which Hinchliff replied, "I don't care, I just want a room and I just want to rest and I'd like to have my meals here."[12] The little old lady agreed and he promptly moved in to the cottage. Hinchliff later described how he passed his first few days:

> All I can remember is that I did get a bottle of booze and I put it beside the bed and I don't remember how many days – probably two or three – and all I did was lay in there and have my meals brought to me and sack out. That's how I relaxed after Normandy.[13]

As soon as they could get away from camp, Bob Davis and two other troopers went to Plumtree to visit Griffin's Inn. Of the original 'Plumtree Eight' only three returned from Normandy. When the three combat veterans entered the pub, they were greeted "as long lost progeny."[14] There were hugs and kisses all around as the three survivors were welcomed back. When they told of the fate of the five troopers who were not lucky enough to make it, tears were much in evidence. After the bittersweet reunion at Griffin's Inn, Davis caught a train to Llandudno, Wales – a resort community on the Irish Sea. "The place was a sort of time warp, I mean to say I don't remember seeing one other uniform there," he recalled.[15] In Llandudno the hotels were fully booked with civilian vacationers and it seemed hard to believe that a great military struggle was raging on the continent. According to Davis, the next week was a "bacchanalian carousal."[16]

For the men of the 507th who were wounded during the regiment's battles at Vindefontaine, Fauvrerie and La Poterie, the

The 507th PIR's combat attrition was very high during the Normandy campaign; a fact that is well illustrated by what happened to the men in this photo, which was taken in Alliance in 1943. The troopers pictured are (*standing*) Sgt. John Carson Smith – wounded in action, Pvt. William H. Witt – killed in action, Pvt. Lewis S. Toye– killed in action, (*kneeling*) Cpl. Walter L. Choquette – murdered at Graignes, Pfc. John D. Williams – injured in training, Pvt. William McDade – wounded in action and (*lying*) Pvt. Bernard E. Kelly – prisoner of war. (*Courtesy of Albert "Bud" Parker*)

507th PIR color guard passes in review during the 82nd Airborne Division awards ceremony in England following the Normandy campaign. *(Courtesy of William D. Bowell, Sr.)*

Major General Matthew B. Ridgway, commanding general of the 82nd Airborne Division, decorating 507th paratroopers during the 82nd Airborne awards ceremony. *(Courtesy of William D. Bowell, Sr.)*

Brigadier General James Gavin leads the 82nd Airborne Division in review in England after the Normandy campaign. *(Courtesy of William D. Bowell, Sr.)*

The shoulder patch of the 17th Airborne Division. After Normandy, the 507th was detached from the 82nd Airborne Division and attached to the 17th Airborne Division on August 27, 1944. (*Author's Collection, photo by Scott Carroll*)

General Dwight D. Eisenhower, the Supreme Commander of the Allied Expeditionary Force, was also present for the ceremony. (*Courtesy of William D. Bowell, Sr.*)

Some famous U.S. Army general officers review the 82nd Airborne Division. They are (*right to left*) Lt. Gen. Lewis Brereton of the 9th Air Force, Major General Matthew B. Ridgway, General Dwight D. Eisenhower and Brigadier General James Gavin. (*Courtesy of William D. Bowell, Sr.*)

After Normandy, the 507th fought in the Battle of the Bulge from December 24, 1944 through February 11, 1945. At the conclusion of that battle, the regiment held a memorial service at Châlons-sur-Marne, France, 116 miles east of Paris, to remember the 741 507th men that were killed and wounded in the Bulge. *(Courtesy of William D. Bowell, Sr.)*

last two weeks of July were spent in recovery rather than on leave. Lt. Johnny Marr was wounded in the pre-dawn hours of the 4th of July on *Hill 95* (La Poterie Ridge) by fragments from a German hand grenade. Later that morning, he was evacuated to the 82nd Airborne Division aid station. The next day, he was given a sedative at the aid station that put him to sleep. He woke up the following morning and was shortly thereafter placed aboard an LST at Utah Beach for the trip back to England. He had a speedy recovery and re-joined the regiment in Nottingham.[17] During the fighting for *Hill 95*, Lt. Col. Maloney was seriously wounded in both legs. He was quickly evacuated back to England and then finally to Ashford General Hospital in West Virginia. From there, he was able to convalesce on extended leave at home with his wife and two sons in Hartford, Connecticut.

• • •

The 507th began to put itself back together beginning in August 1944. Because the regiment sustained such high casualties during combat in Normandy, its ranks had to be replenished with replacements. Replacements were selected from volunteers from other units already in England and they were put through a rigorous airborne training program that included an accelerated Jump School there in England. As soon as the number of jump-qualified paratroopers was brought back up to the required level, the 507th began to train as a regiment again. At about the same time that the regiment began to regain its strength as a unit, it was detached from the 82nd Airborne Division and temporarily attached to the 17th Airborne Division on August 27, 1944. It was also during this time frame that the 507th moved from Tollerton Hall to first Tidworth Barracks and then on to Barton Stacy in southern England. Since the 507th had been detached from the 82nd Airborne Division the previous month, it did not participate in the Operation Market-Garden jump in September.

Throughout October and November, training the replacements continued in full force until just before Christmas. On December 16th, German forces in the Ardennes forest area launched a major offensive that would ultimately come to be known as the Battle of the Bulge. On Christmas Eve 1944 the men of the 507th boarded C-47s in England that flew them to Chartres southwest of Paris, France. From there they boarded trucks that carried them east. The convoy passed into Belgium on Christmas day and the 507th deployed directly into action against the enemy from their trucks (something that the men sarcastically referred to as a *tailgate jump*). Over the course of next forty-five days, the 507th fought the enemy on an almost continuous basis in the snow-covered forests of Belgium and Luxembourg. When it returned to France on February 11, 1945, the regiment had suffered 741 casualties.[18]

After returning from Belgium, the 507th was headquartered at Châlons-sur-Marne 116 miles east of Paris where it had to go through the process yet again of taking-on and training new personnel to replace its losses from the Battle of the Bulge. At that point, the 507th was permanently assigned to the 17th Airborne Division. Then on March 24, 1945, the 17th and the British 6th Airborne Division, comprising the Allied XVIII Airborne Corps, conducted the Operation Varsity jump across the Rhine River. In this operation, the

F Company Commander Capt. Paul F. Smith during the 507th memorial service at Châlons-sur-Marne on February 16, 1945. *(Courtesy of William D. Bowell, Sr.)*

Cpl. Howard R. Huebner of C Company/507th poses with an M1A1 Thompson submachine gun in Germany near the end of the war. *(Courtesy of Howard R. Huebner)*

507th assaulted a drop zone in the vicinity of Wesel, Germany. The regiment was then actively engaged in combat through early April, after which time it performed occupation duties for eight weeks in the city of Essen. The 507th was still occupying Essen when the war in Europe ended in May. On June 15th, the regiment moved from Essen to an encampment area on the outskirts of Rambervillers in western France near Nancy. There it remained until early September when it received orders to return to the United States.

On September 7, 1945, the 507th boarded the SS *Mariposa* at Marseille on the Mediterranean for its trip home. Eight days later, on September 15th, the *Mariposa* entered Boston harbor with several fireboats leading the way, their pumps spewing water sky high in celebration. The week prior, the *Boston Globe* ran an announcement about the arrival of the ship with the names of the New Englanders that would be aboard. Bob Davis's parents, who lived in

Vermont, had seen that announcement. "They drove down to Boston, there to stand with a host of others on an overpass directly in front of the ship at the dock," Davis remembered.[19] He was standing on "A" deck as the *Mariposa* pulled up to the quay and, as if by miracle, he looked in the direction of that overpass and saw his mother and father waving to him. "It was a very emotional experience," he recalled.[20] The *Mariposa* then docked at the Boston Port of Embarkation and the 507th was home after having spent twenty-one months overseas. The men disembarked and were ordered to board a train parked on the pier that took them directly to nearby Camp Miles Standish. There, they spent one last night as the 507th. The following day, September 16, 1945, the 507th Parachute Infantry Regiment was unceremoniously disbanded. There was no fanfare, no inspiring farewell address and no great expression of appreciation for what the men had done. Paul Smith was still with the regiment that day and he described what it was like:

Cpl. Huebner in German near the end of the war. He was among the lucky few who survived Normandy, the Bulge and Operation Varsity. *(Courtesy of Howard R. Huebner)*

Lou Horn of C Company/507th poses with a puppy in Germany shortly before the end of the war in Europe. *(Courtesy of Lou Horn)*

Nobody called the men together and said, "Guys, you did a great job – thank you." Nothing. They said, "Here's your ticket – goodbye."[21]

Such was the anticlimactic end of one of the units that helped win the war.

. . .

Some of the men of the 507th continued on with their careers in the military after the war. Paul Smith retired from the Army at the rank of Major General in 1968 after having served his country for thirty years. Johnny Marr remained in the Army as well and ultimately served in Army aviation during Vietnam. To this day, he still carries fragments from the German grenade that got him on La Poterie Ridge on the 4th of July, 1944. Frank Naughton served in

Vietnam too. Before that, he completed a tour of combat duty in Korea as a battalion commander and then went to the Republic of Vietnam in 1965 as Senior Advisor to the Vietnamese Airborne Division. During his thirty-three-year Army career, Naughton made three combat jumps: Normandy, Operation Varsity and finally one in Vietnam. After retiring as a Colonel in 1974, he went to law school, practiced for eight years and then went on to become a state court judge. Like Naughton, Roy Creek also completed a distinguished career in the Army. He did a tour of duty in Vietnam in 1956 as an advisor and, when he returned to the U.S., he went into Army aviation. As if being in the parachute infantry was not dangerous enough, he went to Fort Rucker and learned to fly both fixed-wing aircraft and helicopters. After that, he did a tour of duty in Germany as a divisional aviation officer and then went back to Vietnam again in 1966. In August 1967, Creek retired from the Army as a Colonel after twenty-eight years of service. In his retirement, he

Paul F. Smith retired from the U.S. Army as a Major General after a career that spanned 30 years. *(Courtesy of Albert "Bud" Parker)*

Frank Naughton as a Captain during the Battle of the Bulge. This photo was taken in January 1945 while the 507th was fighting in Belgium. *(Courtesy of Frank Naughton)*

worked for a few years at Fort Leavenworth with a military contractor and then in 1971 he went to work for the University of Kansas. He retired from UKans in 1986 so that he could spend more time with his four children and fourteen grandchildren. Major Gordon K. Smith, who was wounded and captured on D-Day, spent the rest of the war in German prison camps. He was first taken to Oflag 64 in Poland and later to Stalag III-A, where he remained until the end of the war. He stayed in the Army after 1945 and did a tour of duty in Korea in 1953. In 1968 he retired from active duty at the rank of Lieutenant Colonel and moved to Baton Rouge, Louisiana where he took over the ROTC program at Louisiana State University. While a prisoner at Oflag 64 in Poland, Smith was reunited with the regiment's commanding officer, Col. Millett. On January 21, 1945, Millett escaped from Oflag 64 and made his way across the Ukraine to the Black Sea port of Odessa. From there, he managed to get to Naples, Italy and was back in the United States be-

fore VE Day. After the war, Col. Millett was given command of the 4th Infantry Regiment and, in 1946, he was transferred to the Airborne School. He was serving as military attaché to Jordan in 1955 when he was diagnosed with leukemia. He died in Germany later that year.[22]

While several 507th men went on to have full and productive careers as Army officers, most of the men of the 507th were citizen soldiers. When they got out of the Army at the end of the war, they went back to jobs, families and school. Jack Summer was discharged from the Army as a Staff Sergeant and returned to Atlanta whereupon he enrolled in the Georgia Institute of Technology, ultimately completing a bachelor's degree in architecture. After graduating from Georgia Tech, he began a highly successful career in that field. Silver Star recipient George Leidenheimer went on to college as well. He was discharged from the Army at Camp Shelby, Mississippi on September 29, 1945 with the rank of Technical Sergeant

Frank Naughton as a Captain soon after the end of World War II. *(Courtesy of Frank Naughton)*

Frank and Ruth Naughton on their wedding day in 1947 at Fort Benning. Like so many thousands of other Americans, Naughton came back from the war and started a family. *(Courtesy of Frank Naughton)*

Colonel Frank Naughton suits up for a training jump in Vietnam in 1966. During his tour of duty there (which lasted from April 1965 to April 1966), Naughton served as the Senior Military Advisor for the Vietnamese Airborne Division. His bodyguard is helping him put on his T-10 parachute. *(Courtesy of Frank Naughton)*

A very lean Colonel Naughton talking with a Vietnamese paratrooper in late 1965. Due to illness, Naughton lost 40 pounds during his tour of duty in the Republic of Vietnam. *(Courtesy of Frank Naughton)*

Colonel Naughton speaking with another American advisor in the field in 1965. *(Courtesy of Frank Naughton)*

Frank Naughton as a Colonel during his last tour in the Pentagon in 1970. *(Courtesy of Frank Naughton)*

after which he returned to New Orleans, enrolled at Tulane University and graduated in 1949 with a degree in Business Administration. After college, he went into the construction general contracting business. Carson Smith went on to have a very colorful and interesting life after the war. He started racing cars in 1946 and was a charter member of NASCAR when it was formed in 1948. After a brief career in stock car racing, he became involved in the rodeo circuit, although the shrapnel in his leg from Normandy troubled him from time to time. After the war, G Company Commander, Captain Floyd "Ben" Schwartzwalder went on to have a very successful career in college athletics. He became head football coach at Syracuse University in 1949 and led that team to a National Collegiate Championship in 1959. The men of the 507th were winners on many levels. After the war, Bob Davis accepted a major oil company's offer as a marketing intern, the genesis of his career as an oil marketer in New England and the Midwest. Following his retirement in Oklahoma in 1983, Davis returned to his native Ver-

Above right: Capt. Roy E. Creek of E Company/507th receives his promotion to the rank of Major from Col. Edson D. Raff. Right: Roy Creek remained in the Army until 1967 and, like so many other men, started a family during that time. *(both photos Courtesy of Roy Creek)*

Above: After being wounded and captured in Normandy, 507th Regimental Supply Officer Major Gordon K. Smith spent the duration of the war in Europe as a prisoner of war. The Germans issued him this PW dog tag during that time. *(Courtesy of Gordon K. Smith)* Left: Dave Brummitt or 3rd Battalion/507th also remained in the Army after the war. He is pictured here in front of a C-130 *Hercules* while he was attached to the 101st Airborne Division. *(Courtesy of Dominique François)*

Gregg Howarth was the squad leader of 2nd Squad, 2nd Platoon, C Company, 1st Battalion/507th. He had been on the ground for less than 24 hours in Normandy when he was captured by the Germans. He spent the next eleven months as a prisoner. *(Photo by author)*

507th Regimental Supply Officer Major Gordon K. Smith *(third from left)* poses with other prisoners in Germany in late 1944. *(Courtesy of Dominique François)*

Forced to exist on a diet of turnips and cabbage, Sgt. Howarth dreamed of all of his favorite foods while in solitary confinement, evidence of which can be seen in the etchings in his mess tin. *(Photo by author)*

Howarth also etched a likeness of the jump wings he earned at Fort Benning in 1942. *(Photo by author)*

Sgt. Howarth was obviously preoccupied with dreams of pecan-vanilla ice cream cones and Coca Cola while he was in solitary confinement in October and November 1944. *(Photo by author)*

Corporal Jack Summer in his Class "A" uniform after the Normandy campaign. *(Courtesy of Albert "Bud" Parker via Jump/Cut Productions)*

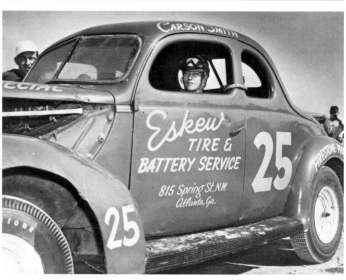

After the war, Carson Smith went on to have a brief career in car racing and was a charter member of NASCAR when it was formed in 1948. *(Courtesy of Albert "Bud" Parker via Jump/Cut Productions)*

After the end of the war, George H. Leidenheimer was discharged from the Army at Camp Shelby, Mississippi in September 1945 and returned to New Orleans a civilian. *(Courtesy of George H. Leidenheimer)*

Bob Davis (*standing, second from left*) was a citizen soldier like so many thousands of the other Americans who served during World War II. He worked in the oil business until his retirement in 1983 whereupon he returned to his native Vermont. *(Courtesy of Robert S. Davis)*

Like so many other 507th men, following his Army discharge Bob Davis started a family. On May 28, 1948, he married the former Marsha Dalton Murray. This photo of the couple was taken at the Queen Elizabeth Hotel in Montreal, Quebec, two days after the wedding. *(Courtesy of Robert S. Davis)*

mont where he is still active in business pursuits.[23] Robert D. Rae was discharged from the Army on Christmas Eve 1945 as a Captain. He left active duty service authorized to wear the Distinguished Service Cross for the superior leadership he displayed on the La Fière causeway and the Purple Heart for wounds he sustained during the Battle of the Bulge. After the war, he served as a Major in the U.S. Army Reserve until 1954. That same year Rae moved his family to Birmingham, Alabama where he went to work for Longview Lime Company. He retired as the company's Vice President in 1978, served as an active member of St. Luke's Episcopal Church in Mountain Brook, Alabama and, until his health began to fail, was an active tennis player. Sadly, Bob Rae died on Friday, September 5, 2003 as this book was being finished. He was only six days away from his 90th birthday.

• • •

The incredible events that took place in Normandy in 1944 resounded with such deep meaning to so many people that, with each passing anniversary, there was ever-increasing interest in commemorating what happened there. For the Norman people, D-Day commemorative activities soon became an annual calendar event of great importance. At first, American D-Day veterans were not a part of these activities because, for the most part, they were attending to the demands of careers and family obligations. On Armistice Day 1948, just four years after the tragedy, a ceremony was held in

Graignes during which the French government awarded the community the Croix de Guerre with Silver Star for its role in assisting the American paratroopers during the invasion. The following year, a ceremony was held there to dedicate the Franco-American memorial that now stands in the ruins of the village's XIIth century Roman Catholic Church.

Inevitably though, veterans of the regiment began finding their way back to Normandy to visit Chef du Pont, La Fière, and Graignes. Most 507th men did not start coming back until the 40th anniversary of the invasion in 1984. It was then that Frank Naughton returned to Graignes for the first time where he was reunited with Marthe and Odette. That reunion was especially meaningful because Marthe and Odette had never known the fate of the paratroopers they had gone to such lengths to help. It was only in 1984 that they learned they had saved the life of every man they had hidden in their barn. Like so many of the other citizens of Graignes, Marthe and Odette performed the most noble and honorable act of bravery possible: they gave life to those who would otherwise have

In February 1986, Frank Naughton and Earcle "Pip" Reed submitted recommendations to the Secretary of the Army to recognize eleven citizens of the village of Graignes for their assistance of 507th paratroopers in June 1944. Those recommendations were approved, and on July 6, 1986, the awards were distributed in a ceremony at the Graignes memorial site. *(Courtesy of Marthe Rigault-His)*

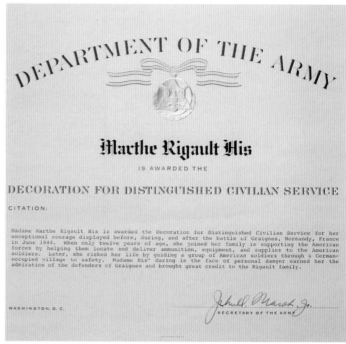

Marthe's Decoration for Distinguished Civilian Service citation. *(Courtesy of Marthe Rigault-His)*

Marthe Rigault-His at the Graignes memorial on July 6, 1986. In this photo, she has just been awarded the Decoration for Distinguished Civilian Service. *(Courtesy of Marthe Rigault-His)*

507th Parachute Infantry Regiment veterans in Normandy in July 2002. They came to dedicate a monument to their regiment. *(Photo by Jeff Petry)*

Frenchmen awaiting the arrival of 507th veterans in front of the Graignes memorial in July 2002. At Graignes, the French greeted the 507th with a moving display of sincere appreciation. *(Photo by author)*

Bob Rae talks to family and friends at the La Fière bridge during his final visit there in July 2002. (*Photo by Jeff Petry***)**

been killed. Col. Naughton returned from that trip determined to see to it that the people of Graignes received some sort of official recognition from the U.S. government for what they had done. During the two years that followed, Naughton and Earcle "Pip" Reed composed a document recommending several citizens of Graignes for awards. This document was presented to the Secretary of the Army in February 1986 and was approved. On July 6, 1986 a ceremony was held at the Graignes memorial site during which eleven villagers were presented with the Award for Distinguished Civilian Service for their role in assisting the men of 3rd Battalion/507th. Six of those awards were posthumous.

During the summer of 2002, those 507th veterans that could make the journey returned to France to dedicate a monument to the regiment they so proudly served. That monument was no small

Bob Rae talking with admirers at the 507th monument site in July 2002. (*Photo by Jeff Petry***)**

During the July 2002 reunion in Normandy, Bob Rae crossed the La Fière causeway one final time. In this photograph, he is on the far west end of the causeway at Cauquigny. (*Photo by Jeff Petry***)**

Bob Rae In the church at Cauquigny. He passed away on September 5, 2003, in Birmingham, Alabama. (*Photo by Jeff Petry***)**

During the Normandy reunion, the veterans visited the American Cemetery at Colleville-Sur-Mer to pay respects to the 129 507th troopers buried there. (*Photo by Jeff Petry*)

507th veterans Joseph J. Stefaniak and Marty Tougher during one of the many ceremonies held as a part of the July 2002 reunion. (*Photo by Jeff Petry*)

undertaking and represents the culmination of an effort that was years in the making. During the 1980s and 1990s when 507th veterans first began their pilgrimages to Normandy, they realized that no commemorative markers or interpretive signs specifically told the story of what the 507th had done there. As a consequence of that fact, several veterans of the regiment came out of retirement to make a 507th monument a reality. Through the tireless efforts of Paul Smith, Frank Naughton, Roy Creek and others, a corporation was formed, a sculpture was commissioned and a parcel of land was purchased – significant accomplishments even to men half their age. Paul Smith, who had been enjoying the life of a retired Major General, ended up devoting about thirty hours a week for two years to the 507th monument project.[24] They selected a site near Amfreville, a few kilometers to the west of Ste.-Mère-Église on the

west bank of the Merderet River. That site was particularly chosen because of its proximity Drop Zone "T" – the area where the regiment was supposed to have landed on D-Day. During their weeklong reunion in Normandy, the remaining men of the 507th visited such significant sites as Chef du Pont and Graignes. During a visit to La Fière, Bob Rae crossed the La Fière causeway for the last time. The crowning moment of the trip came on July 22, 2002 when the monument was dedicated before an assembled crowd of dignitaries, friends and family. Also among the crowd that day were two sisters named Marthe and Odette. They expected no attention, demanded no acknowledgement and attended only to show their respect for the men of the regiment.

The guests of honor that day were the surviving veterans of the 507th Parachute Infantry Regiment. Although 2,004 of them had

SFC Derek S. Gondek of Lewiston, Maine, a "black hat" with the 1st-507th Infantry (Abn), talks with Robert L. Bearden during the 507th monument dedication ceremony. During World War II, Bearden served as a Sergeant in H Company/507th. (*Photo by Jeff Petry*)

507th veterans Robert L. Bearden and Howard R. Huebner pose for a candid photograph during the 507th monument dedication ceremony. Huebner served in C Company/507th and Bearden served in H Company/507th. (*Photo by Jeff Petry*)

For many 507th veterans, the monument dedication ceremony was a very emotional experience. (*Photo by Jeff Petry*)

Bob Rae poses with his grandson Robert Rae Parker in front of the 507th monument just after the dedication ceremony. (*Photo by the author*)

come to Normandy in 1944, barely a busload was on hand in 2002. Fate had placed these men in unusual circumstances fifty-eight years earlier. Their destiny had not been to live civilian lives of office or factory work. They were not destined to support the war effort because they were the spearhead of the war effort. They had been sent to Normandy in the prime of their youth with steel in their hands. That steel had been hewn by the mills of Pittsburgh and Birmingham and fashioned into rifles and sub-machine guns. In 1944 the men of the 507th carried those weapons to Normandy not to conquer, oppress or occupy, but rather to advance the noble work of liberation and to defend the principles of free democratic government. After Pearl Harbor, their generation responded unanimously and literally lined up for the chance to represent that concept. Beginning on June 6, 1944, fate placed the officers and men of the 507th Parachute Infantry Regiment where their dedication to that crusade was rigorously tested during thirty-five arduous days in combat. In Normandy, more than 400 sons of the regiment paid the last full measure of devotion for that cause. Those men forfeited their tomorrows to end the totalitarian rule of tyrants. Those men forfeited their tomorrows to liberate the French people. Of noble causes, you will find none higher. Many of the sons of the regiment who lost their lives during the battle of Normandy lay buried on a now tranquil bluff overlooking Omaha Beach, just a

few miles away from the monument that honors their memory. Those men never left the soil they came to save.

During the dedication of the 507th monument, a number of distinguished speakers offered remarks to give context and perspective to the occasion. Among those speakers was M. Alain Maitre, the Mayor of Amfreville, who delivered an eloquent and moving address that concluded with these words:

> This monument, standing like a sentinel at the entrance to our community, proclaims a message: Vigilance. Democracy is a value incessantly challenged by men with destructive ideologies that lead to the abyss. Democracy is something we must defend. Democracy is something we must deserve. Thank you to the United States of America. Honor and glory to the 507th Parachute Infantry.[25]

The 507th Parachute Infantry Regiment monument near Amfreville. Years in the making, it recognizes the 2,004 sons of the regiment who jumped, fought, and died in Normandy during the summer of 1944. (*Photo by the author*)

Bibliography

Primary sources

After Action Report of the 82nd Airborne Division titled *82nd Airborne Division, Action in Normandy, France in Four Sections.* Medal of Honor Citation of Charles N. Deglopper (G.O. No.: 22, 28 February 1946).

Distinguished Service Cross Citation of Arthur A. Maloney written by General James M. Gavin.

Distinguished Service Cross Citation of Robert D. Rae written by General James M. Gavin.

Memorandum titled "Recommendations for Awards" prepared by Earcle R. Reed and Francis E. Naughton, to John O. Marsh, Secretary of the Army, dated February 13, 1986.

Letter from James M. Gavin, Cambridge, Massachusetts , to Albert "Bud" Parker, Atlanta, Georgia, 31 March 1981.

Unpublished material

Barnes, Edward R. Recorded personal history narrative. Oral History Collection of The Eisenhower Center for American Studies, New Orleans, Louisiana.

Barnes, Edward R. Interview by Martin K.A. Morgan, 16 March 2003, Atlanta, Georgia. Audio recording in the Oral History Collection of The National D-Day Museum, New Orleans, Louisiana.

Blakey, Thomas J. Interview by Martin K.A. Morgan, 22 January 2003. Audio recording in the Oral History Collection of The National D-Day Museum, New Orleans, Louisiana.

Bosworth, Donald. Written personal history narrative, 24 March 1992. Oral History Collection of The Eisenhower Center for American Studies, New Orleans, Louisiana.

Creek, Roy E. Interview by Martin K.A. Morgan, 22 July 2002, Cherbourg, Normandy, France. Audio recording in the Oral History Collection of The National D-Day Museum, New Orleans, Louisiana.

Creek, Roy E. Recorded personal history narrative. Oral History Collection of The Eisenhower Center for American Studies, New Orleans, Louisiana.

Dahlia, Joseph A. Recorded personal history narrative. Oral History Collection of The Eisenhower Center for American Studies, New Orleans, Louisiana.

Davis, Robert S. Interview by Martin K.A. Morgan, 23 July 2002, Cherbourg, Normandy, France. Audio recording in the Oral History Collection of The National D-Day Museum, New Orleans, Louisiana.

Davis, Robert S. Letter to Martin K.A. Morgan, 1 July 2003.

Davis, Robert S. Letter to Martin K.A. Morgan, 11 August 2003.

Davis, Robert S. Letter to Martin K.A. Morgan, 12 August 2003.

Davis, Robert S. Letter to Martin K.A. Morgan, 17 August 2003.

Davis, Robert S. Letter to Martin K.A. Morgan, 18 August 2003.

Dillon, Gerard M. Recorded personal history narrative. Oral History Collection of The Eisenhower Center for American Studies, New Orleans, Louisiana.

François, Fernand. Interview by Martin K.A. Morgan, 26 July 2002, Cherbourg, Normandy, France. Translated by Deborah L. Stoddard. Audio recording in the Oral History Collection of The National D-Day Museum, New Orleans, Louisiana.

Gockel, Franz. "Memoir" written personal history narrative translated by Derek S. Zumbro. Oral History Collection of The Eisenhower Center for American Studies, New Orleans, Louisiana.

Le Goupil, Paul. Interview by Martin K.A. Morgan, 26 July 2002, Cherbourg, Normandy, France. Translated by Deborah L. Stoddard. Audio recording in the Oral History Collection of The National D-Day Museum, New Orleans, Louisiana.

Hinchliff, John J. Interview by Martin K.A. Morgan, 22 July 2002, Cherbourg, Normandy, France. Audio recording in the Oral History Collection of The National D-Day Museum, New Orleans, Louisiana.

Hinchliff, John J. Interview by Martin K.A. Morgan, 16 March 2003, Atlanta, Georgia. Audio recording in the Oral History Collection of The National D-Day Museum, New Orleans, Louisiana.

His, Marthe. Written personal history narrative. Oral History Collection of The National D-Day Museum, New Orleans, Louisiana.

His, Marthe. Interview by Martin K.A. Morgan, translated by Deborah L. Stoddard, 16 May 2003, Vierville-Sur-Mer, Normandy, France. Audio recording in the Oral History Collection of The National D-Day Museum, New Orleans, Louisiana.

Horne, Lou. Interview by Larry Gordon, 23 July 2002, Cherbourg, Normandy, France. Audio recording in the Oral History Collection of The National D-Day Museum, New Orleans, Louisiana.

Hughart, Clarence S. Interview by Patrick O'Donnell.

Jeziorski, Edward J. Recorded personal history narrative. Oral History Collection of The Eisenhower Center for American Studies, New Orleans, Louisiana.

Kanaras, Chris C. Recorded personal history narrative. Oral History Collection of The Eisenhower Center for American Studies, New Orleans, Louisiana.

Lelavechef, Odette. Interview by Martin K.A. Morgan, translated by Deborah L. Stoddard, 16 May 2003, Vierville-Sur-Mer, Normandy, France. Audio recording in the Oral History Collection of The National D-Day Museum, New Orleans, Louisiana.

Marr, John W. Interview by Martin K.A. Morgan, 16 March 2003, Atlanta, Georgia. Audio recording in the Oral History Collection of The National D-Day Museum, New Orleans, Louisiana.

Naughton, Francis E. Interview by Martin K.A. Morgan, 21 July 2002, Cherbourg, Normandy, France. Audio recording in the Oral History Collection of The National D-Day Museum, New Orleans, Louisiana.

Naughton, Francis E. Telephone interview by Martin K.A. Morgan, 3 April 2003. Audio recording in the Oral History Collection of The National D-Day Museum, New Orleans, Louisiana.

Naughton, Francis E. Telephone interview by Martin K.A. Morgan, 22 April 2003. Audio recording in the Oral History Collection of The National D-Day Museum, New Orleans, Louisiana.

Oppenheimer, Harry. Interview by Martin K.A. Morgan, 11 February 2003, The National D-Day Museum, New Orleans, Louisiana. Audio recording in the Oral History Collection of The National D-Day Museum, New Orleans, Louisiana.

Parks, Robert H. "An Unforgettable Memory." Written personal history narrative. Oral History Collection of The National D-Day Museum, New Orleans, Louisiana.

Rae, Robert D. Interview by Martin K.A. Morgan, 27 July 2002, Normandy, France. Audio recording in the Oral History Collection of The National D-Day Museum, New Orleans, Louisiana.

Robinson, Kenneth F. Interview by Bob Dunn. Audio recording in the Curatorial Collection of The National D-Day Museum, New Orleans, Louisiana.

Smith, John Carson. Interview by Martin K.A. Morgan, 21 July 2002, Cherbourg, Normandy, France. Audio recording in the Oral History Collection of The National D-Day Museum, New Orleans, Louisiana.

Smith, John Carson. Interview by Robert J. Carr, 28 July 2002, Air France Flight 316 from Paris to Atlanta. Audio recording in the Oral History Collection of The National D-Day Museum, New Orleans, Louisiana.

Smith, Paul F. Interview by Martin K.A. Morgan, 25 July 2002, Cherbourg, Normandy, France. Audio recording in the Oral History Collection of The National D-Day Museum, New Orleans, Louisiana.

Smith, Paul F. Letter to Martin K.A. Morgan, 8 July 2003.

Summer, Jack. Interview by Martin K.A. Morgan, 22 July 2002, Cherbourg, Normandy, France. Audio recording in the Oral History Collection of The National D-Day Museum, New Orleans, Louisiana.

Ulan, Sidney M. Recorded personal history narrative, September 1989. Oral History Collection of The Eisenhower Center for American Studies, New Orleans, Louisiana.

Secondary sources
Books

507th Parachute Infantry Regiment: 1943 (yearbook). Denver: The Bradford-Robinson Printing Co., 1943.

A Historical and Pictorial Review of the Parachute Battalions, United States Army: Fort Benning, Georgia: 1942. Baton Rouge: The Army and Navy Publishing Company, Inc., 1942.

Ambrose, Stephen E. *Band of Brothers: E Company, 506th Regiment, 101st Airborne from Normandy to Hitler's Eagle's Nest.* New York: Simon & Schuster, 1992.

Ambrose, Stephen E. *D-Day June 6, 1944: The Climactic Battle of World War II.* New York: Simon & Schuster, 1994.

Ambrose, Stephen E. *Citizen Soldiers: The U.S. Army from the Normandy Beaches to the Bulge to the Surrender of Germany.* New York: Simon & Schuster, 1997.

Bando, Mark. *101st Airborne: The Screaming Eagles At Normandy.* Osceola, WI: MBI Publishing Company, 2001.

Bernage, Georges. *The Panzers and the Battle of Normandy.* Bayeux, France: Editions Heimdal, 2000.

Burgett, Donald R. *Curahee!* Boston: Houghton Mifflin Company, 1967.

Callahan, Robert E. *On Wings of Troop Carriers In World War II: Selected Accounts of Events Relating to the 50th Troop Carrier Squadron in Africa and Europe in World War II.* San Antonio, Texas: Burke Publishing Company, 1997.

Canfield, Bruce N. *U.S. Infantry Weapons of World War II.* Lincoln, Rhode Island: Andrew Mowbray Publishers, 1994.

Clark, Gloria. *World War II Prairie Invasion.* Kearney, Nebraska: Morris Publishing, 1999.

Davis, Larry. *C-47 Skytrain In Action.* Carrollton, TX: Squadron/Signal Publications, Inc., 1995.

François, Dominique. *507th Parachute Infantry Regiment: Normandie, Ardennes, Allemagne 1942-1945.* Bayeux, France: Editions Heimdal, 2000.

Fox, Gary N. *Graignes: the Franco-American Memorial*. Fostoria, Ohio: DZ Publishing Company, 1990.

Gavin, General James M. *On To Berlin: Battles of an Airborne Commander 1943-1946*. New York: The Viking Press, 1978.

Gawne, Jonathan. *Spearheading D-Day: American Special Units in Normandy*. Paris: Histoire & Collections, 1998.

Hamlin, John F. *Support and Strike: A Concise History of the U.S. Ninth Air Force in Europe*. Peterborough, England: GMS Enterprises, 1991.

Holt, Tonie and Valmai. *Major & Mrs. Holt's Battlefield Guide to the Normandy Landing Beaches*. Barnsley, South Yorkshire: Pen & Sword Ltd., 2000.

Heisler, Walter G., ed. *In Their Own Words*. Privately printed, 2000.

Marshall, S.L.A. *Night Drop: The American Airborne Invasion of Normandy*. Boston: Little, Brown and Company, 1962.

Mrozek, Steven J. *82nd Airborne Division*. Paducah, KY: Turner Publishing Company, 1997.

Murphy, Robert M. *No Better Place To Die*. Croton Falls, NY: Critical Hit, Inc., 1999.

Rentz, Bill. *Geronimo! U.S. Airborne Uniforms, Insignia & Equipment in World War II*. Atglen, PA: Schiffer Military History, 1999.

Reynosa, Mark A. *The M-1 Helmet: A History of the U.S. M-1 Helmet in World War II*. Atglen, PA: Schiffer Military History, 1996.

Stanton, Shelby L. *Order of Battle*. New York: Galahad Books/ Presidio, 1984.

Tent, James F. *E-Boat Alert: Defending the Normandy Invasion Fleet*. Annapolis, Maryland: U.S. Naval Institute Press, 1996.

Articles

Bando, Mark. "The Controversy Over Troop Carrier." (November 2000)

Booth, T. Michael and Duncan Spencer. "The Airborne's Watery Triumph." *The Quarterly Journal of Military History* Volume 6, Number 3 (Spring 1994).

Films

Gugenheim, Charles. *D-Day Remembered*. Produced and directed by Charles Gugenheim . 53 min. Gugenheim Poductions, Inc., 1994.

Walker, Phil and David Druckenmiller. *D-Day Down to Earth: Return of the 507th*. Produced by Phil Walker and David Druckenmiller. 46 min. Jump/Cut Productions, Inc., 2003.

Notes

Chapter 1: The Beginning

[1] Francis E. Naughton, Interview by Martin K.A. Morgan, 21 July 2002, Cherbourg, France, transcript, Oral History Collection, The National D-Day Museum, New Orleans, Louisiana.

[2] Paul F. Smith, Interview by Martin K.A. Morgan, 25 July 2002, Cherbourg, France, transcript, Oral History Collection, The National D-Day Museum, New Orleans, Louisiana.

[3] Ibid.

[4] Ibid.

[5] *Life* magazine, 12 May 1941, 110.

[6] Ibid.

[7] John W. Marr, Interview by Martin K.A. Morgan, 16 March 2003, Atlanta, Georgia, transcript, Oral History Collection, The National D-Day Museum, New Orleans, Louisiana.

[8] John J. Hinchliff, Interview by Martin K.A. Morgan, 22 July 2002, Cherbourg, Normandy, France, transcript, Oral History Collection, The National D-Day Museum, New Orleans, Louisiana.

[9] Edward R. Barnes, Interview by Martin K.A. Morgan, 16 March 2003, Atlanta, Georgia, transcript, Oral History Collection, The National D-Day Museum, New Orleans, Louisiana.

[10] Stephen E. Ambrose, *Band of Brothers: E Company, 506th Regiment, 101st Airborne from Normandy to Hitler's Eagle's Nest* (New York: Simon & Schuster, 1992), 16.

[11] John J. Hinchliff oral history, The National D-Day Museum.

[12] Robert S. Davis, Interview by Martin K.A. Morgan, 23 July 2002, Cherbourg, France, transcript, Oral History Collection, The National D-Day Museum, New Orleans, Louisiana.

[13] Lou Horne, Interview by Larry Gordon, 23 July 2002, Cherbourg, Normandy, France, transcript, Oral History Collection, The National D-Day Museum, New Orleans, Louisiana.

[14] Roy E. Creek, Interview by Martin K.A. Morgan, 22 July 2002, Cherbourg, France, transcript, Oral History Collection, The National D-Day Museum, New Orleans, Louisiana.

[15] John Carson Smith, Interview by Martin K.A. Morgan, 21 July 2002, Cherbourg, France, transcript, Oral History Collection, The National D-Day Museum, New Orleans, Louisiana.

[16] Lou Horne oral history, The National D-Day Museum.

[17] Jack Summer, Interview by Martin K.A. Morgan, 21 July 2002, Cherbourg, France, transcript, Oral History Collection, The National D-Day Museum, New Orleans, Louisiana.

[18] Roy Creek oral history, The National D-Day Museum.

[19] *Life* magazine, 12 May 1941, 111.

[20] Carson Smith oral history, The National D-Day Museum.

[21] *Life* magazine, 12 May 1941, 110.

[22] George H. Leidenheimer, Personal History Narrative, Oral History Collection, The National D-Day Museum, New Orleans, Louisiana.

[23] Ibid.

[24] Ibid.

[25] Ibid.

[26] Ibid.

[27] *507th Parachute Infantry Regiment: 1943* (Denver: The Bradford-Robinson Printing Co., 1943), 37.

[28] Ibid., 70.

[29] Ibid., 52-57.

[30] Francis E. Naughton, Telephone interview by Martin K.A. Morgan, 3 April 2003, transcript, Oral History Collection, The National D-Day Museum, New Orleans, Louisiana.

[31] Ibid.

[32] Ibid.

[33] *507th Parachute Infantry Regiment: 1943* (Denver: The Bradford-Robinson Printing Co., 1943), 130-131.

[34] Ibid., 164.

Chapter 2: After the Night of Darkness

[1] Gloria Clark, *World War II Prairie Invasion* (Kearney, Nebraska: Morris Publishing, 1999), 16.

[2]   Ibid.

[3]   Ibid.

[4]   Donald R. Burgett, *Curahee!* (Boston: Houghton Mifflin Company, 1967), 10.

[5]   *507th Parachute Infantry Regiment: 1943* (Denver: The Bradford-Robinson Printing Co., 1943), 62-63.

[6]   Ibid., 119.

[7]   Ibid.

[8]   Ibid., 121.

[9]   Robert S. Davis oral history, The National D-Day Museum.

[10] Ibid.

[11] *507th Parachute Infantry Regiment: 1943* (Denver: The Bradford-Robinson Printing Co., 1943), 113.

[12] *Alliance Times and Herald* (Alliance, Nebraska), 10 August 1943.

[13] Ibid., 24 August 1943.

[14] Ibid.

[15] Ibid.

[16] Dorothy and Robert D. Rae, Interview by Martin K.A. Morgan, 27 July 2002, France, transcript, Oral History Collection, The National D-Day Museum, New Orleans, Louisiana.

[17] Ibid.

[18] John J. Hinchliff, Interview by Martin K.A. Morgan, 16 March 2003, Atlanta, Georgia, transcript, Oral History Collection, The National D-Day Museum, New Orleans, Louisiana.

[19] Ibid.

[20] George H. Leidenheimer personal history narrative, The National D-Day Museum.

[21] *507th Parachute Infantry Regiment: 1943* (Denver: The Bradford-Robinson Printing Co., 1943), 88-91.

[22] Ibid., 94.

[23] Francis E. Naughton, Telephone interview by Martin K.A. Morgan, 3 April 2003, transcript, Oral History Collection, The National D-Day Museum, New Orleans, Louisiana.

[24] Ibid.

[25] Walter G. Heisler, ed. *In Their Own Words*. (Privately printed, 2000), 91.

[26] *507th Parachute Infantry Regiment: 1943* (Denver: The Bradford-Robinson Printing Co., 1943), 5.

Chapter 3: An Honorary Catholic

[1]   Robert S. Davis oral history, The National D-Day Museum.

[2]   Francis E. Naughton, Telephone interview by Martin K.A. Morgan, 3 April 2003, transcript, Oral History Collection, The National D-Day Museum, New Orleans, Louisiana.

[3]   Ibid.

[4]   *D-Day Down to Earth: Return of the 507th*, Produced by Phil Walker and David Druckenmiller, 46 min., Jump/Cut Productions, Inc., 2003.

[5]   Francis E. Naughton oral history, The National D-Day Museum.

[6]   Francis E. Naughton, Telephone interview by Martin K.A. Morgan, 22 April 2003, transcript, Oral History Collection, The National D-Day Museum, New Orleans, Louisiana.

[7]   Ibid.

[8]   Ibid.

[9]   Robert S. Davis oral history, The National D-Day Museum.

[10] John J. Hinchliff, Interview by Martin K.A. Morgan, 16 March 2003, Atlanta, Georgia. transcript, Oral History Collection, The National D-Day Museum, New Orleans, Louisiana.

[11] John W. Marr oral history, The National D-Day Museum.

[12] George H. Leidenheimer, Personal History Narrative, Oral History Collection, The National D-Day Museum, New Orleans, Louisiana.

[13] Ibid.

[14] Ibid.

[15] John J. Hinchliff, Interview by Martin K.A. Morgan, 16 March 2003, Atlanta, Georgia, transcript, Oral History Collection, The National D-Day Museum, New Orleans, Louisiana.

[16] Robert S. Davis oral history, The National D-Day Museum.

[17] Ibid.

[18] Ibid.

[19] Ibid.

[20] Francis E. Naughton telephone interview (22 April 2003), The National D-Day Museum.

[21] Joseph A. Dahlia, Personal history narrative, transcript, Oral History Collection, Eisenhower Center for American Studies, New Orleans, Louisiana.

[22] George H. Leidenheimer personal history narrative, The National D-Day Museum.

[23] Ibid.

[24] Ibid.

[25] Robert S. Davis oral history, The National D-Day Museum.

[26] George H. Leidenheimer personal history narrative, The National D-Day Museum.

[27] *In Their Own Words*, 92.

[28] George H. Leidenheimer personal history narrative, The National D-Day Museum.

[29] Ibid.

[30] Ibid.

[31] Ibid.

[32] Ibid.

[33] Edward J. Jeziorski, Recorded personal history narrative, transcript, Oral History Collection, Eisenhower Center for American Studies, New Orleans, Louisiana. Louisiana.

[34] Ibid.

[35] Ibid.

[36] Ibid.

[37] Ibid.

[38] Ibid.

[39] Ibid.

[40] Shelby L. Stanton, *Order of Battle* (New York: Galahad Books/ Presidio, 1984), 151-153.

[41] Ibid.

[42] Chris C. Kanaras, Recorded personal history narrative, transcript, Oral History Collection, Eisenhower Center for American Studies, New Orleans, Louisiana. Louisiana.

[43] Robert S. Davis oral history, The National D-Day Museum.

[44] Ibid.

45 Chris C. Kanaras personal history narrative, Eisenhower Center for American Studies.

46 Francis E. Naughton oral history, The National D-Day Museum.

47 George H. Leidenheimer personal history narrative, The National D-Day Museum.

48 Ibid.

49 Ibid.

50 Robert S. Davis, "British Showed Americans the Way," *The Sunday Rutland Herald* (Vermont), 16 July 2000.

51 Ibid.

52 Ibid.

Chapter 4: Death by Labor

1 Harry Oppenheimer, Interview by Martin K.A. Morgan, 11 February 2003, transcript, Oral History Collection, The National D-Day Museum, New Orleans, Louisiana.

2 Ibid.

3 Ibid.

4 Ibid.

5 *507th Parachute Infantry Regiment: 1943* (Denver: The Bradford-Robinson Printing Co., 1943), 133.

6 Le Goupil, Paul. Interview by Martin K.A. Morgan, 26 July 2002, Cherbourg, France, transcript, Oral History Collection, The National D-Day Museum, New Orleans, Louisiana.

7 Ibid.

8 Ibid.

9 Ibid.

10 Ibid.

11 Ibid.

12 Ibid.

13 Ibid.

14 Ibid.

15 Ibid.

16 Ibid.

17 Ibid.

18 Ibid.

19 Fernand François, Interview by Martin K.A. Morgan, 26 July 2002, Cherbourg, France, transcript, Oral History Collection, The National D-Day Museum, New Orleans, Louisiana.

20 Ibid.

21 Tonie and Valmai Holt. *Major & Mrs. Holt's Battlefield Guide to the Normandy Landing Beaches* (Barnsley, South Yorkshire: Pen & Sword Ltd., 2000), 73.

22 Fernand François oral history, The National D-Day Museum, New Orleans, Louisiana.

23 Ibid.

24 Ibid.

25 Ibid.

26 Ibid.

27 Ibid.

28 Ibid.

29 Odette Lelavechef, Interview by Martin K.A. Morgan, 16 May 2003, Vierville-Sur-Mer, France, transcript, Oral History Collection, The National D-Day Museum, New Orleans, Louisiana.

30 Marthe His, Interview by Martin K.A. Morgan, 16 May 2003, Vierville-Sur-Mer, France, transcript, Oral History Collection, The National D-Day Museum, New Orleans, Louisiana.

31 Ibid.

32 Ibid.

33 Ibid.

34 Ibid.

35 Odette Lelavechef oral history, The National D-Day Museum.

36 Marthe His oral history, The National D-Day Museum.

37 Ibid.

38 Odette Lelavechef oral history, The National D-Day Museum.

39 Ibid.

Chapter 5: Seize and Destroy

1 Stephen E. Ambrose, *D-Day June 6, 1944: The Climactic Battle of World War II* (New York: Simon & Schuster, 1994), 119.

2 *In Their Own Words*, 14.

3 Ibid.

4 Jonathan Gawne, *Spearheading D-Day: American Special Units in Normandy* (Paris: Histoire & Collections, 1998), 5-39.

5 James F. Tent, *E-Boat Alert: Defending the Normandy Invasion Fleet* (Annapolis, Maryland: U.S. Naval Institute Press, 1996).

6 Stephen E. Ambrose, *D-Day June 6, 1944*, 86.

7 Franz Gockel, "Memoir" written personal history narrative translated by Derek S. Zumbro, transcript, Oral History Collection of The Eisenhower Center for American Studies, New Orleans, Louisiana.

8 Ibid.

9 Robert M. Murphy, *No Better Place To Die* (Croton Falls, NY: Critical Hit, Inc., 1999), 9.

10 Georges Bernage, *The Panzers and the Battle of Normandy* (Bayeux, France: Editions Heimdal, 2000), 10.

11 After Action Report of the 82nd Airborne Division titled *82nd Airborne Division, Action in Normandy, France in Four Sections.*

12 Ibid.

Chapter 6: A Beautiful Sight

1 *In Their Own Words*, 14.

2 Ibid.

3 George H. Leidenheimer personal history narrative, The National D-Day Museum.

4 Edward J. Jeziorski oral history, Eisenhower Center for American Studies.

5 Robert S. Davis oral history, The National D-Day Museum.

6 Clarence S. Hughart, Interview by Patrick O'Donnell.

7 *D-Day Down to Earth: Return of the 507th*, Produced by Phil Walker and David Druckenmiller, 46 min., Jump/Cut Productions, Inc., 2003.

8 Robert S. Davis oral history, The National D-Day Museum.

9   Chris C. Kanaras oral history, Eisenhower Center for American Studies.

10 Ibid.

11 Robert S. Davis oral history, The National D-Day Museum.

12 Ibid.

13 Edward J. Jeziorski oral history, Eisenhower Center for American Studies.

14 Robert S. Davis, letter to Martin K.A. Morgan, 1 July 2003.

15 Ibid.

16 Shelby L. Stanton, *Order of Battle* (New York: Galahad Books/Presidio, 1984), 264.

17 Edward J. Jeziorski oral history, Eisenhower Center for American Studies.

18 Ibid.

19 Ibid.

20 Ibid.

21 Ibid.

22 Joseph A. Dahlia personal history narrative, Eisenhower Center for American Studies.

23 Chris C. Kanaras personal history narrative, Eisenhower Center for American Studies.

24 Ibid.

25 Joseph A. Dahlia personal history narrative, Eisenhower Center for American Studies.

26 Ibid.

27 Ibid.

28 Ibid.

29 Ibid.

30 Robert S. Davis, letter to Martin K.A. Morgan, 1 July 2003.

31 *In Their Own Words*, 67.

32 Ibid., 56.

33 Ibid.

34 Clarence S. Hughart, Interview by Patrick O'Donnell.

35 Robert S. Davis oral history, The National D-Day Museum.

36 *In Their Own Words*, 14.

37 Stephen E. Ambrose, *D-Day June 6, 1944*, 194.

38 Roy E. Creek, Recorded personal history narrative, transcript, Oral History Collection, Eisenhower Center for American Studies, New Orleans, Louisiana.

39 Edward J. Jeziorski oral history, Eisenhower Center for American Studies.

40 Ibid.

41 Chris C. Kanaras personal history narrative, Eisenhower Center for American Studies.

42 Bruce N. Canfield, *U.S. Infantry Weapons of World War II* (Lincoln, Rhode Island: Andrew Mowbray Publishers, 1994), 33.

43 Bill Rentz, *Geronimo! U.S. Airborne Uniforms, Insignia & Equipment in World War II* (Atglen, PA: Schiffer Military History, 1999), 154.

44 Chris C. Kanaras personal history narrative, Eisenhower Center for American Studies.

45 Mark A. Reynosa, *The M-1 Helmet: A History of the U.S. M-1 Helmet in World War II* (Atglen, PA: Schiffer Military History, 1996), 66-67.

46 Ibid., 68.

47 Ibid.

48 Donald Bosworth, written personal history narrative dated 24 March 1992, transcript, Oral History Collection, Eisenhower Center for American Studies, New Orleans, Louisiana.

49 Sidney M. Ulan, recorded personal history narrative dated September 1989, transcript, Oral History Collection, Eisenhower Center for American Studies, New Orleans, Louisiana.

50 Larry Davis, *C-47 Skytrain In Action* (Carrollton, TX: Squadron/Signal Publications, Inc., 1995), 25-28.

51 Sidney M. Ulan oral history, Eisenhower Center for American Studies, New Orleans, Louisiana.

52 Ibid.

53 John F. Hamlin, *Support and Strike: A Concise History of the U.S. Ninth Air Force in Europe* (Peterborough, England: GMS Enterprises, 1991), 6-12.

54 Gary N. Fox, *Graignes: the Franco-American Memorial* (Fostoria, Ohio: DZ Publishing Company, 1990), 21.

55 Ibid.

56 Clarence S. Hughart, Interview by Patrick O'Donnell.

57 Edward J. Jeziorski oral history, Eisenhower Center for American Studies.

58 Ibid.

59 Donald R. Burgett, *Curahee!* (Boston: Houghton Mifflin Company, 1967), 75-77.

60 Edward J. Jeziorski oral history, Eisenhower Center for American Studies.

61 Ibid.

62 Robert H. Parks, "An Unforgettable Memory," written personal history narrative, Oral History Collection, The National D-Day Museum, New Orleans, Louisiana.

63 Robert E. Callahan, *On Wings of Troop Carriers In World War II: Selected Accounts of Events Relating to the 50th Troop Carrier Squadron in Africa and Europe in World War II* (San Antonio, Texas: Burke Publishing Company, 1997), 19-3.

64 Donald Bosworth personal history narrative, Eisenhower Center for American Studies.

Chapter 7: No Turning Back

1   *No Better Place To Die*, 13.

2   Ibid., 11.

3   Paul F. Smith oral history, The National D-Day Museum.

4   T. Michael Booth and Duncan Spencer. "The Airborne's Watery Triumph," *The Quarterly Journal of Military History* Volume 6, Number 3 (Spring 1994): 25.

5   Carson Smith oral history, The National D-Day Museum.

6   Robert H. Parks, "An Unforgettable Memory," The National D-Day Museum.

7   Ibid.

8   Clarence S. Hughart, Interview by Patrick O'Donnell.

9   Sidney M. Ulan personal history narrative, Eisenhower Center for American Studies.

10 Ibid.

11 *No Better Place To Die*, 108.

12 Ibid.

13 Edward J. Jeziorski oral history, Eisenhower Center for American Studies.

14 Carson Smith oral history, The National D-Day Museum.

15 Donald Bosworth personal history narrative, Eisenhower Center for American Studies.

16 Ibid.

17 Mark Bando. "The Controversy Over Troop Carriers," (November 2000).

18 Chris C. Kanaras personal history narrative, Eisenhower Center for American Studies.

19 Ibid.

20 Mark Bando. "The Controversy Over Troop Carriers," (November 2000).

21 *In Their Own Words*, 77.

22 Ibid.

23 Charles Gugenheim, *D-Day Remembered*, produced and directed by Charles Gugenheim, 53 min., Gugenheim Poductions, Inc., 1994.

24 *D-Day Down to Earth: Return of the 507th*, Produced by Phil Walker and David Druckenmiller, 46 min., Jump/Cut Productions, Inc., 2003.

25 *Graignes: the Franco-American Memorial*, 21.

26 Edward J. Jeziorski oral history, Eisenhower Center for American Studies.

27 Robert D. Rae, Interview by Martin K.A. Morgan, 27 July 2002, France, transcript, Oral History Collection, The National D-Day Museum, New Orleans, Louisiana.

28 Mark Bando, *101st Airborne: The Screaming Eagles At Normandy* (Osceola, WI: MBI Publishing Company, 2001), 39.

29 Mark Bando. "The Controversy Over Troop Carriers," (November 2000).

30 Thomas J. Blakey, Interview by Martin K.A. Morgan, 22 January 2003, transcript, Oral History Collection, The National D-Day Museum, New Orleans, Louisiana.

31 Sidney M. Ulan personal history narrative, Eisenhower Center for American Studies.

Chapter 8: Descent into Chaos

1 Joseph A. Dahlia personal history narrative, Eisenhower Center for American Studies.

2 Donald Bosworth personal history narrative, Eisenhower Center for American Studies.

3 Joseph A. Dahlia personal history narrative, Eisenhower Center for American Studies.

4 Edward J. Jeziorski oral history, Eisenhower Center for American Studies.

5 Robert H. Parks, "An Unforgettable Memory," The National D-Day Museum.

6 Carson Smith oral history, The National D-Day Museum.

7 Ibid.

8 Paul F. Smith oral history, The National D-Day Museum.

9 Kenneth F. Robinson, Interview by Bob Dunn, transcript, Curatorial Collection of The National D-Day Museum, New Orleans, Louisiana.

10 Robert E. Callahan *On Wings of Troop Carriers In World War II*, 19-4.

11 Carson Smith oral history, The National D-Day Museum.

12 *D-Day Down to Earth: Return of the 507th*, Produced by Phil Walker and David Druckenmiller, 46 min., Jump/Cut Productions, Inc., 2003.

13 Carson Smith oral history, The National D-Day Museum.

14 Joseph A. Dahlia personal history narrative, Eisenhower Center for American Studies.

15 Chris C. Kanaras personal history narrative, Eisenhower Center for American Studies.

16 Ibid.

17 Ibid.

18 Ibid.

19 Ibid.

20 Edward J. Jeziorski oral history, Eisenhower Center for American Studies.

21 Ibid.

22 Ibid.

23 Ibid.

24 Ibid.

25 Ibid.

26 Ibid.

27 Ibid.

28 Ibid.

29 Ibid.

30 Ibid.

31 Clarence S. Hughart, Interview by Patrick O'Donnell.

32 Ibid.

33 Ibid.

34 Ibid.

35 Ibid.

36 Ibid.

37 *In Their Own Words*, 18.

38 Ibid.

39 Ibid., 19.

40 Ibid.

41 Ibid., 20.

42 Robert H. Parks, "An Unforgettable Memory," The National D-Day Museum.

43 Ibid.

44 Ibid.

45 Ibid.

46 Ibid.

47 Ibid.

48 Ibid.

49 Ibid.

50 Ibid.

51 Ibid.

52 Ibid.

53 Ibid.

54 George H. Leidenheimer personal history narrative, The National D-Day Museum.

55 Ibid.

56 Ibid.

57 Ibid.

58 Ibid.

59 Ibid.

60 Ibid.

61 Paul F. Smith oral history, The National D-Day Museum.

62 Ibid.

63 Ibid.

64 Ibid.

65 Ibid.

66 Ibid.

67 Ibid.

68 Stephen E. Ambrose, *Citizen Soldiers: The U.S. Army from the Normandy Beaches to the Bulge to the Surrender of Germany* (New York: Simon & Schuster, 1997), 18-19.

69 Donald Bosworth personal history narrative, Eisenhower Center for American Studies.

70 Ibid.

71 *In Their Own Words*, 77.

72 Ibid.

73 Robert S. Davis oral history, The National D-Day Museum.

74 Ibid.

75 Ibid.

76 Ibid.

77 *On To Berlin: Battles of an Airborne Commander 1943-1946*, 115.

78 Ibid., 116.

79 "The Airborne's Watery Triumph," 24.

80 *On To Berlin: Battles of an Airborne Commander 1943-1946*, 118.

81 Ibid.

82 Ibid.

83 Robert S. Davis oral history, The National D-Day Museum.

84 *In Their Own Words*, 77.

85 Ibid., 78.

86 Ibid.

87 Ibid.

88 Ibid., 79.

89 George H. Leidenheimer personal history narrative, The National D-Day Museum.

90 Ibid.

91 Ibid.

92 Ibid.

93 Ibid.

94 Ibid.

95 Ibid.

96 Ibid.

97 Ibid.

98 Ibid.

99 Ibid.

100 Ibid.

101 Ibid.

102 Ibid.

103 Ibid.

104 Ibid.

105 Ibid.

106 Ibid.

107 Ibid.

108 Ibid.

109 Ibid.

110 Ibid.

111 Ibid.

112 Ibid.

113 Ibid.

114 Ibid.

115 Ibid.

116 Ibid.

Chapter 9: To Cross the Merderet

1 "The Airborne's Watery Triumph," 26.

2 *No Better Place To Die*, 10.

3 Stephen E. Ambrose, *D-Day June 6, 1944*, 119.

4 Ibid., 120.

5 Ibid., 308.

6 *Night Drop*, 63.

7 Ibid.

8 Ibid.

9 *No Better Place To Die*, 22.

10 S.L.A. Marshall, *Night Drop: The American Airborne Invasion of Normandy* (Boston: Little, Brown and Company, 1962), 55.

11 John W. Marr oral history, The National D-Day Museum.

12 S.L.A. Marshall, *Night Drop: The American Airborne Invasion of Normandy* (Boston: Little, Brown and Company, 1962), 54.

13 John W. Marr oral history, The National D-Day Museum.

14 *Night Drop*, 60.

15 Ibid., 58.

16 *No Better Place To Die*, 29.

17 John W. Marr oral history, The National D-Day Museum.

18 Ibid.

19 *Night Drop*, 67.

20 John W. Marr oral history, The National D-Day Museum.

21 Robert S. Davis oral history, The National D-Day Museum.

22 *On To Berlin*, 124.

23 *Night Drop*, 82.

Chapter 10: Hold At All Costs

1 *In Their Own Words*, 54.

2 Ibid.

3 Ibid.

4 Ibid., 56.

5 Ibid.

6 Ibid.

7 Ibid.

8 Ibid.

9 Roy E. Creek personal history narrative, The Eisenhower Center for American Studies.

10 Ibid.

11 "The Airborne's Watery Triumph," 25.

[12] Roy E. Creek personal history narrative, The Eisenhower Center for American Studies.

[13] Roy Creek oral history, The National D-Day Museum.

[14] Roy E. Creek personal history narrative, The Eisenhower Center for American Studies.

[15] Ibid.

[16] Ibid.

[17] "The Airborne's Watery Triumph," 25.

[18] Ibid., 26.

[19] Roy Creek oral history, The National D-Day Museum.

[20] Roy E. Creek personal history narrative, The Eisenhower Center for American Studies.

[21] Ibid.

[22] Ibid.

[23] "The Airborne's Watery Triumph," 26.

[24] Roy E. Creek personal history narrative, The Eisenhower Center for American Studies.

Chapter 11: No Better Place to Die

[1] *On To Berlin*, 124.

[2] *Night Drop*, 65.

[3] Ibid.

[4] Ibid., 68.

[5] Ibid.

[6] Ibid., 69.

[7] Ibid., 70.

[8] Ibid.

[9] Ibid.

[10] Ibid.

[11] Ibid.

[12] Ibid., 71.

[13] Ibid., 72.

[14] Ibid., 73.

[15] Ibid., 73.

[16] Carson Smith oral history, The National D-Day Museum.

[17] Robert S. Davis oral history, The National D-Day Museum.

[18] *On To Berlin*, 124.

[19] *Night Drop*, 83.

[20] Ibid.

[21] *On To Berlin*, 124.

[22] Ibid., 125.

[23] Ibid.

[24] Ibid.

[25] "The Airborne's Watery Triumph," 28.

[26] *On To Berlin*, 125.

[27] "The Airborne's Watery Triumph," 29.

[28] *On To Berlin*, 126.

[29] Ibid.

[30] Ibid.

Chapter 12: Stabbing Westward

[1] *In Their Own Words*, 22.

[2] Ibid.

[3] Ibid.

[4] Ibid.

[5] Ibid., 23.

[6] Ibid.

[7] Ibid.

[8] Ibid.

[9] Ibid., 25.

[10] Ibid., 26.

[11] Ibid.

[12] Ibid., 27.

[13] Ibid., 28.

[14] Ibid.

[15] Ibid.

[16] Ibid., 29.

[17] Ibid.

[18] *No Better Place To Die*, 60.

[19] Ibid. 61.

[20] Charles N. Deglopper Medal of Honor Citation.

[21] *On To Berlin*, 127.

[22] Ibid., 128.

[23] Robert D. Rae oral history, The National D-Day Museum.

[24] Ibid.

[25] Ibid.

[26] Ibid.

[27] Ibid.

[28] Ibid.

[29] Ibid.

[30] Ibid.

Chapter 13: You've Got to Go

[1] "The Airborne's Watery Triumph," 31.

[2] *On To Berlin*, 128.

[3] "The Airborne's Watery Triumph," 31.

[4] Robert D. Rae oral history, The National D-Day Museum.

[5] Ibid.

[6] *Night Drop*, 153.

[7] Ibid., 155.

[8] Ibid., 154.

[9] *No Better Place To Die*, 63.

[10] *Night Drop*, 156.

[11] *No Better Place To Die*, 64.

[12] Ibid., 63.

[13] *Night Drop*, 156.

[14] *No Better Place To Die*, 64.

[15] Ibid., 68.

[16] Ibid., 66.

[17] *Night Drop*, 168.

[18] Robert D. Rae oral history, The National D-Day Museum.

[19] *Night Drop*, 168.

Chapter 14: Into the Mouth of Hell

[1] *Night Drop*, 168.

[2] Ibid.

[3] Ibid., 170.

[4] "The Airborne's Watery Triumph," 31.

[5] Ibid., 30.

[6] Ibid., 31.

7   Carson Smith oral history, The National D-Day Museum.

8   Robert D. Rae Distinguished Service Cross citation.

9   *Night Drop*, 171.

10   Ibid., 170

11   Robert D. Rae oral history, The National D-Day Museum.

12   Robert D. Rae Distinguished Service Cross citation.

13   *Night Drop*, 176.

14   Ibid.

15   *No Better Place To Die*, 70.

16   *Night Drop*, 182.

17   Ibid.

18   Ibid., 190.

19   Ibid.

20   Ibid.

21   *No Better Place To Die*, 71.

22   Ibid., 72.

23   Ibid., 74.

24   *Night Drop*, 192.

25   *No Better Place To Die*, 6.

26   *Night Drop*, 53.

27   Ibid., 193.

28   James M. Gavin, Cambridge, Massachusetts, letter to Albert "Bud" Parker, Atlanta, Georgia, 31 March 1981.

Chapter 15: Graignes

1   *Graignes: the Franco-American Memorial*, 18.

2   Ibid.

3   Odette Lelavechef and Marthe His, Interview by Martin K.A. Morgan, 16 May 2003, Vierville-Sur-Mer, France, transcript, Oral History Collection, The National D-Day Museum, New Orleans, Louisiana.

4   Ibid.

5   Marthe His. Written personal history narrative. Oral History Collection of The National D-Day Museum, New Orleans, Louisiana.

6   Ibid.

7   Ibid.

8   Ibid.

9   *Graignes: the Franco-American Memorial*, 18.

10   Francis E. Naughton oral history. The National D-Day Museum.

11   John J. Hinchliff oral history, The National D-Day Museum.

12   Ibid.

13   Odette Lelavechef and Marthe His oral history. The National D-Day Museum.

14   Ibid.

15   Marthe His. Written personal history narrative. Oral History Collection of The National D-Day Museum, New Orleans, Louisiana.

16   Odette Lelavechef and Marthe His oral history. The National D-Day Museum.

17   Ibid.

18   Ibid.

19   Ibid.

20   Ibid.

21   Marthe His. Written personal history narrative. Oral History Collection of The National D-Day Museum, New Orleans, Louisiana.

22   Memorandum titled "Recommendations for Awards" prepared by Earcle R. Reed and Francis E. Naughton, to John O. Marsh, Secretary of the Army, dated February 13, 1986.

23   *Graignes: the Franco-American Memorial*, 23.

24   Dominique François, *507th Parachute Infantry Regiment: Normandie, Ardennes, Allemagne 1942-1945* (Bayeux, France: Editions Heimdal, 2000), 65.

25   Ibid.

26   Ibid.

27   *Graignes: the Franco-American Memorial*, 24.

28   Francis E. Naughton oral history. The National D-Day Museum.

29   *Graignes: the Franco-American Memorial*, 24.

30   Ibid., 28.

31   Odette Lelavechef and Marthe His oral history. The National D-Day Museum.

32   Francis E. Naughton oral history. The National D-Day Museum.

33   "Recommendations for Awards" prepared by Earcle R. Reed and Francis E. Naughton, to John O. Marsh, Secretary of the Army, dated February 13, 1986.

34   Ibid.

35   *Graignes: the Franco-American Memorial*, 29.

36   Ibid.

37   François, *507th Parachute Infantry Regiment: Normandie, Ardennes, Allemagne 1942-1945*, 66.

38   Odette Lelavechef and Marthe His oral history. The National D-Day Museum.

39   Ibid.

40   François, *507th Parachute Infantry Regiment: Normandie, Ardennes, Allemagne 1942-1945*, 66.

41   Odette Lelavechef and Marthe His oral history. The National D-Day Museum.

42   François, *507th Parachute Infantry Regiment: Normandie, Ardennes, Allemagne 1942-1945*, 65.

43   "Recommendations for Awards" prepared by Earcle R. Reed and Francis E. Naughton, to John O. Marsh, Secretary of the Army, dated February 13, 1986.

44   Graignes: the Franco-American Memorial, 31.

45   Ibid.

46   Ibid.

47   Ibid., 32.

48   Ibid.

49   Ibid.

50   Ibid.

51   Ibid.

52   Ibid.

53   Ibid.

Chapter 16: Ten to One

1   François, *507th Parachute Infantry Regiment: Normandie, Ardennes, Allemagne 1942-1945*, 66.

2   "Recommendations for Awards" prepared by Earcle R. Reed and Francis E. Naughton, to John O. Marsh, Secretary of the Army, dated February 13, 1986.

3   Odette Lelavechef and Marthe His oral history. The National D-Day Museum.

4   Marthe His. Written personal history narrative. Oral History Collection of The National D-Day Museum.

5   John J. Hinchliff oral history, The National D-Day Museum.

6   Odette Lelavechef and Marthe His oral history. The National D-Day Museum.

7   *Graignes: the Franco-American Memorial*, 38.

8   Odette Lelavechef and Marthe His oral history. The National D-Day Museum.

9   *Graignes: the Franco-American Memorial*, 38.

10 Ibid.

11 Odette Lelavechef and Marthe His oral history. The National D-Day Museum.

12 *Graignes: the Franco-American Memorial*, 38.

13 "Recommendations for Awards" prepared by Earcle R. Reed and Francis E. Naughton, to John O. Marsh, Secretary of the Army, dated February 13, 1986.

14 Ambrose, *Band of Brothers*, 97.

15 Odette Lelavechef and Marthe His oral history. The National D-Day Museum.

16 Marthe His personal history narrative. Oral History Collection of The National D-Day Museum.

17 Odette Lelavechef and Marthe His oral history. The National D-Day Museum.

18 Marthe His personal history narrative. Oral History Collection of The National D-Day Museum.

19 Odette Lelavechef and Marthe His oral history. The National D-Day Museum.

20 Marthe His personal history narrative. Oral History Collection of The National D-Day Museum.

21 Ibid.

22 Ibid.

23 Ibid.

24 Odette Lelavechef and Marthe His oral history. The National D-Day Museum.

25 Marthe His personal history narrative. Oral History Collection of The National D-Day Museum.

26 Odette Lelavechef and Marthe His oral history. The National D-Day Museum.

27 *Graignes: the Franco-American Memorial*, 39.

28 Ibid., 43.

29 Ibid., 39.

30 Ibid.

31 Ibid.

32 Ibid., 40

33 Odette Lelavechef and Marthe His oral history. The National D-Day Museum.

34 *Graignes: the Franco-American Memorial*, 40.

35 John J. Hinchliff oral history, The National D-Day Museum.

36 *Graignes: the Franco-American Memorial*, 42.

37 Ibid.

38 Ibid., 43.

39 Ibid.

40 John J. Hinchliff oral history, The National D-Day Museum.

41 *Graignes: the Franco-American Memorial*, 43.

42 John J. Hinchliff oral history, The National D-Day Museum.

Chapter 17: We Lived Only to Save

1   Odette Lelavechef and Marthe His, Interview by Martin K.A. Morgan, 16 May 2003, Vierville-Sur-Mer, France, transcript, Oral History Collection, The National D-Day Museum, New Orleans, Louisiana.

2   Ibid.

3   Odette Lelavechef and Marthe His oral history. The National D-Day Museum.

4   Marthe His personal history narrative. Oral History Collection of The National D-Day Museum.

5   Francis E. Naughton oral history, The National D-Day Museum.

6   Odette Lelavechef and Marthe His oral history. The National D-Day Museum.

7   Ibid.

8   Ibid.

9   **Graignes: the Franco-American Memorial**, 44.

10 Ibid.

11 Ibid.

12 Ibid.

13 Ibid.

14 Ibid.

15 Ibid.

16 Ibid.

17 Ibid.

18 Odette Lelavechef and Marthe His oral history. The National D-Day Museum.

19 Marthe His personal history narrative. Oral History Collection of The National D-Day Museum.

20 **Graignes: the Franco-American Memorial**, 45.

21 Odette Lelavechef and Marthe His oral history. The National D-Day Museum.

22 Ibid.

23 Marthe His personal history narrative. Oral History Collection of The National D-Day Museum.

24 Ibid.

25 **Graignes: the Franco-American Memorial**, 45.

26 Ibid.

27 Ibid.

28 Odette Lelavechef and Marthe His oral history. The National D-Day Museum.

29 **Graignes: the Franco-American Memorial**, 45.

30 Ibid.

31 Ibid.

[32] Ibid.

[33] Marthe His personal history narrative. Oral History Collection of The National D-Day Museum.

[34] Ibid.

[35] **Graignes: the Franco-American Memorial**, 45.

[36] Ibid.

[37] Ibid.

[38] Ibid.

[39] Ibid.

[40] Ibid.

[41] Ibid.

[42] Ibid.

[43] Ibid.

[44] Ibid.

[45] Odette Lelavechef and Marthe His oral history. The National D-Day Museum.

[46] **Narrative** (Report), dated 28 June 1947, prepared by 1ˢᵗ Lt. James A. Hoovler, U.S. Army.

[47] Translation of Statement by Jean Poullain, Mayor of Le Mesnil Angot, dated 28 June 1947, translated by J. Leseigneur.

[48] Translation of Statement by Alphonse Voydie, Mayor of Graignes, dated 28 June 1947, translated by J. Leseigneur.

[49] Translation of Statement by Jean Poullain, Mayor of Le Mesnil Angot, dated 28 June 1947, translated by J. Leseigneur.

[50] **Narrative** (Report), dated 28 June 1947, prepared by 1ˢᵗ Lt. James A. Hoovler, U.S. Army.

[51] Marthe His personal history narrative. Oral History Collection of The National D-Day Museum.

[52] Ibid.

[53] **Graignes: the Franco-American Memorial**, 52.

[54] Odette Lelavechef and Marthe His oral history. The National D-Day Museum.

[55] Ibid.

[56] Marthe His personal history narrative. Oral History Collection of The National D-Day Museum.

[57] Odette Lelavechef and Marthe His oral history. The National D-Day Museum.

[58] Ibid.

[59] Ibid.

Chapter 18: Here's Your Ticket, Goodbye

[1] François, *507th Parachute Infantry Regiment: Normandie, Ardennes, Allemagne 1942-1945*, 69.

[2] Robert S. Davis oral history, The National D-Day Museum.

[3] Robert S. Davis, letter to Martin K.A. Morgan, 11 August 2003.

[4] Ibid.

[5] George H. Leidenheimer personal history narrative, The National D-Day Museum.

[6] Ibid.

[7] Robert S. Davis oral history, The National D-Day Museum.

[8] Robert S. Davis, letter to Martin K.A. Morgan, 11 August 2003.

[9] Robert S. Davis oral history, The National D-Day Museum.

[10] Ibid.

[11] John J. Hinchliff oral history, The National D-Day Museum.

[12] Ibid.

[13] Ibid.

[14] Robert S. Davis, "British Showed Americans the Way," *The Sunday Rutland Herald* (Vermont), 16 July 2000.

[15] Robert S. Davis, letter to Martin K.A. Morgan, 12 August 2003.

[16] Ibid.

[17] John W. Marr oral history, The National D-Day Museum.

[18] 507th Parachute Infantry Regiment Monument, Amfreville, France.

[19] Robert S. Davis, letter to Martin K.A. Morgan, 12 August 2003.

[20] Ibid.

[21] Paul F. Smith oral history, The National D-Day Museum.

[22] *In Their Own Words*, 33.

[23] Robert S. Davis, letter to Martin K.A. Morgan, 17 August 2003.

[24] Paul F. Smith oral history, The National D-Day Museum.

[25] 507th Parachute Infantry Regiment Monument Dedication Ceremony, 22 July 2002, Amfreville, France, transcript, Oral History Collection, The National D-Day Museum, New Orleans, Louisiana.

Index

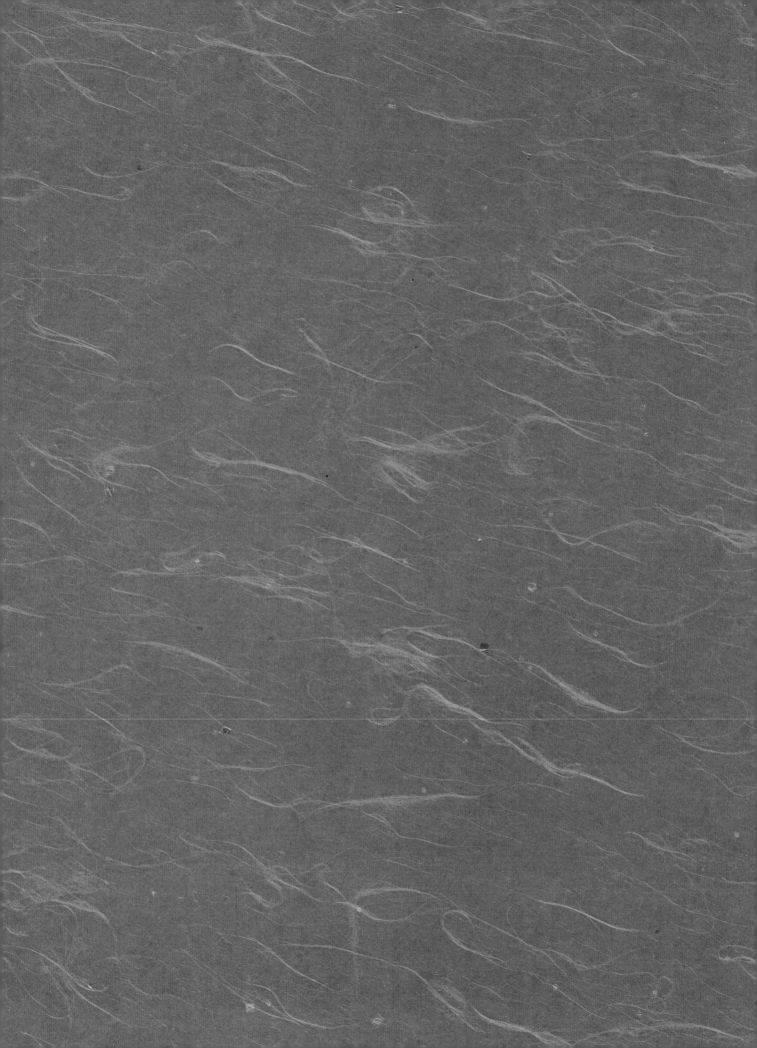